VERBAL
REVIEW
2ND EDITION

The only study guide with

300 past GMAT® questions

—and their answers—

by the creators

of the test.

~The~
OFFICIAL
Guide

THE OFFICIAL GUIDE FOR
GMAT® VERBAL REVIEW
2ND EDITION

- Actual questions from past GMAT tests,
  including more than 75 questions new to this edition
- 300 past questions, answers, and explanations in
  Reading Comprehension, Critical Reasoning,
  and Sentence Correction
- Questions organized in order of difficulty to save study time

From the Graduate Management Admission Council®

THE OFFICIAL GUIDE FOR GMAT® VERBAL REVIEW, 2ND EDITION

For general information on our other products and services or to obtain technical support please contact our Customer Care Department within the U.S. at (877) 762-2974, outside the U.S. at (317) 572-3993 or fax (317) 572-4002.

Wiley also publishes its books in a variety of electronic formats. Some content that appears in print may not be available in electronic books. For more information about Wiley products, please visit our Web site at www.wiley.com.

Library of Congress Control Number: 2009922580

ISBN: 978-0-470-44975-2

Printed in the United States of America

10   9   8   7

Book production by Wiley Publishing, Inc. Composition Services
Charles Forster, Designer
Mike Wilson, Production Designer

Table of Contents

1.0   What Is the GMAT®?

1.0 What Is the GMAT®?

The Graduate Management Admission Test® (GMAT®) is a standardized, three-part test delivered in English. The test was designed to help admissions officers evaluate how suitable individual applicants are for their graduate business and management programs. It measures basic verbal, mathematical, and analytical writing skills that a test taker has developed over a long period of time through education and work.

The GMAT test does not measure a person's knowledge of specific fields of study. Graduate business and management programs enroll people from many different undergraduate and work backgrounds, so rather than test your mastery of any particular subject area, the GMAT test will assess your acquired skills. Your GMAT score will give admissions officers a statistically reliable measure of how well you are likely to perform academically in the core curriculum of a graduate business program.

Of course, there are many other qualifications that can help people succeed in business school and in their careers—for instance, job experience, leadership ability, motivation, and interpersonal skills. The GMAT test does not gauge these qualities. That is why your GMAT score is intended to be used as one standard admissions criterion among other, more subjective, criteria, such as admissions essays and interviews.

1.1 Why Take the GMAT® Test?

GMAT scores are used by admissions officers in roughly 1,800 graduate business and management programs worldwide. Schools that require prospective students to submit GMAT scores in the application process are generally interested in admitting the best-qualified applicants for their programs, which means that you may find a more beneficial learning environment at schools that require GMAT scores as part of your application.

Because the GMAT test gauges skills that are important to successful study of business and management at the graduate level, your scores will give you a good indication of how well prepared you are to succeed academically in a graduate management program; how well you do on the test may also help you choose the business schools to which you apply. Furthermore, the percentile table you receive with your scores will tell you how your performance on the test compares to the performance of other test takers, giving you one way to gauge your competition for admission to business school.

Myth -vs- FACT

M – If I don't score in the 90th percentile, I won't get into any school I choose.

F – Very few people get very high scores.

Fewer than 50 of the more than 200,000 people taking the GMAT test each year get a perfect score of 800. Thus, while you may be exceptionally capable, the odds are against your achieving a perfect score. Also, the GMAT test is just one piece of your application packet. Admissions officers use GMAT scores in conjunction with undergraduate records, application essays, interviews, letters of recommendation, and other information when deciding whom to accept into their programs.

Schools consider many different aspects of an application before making an admissions decision, so even if you score well on the GMAT test, you should contact the schools that interest you to learn more about them and to ask about how they use GMAT scores and other admissions criteria (such as your undergraduate grades, essays, and letters of recommendation) to evaluate candidates for admission. School admissions offices, school Web sites, and materials published by the school are the best sources for you to tap when you are doing research about where you might want to go to business school.

For more information about how schools should use GMAT scores in admissions decisions, please read Appendix A of this book. For more information on the GMAT, registering to take the test, sending your scores to schools, and applying to business school, please visit our Web site at www.mba.com.

1.2 GMAT® Test Format

The GMAT test consists of four separately timed sections (see the table on the next page). You start the test with two 30-minute Analytical Writing Assessment (AWA) questions that require you to type your responses using the computer keyboard. The writing section is followed by two 75-minute, multiple-choice sections: the Quantitative and Verbal sections of the test.

The GMAT is a computer-adaptive test (CAT), which means that in the multiple-choice sections of the test, the computer constantly gauges how well you are doing on the test and presents you with questions that are appropriate to your ability level. These questions are drawn from a huge pool of possible test questions. So, although we talk about the GMAT as one test, the GMAT test you take may be completely different from the test of the person sitting next to you.

Here's how it works. At the start of each GMAT multiple-choice section (Verbal and Quantitative), you will be presented with a question of moderate difficulty. The computer uses your response to that first question to determine which question to present next. If you respond correctly, the test usually will give you questions of increasing difficulty. If you respond incorrectly, the next question you see usually will be easier than the one you answered incorrectly. As you continue to respond to the questions presented, the computer will narrow your score to the number that best characterizes your ability. When you complete each section, the computer will have an accurate assessment of your ability.

Myth -vs- **FACT**

M – **Getting an easier question means I answered the last one wrong.**

F – **Getting an easier question does not necessarily mean you got the previous question wrong.**

To ensure that everyone receives the same content, the test selects a specific number of questions of each type. The test may call for your next question to be a relatively hard problem-solving item involving arithmetic operations. But, if there are no more relatively difficult problem-solving items involving arithmetic, you might be given an easier item.

Most people are not skilled at estimating item difficulty, so don't worry when taking the test or waste valuable time trying to determine the difficulty of the questions you are answering.

Because each question is presented on the basis of your answers to all previous questions, you must answer each question as it appears. You may not skip, return to, or change your responses to previous questions. Random guessing can significantly lower your scores. If you do not know the answer to a question, you should try to eliminate as many choices as possible, then select the answer you think is best. If you answer a question incorrectly by mistake—or correctly by lucky guess— your answers to subsequent questions will lead you back to questions that are at the appropriate level of difficulty for you.

Each multiple-choice question used in the GMAT test has been thoroughly reviewed by professional test developers. New multiple-choice questions are tested each time the test is administered. Answers to trial questions are not counted in the scoring of your test, but the trial questions are not identified and could appear anywhere in the test. Therefore, you should try to do your best on every question.

The test includes the types of questions found in this guide, but the format and presentation of the questions are different on the computer. When you take the test:

- Only one question at a time is presented on the computer screen.

- The answer choices for the multiple-choice questions will be preceded by circles, rather than by letters.

- Different question types appear in random order in the multiple-choice sections of the test.

- You must select your answer using the computer.

- You must choose an answer and confirm your choice before moving on to the next question.

- You may not go back to change answers to previous questions.

Format of the GMAT®		
	Questions	Timing

Analytical Writing
    Analysis of an Argument
    Analysis of an Issue
	1
	1
		30 min.
		30 min.

Optional break		

Quantitative
    Problem Solving
    Data Sufficiency
	37	75 min.

Optional break		

Verbal
    Reading Comprehension
    Critical Reasoning
    Sentence Correction
	41	75 min.

	Total Time:	210 min.

1.3 What Is the Content of the Test Like?

It is important to recognize that the GMAT test evaluates skills and abilities developed over a relatively long period of time. Although the sections contain questions that are basically verbal and mathematical, the complete test provides one method of measuring overall ability.

Keep in mind that although the questions in this guide are arranged by question type and ordered from easy to difficult, the test is organized differently. When you take the test, you may see different types of questions in any order.

1.4 Quantitative Section

The GMAT Quantitative section measures your ability to reason quantitatively, solve quantitative problems, and interpret graphic data.

Two types of multiple-choice questions are used in the Quantitative section:

- Problem solving
- Data sufficiency

Problem solving and data sufficiency questions are intermingled throughout the Quantitative section. Both types of questions require basic knowledge of:

- Arithmetic
- Elementary algebra
- Commonly known concepts of geometry

To review the basic mathematical concepts that will be tested in the GMAT Quantitative questions and for test-taking tips specific to the question types in the Quantitative section of the GMAT test, sample questions, and answer explanations, see *The Official Guide for GMAT® Review*, 12th Edition, or *The Official Guide for GMAT® Quantitative Review*, 2nd Edition; both are available for purchase at www.mba.com.

1.5 Verbal Section

The GMAT Verbal section measures your ability to read and comprehend written material, to reason and evaluate arguments, and to correct written material to conform to standard written English. Because the Verbal section includes reading sections from several different content areas, you may be generally familiar with some of the material; however, neither the reading passages nor the questions assume detailed knowledge of the topics discussed.

Three types of multiple-choice questions are used in the Verbal section:

- Reading comprehension
- Critical reasoning
- Sentence correction

These question types are intermingled throughout the Verbal section.

For test-taking tips specific to each question type in the Verbal section, sample questions, and answer explanations, see chapters 3 through 5.

1.6 What Computer Skills Will I Need?

You only need minimal computer skills to take the GMAT Computer-Adaptive Test (CAT). You will be required to type your essays on the computer keyboard using standard word-processing keystrokes. In the multiple-choice sections, you will select your responses using either your mouse or the keyboard.

To learn more about the specific skills required to take the GMAT CAT, download the free test-preparation software available at www.mba.com.

1.7 What Are the Test Centers Like?

The GMAT test is administered at a test center providing the quiet and privacy of individual computer workstations. You will have the opportunity to take two optional breaks—one after completing the essays and another between the Quantitative and Verbal sections. An erasable notepad will be provided for your use during the test.

1.8 How Are Scores Calculated?

Your GMAT scores are determined by:

- The number of questions you answer
- Whether you answer correctly or incorrectly
- The level of difficulty and other statistical characteristics of each question

Your Verbal, Quantitative, and Total GMAT scores are determined by a complex mathematical procedure that takes into account the difficulty of the questions that were presented to you and how you answered them. When you answer the easier questions correctly, you get a chance to answer harder questions—making it possible to earn a higher score. After you have completed all the questions on the test—or when your time is up—the computer will calculate your scores. Your scores on the Verbal and Quantitative sections are combined to produce your Total score. If you have not responded to all the questions in a section (37 Quantitative questions or 41 Verbal questions), your score is adjusted, using the proportion of questions answered.

Appendix A contains the 2007 percentile ranking tables that explain how your GMAT scores compare with scores of other 2007 GMAT test takers.

1.9 Analytical Writing Assessment Scores

The Analytical Writing Assessment consists of two writing tasks: Analysis of an Issue and Analysis of an Argument. The responses to each of these tasks are scored on a 6-point scale, with 6 being the highest score and 1, the lowest. A score of zero (0) is given to responses that are off-topic, are in a foreign language, merely attempt to copy the topic, consist only of keystroke characters, or are blank.

The readers who evaluate the responses are college and university faculty members from various subject matter areas, including management education. These readers read holistically—that is, they respond to the overall quality of your critical thinking and writing. (For details on how readers are qualified, visit www.mba.com.) In addition, responses may be scored by an automated scoring program designed to reflect the judgment of expert readers.

Each response is given two independent ratings. If the ratings differ by more than a point, a third reader adjudicates. (Because of ongoing training and monitoring, discrepant ratings are rare.)

Your final score is the average (rounded to the nearest half point) of the four scores independently assigned to your responses—two scores for the Analysis of an Issue and two for the Analysis of an Argument. For example, if you earned scores of 6 and 5 on the Analysis of an Issue and 4 and 4 on the Analysis of an Argument, your final score would be 5: $(6 + 5 + 4 + 4) \div 4 = 4.75$, which rounds up to 5.

Your Analytical Writing Assessment scores are computed and reported separately from the multiple-choice sections of the test and have no effect on your Verbal, Quantitative, or Total scores. The schools that you have designated to receive your scores may receive your responses to the Analytical Writing Assessment with your score report. Your own copy of your score report will not include copies of your responses.

1.10 Test Development Process

The GMAT test is developed by experts who use standardized procedures to ensure high-quality, widely appropriate test material. All questions are subjected to independent reviews and are revised or discarded as necessary. Multiple-choice questions are tested during GMAT test administrations. Analytical Writing Assessment tasks are tried out on first-year business school students and then assessed for their fairness and reliability. For more information on test development, see www.mba.com.

To register for the GMAT test go to www.mba.com

2.0 How to Prepare

2.0 How to Prepare

2.1 How Can I Best Prepare to Take the Test?

We at the Graduate Management Admission Council® (GMAC®) firmly believe that the test-taking skills you can develop by using this guide—and *The Official Guide for GMAT® Review*, 12th Edition, and *The Official Guide for GMAT® Quantitative Review*, 2nd Edition, if you want additional practice—are all you need to perform your best when you take the GMAT® test. By answering questions that have appeared on the GMAT test before, you will gain experience with the types of questions you may see on the test when you take it. As you practice with this guide, you will develop confidence in your ability to reason through the test questions. No additional techniques or strategies are needed to do well on the standardized test if you develop a practical familiarity with the abilities it requires. Simply by practicing and understanding the concepts that are assessed on the test, you will learn what you need to know to answer the questions correctly.

2.2 What About Practice Tests?

Because a computer-adaptive test cannot be presented in paper form, we have created GMATPrep software to help you prepare for the test. The software is available for download at no charge for those who have created a user profile on www.mba.com. It is also provided on a disk, by request, to anyone who has registered for the GMAT test. The software includes two practice GMAT tests plus additional practice questions, information about the test, and tutorials to help you become familiar with how the GMAT test will appear on the computer screen at the test center.

We recommend that you download the software as you start to prepare for the test. Take one practice test to familiarize yourself with the test and to get an idea of how you might score. After you have studied using this book, and as your test date approaches, take the second practice test to determine whether you need to shift your focus to other areas you need to strengthen.

Myth -vs- **FACT**

M – **You need very advanced math skills to get a high GMAT score.**

F – **The math skills tested on the GMAT test are quite basic.**

The GMAT test only requires basic quantitative analytic skills. You should review the math skills (algebra, geometry, basic arithmetic) presented in both *The Official Guide for GMAT® Review*, 12th Edition and *The Official Guide for GMAT® Quantitative Review*, 2nd Edition, but the required skill level is low. The difficulty of GMAT Quantitative questions stems from the logic and analysis used to solve the problems and not the underlying math skills.

2.3 Where Can I Get Additional Practice?

If you complete all the questions in this guide and think you would like additional practice, you may purchase *The Official Guide for GMAT® Review*, 12th Edition, or *The Official Guide for GMAT® Quantitative Review*, 2nd Edition, at www.mba.com.

Note: There may be some overlap between this book and the review sections of the GMATPrep® software.

2.4 General Test-Taking Suggestions

Specific test-taking strategies for individual question types are presented later in this book. The following are general suggestions to help you perform your best on the test.

1. Use your time wisely.

Although the GMAT test stresses accuracy more than speed, it is important to use your time wisely. On average, you will have about 1¾ minutes for each verbal question and about 2 minutes for each quantitative question. Once you start the test, an onscreen clock will continuously count the time you have left. You can hide this display if you want, but it is a good idea to check the clock periodically to monitor your progress. The clock will automatically alert you when 5 minutes remain in the allotted time for the section you are working on.

2. Answer practice questions ahead of time.

After you become generally familiar with all question types, use the sample questions in this book to prepare for the actual test. It may be useful to time yourself as you answer the practice questions to get an idea of how long you will have for each question during the actual GMAT test as well as to determine whether you are answering quickly enough to complete the test in the time allotted.

3. Read all test directions carefully.

The directions explain exactly what is required to answer each question type. If you read hastily, you may miss important instructions and lower your scores. To review directions during the test, click on the Help icon. But be aware that the time you spend reviewing directions will count against the time allotted for that section of the test.

4. Read each question carefully and thoroughly.

Before you answer a multiple-choice question, determine exactly what is being asked, then eliminate the wrong answers and select the best choice. Never skim a question or the possible answers; skimming may cause you to miss important information or nuances.

5. Do not spend too much time on any one question.

If you do not know the correct answer, or if the question is too time-consuming, try to eliminate choices you know are wrong, select the best of the remaining answer choices, and move on to the next question. Try not to worry about the impact on your score—guessing may lower your score, but not finishing the section will lower your score more.

Bear in mind that if you do not finish a section in the allotted time, you will still receive a score.

6. Confirm your answers ONLY when you are ready to move on.

Once you have selected your answer to a multiple-choice question, you will be asked to confirm it. Once you confirm your response, you cannot go back and change it. You may not skip questions, because the computer selects each question on the basis of your responses to preceding questions.

7. Plan your essay answers before you begin to write.

The best way to approach the two writing tasks that comprise the Analytical Writing Assessment is to read the directions carefully, take a few minutes to think about the question, and plan a response before you begin writing. Take care to organize your ideas and develop them fully, but leave time to reread your response and make any revisions that you think would improve it.

Myth -vs- **FACT**

M – **It is more important to respond correctly to the test questions than it is to finish the test.**

F – **There is a severe penalty for not completing the GMAT test.**

If you are stumped by a question, give it your best guess and move on. If you guess incorrectly, the computer program will likely give you an easier question, which you are likely to answer correctly, and the computer will rapidly return to giving you questions matched to your ability. If you don't finish the test, your score will be reduced greatly. Failing to answer five verbal questions, for example, could reduce your score from the 91st percentile to the 77th percentile. Pacing is important.

Myth -vs- **FACT**

M – **The first 10 questions are critical and you should invest the most time on those.**

F – **All questions count.**

It is true that the computer-adaptive testing algorithm uses the first 10 questions to obtain an initial estimate of your ability; however, that is only an *initial* estimate. As you continue to answer questions, the algorithm self-corrects by computing an updated estimate on the basis of all the questions you have answered, and then administers items that are closely matched to this new estimate of your ability. Your final score is based on all your responses and considers the difficulty of all the questions you answered. Taking additional time on the first 10 questions will not game the system and can hurt your ability to finish the test.

3.0   Reading Comprehension

3.0 Reading Comprehension

Reading comprehension questions appear in the Verbal section of the GMAT® test. The Verbal section uses multiple-choice questions to measure your ability to read and comprehend written material, to reason and evaluate arguments, and to correct written material to conform to standard written English. Because the Verbal section includes content from a variety of topics, you may be generally familiar with some of the material; however, neither the passages nor the questions assume knowledge of the topics discussed. Reading comprehension questions are intermingled with critical reasoning and sentence correction questions throughout the Verbal section of the test.

You will have 75 minutes to complete the Verbal section, or an average of about 1¾ minutes to answer each question. Keep in mind, however, that you will need time to read the written passages—and that time is not factored into the 1¾ minute average. You should therefore plan to proceed more quickly through the reading comprehension questions in order to give yourself enough time to read the passages thoroughly.

Reading comprehension questions begin with written passages up to 350 words long. The passages discuss topics from the social sciences, humanities, the physical or biological sciences, and such business-related fields as marketing, economics, and human resource management. The passages are accompanied by questions that will ask you to interpret the passage, apply the information you gather from the reading, and make inferences (or informed assumptions) based on the reading. For these questions, you will see a split computer screen. The written passage will remain visible on the left side as each question associated with that passage appears in turn on the right side. You will see only one question at a time, however. The number of questions associated with each passage may vary.

As you move through the reading comprehension sample questions, try to determine a process that works best for you. You might begin by reading a passage carefully and thoroughly, though some test takers prefer to skim the passages the first time through, or even to read the first question before reading the passage. You may want to reread any sentences that present complicated ideas or introduce terms that are new to you. Read each question and series of answers carefully. Make sure you understand exactly what the question is asking and what the answer choices are.

If you need to, you may go back to the passage and read any parts that are relevant to answering the question. Specific portions of the passages may be highlighted in the related questions.

The following pages describe what reading comprehension questions are designed to measure, present the directions that will precede questions of this type, and describe the various question types. This chapter also provides test-taking strategies, sample questions, and detailed explanations of all the questions. The explanations further illustrate the ways in which reading comprehension questions evaluate basic reading skills.

3.1 What Is Measured

Reading comprehension questions measure your ability to understand, analyze, and apply information and concepts presented in written form. All questions are to be answered on the basis of what is stated or implied in the reading material, and no specific prior knowledge of the material is required.

The GMAT reading comprehension questions evaluate your ability to do the following:

- **Understand words and statements.**
  Although the questions do not test your vocabulary (they will not ask you to define terms), they do test your ability to interpret special meanings of terms as they are used in the reading passages. The questions will also test your understanding of the English language. These questions may ask about the overall meaning of a passage.

- **Understand logical relationships between points and concepts.**
  This type of question may ask you to determine the strong and weak points of an argument or evaluate the relative importance of arguments and ideas in a passage.

- **Draw inferences from facts and statements.**
  The inference questions will ask you to consider factual statements or information presented in a reading passage and, on the basis of that information, reach conclusions.

- **Understand and follow the development of quantitative concepts as they are presented in written material.**
  This may involve the interpretation of numerical data or the use of simple arithmetic to reach conclusions about material in a passage.

There are six kinds of reading comprehension questions, each of which tests a different skill. The reading comprehension questions ask about the following areas:

Main idea

Each passage is a unified whole—that is, the individual sentences and paragraphs support and develop one main idea or central point. Sometimes you will be told the central point in the passage itself, and sometimes it will be necessary for you to determine the central point from the overall organization or development of the passage. You may be asked in this kind of question to

- recognize a correct restatement, or paraphrasing, of the main idea of a passage

- identify the author's primary purpose or objective in writing the passage

- assign a title that summarizes, briefly and pointedly, the main idea developed in the passage

Supporting ideas

These questions measure your ability to comprehend the supporting ideas in a passage and differentiate them from the main idea. The questions also measure your ability to differentiate ideas that are *explicitly stated* in a passage from ideas that are *implied* by the author but that are not explicitly stated. You may be asked about

- facts cited in a passage

- the specific content of arguments presented by the author in support of his or her views

- descriptive details used to support or elaborate on the main idea

Whereas questions about the main idea ask you to determine the meaning of a passage *as a whole*, questions about supporting ideas ask you to determine the meanings of individual sentences and paragraphs that *contribute* to the meaning of the passage as a whole. In other words, these questions ask for the main point of *one small part* of the passage.

Inferences

These questions ask about ideas that are not explicitly stated in a passage but are *implied* by the author. Unlike questions about supporting details, which ask about information that is directly stated in a passage, inference questions ask about ideas or meanings that must be inferred from information that is directly stated. Authors can make their points in indirect ways, suggesting ideas without actually stating them. Inference questions measure your ability to understand an author's intended meaning in parts of a passage where the meaning is only suggested. These questions do not ask about meanings or implications that are remote from the passage; rather, they ask about meanings that are developed indirectly or implications that are specifically suggested by the author.

To answer these questions, you may have to

- logically take statements made by the author one step beyond their literal meanings

- recognize an alternative interpretation of a statement made by the author

- identify the intended meaning of a word used figuratively in a passage

If a passage explicitly states an effect, for example, you may be asked to infer its cause. If the author compares two phenomena, you may be asked to infer the basis for the comparison. You may be asked to infer the characteristics of an old policy from an explicit description of a new one. When you read a passage, therefore, you should concentrate not only on the explicit meaning of the author's words, but also on the more subtle meaning implied by those words.

Applying information to a context outside the passage itself

These questions measure your ability to discern the relationships between situations or ideas presented by the author and other situations or ideas that might parallel those in the passage. In this kind of question, you may be asked to

- identify a hypothetical situation that is comparable to a situation presented in the passage

- select an example that is similar to an example provided in the passage

- apply ideas given in the passage to a situation not mentioned by the author

- recognize ideas that the author would probably agree or disagree with on the basis of statements made in the passage

Unlike inference questions, application questions use ideas or situations *not* taken from the passage. Ideas and situations given in a question are *like* those given in the passage, and they parallel ideas and situations in the passage; therefore, to answer the question, you must do more than recall what you read. You must recognize the essential attributes of ideas and situations presented in the passage when they appear in different words and in an entirely new context.

Logical structure

These questions require you to analyze and evaluate the organization and logic of a passage. They may ask you

- how a passage is constructed—for instance, does it define, compare or contrast, present a new idea, or refute an idea?

- how the author persuades readers to accept his or her assertions

- the reason behind the author's use of any particular supporting detail

- to identify assumptions that the author is making

- to assess the strengths and weaknesses of the author's arguments

- to recognize appropriate counterarguments

These questions measure your ability not only to comprehend a passage but also to evaluate it critically. However, it is important for you to realize that logical structure questions do not rely on any kind of formal logic, nor do they require you to be familiar with specific terms of logic or argumentation. You can answer these questions using only the information in the passage and careful reasoning.

About the style and tone

Style and tone questions ask about the expression of a passage and about the ideas in a passage that may be expressed through its diction—the author's choice of words. You may be asked to deduce the author's attitude to an idea, a fact, or a situation from the words that he or she uses to describe it. You may also be asked to select a word that accurately describes the tone of a passage—for instance, "critical," "questioning," "objective," or "enthusiastic."

To answer this type of question, you will have to consider the language of the passage as a whole. It takes more than one pointed, critical word to make the tone of an entire passage "critical." Sometimes, style and tone questions ask what audience the passage was probably intended for or what type of publication it probably appeared in. Style and tone questions may apply to one small part of the passage or to the passage as a whole. To answer them, you must ask yourself what meanings are contained in the words of a passage beyond the literal meanings. Did the author use certain words because of their emotional content, or because a particular audience would expect to hear them? Remember, these questions measure your ability to discern meaning expressed by the author through his or her choice of words.

3.2 Test-Taking Strategies

1. **Do not expect to be completely familiar with any of the material presented in reading comprehension passages.**

   You may find some passages easier to understand than others, but all passages are designed to present a challenge. If you have some familiarity with the material presented in a passage, do not let this knowledge influence your choice of answers to the questions. Answer all questions on the basis of what is *stated* or *implied* in the passage itself.

2. **Analyze each passage carefully, because the questions require you to have a specific and detailed understanding of the material.**

   You may find it easier to do the analysis first, before moving to the questions. Or, you may find that you prefer to skim the passage the first time and read more carefully once you understand what a question asks. You may even want to read the question before reading the passage. You should choose the method most suitable for you.

3. **Focus on key words and phrases, and make every effort to avoid losing the sense of what is discussed in the passage.**

   Keep the following in mind:

   • Note how each fact relates to an idea or an argument.

   • Note where the passage moves from one idea to the next.

   • Separate main ideas from supporting ideas.

   • Determine what conclusions are reached and why.

4. **Read the questions carefully, making certain that you understand what is asked.**

   An answer choice that accurately restates information in the passage may be incorrect if it does not answer the question. If you need to, refer back to the passage for clarification.

5. **Read all the choices carefully.**

   Never assume that you have selected the best answer without first reading all the choices.

6. **Select the choice that answers the question best in terms of the information given in the passage.**

   Do not rely on outside knowledge of the material to help you answer the questions.

7. **Remember that comprehension—not speed—is the critical success factor when it comes to reading comprehension questions.**

3.3 The Directions

These are the directions that you will see for reading comprehension questions when you take the GMAT test. If you read them carefully and understand them clearly before going to sit for the test, you will not need to spend too much time reviewing them once you are at the test center and the test is under way.

The questions in this group are based on the content of a passage. After reading the passage, choose the best answer to each question. Answer all questions following the passage on the basis of what is *stated or implied in the passage.*

3.4 Sample Questions

Each of the <u>reading comprehension</u> questions is based on the content of a passage. After reading the passage answer all questions pertaining to it on the basis of what is <u>stated</u> or <u>implied</u> in the passage. For each question, select the best answer of the choices given.

Line   The Gross Domestic Product (GDP), which
        measures the dollar value of finished goods and
        services produced by an economy during a given
        period, serves as the chief indicator of the
(5)   economic well-being of the United States. The GDP
        assumes that the economic significance of goods
        and services lies solely in their price, and that these
        goods and services add to the national well-being,
        not because of any intrinsic value they may
(10)   possess, but simply because they were produced
        and bought. Additionally, only those goods and
        services involved in monetary transactions are
        included in the GDP. Thus, the GDP ignores the
        economic utility of such things as a clean
(15)   environment and cohesive families and
        communities. It is therefore not merely coincidental,
        since national policies in capitalist and noncapitalist
        countries alike are dependent on indicators such as
        the GDP, that both the environment and the social
(20)   structure have been eroded in recent decades. Not
        only does the GDP mask this erosion, it can actually
        portray it as an economic gain: an oil spill off a
        coastal region "adds" to the GDP because it
        generates commercial activity. In short, the nation's
(25)   central measure of economic well-being works like a
        calculating machine that adds but cannot subtract.

Questions 1–6 refer to the passage above.

1. The primary purpose of the passage is to

(A) identify ways in which the GDP could be modified so that it would serve as a more accurate indicator of the economic well-being of the United States

(B) suggest that the GDP, in spite of certain shortcomings, is still the most reliable indicator of the economic well-being of the United States

(C) examine crucial shortcomings of the GDP as an indicator of the economic well-being of the United States

(D) argue that the growth of the United States economy in recent decades has diminished the effectiveness of the GDP as an indicator of the nation's economic well-being

(E) discuss how the GDP came to be used as the primary indicator of the economic well-being of the United States

2. Which of the following best describes the function of the second sentence of the passage in the context of the passage as a whole?

(A) It describes an assumption about the GDP that is defended in the course of the passage.

(B) It contributes to a discussion of the origins of the GDP.

(C) It clarifies a common misconception about the use of the GDP.

(D) It identifies a major flaw in the GDP.

(E) It suggests a revision to the method of calculating the GDP.

3. It can be inferred that the author of the passage would agree with which of the following about the "economic significance" of those goods and services that are included in the GDP?

(A) It is a comprehensive indicator of a nation's economic well-being.

(B) It is not accurately captured by the price of those goods and services.

(C) It is usually less than the intrinsic value of those goods and services.

(D) It is more difficult to calculate than the economic significance of those goods and services that are not included in the GDP.

(E) It is calculated differently in capitalist countries than in noncapitalist countries.

4. The comparison of the GDP to a calculating machine serves to do which of the following?

(A) Refute an assertion that the calculations involved in the GDP are relatively complex in nature

(B) Indicate that the GDP is better suited to record certain types of monetary transactions than others

(C) Suggest that it is likely that the GDP will be supplanted by other, more sophisticated economic indicators

(D) Illustrate the point that the GDP has no way of measuring the destructive impact of such things as oil spills on the nation's economic well-being

(E) Exemplify an assertion that the GDP tends to exaggerate the amount of commercial activity generated by such things as oil spills

5. The passage implies that national policies that rely heavily on economic indicators such as the GDP tend to

(A) become increasingly capitalistic in nature

(B) disregard the economic importance of environmental and social factors that do not involve monetary transactions

(C) overestimate the amount of commercial activity generated by environmental disasters

(D) overestimate the economic significance of cohesive families and communities

(E) assume that the economic significance of goods and services does not lie solely in the price of those goods and services

6. It can be inferred that the author of the passage would agree with which of the following assessments of the GDP as an indicator of the economic well-being of the United States?

(A) It masks social and environmental erosion more fully than the chief economic indicators of other nations.

(B) It is based on inaccurate estimations of the prices of many goods and services.

(C) It overestimates the amount of commercial activity that is generated in the United States.

(D) It is conducive to error because it conflates distinct types of economic activity.

(E) It does not take into account the economic utility of certain environmental and social conditions.

Line Coral reefs are one of the most fragile, biologically
      complex, and diverse marine ecosystems on Earth.
      This ecosystem is one of the fascinating paradoxes
      of the biosphere: how do clear, and thus nutrient-
(5)   poor, waters support such prolific and productive
      communities? Part of the answer lies within the
      tissues of the corals themselves. Symbiotic cells of
      algae known as zooxanthellae carry out
      photosynthesis using the metabolic wastes of the
(10) corals, thereby producing food for themselves, for
      their coral hosts, and even for other members of
      the reef community. This symbiotic process allows
      organisms in the reef community to use sparse
      nutrient resources efficiently.
(15)   Unfortunately for coral reefs, however, a variety
      of human activities are causing worldwide
      degradation of shallow marine habitats by adding
      nutrients to the water. Agriculture, slash-and-burn
      land clearing, sewage disposal, and manufacturing
(20) that creates waste by-products all increase nutrient
      loads in these waters. Typical symptoms of reef
      decline are destabilized herbivore populations and
      an increasing abundance of algae and filter-feeding
      animals. Declines in reef communities are
(25) consistent with observations that nutrient input is
      increasing in direct proportion to growing human
      populations, thereby threatening reef communities
      sensitive to subtle changes in nutrient input to their
      waters.

Questions 7–11 refer to the passage above.

7. The passage is primarily concerned with

    (A) describing the effects of human activities on algae in coral reefs
    (B) explaining how human activities are posing a threat to coral reef communities
    (C) discussing the process by which coral reefs deteriorate in nutrient-poor waters
    (D) explaining how coral reefs produce food for themselves
    (E) describing the abundance of algae and filter-feeding animals in coral reef areas

8. The passage suggests which of the following about coral reef communities?

    (A) Coral reef communities may actually be more likely to thrive in waters that are relatively low in nutrients.
    (B) The nutrients on which coral reef communities thrive are only found in shallow waters.
    (C) Human population growth has led to changing ocean temperatures, which threatens coral reef communities.
    (D) The growth of coral reef communities tends to destabilize underwater herbivore populations.
    (E) Coral reef communities are more complex and diverse than most ecosystems located on dry land.

9. The author refers to "filter-feeding animals" (lines 23–24) in order to

    (A) provide an example of a characteristic sign of reef deterioration
    (B) explain how reef communities acquire sustenance for survival
    (C) identify a factor that helps herbivore populations thrive
    (D) indicate a cause of decreasing nutrient input in waters that reefs inhabit
    (E) identify members of coral reef communities that rely on coral reefs for nutrients

10. According to the passage, which of the following is a factor that is threatening the survival of coral reef communities?

    (A) The waters they inhabit contain few nutrient resources.

    (B) A decline in nutrient input is disrupting their symbiotic relationship with zooxanthellae.

    (C) The degraded waters of their marine habitats have reduced their ability to carry out photosynthesis.

    (D) They are too biologically complex to survive in habitats with minimal nutrient input.

    (E) Waste by-products result in an increase in nutrient input to reef communities.

11. It can be inferred from the passage that the author describes coral reef communities as paradoxical most likely for which of the following reasons?

    (A) They are thriving even though human activities have depleted the nutrients in their environment.

    (B) They are able to survive in spite of an overabundance of algae inhabiting their waters.

    (C) They are able to survive in an environment with limited food resources.

    (D) Their metabolic wastes contribute to the degradation of the waters that they inhabit.

    (E) They are declining even when the water surrounding them remains clear.

Line   Although genetic mutations in bacteria and viruses
can lead to epidemics, some epidemics are caused
by bacteria and viruses that have undergone no
significant genetic change. In analyzing the latter,
(5)   scientists have discovered the importance of social
and ecological factors to epidemics. Poliomyelitis,
for example, emerged as an epidemic in the United
States in the twentieth century; by then, modern
sanitation was able to delay exposure to polio until
(10)   adolescence or adulthood, at which time polio
infection produced paralysis. Previously, infection
had occurred during infancy, when it typically
provided lifelong immunity without paralysis. Thus,
the hygiene that helped prevent typhoid epidemics
(15)   indirectly fostered a paralytic polio epidemic.
Another example is Lyme disease, which is caused
by bacteria that are transmitted by deer ticks. It
occurred only sporadically during the late
nineteenth century but has recently become
(20)   prevalent in parts of the United States, largely due
to an increase in the deer population that occurred
simultaneously with the growth of the suburbs and
increased outdoor recreational activities in the
deer's habitat. Similarly, an outbreak of dengue
(25)   hemorrhagic fever became an epidemic in Asia in
the 1950s because of ecological changes that
caused *Aedes aegypti*, the mosquito that transmits
the dengue virus, to proliferate. The stage is now
set in the United States for a dengue epidemic
(30)   because of the inadvertent introduction and wide
dissemination of another mosquito, *Aedes
albopictus*.

Questions 12–17 refer to the passage above.

12.   The passage suggests that a lack of modern
sanitation would make which of the following most
likely to occur?

(A)   An outbreak of Lyme disease

(B)   An outbreak of dengue hemorrhagic fever

(C)   An epidemic of typhoid

(D)   An epidemic of paralytic polio among infants

(E)   An epidemic of paralytic polio among
adolescents and adults

13.   According to the passage, the outbreak of dengue
hemorrhagic fever in the 1950s occurred for which of
the following reasons?

(A)   The mosquito *Aedes aegypti* was newly
introduced into Asia.

(B)   The mosquito *Aedes aegypti* became more
numerous.

(C)   The mosquito *Aedes albopictus* became infected
with the dengue virus.

(D)   Individuals who would normally acquire immunity
to the dengue virus as infants were not infected
until later in life.

(E)   More people began to visit and inhabit areas in
which mosquitoes live and breed.

14.   It can be inferred from the passage that Lyme disease
has become prevalent in parts of the United States
because of which of the following?

(A)   The inadvertent introduction of Lyme disease
bacteria to the United States

(B)   The inability of modern sanitation methods to
eradicate Lyme disease bacteria

(C)   A genetic mutation in Lyme disease bacteria that
makes them more virulent

(D)   The spread of Lyme disease bacteria from
infected humans to noninfected humans

(E)   An increase in the number of humans who
encounter deer ticks

15. Which of the following can most reasonably be concluded about the mosquito *Aedes albopictus* on the basis of information given in the passage?

    (A)   It is native to the United States.

    (B)   It can proliferate only in Asia.

    (C)   It transmits the dengue virus.

    (D)   It caused an epidemic of dengue hemorrhagic fever in the 1950s.

    (E)   It replaced *Aedes aegypti* in Asia when ecological changes altered *Aedes aegypti's* habitat.

16. Which of the following best describes the organization of the passage?

    (A)   A paradox is stated, discussed, and left unresolved.

    (B)   Two opposing explanations are presented, argued, and reconciled.

    (C)   A theory is proposed and is then followed by descriptions of three experiments that support the theory.

    (D)   A generalization is stated and is then followed by three instances that support the generalization.

    (E)   An argument is described and is then followed by three counterexamples that refute the argument.

17. Which of the following, if true, would most strengthen the author's assertion about the cause of the Lyme disease outbreak in the United States?

    (A)   The deer population was smaller in the late nineteenth century than in the mid twentieth century.

    (B)   Interest in outdoor recreation began to grow in the late nineteenth century.

    (C)   In recent years the suburbs have stopped growing.

    (D)   Outdoor recreation enthusiasts routinely take measures to protect themselves against Lyme disease.

    (E)   Scientists have not yet developed a vaccine that can prevent Lyme disease.

Line   In 1994, a team of scientists led by David McKay
        began studying the meteorite ALH84001, which had
        been discovered in Antarctica in 1984. Two years
        later, the McKay team announced that ALH84001,
(5)   which scientists generally agree originated on Mars,
        contained compelling evidence that life once
        existed on Mars. This evidence includes the
        discovery of organic molecules in ALH84001, the
        first ever found in Martian rock. Organic
(10)   molecules—complex, carbon-based compounds—
        form the basis for terrestrial life. The organic
        molecules found in ALH84001 are polycyclic
        aromatic hydrocarbons, or PAHs. When microbes
        die, their organic material often decays into PAHs.
(15)   Skepticism about the McKay team's claim
        remains, however. For example, ALH84001 has
        been on Earth for 13,000 years, suggesting to
        some scientists that its PAHs might have resulted
        from terrestrial contamination. However, McKay's
(20)   team has demonstrated that the concentration of
        PAHs increases as one looks deeper into
        ALH84001, contrary to what one would expect from
        terrestrial contamination. The skeptics' strongest
        argument, however, is that processes unrelated to
(25)   organic life can easily produce all the evidence
        found by McKay's team, including PAHs. For
        example, star formation produces PAHs. Moreover,
        PAHs frequently appear in other meteorites, and no
        one attributes their presence to life processes. Yet
(30)   McKay's team notes that the particular combination
        of PAHs in ALH84001 is more similar to the
        combinations produced by decaying organisms than
        to those originating from nonbiological processes.

Questions 18–23 refer to the passage above.

18. The primary purpose of the passage is to

     (A)   describe new ways of studying the possibility
           that life once existed on Mars
     (B)   revise a theory regarding the existence of life on
           Mars in light of new evidence
     (C)   reconcile conflicting viewpoints regarding the
           possibility that life once existed on Mars
     (D)   evaluate a recently proposed argument
           concerning the origin of ALH84001
     (E)   describe a controversy concerning the
           significance of evidence from ALH84001

19. The passage asserts which of the following about the
     claim that ALH84001 originated on Mars?

     (A)   It was initially proposed by the McKay team of
           scientists.
     (B)   It is not a matter of widespread scientific
           dispute.
     (C)   It has been questioned by some skeptics of the
           McKay team's work.
     (D)   It has been undermined by recent work on PAHs.
     (E)   It is incompatible with the fact that ALH84001
           has been on Earth for 13,000 years.

20. The passage suggests that the fact that ALH84001
     has been on Earth for 13,000 years has been used by
     some scientists to support which of the following
     claims about ALH84001?

     (A)   ALH84001 may not have originated on Mars.
     (B)   ALH84001 contains PAHs that are the result of
           nonbiological processes.
     (C)   ALH84001 may not have contained PAHs when it
           landed on Earth.
     (D)   The organic molecules found in ALH84001 are
           not PAHs.
     (E)   The organic molecules found in ALH84001 could
           not be the result of terrestrial contamination.

21. The passage suggests that if a meteorite contained PAHs that were the result of terrestrial contamination, then one would expect which of the following to be true?

    (A) The meteorite would have been on Earth for more than 13,000 years.
    (B) The meteorite would have originated from a source other than Mars.
    (C) The PAHs contained in the meteorite would have originated from nonbiological processes.
    (D) The meteorite would contain fewer PAHs than most other meteorites contain.
    (E) The PAHs contained in the meteorite would be concentrated toward the meteorite's surface.

22. Which of the following best describes the function of the last sentence of the first paragraph?

    (A) It identifies a possible organic source for the PAHs found in ALH84001.
    (B) It describes a feature of PAHs that is not shared by other types of organic molecules.
    (C) It explains how a characteristic common to most meteorites originates.
    (D) It suggests how the terrestrial contamination of ALH84001 might have taken place.
    (E) It presents evidence that undermines the claim that life once existed on Mars.

23. The passage suggests that McKay's team would agree with which of the following regarding the PAHs produced by nonorganic processes?

    (A) These PAHs are not likely to be found in any meteorite that has been on Earth for 13,000 years or more.
    (B) These PAHs are not likely to be found in any meteorite that originated from Mars.
    (C) These PAHs are not likely to be produced by star formation.
    (D) These PAHs are likely to be found in combinations that distinguish them from the PAHs produced by organic processes.
    (E) These PAHs are likely to be found in fewer meteorites than the PAHs produced by organic processes.

Line   Homeostasis, an animal's maintenance of certain
internal variables within an acceptable range,
particularly in extreme physical environments, has
long interested biologists. The desert rat and the
(5)   camel in the most water-deprived environments,
and marine vertebrates in an all-water environment,
encounter the same regulatory problem:
maintaining adequate internal fluid balance.

For desert rats and camels, the problem is
(10)   conservation of water in an environment where
standing water is nonexistent, temperature is high,
and humidity is low. Despite these handicaps,
desert rats are able to maintain the osmotic
pressure of their blood, as well as their total body-
(15)   water content, at approximately the same levels as
other rats. One countermeasure is behavioral: these
rats stay in burrows during the hot part of the day,
thus avoiding loss of fluid through panting or
sweating, which are regulatory mechanisms for
(20)   maintaining internal body temperature by
evaporative cooling. Also, desert rats' kidneys can
excrete a urine having twice as high a salt content
as seawater.

Camels, on the other hand, rely more on simple
(25)   endurance. They cannot store water, and their
reliance on an entirely unexceptional kidney results
in a rate of water loss through renal function
significantly higher than that of desert rats. As a
result, camels must tolerate losses in body water of
(30)   up to 30 percent of their body weight.
Nevertheless, camels do rely on a special
mechanism to keep water loss within a tolerable
range: by sweating and panting only when their
body temperature exceeds that which would kill a
(35)   human, they conserve internal water.

Marine vertebrates experience difficulty with
their water balance because though there is no
shortage of seawater to drink, they must drink a lot
of it to maintain their internal fluid balance. But the
(40)   excess salts from the seawater must be discharged
somehow, and the kidneys of most marine
vertebrates are unable to excrete a urine in which
the salts are more concentrated than in seawater.
Most of these animals have special salt-secreting
(45)   organs outside the kidney that enable them to
eliminate excess salt.

Questions 24–26 refer to the passage above.

24.   Which of the following most accurately states the
purpose of the passage?

(A)   To compare two different approaches to the
study of homeostasis

(B)   To summarize the findings of several studies
regarding organisms' maintenance of internal
variables in extreme environments

(C)   To argue for a particular hypothesis regarding
various organisms' conservation of water in
desert environments

(D)   To cite examples of how homeostasis is
achieved by various organisms

(E)   To defend a new theory regarding the
maintenance of adequate fluid balance

25.   It can be inferred from the passage that some
mechanisms that regulate internal body temperature,
like sweating and panting, can lead to which of the
following?

(A)   A rise in the external body temperature

(B)   A drop in the body's internal fluid level

(C)   A decrease in the osmotic pressure of the blood

(D)   A decrease in the amount of renal water loss

(E)   A decrease in the urine's salt content

26. It can be inferred from the passage that the author characterizes the camel's kidney as "entirely unexceptional" (line 26) primarily to emphasize that it

(A) functions much as the kidney of a rat functions

(B) does not aid the camel in coping with the exceptional water loss resulting from the extreme conditions of its environment

(C) does not enable the camel to excrete as much salt as do the kidneys of marine vertebrates

(D) is similar in structure to the kidneys of most mammals living in water-deprived environments

(E) requires the help of other organs in eliminating excess salt

Line The new school of political history that emerged in the 1960s and 1970s sought to go beyond the traditional focus of political historians on leaders and government institutions by examining directly
(5)   the political practices of ordinary citizens. Like the old approach, however, this new approach excluded women. The very techniques these historians used to uncover mass political behavior in the nineteenth century United States—quantitative analyses of
(10) election returns, for example—were useless in analyzing the political activities of women, who were denied the vote until 1920.
      By redefining "political activity," historian Paula Baker has developed a political history that includes
(15) women. She concludes that among ordinary citizens, political activism by women in the nineteenth century prefigured trends in twentieth century politics. Defining "politics" as "any action taken to affect the course of behavior of
(20) government or of the community," Baker concludes that, while voting and holding office were restricted to men, women in the nineteenth century organized themselves into societies committed to social issues such as temperance and poverty. In other
(25) words, Baker contends, women activists were early practitioners of nonpartisan, issue-oriented politics and thus were more interested in enlisting lawmakers, regardless of their party affiliation, on behalf of certain issues than in ensuring that one
(30) party or another won an election. In the twentieth century, more men drew closer to women's ideas about politics and took up modes of issue-oriented politics that Baker sees women as having pioneered.

Questions 27–32 refer to the passage above.

27. The primary purpose of the passage is to

(A) enumerate reasons why both traditional scholarly methods and newer scholarly methods have limitations

(B) identify a shortcoming in a scholarly approach and describe an alternative approach

(C) provide empirical data to support a long-held scholarly assumption

(D) compare two scholarly publications on the basis of their authors' backgrounds

(E) attempt to provide a partial answer to a long-standing scholarly dilemma

28. The passage suggests which of the following concerning the techniques used by the new political historians described in the first paragraph of the passage?

(A) They involved the extensive use of the biographies of political party leaders and political theoreticians.

(B) They were conceived by political historians who were reacting against the political climates of the 1960s and 1970s.

(C) They were of more use in analyzing the positions of United States political parties in the nineteenth century than in analyzing the positions of those in the twentieth century.

(D) They were of more use in analyzing the political behavior of nineteenth-century voters than in analyzing the political activities of those who could not vote during that period.

(E) They were devised as a means of tracing the influence of nineteenth-century political trends on twentieth-century political trends.

29. It can be inferred that the author of the passage quotes Baker directly in the second paragraph primarily in order to

    (A) clarify a position before providing an alternative to that position
    (B) differentiate between a novel definition and traditional definitions
    (C) provide an example of a point agreed on by different generations of scholars
    (D) provide an example of the prose style of an important historian
    (E) amplify a definition given in the first paragraph

30. According to the passage, Paula Baker and the new political historians of the 1960s and 1970s shared which of the following?

    (A) A commitment to interest group politics
    (B) A disregard for political theory and ideology
    (C) An interest in the ways in which nineteenth-century politics prefigured contemporary politics
    (D) A reliance on such quantitative techniques as the analysis of election returns
    (E) An emphasis on the political involvement of ordinary citizens

31. Which of the following best describes the structure of the first paragraph of the passage?

    (A) Two scholarly approaches are compared, and a shortcoming common to both is identified.
    (B) Two rival schools of thought are contrasted, and a third is alluded to.
    (C) An outmoded scholarly approach is described, and a corrective approach is called for.
    (D) An argument is outlined, and counterarguments are mentioned.
    (E) A historical era is described in terms of its political trends.

32. The information in the passage suggests that a pre-1960s political historian would have been most likely to undertake which of the following studies?

    (A) An analysis of voting trends among women voters of the 1920s
    (B) A study of male voters' gradual ideological shift from party politics to issue-oriented politics
    (C) A biography of an influential nineteenth-century minister of foreign affairs
    (D) An analysis of narratives written by previously unrecognized women activists
    (E) A study of voting trends among naturalized immigrant laborers in a nineteenth-century logging camp

Line At the end of the nineteenth century, a rising
interest in Native American customs and an
increasing desire to understand Native American
culture prompted ethnologists to begin recording
(5) the life stories of Native Americans. Ethnologists
had a distinct reason for wanting to hear the
stories: they were after linguistic or anthropological
data that would supplement their own field
observations, and they believed that the personal
(10) stories, even of a single individual, could increase
their understanding of the cultures that they had
been observing from without. In addition many
ethnologists at the turn of the century believed that
Native American manners and customs were rapidly
(15) disappearing, and that it was important to preserve
for posterity as much information as could be
adequately recorded before the cultures
disappeared forever.
　　There were, however, arguments against this
(20) method as a way of acquiring accurate and
complete information. Franz Boas, for example,
described autobiographies as being "of limited
value, and useful chiefly for the study of the
perversion of truth by memory," while Paul Radin
(25) contended that investigators rarely spent enough
time with the tribes they were observing, and
inevitably derived results too tinged by the
investigator's own emotional tone to be reliable.
　　Even more importantly, as these life stories
(30) moved from the traditional oral mode to recorded
written form, much was inevitably lost. Editors often
decided what elements were significant to the field
research on a given tribe. Native Americans
recognized that the essence of their lives could not
(35) be communicated in English and that events that
they thought significant were often deemed
unimportant by their interviewers. Indeed, the very
act of telling their stories could force Native
American narrators to distort their cultures, as
(40) taboos had to be broken to speak the names of
dead relatives crucial to their family stories.
　　Despite all of this, autobiography remains a
useful tool for ethnological research: such personal
reminiscences and impressions, incomplete as they
(45) may be, are likely to throw more light on the
working of the mind and emotions than any amount
of speculation from an ethnologist or ethnological
theorist from another culture.

Questions 33–38 refer to the passage above.

33. Which of the following best describes the organization of the passage?

    (A) The historical backgrounds of two currently used research methods are chronicled.

    (B) The validity of the data collected by using two different research methods is compared.

    (C) The usefulness of a research method is questioned and then a new method is proposed.

    (D) The use of a research method is described and the limitations of the results obtained are discussed.

    (E) A research method is evaluated and the changes necessary for its adaptation to other subject areas are discussed.

34. Which of the following is most similar to the actions of nineteenth-century ethnologists in their editing of the life stories of Native Americans?

    (A) A witness in a jury trial invokes the Fifth Amendment in order to avoid relating personally incriminating evidence.

    (B) A stockbroker refuses to divulge the source of her information on the possible future increase in a stock's value.

    (C) A sports announcer describes the action in a team sport with which he is unfamiliar.

    (D) A chef purposely excludes the special ingredient from the recipe of his prizewinning dessert.

    (E) A politician fails to mention in a campaign speech the similarities in the positions held by her opponent for political office and by herself.

35. According to the passage, collecting life stories can be a useful methodology because

    (A) life stories provide deeper insights into a culture than the hypothesizing of academics who are not members of that culture

    (B) life stories can be collected easily and they are not subject to invalid interpretations

    (C) ethnologists have a limited number of research methods from which to choose

    (D) life stories make it easy to distinguish between the important and unimportant features of a culture

    (E) the collection of life stories does not require a culturally knowledgeable investigator

36. Information in the passage suggests that which of the following may be a possible way to eliminate bias in the editing of life stories?

    (A) Basing all inferences made about the culture on an ethnological theory

    (B) Eliminating all of the emotion laden information reported by the informant

    (C) Translating the informant's words into the researcher's language

    (D) Reducing the number of questions and carefully specifying the content of the questions that the investigator can ask the informant

    (E) Reporting all of the information that the informant provides regardless of the investigator's personal opinion about its intrinsic value

37. The primary purpose of the passage as a whole is to

    (A) question an explanation

    (B) correct a misconception

    (C) critique a methodology

    (D) discredit an idea

    (E) clarify an ambiguity

38. It can be inferred from the passage that a characteristic of the ethnological research on Native Americans conducted during the nineteenth century was the use of which of the following?

    (A) Investigators familiar with the culture under study

    (B) A language other than the informant's for recording life stories

    (C) Life stories as the ethnologist's primary source of information

    (D) Complete transcriptions of informants' descriptions of tribal beliefs

    (E) Stringent guidelines for the preservation of cultural data

Line   Seeking a competitive advantage, some
       professional service firms (for example, firms
       providing advertising, accounting, or health care
       services) have considered offering unconditional
(5)   guarantees of satisfaction. Such guarantees specify
       what clients can expect and what the firm will do if
       it fails to fulfill these expectations. Particularly with
       first-time clients, an unconditional guarantee can be
       an effective marketing tool if the client is very
(10)   cautious, the firm's fees are high, the negative
       consequences of bad service are grave, or
       business is difficult to obtain through referrals and
       word-of-mouth.

       However, an unconditional guarantee can
(15)   sometimes hinder marketing efforts. With its
       implication that failure is possible, the guarantee
       may, paradoxically, cause clients to doubt the
       service firm's ability to deliver the promised level of
       service. It may conflict with a firm's desire to
(20)   appear sophisticated, or may even suggest that a
       firm is begging for business. In legal and health care
       services, it may mislead clients by suggesting that
       lawsuits or medical procedures will have
       guaranteed outcomes. Indeed, professional service
(25)   firms with outstanding reputations and performance
       to match have little to gain from offering
       unconditional guarantees. And any firm that
       implements an unconditional guarantee without
       undertaking a commensurate commitment to
(30)   quality of service is merely employing a potentially
       costly marketing gimmick.

Questions 39–44 refer to the passage above.

39.   The primary function of the passage as a whole is to

      (A)   account for the popularity of a practice
      (B)   evaluate the utility of a practice
      (C)   demonstrate how to institute a practice
      (D)   weigh the ethics of using a strategy
      (E)   explain the reasons for pursuing a strategy

40.   All of the following are mentioned in the passage as
      circumstances in which professional service firms can
      benefit from offering an unconditional guarantee
      EXCEPT:

      (A)   The firm is having difficulty retaining its clients
            of long standing.
      (B)   The firm is having difficulty getting business
            through client recommendations.
      (C)   The firm charges substantial fees for its
            services.
      (D)   The adverse effects of poor performance by the
            firm are significant for the client.
      (E)   The client is reluctant to incur risk.

41.   Which of the following is cited in the passage as a goal
      of some professional service firms in offering
      unconditional guarantees of satisfaction?

      (A)   A limit on the firm's liability
      (B)   Successful competition against other firms
      (C)   Ability to justify fee increases
      (D)   Attainment of an outstanding reputation in a field
      (E)   Improvement in the quality of the firm's service

42. The passage's description of the issue raised by unconditional guarantees for health care or legal services most clearly implies that which of the following is true?

    (A)   The legal and medical professions have standards of practice that would be violated by attempts to fulfill such unconditional guarantees.

    (B)   The result of a lawsuit or medical procedure cannot necessarily be determined in advance by the professionals handling a client's case.

    (C)   The dignity of the legal and medical professions is undermined by any attempts at marketing of professional services, including unconditional guarantees.

    (D)   Clients whose lawsuits or medical procedures have unsatisfactory outcomes cannot be adequately compensated by financial settlements alone.

    (E)   Predicting the monetary cost of legal or health care services is more difficult than predicting the monetary cost of other types of professional services.

43. Which of the following hypothetical situations best exemplifies the potential problem noted in the second sentence of the second paragraph (lines 15–19)?

    (A)   A physician's unconditional guarantee of satisfaction encourages patients to sue for malpractice if they are unhappy with the treatment they receive.

    (B)   A lawyer's unconditional guarantee of satisfaction makes clients suspect that the lawyer needs to find new clients quickly to increase the firm's income.

    (C)   A business consultant's unconditional guarantee of satisfaction is undermined when the consultant fails to provide all of the services that are promised.

    (D)   An architect's unconditional guarantee of satisfaction makes clients wonder how often the architect's buildings fail to please clients.

    (E)   An accountant's unconditional guarantee of satisfaction leads clients to believe that tax returns prepared by the accountant are certain to be accurate.

44. The passage most clearly implies which of the following about the professional service firms mentioned in lines 24–27?

    (A)   They are unlikely to have offered unconditional guarantees of satisfaction in the past.

    (B)   They are usually profitable enough to be able to compensate clients according to the terms of an unconditional guarantee.

    (C)   They usually practice in fields in which the outcomes are predictable.

    (D)   Their fees are usually more affordable than those charged by other professional service firms.

    (E)   Their clients are usually already satisfied with the quality of service that is delivered.

Line   In a 1918 editorial, W. E. B. Du Bois advised African
        Americans to stop agitating for equality and to
        proclaim their solidarity with White Americans for
        the duration of the First World War. The editorial
(5)   surprised many African Americans who viewed
        Du Bois as an uncompromising African American
        leader and a chief opponent of the accommodationist
        tactics urged by Booker T. Washington. In fact,
        however, Du Bois often shifted positions along the
(10)   continuum between Washington and
        confrontationists such as William Trotter. In 1895,
        when Washington called on African Americans to
        concentrate on improving their communities instead
        of opposing discrimination and agitating for political
(15)   rights, Du Bois praised Washington's speech. In
        1903, however, Du Bois aligned himself with Trotter,
        Washington's militant opponent, less for ideological
        reasons than because Trotter had described to him
        Washington's efforts to silence those in the African
(20)   American press who opposed Washington's
        positions.
            Du Bois's wartime position thus reflected not a
        change in his long-term goals but rather a
        pragmatic response in the face of social pressures:
(25)   government officials had threatened African
        American journalists with censorship if they
        continued to voice grievances. Furthermore,
        Du Bois believed that African Americans'
        contributions to past war efforts had brought them
(30)   some legal and political advances. Du Bois's
        accommodationism did not last, however. Upon
        learning of systematic discrimination experienced
        by African Americans in the military, he called on
        them to "return fighting" from the war.

Questions 45–49 refer to the passage above.

45. The passage is primarily concerned with

  (A) identifying historical circumstances that led
       Du Bois to alter his long-term goals

  (B) defining "accommodationism" and showing how
       Du Bois used this strategy to achieve certain
       goals

  (C) accounting for a particular position adopted by
       Du Bois during the First World War

  (D) contesting the view that Du Bois was significantly
       influenced by either Washington or Trotter

  (E) assessing the effectiveness of a strategy that
       Du Bois urged African Americans to adopt

46. The passage indicates which of the following about
     Du Bois's attitude toward Washington?

  (A) It underwent a shift during the First World War as
       Du Bois became more sympathetic with Trotter's
       views.

  (B) It underwent a shift in 1903 for reasons other
       than Du Bois's disagreement with Washington's
       accommodationist views.

  (C) It underwent a shift as Du Bois made a long-term
       commitment to the strategy of accommodation.

  (D) It remained consistently positive even though
       Du Bois disagreed with Washington's efforts to
       control the African American press.

  (E) It was shaped primarily by Du Bois's appreciation
       of Washington's pragmatic approach to the
       advancement of the interests of African
       Americans.

47. The passage suggests which of the following about the contributions of African Americans to the United States war effort during the First World War?

   (A) The contributions were made largely in response to Du Bois's 1918 editorial.

   (B) The contributions had much the same effect as African Americans' contributions to previous wars.

   (C) The contributions did not end discrimination against African Americans in the military.

   (D) The contributions were made in protest against Trotter's confrontationist tactics.

   (E) The contributions were made primarily by civil rights activists who returned to activism after the war.

48. The author of the passage refers to Washington's call to African Americans in 1895 primarily in order to

   (A) identify Du Bois's characteristic position on the continuum between accommodationism and confrontationism

   (B) explain why Du Bois was sympathetic with Washington's views in 1895

   (C) clarify how Trotter's views differed from those of Washington in 1895

   (D) support an assertion about Du Bois's tendency to shift his political positions

   (E) dismiss the claim that Du Bois's position in his 1918 editorial was consistent with his previous views

49. According to the passage, which of the following is true of the strategy that Du Bois's 1918 editorial urged African Americans to adopt during the First World War?

   (A) It was a strategy that Du Bois had consistently rejected in the past.

   (B) It represented a compromise between Du Bois's own views and those of Trotter.

   (C) It represented a significant redefinition of the long-term goals Du Bois held prior to the war.

   (D) It was advocated by Du Bois in response to his recognition of the discrimination faced by African Americans during the war.

   (E) It was advocated by Du Bois in part because of his historical knowledge of gains African Americans had made during past wars.

Line The fact that superior service can generate a
competitive advantage for a company does not
mean that every attempt at improving service will
create such an advantage. Investments in service,
(5) like those in production and distribution, must be
balanced against other types of investments on the
basis of direct, tangible benefits such as cost
reduction and increased revenues. If a company is
already effectively on a par with its competitors
(10) because it provides service that avoids a damaging
reputation and keeps customers from leaving at an
unacceptable rate, then investment in higher
service levels may be wasted, since service is a
deciding factor for customers only in extreme
(15) situations.
      This truth was not apparent to managers of one
regional bank, which failed to improve its
competitive position despite its investment in
reducing the time a customer had to wait for a
(20) teller. The bank managers did not recognize the
level of customer inertia in the consumer banking
industry that arises from the inconvenience of
switching banks. Nor did they analyze their service
improvement to determine whether it would attract
(25) new customers by producing a new standard of
service that would excite customers or by proving
difficult for competitors to copy. The only merit of
the improvement was that it could easily be
described to customers.

Questions 50–55 refer to the passage above.

50. The primary purpose of the passage is to

(A) contrast possible outcomes of a type of
business investment

(B) suggest more careful evaluation of a type of
business investment

(C) illustrate various ways in which a type of
business investment could fail to enhance
revenues

(D) trace the general problems of a company to a
certain type of business investment

(E) criticize the way in which managers tend to
analyze the costs and benefits of business
investments

51. According to the passage, investments in service are
comparable to investments in production and
distribution in terms of the

(A) tangibility of the benefits that they tend to confer

(B) increased revenues that they ultimately produce

(C) basis on which they need to be weighed

(D) insufficient analysis that managers devote to
them

(E) degree of competitive advantage that they are
likely to provide

52. The passage suggests which of the following about
service provided by the regional bank prior to its
investment in enhancing that service?

(A) It enabled the bank to retain customers at an
acceptable rate.

(B) It threatened to weaken the bank's competitive
position with respect to other regional banks.

(C) It had already been improved after having
caused damage to the bank's reputation in the
past.

(D) It was slightly superior to that of the bank's
regional competitors.

(E) It needed to be improved to attain parity with
the service provided by competing banks.

53. The passage suggests that bank managers failed to consider whether or not the service improvement mentioned in lines 18–20

    (A) was too complicated to be easily described to prospective customers

    (B) made a measurable change in the experiences of customers in the bank's offices

    (C) could be sustained if the number of customers increased significantly

    (D) was an innovation that competing banks could have imitated

    (E) was adequate to bring the bank's general level of service to a level that was comparable with that of its competitors

54. The discussion of the regional bank in the second paragraph serves which of the following functions within the passage as a whole?

    (A) It describes an exceptional case in which investment in service actually failed to produce a competitive advantage.

    (B) It illustrates the pitfalls of choosing to invest in service at a time when investment is needed more urgently in another area.

    (C) It demonstrates the kind of analysis that managers apply when they choose one kind of service investment over another.

    (D) It supports the argument that investments in certain aspects of service are more advantageous than investments in other aspects of service.

    (E) It provides an example of the point about investment in service made in the first paragraph.

55. The author uses the word "only" in line 27 most likely in order to

    (A) highlight the oddity of the service improvement

    (B) emphasize the relatively low value of the investment in service improvement

    (C) distinguish the primary attribute of the service improvement from secondary attributes

    (D) single out a certain merit of the service improvement from other merits

    (E) point out the limited duration of the actual service improvement

Line   In an attempt to improve the overall performance of
        clerical workers, many companies have introduced
        computerized performance monitoring and control
        systems (CPMCS) that record and report a worker's
(5)   computer-driven activities. However, at least one
        study has shown that such monitoring may not be
        having the desired effect. In the study, researchers
        asked monitored clerical workers and their
        supervisors how assessments of productivity
(10)   affected supervisors' ratings of workers'
        performance. In contrast to unmonitored workers
        doing the same work, who without exception
        identified the most important element in their jobs
        as customer service, the monitored workers and
(15)   their supervisors all responded that productivity
        was the critical factor in assigning ratings. This
        finding suggested that there should have been a
        strong correlation between a monitored worker's
        productivity and the overall rating the worker
(20)   received. However, measures of the relationship
        between overall rating and individual elements of
        performance clearly supported the conclusion that
        supervisors gave considerable weight to criteria
        such as attendance, accuracy, and indications of
(25)   customer satisfaction.

        It is possible that productivity may be a
        "hygiene factor"; that is, if it is too low, it will hurt
        the overall rating. But the evidence suggests that
        beyond the point at which productivity becomes
(30)   "good enough," higher productivity per se is unlikely
        to improve a rating.

Questions 56–60 refer to the passage above.

56. According to the passage, before the final results of
     the study were known, which of the following seemed
     likely?

     (A) That workers with the highest productivity would
          also be the most accurate

     (B) That workers who initially achieved high
          productivity ratings would continue to do so
          consistently

     (C) That the highest performance ratings would be
          achieved by workers with the highest
          productivity

     (D) That the most productive workers would be
          those whose supervisors claimed to value
          productivity

     (E) That supervisors who claimed to value
          productivity would place equal value on
          customer satisfaction

57. It can be inferred that the author of the passage
     discusses "unmonitored workers" (line 11) primarily in
     order to

     (A) compare the ratings of these workers with the
          ratings of monitored workers

     (B) provide an example of a case in which
          monitoring might be effective

     (C) provide evidence of an inappropriate use of
          CPMCS

     (D) emphasize the effect that CPMCS may have on
          workers' perceptions of their jobs

     (E) illustrate the effect that CPMCS may have on
          workers' ratings

58. Which of the following, if true, would most clearly have supported the conclusion referred to in lines 22–25?

(A) Ratings of productivity correlated highly with ratings of both accuracy and attendance.

(B) Electronic monitoring greatly increased productivity.

(C) Most supervisors based overall ratings of performance on measures of productivity alone.

(D) Overall ratings of performance correlated more highly with measures of productivity than the researchers expected.

(E) Overall ratings of performance correlated more highly with measures of accuracy than with measures of productivity.

59. According to the passage, a "hygiene factor" (line 27) is an aspect of a worker's performance that

(A) has no effect on the rating of a worker's performance

(B) is so basic to performance that it is assumed to be adequate for all workers

(C) is given less importance than it deserves in rating a worker's performance

(D) is not likely to affect a worker's rating unless it is judged to be inadequate

(E) is important primarily because of the effect it has on a worker's rating

60. The primary purpose of the passage is to

(A) explain the need for the introduction of an innovative strategy

(B) discuss a study of the use of a particular method

(C) recommend a course of action

(D) resolve a difference of opinion

(E) suggest an alternative approach

Line Neotropical coastal mangrove forests are usually
      "zonal," with certain mangrove species found
      predominantly in the seaward portion of the habitat
      and other mangrove species on the more landward
(5)   portions of the coast. The earliest research on
      mangrove forests produced descriptions of species
      distribution from shore to land, without exploring
      the causes of the distributions.
          The idea that zonation is caused by plant
(10) succession was first expressed by J. H. Davis in a
      study of Florida mangrove forests. According to
      Davis' scheme, the shoreline is being extended in a
      seaward direction because of the "land-building" role
      of mangroves, which, by trapping sediments over
(15) time, extend the shore. As a habitat gradually
      becomes more inland as the shore extends, the
      "land-building" species are replaced. This continuous
      process of accretion and succession would be
      interrupted only by hurricanes or storm flushings.
(20)   Recently the universal application of Davis'
      succession paradigm has been challenged. It
      appears that in areas where weak currents and
      weak tidal energies allow the accumulation of
      sediments, mangroves will follow land formation
(25) and accelerate the rate of soil accretion;
      succession will proceed according to Davis'
      scheme. But on stable coastlines, the distribution of
      mangrove species results in other patterns of
      zonation; "land building" does not occur.
(30)   To find a principle that explains the various
      distribution patterns, several researchers have
      looked to salinity and its effects on mangroves.
      While mangroves can develop in fresh water, they
      can also thrive in salinities as high as 2.5 times that
(35) of seawater. However, those mangrove species
      found in freshwater habitats do well only in the
      absence of competition, thus suggesting that
      salinity tolerance is a critical factor in competitive
      success among mangrove species. Research
(40) suggests that mangroves will normally dominate
      highly saline regions, although not because they
      require salt. Rather, they are metabolically efficient
      (and hence grow well) in portions of an environment
      whose high salinity excludes plants adapted to
(45) lower salinities. Tides create different degrees of
      salinity along a coastline. The characteristic
      mangrove species of each zone should exhibit a
      higher metabolic efficiency at that salinity
      than will any potential invader, including other
(50) species of mangrove.

Questions 61–63 refer to the passage above.

61. The primary purpose of the passage is to

    (A) refute the idea that the zonation exhibited in mangrove forests is caused by adaptation to salinity
    (B) describe the pattern of zonation typically found in Florida mangrove forests
    (C) argue that Davis' succession paradigm cannot be successfully applied to Florida mangrove forests
    (D) discuss hypotheses that attempt to explain the zonation of coastal mangrove forests
    (E) establish that plants that do well in saline forest environments require salt to achieve maximum metabolic efficiency

62. According to the passage, the earliest research on mangrove forests produced which of the following?

    (A) Data that implied random patterns of mangrove species distribution
    (B) Descriptions of species distributions suggesting zonation
    (C) Descriptions of the development of mangrove forests over time
    (D) Reclassification of species formerly thought to be identical
    (E) Data that confirmed the "land-building" role of mangroves

63. It can be inferred from the passage that Davis' paradigm does NOT apply to which of the following?

    (A) The shoreline of Florida mangrove forests first studied by Davis

    (B) A shoreline in an area with weak currents

    (C) A shoreline in an area with weak tidal energy

    (D) A shoreline extended by "land-building" species of mangroves

    (E) A shoreline in which few sediments can accumulate

Line Findings from several studies on corporate mergers and acquisitions during the 1970s and 1980s raise questions about why firms initiate and consummate such transactions. One study showed, for example,
(5) that acquiring firms were on average unable to maintain acquired firms' pre-merger levels of profitability. A second study concluded that post-acquisition gains to most acquiring firms were not adequate to cover the premiums paid to obtain
(10) acquired firms. A third demonstrated that, following the announcement of a prospective merger, the stock of the prospective acquiring firm tends to increase in value much less than does that of the firm for which it bids. Yet mergers and acquisitions
(15) remain common, and bidders continue to assert that their objectives are economic ones. Acquisitions may well have the desirable effect of channeling a nation's resources efficiently from less to more efficient sectors of its economy, but the
(20) individual acquisitions executives arranging these deals must see them as advancing either their own or their companies' private economic interests. It seems that factors having little to do with corporate economic interests explain acquisitions. These
(25) factors may include the incentive compensation of executives, lack of monitoring by boards of directors, and managerial error in estimating the value of firms targeted for acquisition. Alternatively, the acquisition acts of bidders may derive from
(30) modeling: a manager does what other managers do.

Questions 64–70 refer to the passage above.

64. The primary purpose of the passage is to

(A) review research demonstrating the benefits of corporate mergers and acquisitions and examine some of the drawbacks that acquisition behavior entails

(B) contrast the effects of corporate mergers and acquisitions on acquiring firms and on firms that are acquired

(C) report findings that raise questions about a reason for corporate mergers and acquisitions and suggest possible alternative reasons

(D) explain changes in attitude on the part of acquiring firms toward corporate mergers and acquisitions

(E) account for a recent decline in the rate of corporate mergers and acquisitions

65. The findings cited in the passage suggest which of the following about the outcomes of corporate mergers and acquisitions with respect to acquiring firms?

(A) They include a decrease in value of many acquiring firms' stocks.

(B) They tend to be more beneficial for small firms than for large firms.

(C) They do not fulfill the professed goals of most acquiring firms.

(D) They tend to be beneficial to such firms in the long term even though apparently detrimental in the short term.

(E) They discourage many such firms from attempting to make subsequent bids and acquisitions.

66. It can be inferred from the passage that the author would be most likely to agree with which of the following statements about corporate acquisitions?

(A) Their known benefits to national economies explain their appeal to individual firms during the 1970s and 1980s.

(B) Despite their adverse impact on some firms, they are the best way to channel resources from less to more productive sectors of a nation's economy.

(C) They are as likely to occur because of poor monitoring by boards of directors as to be caused by incentive compensation for managers.

(D) They will be less prevalent in the future, since their actual effects will gain wider recognition.

(E) Factors other than economic benefit to the acquiring firm help to explain the frequency with which they occur.

67. The author of the passage mentions the effect of acquisitions on national economies most probably in order to

(A) provide an explanation for the mergers and acquisitions of the 1970s and 1980s overlooked by the findings discussed in the passage

(B) suggest that national economic interests played an important role in the mergers and acquisitions of the 1970s and 1980s

(C) support a noneconomic explanation for the mergers and acquisitions of the 1970s and 1980s that was cited earlier in the passage

(D) cite and point out the inadequacy of one possible explanation for the prevalence of mergers and acquisitions during the 1970s and 1980s

(E) explain how modeling affected the decisions made by managers involved in mergers and acquisitions during the 1970s and 1980s

68. According to the passage, during the 1970s and 1980s bidding firms differed from the firms for which they bid in that bidding firms

(A) tended to be more profitable before a merger than after a merger

(B) were more often concerned about the impact of acquisitions on national economies

(C) were run by managers whose actions were modeled on those of other managers

(D) anticipated greater economic advantages from prospective mergers

(E) experienced less of an increase in stock value when a prospective merger was announced

69. According to the passage, which of the following was true of corporate acquisitions that occurred during the 1970s and 1980s?

(A) Few of the acquisitions that firms made were subsequently divested.

(B) Most such acquisitions produced only small increases in acquired firms' levels of profitability.

(C) Most such acquisitions were based on an overestimation of the value of target firms.

(D) The gains realized by most acquiring firms did not equal the amounts expended in acquiring target firms.

(E) About half of such acquisitions led to long-term increases in the value of acquiring firms' stocks.

70. The author of the passage implies that which of the following is a possible partial explanation for acquisition behavior during the 1970s and 1980s?

(A) Managers wished to imitate other managers primarily because they saw how financially beneficial other firms' acquisitions were.

(B) Managers miscalculated the value of firms that were to be acquired.

(C) Lack of consensus within boards of directors resulted in their imposing conflicting goals on managers.

(D) Total compensation packages for managers increased during that period.

(E) The value of bidding firms' stock increased significantly when prospective mergers were announced.

Line Caffeine, the stimulant in coffee, has been called "the most widely used psychoactive substance on Earth." Snyder, Daly, and Bruns have recently proposed that caffeine affects behavior by

(5) countering the activity in the human brain of a naturally occurring chemical called adenosine. Adenosine normally depresses neuron firing in many areas of the brain. It apparently does this by inhibiting the release of neurotransmitters,

(10) chemicals that carry nerve impulses from one neuron to the next.

Like many other agents that affect neuron firing, adenosine must first bind to specific receptors on neuronal membranes. There are at

(15) least two classes of these receptors, which have been designated A_1 and A_2. Snyder et al. propose that caffeine, which is structurally similar to adenosine, is able to bind to both types of receptors, which prevents adenosine from attaching

(20) there and allows the neurons to fire more readily than they otherwise would.

For many years, caffeine's effects have been attributed to its inhibition of the production of phosphodiesterase, an enzyme that breaks down

(25) the chemical called cyclic AMP. A number of neurotransmitters exert their effects by first increasing cyclic AMP concentrations in target neurons. Therefore, prolonged periods at the elevated concentrations, as might be brought about

(30) by a phosphodiesterase inhibitor, could lead to a greater amount of neuron firing and, consequently, to behavioral stimulation. But Snyder et al. point out that the caffeine concentrations needed to inhibit the production of phosphodiesterase in the brain

(35) are much higher than those that produce stimulation. Moreover, other compounds that block phosphodiesterase's activity are not stimulants.

To buttress their case that caffeine acts instead by preventing adenosine binding, Snyder et

(40) al. compared the stimulatory effects of a series of caffeine derivatives with their ability to dislodge adenosine from its receptors in the brains of mice. "In general," they reported, "the ability of the compounds to compete at the receptors correlates

(45) with their ability to stimulate locomotion in the mouse; i.e., the higher their capacity to bind at the receptors, the higher their ability to stimulate locomotion." Theophylline, a close structural relative of caffeine and the major stimulant in tea, was one

(50) of the most effective compounds in both regards.

Line   There were some apparent exceptions to the general correlation observed between adenosine-receptor binding and stimulation. One of these was a compound called 3-isobutyl-1-methylxanthine

(55) (IBMX), which bound very well but actually depressed mouse locomotion. Snyder et al. suggest that this is not a major stumbling block to their hypothesis. The problem is that the compound has mixed effects in the brain, a not unusual occurrence

(60) with psychoactive drugs. Even caffeine, which is generally known only for its stimulatory effects, displays this property, depressing mouse locomotion at very low concentrations and stimulating it at higher ones.

Questions 71–76 refer to the passage above.

71. The primary purpose of the passage is to

    (A) discuss a plan for investigation of a phenomenon that is not yet fully understood

    (B) present two explanations of a phenomenon and reconcile the differences between them

    (C) summarize two theories and suggest a third theory that overcomes the problems encountered in the first two

    (D) describe an alternative hypothesis and provide evidence and arguments that support it

    (E) challenge the validity of a theory by exposing the inconsistencies and contradictions in it

72. According to Snyder et al., caffeine differs from adenosine in that caffeine

    (A) stimulates behavior in the mouse and in humans, whereas adenosine stimulates behavior in humans only

    (B) has mixed effects in the brain, whereas adenosine has only a stimulatory effect

    (C) increases cyclic AMP concentrations in target neurons, whereas adenosine decreases such concentrations

    (D) permits release of neurotransmitters when it is bound to adenosine receptors, whereas adenosine inhibits such release

    (E) inhibits both neuron firing and the production of phosphodiesterase when there is a sufficient concentration in the brain, whereas adenosine inhibits only neuron firing

73. In response to experimental results concerning IBMX, Snyder et al. contended that it is not uncommon for psychoactive drugs to have

    (A) mixed effects in the brain

    (B) inhibitory effects on enzymes in the brain

    (C) close structural relationships with caffeine

    (D) depressive effects on mouse locomotion

    (E) the ability to dislodge caffeine from receptors in the brain

74. According to Snyder et al., all of the following compounds can bind to specific receptors in the brain EXCEPT

    (A) IBMX

    (B) caffeine

    (C) adenosine

    (D) theophylline

    (E) phosphodiesterase

75. Snyder et al. suggest that caffeine's ability to bind to A_1 and A_2 receptors can be at least partially attributed to which of the following?

    (A) The chemical relationship between caffeine and phosphodiesterase

    (B) The structural relationship between caffeine and adenosine

    (C) The structural similarity between caffeine and neurotransmitters

    (D) The ability of caffeine to stimulate behavior

    (E) The natural occurrence of caffeine and adenosine in the brain

76. The author quotes Snyder et al. in lines 43–48 most probably in order to

    (A) reveal some of the assumptions underlying their theory

    (B) summarize a major finding of their experiments

    (C) point out that their experiments were limited to the mouse

    (D) indicate that their experiments resulted only in general correlations

    (E) refute the objections made by supporters of the older theory

Line Historians of women's labor in the United States at first largely disregarded the story of female service workers—women earning wages in occupations such as salesclerk, domestic servant, and office
(5) secretary. These historians focused instead on factory work, primarily because it seemed so different from traditional, unpaid "women's work" in the home, and because the underlying economic forces of industrialism were presumed to be
(10) gender-blind and hence emancipatory in effect. Unfortunately, emancipation has been less profound than expected, for not even industrial wage labor has escaped continued sex segregation in the workplace.
(15)   To explain this unfinished revolution in the status of women, historians have recently begun to emphasize the way a prevailing definition of femininity often determines the kinds of work allocated to women, even when such allocation is
(20) inappropriate to new conditions. For instance, early textile-mill entrepreneurs, in justifying women's employment in wage labor, made much of the assumption that women were by nature skillful at detailed tasks and patient in carrying out repetitive
(25) chores; the mill owners thus imported into the new industrial order hoary stereotypes associated with the homemaking activities they presumed to have been the purview of women. Because women accepted the more unattractive new industrial tasks
(30) more readily than did men, such jobs came to be regarded as female jobs. And employers, who assumed that women's "real" aspirations were for marriage and family life, declined to pay women wages commensurate with those of men. Thus
(35) many lower-skilled, lower-paid, less secure jobs came to be perceived as "female."
        More remarkable than the original has been the persistence of such sex segregation in twentieth-century industry. Once an occupation came to be
(40) perceived as "female," employers showed surprisingly little interest in changing that perception, even when higher profits beckoned. And despite the urgent need of the United States during the Second World War to mobilize its human
(45) resources fully, job segregation by sex characterized even the most important war industries. Moreover, once the war ended, employers quickly returned to men most of the "male" jobs that women had been permitted to
(50) master.

Questions 77–84 refer to the passage above.

77. According to the passage, job segregation by sex in the United States was

(A) greatly diminished by labor mobilization during the Second World War

(B) perpetuated by those textile-mill owners who argued in favor of women's employment in wage labor

(C) one means by which women achieved greater job security

(D) reluctantly challenged by employers except when the economic advantages were obvious

(E) a constant source of labor unrest in the young textile industry

78. According to the passage, historians of women's labor focused on factory work as a more promising area of research than service-sector work because factory work

(A) involved the payment of higher wages

(B) required skill in detailed tasks

(C) was assumed to be less characterized by sex segregation

(D) was more readily accepted by women than by men

(E) fit the economic dynamic of industrialism better

79. It can be inferred from the passage that early historians of women's labor in the United States paid little attention to women's employment in the service sector of the economy because

(A) the extreme variety of these occupations made it very difficult to assemble meaningful statistics about them

(B) fewer women found employment in the service sector than in factory work

(C) the wages paid to workers in the service sector were much lower than those paid in the industrial sector

(D) women's employment in the service sector tended to be much more short-term than in factory work

(E) employment in the service sector seemed to have much in common with the unpaid work associated with homemaking

80. The passage supports which of the following statements about the early mill owners mentioned in the second paragraph?

    (A) They hoped that by creating relatively unattractive "female" jobs they would discourage women from losing interest in marriage and family life.

    (B) They sought to increase the size of the available labor force as a means to keep men's wages low.

    (C) They argued that women were inherently suited to do well in particular kinds of factory work.

    (D) They thought that factory work bettered the condition of women by emancipating them from dependence on income earned by men.

    (E) They felt guilty about disturbing the traditional division of labor in the family.

81. It can be inferred from the passage that the "unfinished revolution" the author mentions in line 15 refers to the

    (A) entry of women into the industrial labor market

    (B) recognition that work done by women as homemakers should be compensated at rates comparable to those prevailing in the service sector of the economy

    (C) development of a new definition of femininity unrelated to the economic forces of industrialism

    (D) introduction of equal pay for equal work in all professions

    (E) emancipation of women wage earners from gender-determined job allocation

82. The passage supports which of the following statements about hiring policies in the United States?

    (A) After a crisis many formerly "male" jobs are reclassified as "female" jobs.

    (B) Industrial employers generally prefer to hire women with previous experience as homemakers.

    (C) Post–Second World War hiring policies caused women to lose many of their wartime gains in employment opportunity.

    (D) Even war industries during the Second World War were reluctant to hire women for factory work.

    (E) The service sector of the economy has proved more nearly gender-blind in its hiring policies than has the manufacturing sector.

83. Which of the following words best expresses the opinion of the author of the passage concerning the notion that women are more skillful than men in carrying out detailed tasks?

    (A) "patient" (line 24)

    (B) "repetitive" (line 24)

    (C) "hoary" (line 26)

    (D) "homemaking" (line 27)

    (E) "purview" (line 28)

84. Which of the following best describes the relationship of the final paragraph to the passage as a whole?

    (A) The central idea is reinforced by the citation of evidence drawn from twentieth-century history.

    (B) The central idea is restated in such a way as to form a transition to a new topic for discussion.

    (C) The central idea is restated and juxtaposed with evidence that might appear to contradict it.

    (D) A partial exception to the generalizations of the central idea is dismissed as unimportant.

    (E) Recent history is cited to suggest that the central idea's validity is gradually diminishing.

Line   Two modes of argumentation have been used on
       behalf of women's emancipation in Western
       societies. Arguments in what could be called the
       "relational" feminist tradition maintain the doctrine
(5)   of "equality in difference," or equity as distinct from
       equality. They posit that biological distinctions
       between the sexes result in a necessary sexual
       division of labor in the family and throughout society
       and that women's procreative labor is currently
(10)   undervalued by society, to the disadvantage of
       women. By contrast, the individualist feminist
       tradition emphasizes individual human rights and
       celebrates women's quest for personal autonomy,
       while downplaying the importance of gender roles
(15)   and minimizing discussion of childbearing and its
       attendant responsibilities.
           Before the late nineteenth century, these views
       coexisted within the feminist movement, often
       within the writings of the same individual. Between
(20)   1890 and 1920, however, relational feminism, which
       had been the dominant strain in feminist thought,
       and which still predominates among European and
       non-Western feminists, lost ground in England and
       the United States. Because the concept of individual
(25)   rights was already well established in the Anglo-
       Saxon legal and political tradition, individualist
       feminism came to predominate in English-speaking
       countries. At the same time, the goals of the two
       approaches began to seem increasingly
(30)   irreconcilable. Individualist feminists began to
       advocate a totally gender-blind system with equal
       rights for all. Relational feminists, while agreeing
       that equal educational and economic opportunities
       outside the home should be available for all women,
(35)   continued to emphasize women's special
       contributions to society as homemakers and
       mothers; they demanded special treatment for
       women, including protective legislation for women
       workers, state-sponsored maternity benefits, and
(40)   paid compensation for housework.
           Relational arguments have a major pitfall:
       because they underline women's physiological and
       psychological distinctiveness, they are often
       appropriated by political adversaries and used to
(45)   endorse male privilege. But the individualist
       approach, by attacking gender roles, denying the
       significance of physiological difference, and
       condemning existing familial institutions as
       hopelessly patriarchal, has often simply treated as
(50)   irrelevant the family roles important to many

Line   women. If the individualist framework, with its claim
       for women's autonomy, could be harmonized with
       the family-oriented concerns of relational feminists,
       a more fruitful model for contemporary feminist
(55)   politics could emerge.

Questions 85–90 refer to the passage above.

85. The author of the passage alludes to the well-
     established nature of the concept of individual rights in
     the Anglo-Saxon legal and political tradition in order to

     (A) illustrate the influence of individualist feminist
          thought on more general intellectual trends in
          English history
     (B) argue that feminism was already a part of the
          larger Anglo-Saxon intellectual tradition, even
          though this has often gone unnoticed by critics
          of women's emancipation
     (C) explain the decline in individualist thinking among
          feminists in non-English-speaking countries
     (D) help account for an increasing shift toward
          individualist feminism among feminists in
          English-speaking countries
     (E) account for the philosophical differences
          between individualist and relational feminists in
          English-speaking countries

86. The passage suggests that the author of the passage believes which of the following?

    (A) The predominance of individualist feminism in English-speaking countries is a historical phenomenon, the causes of which have not yet been investigated.

    (B) The individualist and relational feminist views are irreconcilable, given their theoretical differences concerning the foundations of society.

    (C) A consensus concerning the direction of future feminist politics will probably soon emerge, given the awareness among feminists of the need for cooperation among women.

    (D) Political adversaries of feminism often misuse arguments predicated on differences between the sexes to argue that the existing social system should be maintained.

    (E) Relational feminism provides the best theoretical framework for contemporary feminist politics, but individualist feminism could contribute much toward refining and strengthening modern feminist thought.

87. It can be inferred from the passage that the individualist feminist tradition denies the validity of which of the following causal statements?

    (A) A division of labor in a social group can result in increased efficiency with regard to the performance of group tasks.

    (B) A division of labor in a social group causes inequities in the distribution of opportunities and benefits among group members.

    (C) A division of labor on the basis of gender in a social group is necessitated by the existence of sex-linked biological differences between male and female members of the group.

    (D) Culturally determined distinctions based on gender in a social group foster the existence of differing attitudes and opinions among group members.

    (E) Educational programs aimed at reducing inequalities based on gender among members of a social group can result in a sense of greater well-being for all members of the group.

88. According to the passage, relational feminists and individualist feminists agree that

    (A) individual human rights take precedence over most other social claims

    (B) the gender-based division of labor in society should be eliminated

    (C) laws guaranteeing equal treatment for all citizens regardless of gender should be passed

    (D) a greater degree of social awareness concerning the importance of motherhood would be beneficial to society

    (E) the same educational and economic opportunities should be available to both sexes

89. According to the author, which of the following was true of feminist thought in Western societies before 1890?

    (A) Individualist feminist arguments were not found in the thought or writing of non-English-speaking feminists.

    (B) Individualist feminism was a strain in feminist thought, but another strain, relational feminism, predominated.

    (C) Relational and individualist approaches were equally prevalent in feminist thought and writing.

    (D) The predominant view among feminists held that the welfare of women was ultimately less important than the welfare of children.

    (E) The predominant view among feminists held that the sexes should receive equal treatment under the law.

90. The author implies that which of the following was true of most feminist thinkers in England and the United States after 1920?

    (A) They were less concerned with politics than with intellectual issues.

    (B) They began to reach a broader audience and their programs began to be adopted by mainstream political parties.

    (C) They called repeatedly for international cooperation among women's groups to achieve their goals.

    (D) They moderated their initial criticism of the economic systems that characterized their societies.

    (E) They did not attempt to unite the two different feminist approaches in their thought.

Line   In addition to conventional galaxies, the universe contains very dim galaxies that until recently went unnoticed by astronomers. Possibly as numerous as conventional galaxies, these galaxies have the
(5)   same general shape and even the same approximate number of stars as a common type of conventional galaxy, the spiral, but tend to be much larger. Because these galaxies' mass is spread out over larger areas, they have far fewer stars per unit
(10)   volume than do conventional galaxies. Apparently these low-surface-brightness galaxies, as they are called, take much longer than conventional galaxies to condense their primordial gas and convert it to stars—that is, they evolve much more slowly.
(15)   These galaxies may constitute an answer to the long-standing puzzle of the missing baryonic mass in the universe. Baryons—subatomic particles that are generally protons or neutrons—are the source of stellar, and therefore galactic, luminosity, and so
(20)   their numbers can be estimated based on how luminous galaxies are. However, the amount of helium in the universe, as measured by spectroscopy, suggests that there are far more baryons in the universe than estimates based on
(25)   galactic luminosity indicate. Astronomers have long speculated that the missing baryonic mass might eventually be discovered in intergalactic space or as some large population of galaxies that are difficult to detect.

Questions 91–97 refer to the passage above.

91. According to the passage, conventional spiral galaxies differ from low-surface-brightness galaxies in which of the following ways?

   (A)   They have fewer stars than do low-surface-brightness galaxies.

   (B)   They evolve more quickly than low-surface-brightness galaxies.

   (C)   They are more diffuse than low-surface-brightness galaxies.

   (D)   They contain less helium than do low-surface-brightness galaxies.

   (E)   They are larger than low-surface-brightness galaxies.

92. It can be inferred from the passage that which of the following is an accurate physical description of typical low-surface-brightness galaxies?

   (A)   They are large spiral galaxies containing fewer stars than do conventional galaxies.

   (B)   They are compact but very dim spiral galaxies.

   (C)   They are diffuse spiral galaxies that occupy a large volume of space.

   (D)   They are small, young spiral galaxies that contain a high proportion of primordial gas.

   (E)   They are large, dense spirals with low luminosity.

93. It can be inferred from the passage that the "long-standing puzzle" refers to which of the following?

   (A)   The difference between the rate at which conventional galaxies evolve and the rate at which low-surface-brightness galaxies evolve

   (B)   The discrepancy between estimates of total baryonic mass derived from measuring helium and estimates based on measuring galactic luminosity

   (C)   The inconsistency between the observed amount of helium in the universe and the number of stars in typical low-surface-brightness galaxies

   (D)   Uncertainties regarding what proportion of baryonic mass is contained in intergalactic space and what proportion in conventional galaxies

   (E)   Difficulties involved in detecting very distant galaxies and in investigating their luminosity

94. The author implies that low-surface-brightness galaxies could constitute an answer to the puzzle discussed in the second paragraph primarily because

    (A) they contain baryonic mass that was not taken into account by researchers using galactic luminosity to estimate the number of baryons in the universe

    (B) they, like conventional galaxies that contain many baryons, have evolved from massive, primordial gas clouds

    (C) they may contain relatively more helium, and hence more baryons, than do galaxies whose helium content has been studied using spectroscopy

    (D) they have recently been discovered to contain more baryonic mass than scientists had thought when low-surface-brightness galaxies were first observed

    (E) they contain stars that are significantly more luminous than would have been predicted on the basis of initial studies of luminosity in low-surface-brightness galaxies

95. The author mentions the fact that baryons are the source of stars' luminosity primarily in order to explain

    (A) how astronomers determine that some galaxies contain fewer stars per unit volume than do others

    (B) how astronomers are able to calculate the total luminosity of a galaxy

    (C) why astronomers can use galactic luminosity to estimate baryonic mass

    (D) why astronomers' estimates of baryonic mass based on galactic luminosity are more reliable than those based on spectroscopic studies of helium

    (E) how astronomers know bright galaxies contain more baryons than do dim galaxies

96. The author of the passage would be most likely to disagree with which of the following statements?

    (A) Low-surface-brightness galaxies are more difficult to detect than are conventional galaxies.

    (B) Low-surface-brightness galaxies are often spiral in shape.

    (C) Astronomers have advanced plausible ideas about where missing baryonic mass might be found.

    (D) Astronomers have devised a useful way of estimating the total baryonic mass in the universe.

    (E) Astronomers have discovered a substantial amount of baryonic mass in intergalactic space.

97. The primary purpose of the passage is to

    (A) describe a phenomenon and consider its scientific significance

    (B) contrast two phenomena and discuss a puzzling difference between them

    (C) identify a newly discovered phenomenon and explain its origins

    (D) compare two classes of objects and discuss the physical properties of each

    (E) discuss a discovery and point out its inconsistency with existing theory

This passage was adapted from an article published in 1992.

Line   While there is no blueprint for transforming a largely
        government-controlled economy into a free one, the
        experience of the United Kingdom since 1979
        clearly shows one approach that works:
(5)   privatization, in which state-owned industries are
        sold to private companies. By 1979, the total
        borrowings and losses of state-owned industries
        were running at about £3 billion a year. By selling
        many of these industries, the government has
(10)   decreased these borrowings and losses, gained
        over £34 billion from the sales, and now receives
        tax revenues from the newly privatized companies.
        Along with a dramatically improved overall
        economy, the government has been able to repay
(15)   12.5 percent of the net national debt over a two-
        year period.
            In fact, privatization has not only rescued
        individual industries and a whole economy headed
        for disaster, but has also raised the level of
(20)   performance in every area. At British Airways and
        British Gas, for example, productivity per employee
        has risen by 20 percent. At Associated British
        Ports, labor disruptions common in the 1970s and
        early 1980s have now virtually disappeared. At
(25)   British Telecom, there is no longer a waiting list—as
        there always was before privatization—to have a
        telephone installed.
            Part of this improved productivity has come
        about because the employees of privatized
(30)   industries were given the opportunity to buy shares
        in their own companies. They responded
        enthusiastically to the offer of shares: at British
        Aerospace, 89 percent of the eligible work force
        bought shares; at Associated British Ports, 90
(35)   percent; and at British Telecom, 92 percent. When
        people have a personal stake in something, they
        think about it, care about it, work to make it
        prosper. At the National Freight Consortium, the
        new employee-owners grew so concerned about
(40)   their company's profits that during wage
        negotiations they actually pressed their union to
        lower its wage demands.
            Some economists have suggested that giving
        away free shares would provide a needed
(45)   acceleration of the privatization process. Yet they

Line   miss Thomas Paine's point that "what we obtain too
        cheap we esteem too lightly." In order for the far-
        ranging benefits of individual ownership to be
        achieved by owners, companies, and countries,
(50)   employees and other individuals must make their
        own decisions to buy, and they must commit some
        of their own resources to the choice.

Questions 98–104 refer to the passage above.

98. According to the passage, all of the following were benefits of privatizing state-owned industries in the United Kingdom EXCEPT:

    (A) Privatized industries paid taxes to the government.

    (B) The government gained revenue from selling state-owned industries.

    (C) The government repaid some of its national debt.

    (D) Profits from industries that were still state-owned increased.

    (E) Total borrowings and losses of state-owned industries decreased.

99. According to the passage, which of the following resulted in increased productivity in companies that have been privatized?

    (A) A large number of employees chose to purchase shares in their companies.

    (B) Free shares were widely distributed to individual shareholders.

    (C) The government ceased to regulate major industries.

    (D) Unions conducted wage negotiations for employees.

    (E) Employee-owners agreed to have their wages lowered.

100. It can be inferred from the passage that the author considers labor disruptions to be

    (A) an inevitable problem in a weak national economy

    (B) a positive sign of employee concern about a company

    (C) a predictor of employee reactions to a company's offer to sell shares to them

    (D) a phenomenon found more often in state-owned industries than in private companies

    (E) a deterrence to high performance levels in an industry

101. The passage supports which of the following statements about employees buying shares in their own companies?

    (A) At three different companies, approximately nine out of ten of the workers were eligible to buy shares in their companies.

    (B) Approximately 90 percent of the eligible workers at three different companies chose to buy shares in their companies.

    (C) The opportunity to buy shares was discouraged by at least some labor unions.

    (D) Companies that demonstrated the highest productivity were the first to allow their employees the opportunity to buy shares.

    (E) Eligibility to buy shares was contingent on employees' agreeing to increased work loads.

102. Which of the following statements is most consistent with the principle described in lines 35–38?

    (A) A democratic government that decides it is inappropriate to own a particular industry has in no way abdicated its responsibilities as guardian of the public interest.

    (B) The ideal way for a government to protect employee interests is to force companies to maintain their share of a competitive market without government subsidies.

    (C) The failure to harness the power of self-interest is an important reason that state-owned industries perform poorly.

    (D) Governments that want to implement privatization programs must try to eliminate all resistance to the free-market system.

    (E) The individual shareholder will reap only a minute share of the gains from whatever sacrifices he or she makes to achieve these gains.

103. Which of the following can be inferred from the passage about the privatization process in the United Kingdom?

   (A)   It depends to a potentially dangerous degree on individual ownership of shares.

   (B)   It conforms in its most general outlines to Thomas Paine's prescription for business ownership.

   (C)   It was originally conceived to include some giving away of free shares.

   (D)   It has been successful, even though privatization has failed in other countries.

   (E)   It is taking place more slowly than some economists suggest is necessary.

104. The quotation in lines 46–47 is most probably used to

   (A)   counter a position that the author of the passage believes is incorrect

   (B)   state a solution to a problem described in the previous sentence

   (C)   show how opponents of the viewpoint of the author of the passage have supported their arguments

   (D)   point out a paradox contained in a controversial viewpoint

   (E)   present a historical maxim to challenge the principle introduced in the third paragraph

3.5 Answer Key

1.	C	27.	B	53.	D	79.	E
2.	D	28.	D	54.	E	80.	C
3.	B	29.	B	55.	B	81.	E
4.	D	30.	E	56.	C	82.	C
5.	B	31.	A	57.	D	83.	C
6.	E	32.	C	58.	E	84.	A
7.	B	33.	D	59.	D	85.	D
8.	A	34.	C	60.	B	86.	D
9.	A	35.	A	61.	D	87.	C
10.	E	36.	E	62.	B	88.	E
11.	C	37.	C	63.	E	89.	B
12.	C	38.	B	64.	C	90.	E
13.	B	39.	B	65.	C	91.	B
14.	E	40.	A	66.	E	92.	C
15.	C	41.	B	67.	D	93.	B
16.	D	42.	B	68.	E	94.	A
17.	A	43.	D	69.	D	95.	C
18.	E	44.	E	70.	B	96.	E
19.	B	45.	C	71.	D	97.	A
20.	C	46.	B	72.	D	98.	D
21.	E	47.	C	73.	A	99.	A
22.	A	48.	D	74.	E	100.	E
23.	D	49.	E	75.	B	101.	B
24.	D	50.	B	76.	B	102.	C
25.	B	51.	C	77.	B	103.	E
26.	B	52.	A	78.	C	104.	A

3.6 Answer Explanations

The following discussion of reading comprehension is intended to familiarize you with the most efficient and effective approaches to the kinds of problems common to reading comprehension. The particular questions in this chapter are generally representative of the kinds of reading comprehension questions you will encounter on the GMAT. Remember that it is the problem solving strategy that is important, not the specific details of a particular question.

Questions 1–6 refer to the passage on page 22.

1. The primary purpose of the passage is to

    (A) identify ways in which the GDP could be modified so that it would serve as a more accurate indicator of the economic well-being of the United States

    (B) suggest that the GDP, in spite of certain shortcomings, is still the most reliable indicator of the economic well-being of the United States

    (C) examine crucial shortcomings of the GDP as an indicator of the economic well-being of the United States

    (D) argue that the growth of the United States economy in recent decades has diminished the effectiveness of the GDP as an indicator of the nation's economic well-being

    (E) discuss how the GDP came to be used as the primary indicator of the economic well-being of the United States

Main idea

This question requires determining the main purpose of the passage as a whole. The passage begins by broadly defining GDP and describing how it is used as an indicator of the economic well-being of the United States. The passage then describes in more detail what is and is not taken into account by the GDP and then draws a causal connection between the limitations of what the GDP measures and disturbing trends within the U.S. in recent decades.

A   There is no discussion in the passage about modifying how the GDP is calculated.

B   The passage makes no judgment about the merits of using the GDP in relation to other economic indicators.

C   **Correct.** The passage portrays the GDP as having limitations that make it a problematic indicator of real economic well-being.

D   The passage does not portray the GDP as being any less useful as an economic indicator than it ever was.

E   There is no discussion in the passage of the history of how the GDP came to be used as an economic indicator.

The correct answer is C.

2. Which of the following best describes the function of the second sentence of the passage in the context of the passage as a whole?

    (A) It describes an assumption about the GDP that is defended in the course of the passage.

    (B) It contributes to a discussion of the origins of the GDP.

    (C) It clarifies a common misconception about the use of the GDP.

    (D) It identifies a major flaw in the GDP.

    (E) It suggests a revision to the method of calculating the GDP.

Evaluation

Answering this question requires understanding how a particular part of the passage functions in the passage as a whole. The second sentence describes the GDP as being solely concerned with the prices of goods and services produced in the United States, aside from any other kind of value. The passage then goes on to imply that by ignoring value other than price, the GDP may actually mask problems present in the nation's overall economy.

A   The passage is concerned with calling into question the use of the GDP, not defending it.

B   The passage does not mention how the GDP came to be used as a primary economic indicator.

C   The passage does not describe the function of the GDP as being commonly misunderstood.

D   Correct. The limitations of the GDP as described in the second sentence are then, in the rest of the passage, tied to problems in the United States.

E   The passage makes no explicit recommendations about revising how the GDP is measured.

The correct answer is D.

3.   It can be inferred that the author of the passage would agree with which of the following about the "economic significance" of those goods and services that are included in the GDP?

(A)   It is a comprehensive indicator of a nation's economic well-being.

(B)   It is not accurately captured by the price of those goods and services.

(C)   It is usually less than the intrinsic value of those goods and services.

(D)   It is more difficult to calculate than the economic significance of those goods and services that are not included in the GDP.

(E)   It is calculated differently in capitalist countries than in noncapitalist countries.

Inference

This question asks what the author implies about a piece of information given in the passage. The passage states that *the GDP assumes that the economic significance of goods and services lies solely in their price* (lines 5–7) and that *the GDP ignores the economic utility* (lines 13–14) of things such as a healthy environment and a cohesive social structure. The passage then implies that the worsening problems with the environment and social structure in recent decades are due to the way the GDP is calculated.

A   In describing the GDP as limited in what it measures, the author would not agree that the GDP is a comprehensive indicator.

B   Correct. The author implies that because the GDP ignores the economic utility of certain things, it is an inaccurate indicator of economic well-being.

C   The author makes no comparison between the economic value and the intrinsic value of goods and services.

D   The author makes no judgment about the difficulty of measuring the value of goods and services not measured by the GDP.

E   The author does not indicate how noncapitalist countries calculate GDP.

The correct answer is B.

4.   The comparison of the GDP to a calculating machine serves to do which of the following?

(A)   Refute an assertion that the calculations involved in the GDP are relatively complex in nature

(B)   Indicate that the GDP is better suited to record certain types of monetary transactions than others

(C)   Suggest that it is likely that the GDP will be supplanted by other, more sophisticated economic indicators

(D)   Illustrate the point that the GDP has no way of measuring the destructive impact of such things as oil spills on the nation's economic well-being

(E)   Exemplify an assertion that the GDP tends to exaggerate the amount of commercial activity generated by such things as oil spills

Evaluation

This question asks how a certain statement in the passage functions in the passage as a whole. In lines 13–16 and 19–24, respectively, the passage indicates that the GDP not only ignores problems affecting a nation's economy but that it actually can portray these problems as economic gains, and it subsequently uses the example of an oil spill adding to the GDP to illustrate this. The passage then closes by describing the GDP as a calculating machine that can add but not subtract.

A   The passage does not discuss the complexities of calculating the GDP.

B   The passage makes no judgment about the relative successes of the GDP in recording different types of monetary transactions.

C   The passage makes no mention of other economic indicators aside from the GDP.

D   **Correct.** By characterizing the GDP as a calculating machine that cannot subtract, the passage helps illustrate why something like an oil spill is misrepresented by the GDP.

E   While the passage does mention that the GDP measures commercial activity generated by an oil spill, it does not suggest that the GDP exaggerates the amount of that activity.

The correct answer is D.

5.   The passage implies that national policies that rely heavily on economic indicators such as the GDP tend to

(A)   become increasingly capitalistic in nature

(B)   disregard the economic importance of environmental and social factors that do not involve monetary transactions

(C)   overestimate the amount of commercial activity generated by environmental disasters

(D)   overestimate the economic significance of cohesive families and communities

(E)   assume that the economic significance of goods and services does not lie solely in the price of those goods and services

Inference

This question requires understanding what the passage implies about the main issue it discusses. In lines 13–14, the passage states that *the GDP ignores the economic utility* of things such as a clean environment and social cohesiveness. It then indicates that in countries that are dependent on economic indicators such as the GDP, *the environment and the social structure have been eroded in recent decades* (lines 19–20).

A   The passage does not mention how or if the GDP affects the capitalist nature of national policies.

B   **Correct.** In indicating that the GDP ignores environmental and social factors, the passage implies that policies dependent on the GDP will also ignore these issues.

C   The passage indicates that the GDP takes into account the commercial activity generated by environmental disasters but does not suggest that the amount of that activity is overestimated.

D   The passage indicates that the GDP ignores the value of social cohesion.

E   The passage indicates that *the GDP assumes that the economic significance of goods and services lies solely in their price* (lines 5–7).

The correct answer is B.

6.   It can be inferred that the author of the passage would agree with which of the following assessments of the GDP as an indicator of the economic well-being of the United States?

(A)   It masks social and environmental erosion more fully than the chief economic indicators of other nations.

(B)   It is based on inaccurate estimations of the prices of many goods and services.

(C)   It overestimates the amount of commercial activity that is generated in the United States.

(D)   It is conducive to error because it conflates distinct types of economic activity.

(E)   It does not take into account the economic utility of certain environmental and social conditions.

Inference

This question requires understanding what the author implies about information in the passage. The passage states that the GDP is *the chief indicator of the economic well-being of the United States* (lines 4–5). It also states that *the GDP ignores the economic utility* (lines 13–16) of things such as a clean environment and social cohesiveness. Therefore, the GDP does not take into account the economic utility of certain environmental and social conditions.

A   The passage makes no comparisons among different nations' economic indicators.
B   The passage does not describe the GDP as being inaccurate in its estimates of the prices of goods and services.
C   The passage does not describe the GDP as overestimating amounts of commercial activity.
D   The passage does not describe the GDP as confusing different types of economic activity.
E   **Correct.** The passage states that the GDP ignores the economic utility of a clean environment and social cohesiveness.

The correct answer is E.

Questions 7–11 refer to the passage on page 24.

7.   The passage is primarily concerned with

(A)   describing the effects of human activities on algae in coral reefs
(B)   explaining how human activities are posing a threat to coral reef communities
(C)   discussing the process by which coral reefs deteriorate in nutrient-poor waters
(D)   explaining how coral reefs produce food for themselves
(E)   describing the abundance of algae and filter-feeding animals in coral reef areas

Main idea

This question concerns the author's main point, the focus of the passage as a whole. The first paragraph describes the symbiotic process of coral reefs so that readers will understand how human activities are degrading this fragile ecosystem, as explained in the second paragraph. The author focuses on how harmful these human activities are to coral reefs.

A   The increased abundance of algae (line 23) is a detail supporting the main point.
B   **Correct.** Human activities are threatening complex coral reef communities.
C   The first paragraph explains how coral reefs thrive in nutrient-poor waters.
D   The zooxanthellae cells of algae feed the coral reefs (lines 7–12); this point is a detail that supports the main idea.
E   This abundance is a detail supporting the main idea, not the main idea itself.

The correct answer is B.

8.   The passage suggests which of the following about coral reef communities?

(A)   Coral reef communities may actually be more likely to thrive in waters that are relatively low in nutrients.
(B)   The nutrients on which coral reef communities thrive are only found in shallow waters.
(C)   Human population growth has led to changing ocean temperatures, which threatens coral reef communities.
(D)   The growth of coral reef communities tends to destabilize underwater herbivore populations.
(E)   Coral reef communities are more complex and diverse than most ecosystems located on dry land.

Inference

The word *suggests* in the question indicates that the answer will be an inference based on what the passage says about coral reef communities. The beginning of the passage states that *nutrient-poor* waters (lines 4–5) sustain the thriving life of a coral reef. Lines 25–27 show that *nutrient input is increasing* because of human activities, with consequent *declines in reef communities* (line 24). Given this information, it is reasonable to conclude that coral reefs thrive in nutrient-poor, rather than nutrient-rich, waters.

A   **Correct.** Coral reefs flourish in clear, nutrient-poor waters.

B   Shallow waters are mentioned only in the context of deteriorating marine habitats (line 17), not as a source of nutrients; the passage does not indicate that the nutrients are unique to shallow waters.

C   Ocean temperatures are not mentioned in the passage.

D   Reef decline, not reef growth, leads to destabilized herbivore populations (lines 21–22).

E   No comparisons are made between ecosystems in water and on land.

The correct answer is A.

9.   The author refers to "filter-feeding animals" (lines 23–24) in order to

(A)   provide an example of a characteristic sign of reef deterioration

(B)   explain how reef communities acquire sustenance for survival

(C)   identify a factor that helps herbivore populations thrive

(D)   indicate a cause of decreasing nutrient input in waters that reefs inhabit

(E)   identify members of coral reef communities that rely on coral reefs for nutrients

Logical structure

This question concerns why the author has included a particular detail. Look at the context for the phrase *filter-feeding animals*. The complete sentence (lines 21–24) shows that a higher population of filter-feeding animals is a symptom of reef decline.

A   **Correct.** An *increasing abundance* of these animals is a *typical* sign of reef decline.

B   Zooxanthellae cells of algae, not filter-feeding animals, provide sustenance for reef communities (lines 7–12).

C   An increase in filter-feeding animals is associated with *destabilized*, not thriving, herbivore populations.

D   An increase in nutrients, rather than a decrease, causes reef decline, when the population of filter-feeding animals then grows.

E   The author includes filter-feeding animals in the context of the decline of coral reefs, not the symbiotic process of coral reefs.

The correct answer is A.

10.   According to the passage, which of the following is a factor that is threatening the survival of coral reef communities?

(A)   The waters they inhabit contain few nutrient resources.

(B)   A decline in nutrient input is disrupting their symbiotic relationship with zooxanthellae.

(C)   The degraded waters of their marine habitats have reduced their ability to carry out photosynthesis.

(D)   They are too biologically complex to survive in habitats with minimal nutrient input.

(E)   Waste by-products result in an increase in nutrient input to reef communities.

Supporting ideas

The phrase *according to the passage* indicates that the necessary information is explicitly stated in the passage. Look at the threats to coral reefs listed in lines 18–21 and match them against the possible answers. Waste by-products increase nutrients in the water, and reefs decline as nutrients grow more plentiful (lines 21–24).

A   Coral reefs thrive in nutrient-poor waters, as the first paragraph explains.

B   Nutrient input is increasing, not decreasing (lines 20–21).

C   The passage does not say that the degraded waters inhibit photosynthesis.

D   The complex ecosystem of coral reefs thrives in nutrient-poor waters.

E   **Correct.** Waste by-products contribute to increased nutrient input, which causes reef decline.

The correct answer is E.

11. It can be inferred from the passage that the author describes coral reef communities as paradoxical most likely for which of the following reasons?

(A) They are thriving even though human activities have depleted the nutrients in their environment.

(B) They are able to survive in spite of an overabundance of algae inhabiting their waters.

(C) They are able to survive in an environment with limited food resources.

(D) Their metabolic wastes contribute to the degradation of the waters that they inhabit.

(E) They are declining even when the water surrounding them remains clear.

Inference

A paradox is a puzzling statement that seems to contradict itself. To answer this question, look for information that appears puzzling. The author calls coral reefs *one of the fascinating paradoxes of the biosphere* because the reefs are *prolific and productive* despite inhabiting clear waters with few nutrients. The paradox is that the reefs seem to flourish with little food.

A   Human activities have harmed coral reefs by increasing nutrient input (lines 24–29).

B   An increase in algae is a sign of reef decline, not reef survival (lines 21–23).

C   **Correct.** Coral reefs thrive in waters that provide little food.

D   Algae cells use the metabolic wastes of the corals to carry out photosynthesis; the result is sustenance for the reef community, not a degradation of waters (lines 9–12).

E   Coral reefs thrive in clear, nutrient-poor water and decline in nutrient-rich water.

The correct answer is C.

Questions 12–17 refer to the passage on page 26.

12. The passage suggests that a lack of modern sanitation would make which of the following most likely to occur?

(A) An outbreak of Lyme disease

(B) An outbreak of dengue hemorrhagic fever

(C) An epidemic of typhoid

(D) An epidemic of paralytic polio among infants

(E) An epidemic of paralytic polio among adolescents and adults

Inference

Since the question asks for an inference about a lack of modern sanitation, begin by examining what the passage says about the presence of modern sanitation. Lines 8–11 explain the role of modern sanitation in delaying the onset of polio. Lines 14–15 state that *the hygiene that helped prevent typhoid epidemics indirectly fostered a paralytic polio epidemic.* It is reasonable to infer from this statement that a lack of modern sanitation could lead to a typhoid epidemic.

A   Lyme disease is caused by the bacteria carried by deer ticks, not by a lack of sanitation.

B   The dengue virus is transmitted by a mosquito, not by a lack of sanitation.

C   **Correct.** Lines 14–15 show that typhoid epidemics were prevented by modern sanitation; therefore, typhoid might break out in the absence of modern sanitation.

D   Lines 11–13 show that infants did not typically suffer paralysis with polio.

E   When modern sanitation is not present, the polio infection occurs in infancy and *typically* provides *lifelong immunity without paralysis* (lines 12–13); adolescents and adults then were not affected.

The correct answer is C.

13. According to the passage, the outbreak of dengue hemorrhagic fever in the 1950s occurred for which of the following reasons?

    (A) The mosquito *Aedes aegypti* was newly introduced into Asia.

    (B) The mosquito *Aedes aegypti* became more numerous.

    (C) The mosquito *Aedes albopictus* became infected with the dengue virus.

    (D) Individuals who would normally acquire immunity to the dengue virus as infants were not infected until later in life.

    (E) More people began to visit and inhabit areas in which mosquitoes live and breed.

Supporting ideas

The question asks for information explicitly stated in the passage, although in slightly different language. Look at lines 24–28, where the 1950s outbreak of dengue hemorrhagic fever is discussed. The outbreak became an epidemic in Asia *because of ecological changes that caused* Aedes aegypti, *the mosquito that transmits the dengue virus, to proliferate.*

A   The passage does not say that the mosquito was newly introduced into Asia.

B   **Correct.** Ecological conditions in Asia at that time allowed the mosquito *Aedes aegypti* to proliferate, that is, to grow numerous.

C   *Aedes albopictus* is another mosquito (lines 28–32) more recently connected with a potential epidemic; the passage does not suggest this mosquito was connected to the 1950s Asian epidemic.

D   Immunity to polio is acquired in infancy (lines 12–13), but no mention is made of a similar immunity to the dengue virus.

E   Population shifts may explain the prevalence of Lyme disease in parts of the United States (lines 18–24), but they are not cited as the cause of the Asian epidemic.

The correct answer is B.

14. It can be inferred from the passage that Lyme disease has become prevalent in parts of the United States because of which of the following?

    (A) The inadvertent introduction of Lyme disease bacteria to the United States

    (B) The inability of modern sanitation methods to eradicate Lyme disease bacteria

    (C) A genetic mutation in Lyme disease bacteria that makes them more virulent

    (D) The spread of Lyme disease bacteria from infected humans to noninfected humans

    (E) An increase in the number of humans who encounter deer ticks

Inference

To make an inference about Lyme disease, examine the discussion of Lyme disease in lines 16–24. The disease is caused by bacteria carried by deer ticks. It has become prevalent in parts of the United States as the deer population has grown. This population growth has occurred at the same time that the suburbs have expanded and outdoor activities in the deer's habitat have increased. What can be inferred about the growing prevalence of Lyme disease? It is logical to infer that more people are encountering the deer ticks that carry the disease.

A   No inadvertent introduction of the bacteria is mentioned in the passage.

B   Modern sanitation plays a role in typhoid and polio epidemics, but it is not linked to Lyme disease.

C   No genetic mutation of bacteria is discussed in the context of Lyme disease.

D   Transmission by deer ticks is discussed, but not human-to-human transmission.

E   **Correct.** As the deer population grows and as humans encroach on the deer habitat, more people encounter deer ticks and become infected with the disease.

The correct answer is E.

15. Which of the following can most reasonably be concluded about the mosquito *Aedes albopictus* on the basis of information given in the passage?

    (A) It is native to the United States.

    (B) It can proliferate only in Asia.

    (C) It transmits the dengue virus.

    (D) It caused an epidemic of dengue hemorrhagic fever in the 1950s.

    (E) It replaced *Aedes aegypti* in Asia when ecological changes altered *Aedes aegypti's* habitat.

Inference

An inference is drawn from stated information rather than explicitly stated. Begin by finding the information given about this mosquito. The mosquito *Aedes albopictus* is mentioned in the final sentence of the passage, which says that this mosquito was inadvertently introduced into the United States and has spread widely. Because of this, the author states that *the stage is now set in the United States for a dengue epidemic*. It is reasonable to infer that this mosquito can transmit the dengue virus.

A   It has been inadvertently introduced into the United States.

B   The mosquito that proliferated in Asia during the 1950s was *Aedes aegypti*.

C   **Correct.** The mosquito *Aedes albopictus* transmits the dengue virus.

D   The mosquito *Aedes aegypti* caused the epidemic in the 1950s, not *Aedes albopictus*.

E   No information in the passage supports this statement.

The correct answer is C.

16. Which of the following best describes the organization of the passage?

    (A) A paradox is stated, discussed, and left unresolved.

    (B) Two opposing explanations are presented, argued, and reconciled.

    (C) A theory is proposed and is then followed by descriptions of three experiments that support the theory.

    (D) A generalization is stated and is then followed by three instances that support the generalization.

    (E) An argument is described and is then followed by three counterexamples that refute the argument.

Logical structure

Analyze the structure of the passage in order to answer a question about how the passage is organized. The passage begins by explaining that some epidemics are not caused by genetic mutations in bacteria and viruses, but rather by social and ecological changes in an environment. Three specific examples—polio, Lyme disease, and dengue hemorrhagic fever—are then used to support this general statement.

A   The passage opens by showing that epidemics may be caused by different means; this is not a paradox.

B   Only one explanation, having three supporting examples, is given.

C   The three examples of epidemics are not experiments conducted to support a theory; they are documented cases of disease.

D   **Correct.** A generalization is stated: *scientists have discovered the importance of social and ecological factors to epidemics* (lines 5–6). Three examples—polio, Lyme disease, and dengue hemorrhagic fever—support the generalization.

E   The examples in the passage support the author's generalization or argument; no counterexamples refuting the argument are included.

The correct answer is D.

17. Which of the following, if true, would most strengthen the author's assertion about the cause of the Lyme disease outbreak in the United States?

(A) The deer population was smaller in the late nineteenth century than in the mid twentieth century.

(B) Interest in outdoor recreation began to grow in the late nineteenth century.

(C) In recent years the suburbs have stopped growing.

(D) Outdoor recreation enthusiasts routinely take measures to protect themselves against Lyme disease.

(E) Scientists have not yet developed a vaccine that can prevent Lyme disease.

Logical structure

Examine the author's argument about the cause of Lyme disease. The author blames the recent prevalence of Lyme disease on the rise in the deer population and the growth of the suburbs, with people spending more time outside in the deer's habitat. The disease had appeared *only sporadically* during the late nineteenth century.

A   **Correct.** If the deer population was smaller when the disease occurred *only sporadically*, then the author's claim that the mid-century rise in deer population is one of the causes of Lyme disease is strengthened.

B   An *interest* in outdoor recreation, such as an interest in hiking, may be an appreciation for that activity without being an engagement in that activity; even if *interest* here did mean engagement, an increased interest in outdoor recreation does not entail that people engaged in outdoor activities in the deer's habitat; the assertion is not strengthened.

C   The lack of growth of the suburbs weakens, rather than strengthens, the author's assertion.

D   Protective measures against the disease are not relevant to an assertion about what causes the disease.

E   The lack of a vaccine is irrelevant to an assertion about what causes the disease.

The correct answer is A.

Questions 18–23 refer to the passage on page 28.

18. The primary purpose of the passage is to

(A) describe new ways of studying the possibility that life once existed on Mars

(B) revise a theory regarding the existence of life on Mars in light of new evidence

(C) reconcile conflicting viewpoints regarding the possibility that life once existed on Mars

(D) evaluate a recently proposed argument concerning the origin of ALH84001

(E) describe a controversy concerning the significance of evidence from ALH84001

Main idea

Answering this question requires determining the purpose of the passage as a whole. In the first paragraph, the passage indicates that a research team found that a Martian meteorite in Antarctica contains compelling evidence that life existed on Mars. The rest of the passage then describes arguments by skeptics against the research team's conclusion together with the research team's rebuttals to the skeptics' arguments.

A   While the passage discusses one type of evidence that life might have existed on Mars, it does not describe multiple ways of studying the possibility of Martian life, nor characterize any method of study as *new*.

B   The passage merely reports and does not make any attempt at revising existing theories.

C   The passage describes but does not try to reconcile conflicting viewpoints concerning life on Mars.

D   The origin of ALH84001 is generally agreed upon (line 5), not a recently proposed hypothesis evaluated by the passage.

E   **Correct.** The passage describes opposing arguments about whether ALH84001 suggests life ever existed on Mars.

The correct answer is E.

19. The passage asserts which of the following about the claim that ALH84001 originated on Mars?

    (A) It was initially proposed by the McKay team of scientists.
    (B) It is not a matter of widespread scientific dispute.
    (C) It has been questioned by some skeptics of the McKay team's work.
    (D) It has been undermined by recent work on PAHs.
    (E) It is incompatible with the fact that ALH84001 has been on Earth for 13,000 years.

Supporting ideas

This question requires recognizing what the passage indicates about a piece of information it offers. The passage states that *scientists generally agree* (line 5) that ALH84001 originated on Mars, which strongly suggests that there is not much dispute about it.

A   While it is possible that McKay's team initially made the proposal, the passage does not say so.
B   Correct. In stating that scientists generally agree ALH84001 originated on Mars, the passage indicates there is no real controversy on this matter.
C   The skeptics mentioned in the passage are not described as calling into question that ALH84001 originated on Mars.
D   The passage does not tie the existence of PAHs in ALH84001 to questions about its Martian origins.
E   The passage makes no connection between the time ALH84001 has been on the Earth and questions as to its Martian origins.

The correct answer is B.

20. The passage suggests that the fact that ALH84001 has been on Earth for 13,000 years has been used by some scientists to support which of the following claims about ALH84001?

    (A) ALH84001 may not have originated on Mars.
    (B) ALH84001 contains PAHs that are the result of nonbiological processes.
    (C) ALH84001 may not have contained PAHs when it landed on Earth.
    (D) The organic molecules found in ALH84001 are not PAHs.
    (E) The organic molecules found in ALH84001 could not be the result of terrestrial contamination.

Supporting ideas

This question requires recognizing how a particular fact is used to support a particular point of view reported in the passage. In the second paragraph, the passage presents various skeptics' arguments about whether the PAHs in ALH84001 originated on Mars. In lines 15–19, the passage indicates that some scientists see the fact that ALH84001 has been on Earth for 13,000 years as raising the possibility that the PAHs in ALH84001 *resulted from terrestrial contamination* or in other words that it did not contain PAHs when it landed on Earth.

A   The passage indicates only that most scientists believe that ALH84001 originated on Mars.
B   Although the passage indicates that skeptics have pointed out that PAHs can be formed by nonbiological processes, their point is not related to the length of time ALH84001 has been on Earth.
C   Correct. The passage indicates that some scientists believe that the PAHs in ALH84001 may have been transferred to it during its 13,000 years on Earth.
D   The passage does not indicate that any scientists doubt the presence of PAHs in ALH84001.
E   The passage indicates that the fact that ALH84001 has been on Earth for 13,000 years is used by some scientists to support the idea of terrestrial contamination.

The correct answer is C.

21. The passage suggests that if a meteorite contained PAHs that were the result of terrestrial contamination, then one would expect which of the following to be true?

   (A)   The meteorite would have been on Earth for more than 13,000 years.

   (B)   The meteorite would have originated from a source other than Mars.

   (C)   The PAHs contained in the meteorite would have originated from nonbiological processes.

   (D)   The meteorite would contain fewer PAHs than most other meteorites contain.

   (E)   The PAHs contained in the meteorite would be concentrated toward the meteorite's surface.

Application

Answering this question involves applying information contained in the passage to a situation that is not described in the passage. According to the passage, some scientists believe that because ALH84001 has been on Earth for as long as 13,000 years, any PAHs contained in it may have been transferred from the Earth, a process the passage describes as *terrestrial contamination* (line 19). The passage also indicates that if terrestrial contamination occurred with ALH84001, then, contrary to the findings of McKay's team that showed PAH concentrations increasing *as one looks deeper into ALH84001* (lines 21–22), the PAHs would be expected to be concentrated more toward the outer parts, or surface, of ALH84001.

   A   The passage indicates that scientists believe that 13,000 years is sufficient time for terrestrial contamination to happen.

   B   The passage does not suggest that the origin of a meteorite affects its ability to become contaminated with terrestrial PAHs.

   C   The passage does not indicate whether PAHs resulting from terrestrial contamination would be nonbiological or not.

   D   The passage does not mention that different meteorites may contain different amounts of PAHs.

   E   **Correct.** The passage suggests that if ALH84001 experienced terrestrial contamination, then the PAHs would be more concentrated toward the outer surface of the meteorite.

The correct answer is E.

22. Which of the following best describes the function of the last sentence of the first paragraph?

   (A)   It identifies a possible organic source for the PAHs found in ALH84001.

   (B)   It describes a feature of PAHs that is not shared by other types of organic molecules.

   (C)   It explains how a characteristic common to most meteorites originates.

   (D)   It suggests how the terrestrial contamination of ALH84001 might have taken place.

   (E)   It presents evidence that undermines the claim that life once existed on Mars.

Evaluation

This question requires understanding how a part of the passage functions within the passage as a whole. The first paragraph begins by establishing that McKay's team believes that the PAHs found in ALH84001 provide compelling evidence that life existed on Mars. To explain this, the passage indicates that PAHs are a type of organic molecules, which form the basis for life. Furthermore, to connect PAHs to possible life on Mars, the final sentence of the first paragraph indicates that one source of PAHs is the decay of dead microbes.

   A   **Correct.** Without evidence of an organic source for the PAHs in ALH84001, the team's argument would not make sense.

   B   The passage indicates that PAHs can be formed by the decay of organic material from microbes but does not imply that other organic molecules cannot be formed this way.

   C   The sentence referred to explains one possible origin of a molecule found in ALH84001 but does not imply that most meteorites contain that molecule.

   D   The sentence referred to does not involve the process of terrestrial contamination.

   E   The sentence referred to provides information necessary to the team's argument that life may have existed on Mars.

The correct answer is A.

23. The passage suggests that McKay's team would agree with which of the following regarding the PAHs produced by nonorganic processes?

    (A) These PAHs are not likely to be found in any meteorite that has been on Earth for 13,000 years or more.
    (B) These PAHs are not likely to be found in any meteorite that originated from Mars.
    (C) These PAHs are not likely to be produced by star formation.
    (D) These PAHs are likely to be found in combinations that distinguish them from the PAHs produced by organic processes.
    (E) These PAHs are likely to be found in fewer meteorites than the PAHs produced by organic processes.

Inference

This question involves understanding a particular point of view presented in the passage. The passage indicates in lines 11–13 that the organic molecules found in ALH84001 are PAHs. In lines 23–27, skeptics of McKay's team's findings point out that processes unrelated to organic life, including star formation, can produce PAHs. In the final sentence of the passage, McKay's team notes that the type of PAHs found in ALH84001 are more similar to those produced by organic processes than to those produced by nonorganic processes.

A   McKay's team does not tie the presence of nonorganic PAHs in meteorites to the length of time the meteorites have been on Earth.
B   McKay's team does not deny the possibility that at least some of the PAHs found in Martian meteorites are nonorganic in origin.
C   McKay's team does not deny that PAHs can be produced by the formation of stars.
D   **Correct.** McKay's team notes in lines 29–34 that the PAH combinations produced by organic processes can be distinguished from those produced by nonorganic processes.
E   McKay's team does not address the probability of nonorganic PAHs being found in meteorites.

The correct answer is D.

Questions 24–26 refer to the passage on page 30.

24. Which of the following most accurately states the purpose of the passage?

    (A) To compare two different approaches to the study of homeostasis
    (B) To summarize the findings of several studies regarding organisms' maintenance of internal variables in extreme environments
    (C) To argue for a particular hypothesis regarding various organisms' conservation of water in desert environments
    (D) To cite examples of how homeostasis is achieved by various organisms
    (E) To defend a new theory regarding the maintenance of adequate fluid balance

Main idea

To answer this question, look at the passage as a whole. The first paragraph defines homeostasis and names three animals that must maintain internal fluid balance in difficult circumstances. The topic of the second paragraph is how desert rats maintain fluid balance. The third paragraph discusses how camels maintain fluid balance, while the final paragraph describes maintenance of water balance in marine vertebrates. Thus, the overall purpose is to give three examples of how homeostasis is achieved.

A   Examples of homeostasis are given, but different approaches to studying it are not discussed.
B   The passage describes examples, but it does not summarize studies.
C   While the passage does discuss two desert animals, it does not present any argument for a particular hypothesis.
D   **Correct.** The passage discusses the examples of desert rats, camels, and marine vertebrates to show how these organisms are able to achieve homeostasis.
E   The passage describes how three organisms maintain water balance, but it presents no theory about it.

The correct answer is D.

25. It can be inferred from the passage that some mechanisms that regulate internal body temperature, like sweating and panting, can lead to which of the following?

    (A) A rise in the external body temperature
    (B) A drop in the body's internal fluid level
    (C) A decrease in the osmotic pressure of the blood
    (D) A decrease in the amount of renal water loss
    (E) A decrease in the urine's salt content

Inference

An inference is drawn from stated information. To answer this question, look at the information about sweating and panting in lines 18–21 and 33–35. The passage states that desert rats avoid *loss of fluid through panting or sweating, which are regulatory mechanisms for maintaining internal body temperature by evaporative cooling*. These mechanisms reduce internal body temperatures. Additionally, camels *conserve internal water* (line 35) when they avoid sweating and panting, except at very high body temperatures. Therefore, they must lose internal water when they do sweat and pant.

A   The passage does not discuss *external body temperature*; sweating and panting lower internal body temperature, and there is no reason to infer external body temperatures might rise.

B   **Correct.** Sweating and panting lead to *loss of fluid*. Desert rats avoid sweating and panting by staying in burrows, and camels do not employ these mechanisms except at very high body temperatures (lines 33–35) and thus *conserve internal water*.

C   The passage states that *desert rats are able to maintain the osmotic pressure of their blood, as well as their total body-water content* (lines 13–15) and does not connect changes in osmotic pressure to temperature-regulating mechanisms such as sweating and panting.

D   While the passage does discuss renal water loss, it does not relate this to temperature-regulating mechanisms like sweating and panting.

E   The passage does not relate body temperature regulators like sweating and panting to changes in the urine's salt content.

The correct answer is B.

26. It can be inferred from the passage that the author characterizes the camel's kidney as "entirely unexceptional" (line 26) primarily to emphasize that it

    (A) functions much as the kidney of a rat functions
    (B) does not aid the camel in coping with the exceptional water loss resulting from the extreme conditions of its environment
    (C) does not enable the camel to excrete as much salt as do the kidneys of marine vertebrates
    (D) is similar in structure to the kidneys of most mammals living in water-deprived environments
    (E) requires the help of other organs in eliminating excess salt

Inference

To answer this question, look at the phrase *entirely unexceptional* in the context of the passage. Desert rats and camels share the problem of conserving water in an environment where water is lacking, *temperature is high, and humidity is low* (lines 10–12). Desert rats have as part of their coping mechanisms exceptional kidneys that produce urine with a high salt content. The author compares camels' kidneys to those of desert rats and shows that the camels have ordinary kidneys that do not help the camels conserve water.

A   Since a contrast is drawn between the kidneys of camels and those of desert rats, the two must function differently; the passage makes no reference to the kidneys of other rats.

B   **Correct.** The camel's kidney does nothing special to help the camel cope with its difficult environment.

C   No comparison between the kidneys of camels and the kidneys of marine vertebrates is made.

D   There is no information given about the kidney structure of most mammals in desert environments so this conclusion is not justified.

E   Marine vertebrates have other organs that help eliminate extra salt; camels do not.

The correct answer is B.

Questions 27–32 refer to the passage on page 32.

27.   The primary purpose of the passage is to

(A)   enumerate reasons why both traditional scholarly methods and newer scholarly methods have limitations

(B)   identify a shortcoming in a scholarly approach and describe an alternative approach

(C)   provide empirical data to support a long-held scholarly assumption

(D)   compare two scholarly publications on the basis of their authors' backgrounds

(E)   attempt to provide a partial answer to a long-standing scholarly dilemma

Main idea

To find the primary purpose, look at what the author is doing in the entire passage. In the first paragraph, the author examines two approaches to political history, both of which suffer from the same flaw, the exclusion of women. In the second paragraph, the author reviews an alternative, more inclusive way to understand political history.

A   The first paragraph identifies only one reason that the two approaches are flawed; an alternative approach is discussed in the second paragraph.

B   Correct. The author points to the flaw in earlier approaches to history and shows an alternative way of thinking about political history.

C   No data are offered to support an assumption.

D   Only one historian is mentioned by name; her background is not mentioned.

E   No long-standing dilemma is discussed.

The correct answer is B.

28.   The passage suggests which of the following concerning the techniques used by the new political historians described in the first paragraph of the passage?

(A)   They involved the extensive use of the biographies of political party leaders and political theoreticians.

(B)   They were conceived by political historians who were reacting against the political climates of the 1960s and 1970s.

(C)   They were of more use in analyzing the positions of United States political parties in the nineteenth century than in analyzing the positions of those in the twentieth century.

(D)   They were of more use in analyzing the political behavior of nineteenth-century voters than in analyzing the political activities of those who could not vote during that period.

(E)   They were devised as a means of tracing the influence of nineteenth-century political trends on twentieth-century political trends.

Inference

The question's use of the verb *suggests* is an indication that an inference must be made. Examine the first paragraph, where the *new school of political history* is discussed. These historians used techniques such as *quantitative analyses of election returns* that the author describes as *useless in analyzing the political activities of women, who were denied the vote until 1920* (lines 9–12). It can, however, be assumed that the same techniques did prove useful in understanding the *mass political behavior* of voters.

A   The first sentence explains that these historians *sought to go beyond the traditional focus . . . on leaders and government institutions.*

B   The passage does not indicate that the new historians were reacting against the political climate of their own time.

C   The new historians examined the *political practices of ordinary citizens* (line 5), not the positions of political parties.

D   Correct. Lines 7–12 explicitly state that the new historians' techniques were *useless* in analyzing the political activities of those not allowed to vote; the same lines imply that the techniques were useful in analyzing the political behavior of voters.

E   No information in the passage supports this explanation.

The correct answer is D.

29. It can be inferred that the author of the passage quotes Baker directly in the second paragraph primarily in order to

    (A) clarify a position before providing an alternative to that position
    (B) differentiate between a novel definition and traditional definitions
    (C) provide an example of a point agreed on by different generations of scholars
    (D) provide an example of the prose style of an important historian
    (E) amplify a definition given in the first paragraph

Logical structure

To analyze why the author uses a direct quotation, look at the logical structure of the passage in relation to the quotation. The historians discussed in the first paragraph define political activity as voting. Paula Baker, however, has a new definition of political activity, one that includes the activities of those who were not allowed to vote. It is reasonable to infer that the author quotes Baker to draw attention to this new definition, which provides an innovative, alternative way of thinking about political history.

A   Paula Baker's is the alternative position offered; no alternative to hers is discussed.
B   **Correct.** Baker is quoted to emphasize that her definition is new and that it differs significantly from the traditional definition used by other historians.
C   The contrasting views expressed in the first and second paragraphs show that different generations of scholars have not agreed.
D   The author does not comment on Baker's prose style.
E   Baker's definition contrasts with, rather than amplifies, the one offered in the first paragraph.

The correct answer is B.

30. According to the passage, Paula Baker and the new political historians of the 1960s and 1970s shared which of the following?

    (A) A commitment to interest group politics
    (B) A disregard for political theory and ideology
    (C) An interest in the ways in which nineteenth-century politics prefigured contemporary politics
    (D) A reliance on such quantitative techniques as the analysis of election returns
    (E) An emphasis on the political involvement of ordinary citizens

Supporting ideas

Since the question uses the phrase *according to the passage*, the answer is explicitly stated in the passage. Look for a point on which the new political historians and Baker agree. The first sentence of the passage says that these new historians were interested in the political activities of *ordinary citizens* (line 5). Paula Baker is similarly interested in the political activities of *ordinary citizens* (lines 15–16), especially of female citizens, who were not allowed to vote.

A   No mention at all is made of interest group politics, neither in relation to Baker nor in relation to the new historians.
B   The passage does not show that they disregarded political theory and ideology.
C   The passage only discusses Baker's interest in the way women's political activities in the nineteenth century prefigured twentieth-century trends (lines 16–18).
D   The passage explains that new historians relied on such techniques, but that Baker did not.
E   **Correct.** Both the new historians and Baker are said to have studied the political activities of *ordinary citizens*.

The correct answer is E.

31. Which of the following best describes the structure of the first paragraph of the passage?

    (A) Two scholarly approaches are compared, and a shortcoming common to both is identified.

    (B) Two rival schools of thought are contrasted, and a third is alluded to.

    (C) An outmoded scholarly approach is described, and a corrective approach is called for.

    (D) An argument is outlined, and counterarguments are mentioned.

    (E) A historical era is described in terms of its political trends.

Logical structure

To answer this question, analyze the structure of the first paragraph. It compares *the old approach* of studying political history through emphasis on leaders and government institutions with *the new school of political history*, which turned instead to the political practices of ordinary citizens. Both approaches suffered from the same drawback: the failure to include women in their analyses.

A **Correct.** Two approaches to history are discussed, and a flaw shared by both, the exclusion of women, is identified.

B The first paragraph does not allude to a third school of thought.

C A corrective approach is not discussed in the first paragraph.

D The first paragraph does present an argument, but no counterarguments are made.

E The political trends of an historical era are not detailed in the first paragraph.

The correct answer is A.

32. The information in the passage suggests that a pre-1960s political historian would have been most likely to undertake which of the following studies?

    (A) An analysis of voting trends among women voters of the 1920s

    (B) A study of male voters' gradual ideological shift from party politics to issue-oriented politics

    (C) A biography of an influential nineteenth-century minister of foreign affairs

    (D) An analysis of narratives written by previously unrecognized women activists

    (E) A study of voting trends among naturalized immigrant laborers in a nineteenth-century logging camp

Inference

In using *suggests*, this question asks the reader to apply information stated in the passage to make an inference about the methods of historians before the 1960s. These methods are discussed in the first paragraph. Lines 3–4 say that the *traditional focus of political historians* (before the advent of the new school of historians in the 1960s and 1970s) was *on leaders and government institutions*. It is reasonable to infer that the pre-1960s historian was likely to focus on a leader or government institution.

A Traditional historians did not focus on ordinary citizens, but on their leaders.

B Baker is interested in this group shift, but traditional historians were not.

C **Correct.** Traditional historians emphasized the work of leaders and government institutions; a biography of a foreign affairs minister fits this focus perfectly.

D Such an analysis would be of interest to Baker, but not to traditional historians focusing on leaders and government.

E The new historians would be interested in such a study, but not traditional historians, who did not look at the activities of ordinary citizens.

The correct answer is C.

Questions 33–38 refer to the passage on page 34.

33. Which of the following best describes the organization of the passage?

   (A) The historical backgrounds of two currently used research methods are chronicled.

   (B) The validity of the data collected by using two different research methods is compared.

   (C) The usefulness of a research method is questioned and then a new method is proposed.

   (D) The use of a research method is described and the limitations of the results obtained are discussed.

   (E) A research method is evaluated and the changes necessary for its adaptation to other subject areas are discussed.

Logical structure

To answer a question about organization, determine the function of each paragraph in order to see the overall structure of the whole passage. The first paragraph introduces a research method, recording life stories. The second and third paragraphs discuss the problems of this method. According to the final paragraph, the method remains useful despite its limitations.

A   Only one research method is discussed in the passage.

B   The validity of data is questioned, but only one research method is discussed.

C   While the usefulness of the method is questioned, no new one is proposed.

D   Correct. The method of recording life stories is described, its limitations acknowledged, and its usefulness recognized.

E   A research method is evaluated, but no changes are proposed.

The correct answer is D.

34. Which of the following is most similar to the actions of nineteenth-century ethnologists in their editing of the life stories of Native Americans?

   (A) A witness in a jury trial invokes the Fifth Amendment in order to avoid relating personally incriminating evidence.

   (B) A stockbroker refuses to divulge the source of her information on the possible future increase in a stock's value.

   (C) A sports announcer describes the action in a team sport with which he is unfamiliar.

   (D) A chef purposely excludes the special ingredient from the recipe of his prizewinning dessert.

   (E) A politician fails to mention in a campaign speech the similarities in the positions held by her opponent for political office and by herself.

Application

To answer the question, determine what the author says about the ethnologists and apply the information to the examples given in the answer choices. Ethnologists believed that recording personal stories *could increase their understanding of the cultures that they had been observing from without* (lines 10–12). But they were criticized for not spending enough time in these cultures (lines 25–26) and thus not understanding the cultures well enough. Their position is most like that of the sports announcer, who is also an observer, but who is not familiar with the game (or, in the case of the ethnologists, the culture) being observed.

A   The passage does not suggest that the ethnographers deliberately withheld evidence for personal reasons.

B   The ethnologists were faulted for other reasons, not for withholding evidence.

C   Correct. As do the ethnologists, the sports announcer observes and reports, but in neither case is the observer adequately familiar with the subject being observed.

D   The ethnologists did not purposely exclude an item from their studies.

E   The passage does not point to any similarities between the ethnologists and the people they studied.

The correct answer is C.

35. According to the passage, collecting life stories can be a useful methodology because

    (A) life stories provide deeper insights into a culture than the hypothesizing of academics who are not members of that culture

    (B) life stories can be collected easily and they are not subject to invalid interpretations

    (C) ethnologists have a limited number of research methods from which to choose

    (D) life stories make it easy to distinguish between the important and unimportant features of a culture

    (E) the collection of life stories does not require a culturally knowledgeable investigator

Supporting ideas

The phrase *according to the passage* indicates that the answer is stated in the passage. The final paragraph describes collecting life stories as *a useful tool* because the stories *are likely to throw more light on the working of the mind and emotions* of the people the ethnologists study than *any amount of speculation from an ethnologist . . . from another culture.*

A   **Correct.** Because they come from within a culture, the life stories reveal more about the culture than can any of the theories developed by those outside the culture.

B   Neither the ease nor the difficulty of gathering the stories is mentioned, but their vulnerability to misinterpretation is discussed in lines 19–28.

C   The passage does not discuss how many research tools are available.

D   The passage states that ethnologists regarded as *unimportant* some of the events that the people of the stories found *significant* (lines 33–37).

E   According to the passage, ethnologists were criticized for not being culturally knowledgeable enough (lines 25–26).

The correct answer is A.

36. Information in the passage suggests that which of the following may be a possible way to eliminate bias in the editing of life stories?

    (A) Basing all inferences made about the culture on an ethnological theory

    (B) Eliminating all of the emotion laden information reported by the informant

    (C) Translating the informant's words into the researcher's language

    (D) Reducing the number of questions and carefully specifying the content of the questions that the investigator can ask the informant

    (E) Reporting all of the information that the informant provides regardless of the investigator's personal opinion about its intrinsic value

Inference

The question's use of the word *suggests* means that the answer depends on making an inference. Lines 31–33 provide the reference for this question about biased editing: *Editors often decided what elements were significant to the field research on a given tribe.* The editors introduced bias with their choices about what was important. Therefore, it is reasonable to infer that, to eliminate bias, those choices must be eliminated. Reporting all the information, not just what the investigator or editor thinks is important, is a possible way to avoid bias.

A   The passage does not imply that bias results from veering away from a theory.

B   Investigators are criticized for allowing emotion to tinge their reports (lines 27–28), but informants are not criticized for having emotional material.

C   Lines 33–35 reveal that translations are not always possible.

D   The passage does not discuss the number and content of questions, so it cannot be inferred that restricting them would eliminate bias.

E   **Correct.** Reporting all the information, rather than choosing to report only what appears to the observer to be important, is a possible way to eliminate bias in editing life stories.

The correct answer is E.

37. The primary purpose of the passage as a whole is to

   (A) question an explanation
   (B) correct a misconception
   (C) critique a methodology
   (D) discredit an idea
   (E) clarify an ambiguity

Main idea

This question explicitly asks the reader to consider the passage as a whole in order to determine the author's intent. What is the subject of the passage? Collecting life stories is called a *method* (line 20) and a *useful tool* (line 43). The first paragraph introduces this research method, the middle paragraphs offer an extended critique of it, and the final paragraph reaffirms its usefulness.

A   Collecting life stories is not an explanation; it is a method to gain understanding of a culture.
B   The autobiographies may be misinterpreted, but they are not a misconception.
C   Correct. The passage is about a methodology; both its weaknesses and strengths are examined.
D   Collecting the stories is not an idea but a method; though its limitations are revealed, the method is not discredited.
E   The final paragraph implies that ambiguity is inherent in life stories; that ambiguity is not clarified.

The correct answer is C.

38. It can be inferred from the passage that a characteristic of the ethnological research on Native Americans conducted during the nineteenth century was the use of which of the following?

   (A) Investigators familiar with the culture under study
   (B) A language other than the informant's for recording life stories
   (C) Life stories as the ethnologist's primary source of information
   (D) Complete transcriptions of informants' descriptions of tribal beliefs
   (E) Stringent guidelines for the preservation of cultural data

Inference

An inference is drawn from stated information. To answer this question, find what the passage says about the ethnological research on Native American cultures in the nineteenth century. The third paragraph tells us that *much was inevitably lost* (line 31) when investigators wrote the oral stories down. *Native Americans recognized that the essence of their lives could not be communicated in English* (lines 33–35). From these two statements, it is reasonable to infer that the stories were written down in a language different from that of the storyteller.

A   The investigators were criticized for not being suitably familiar with the culture (lines 25–26).
B   Correct. Native Americans believed that English could not express their culture; at least some investigators, therefore, must have written the stories down in English.
C   Ethnologists wanted the stories to *supplement* their fieldwork (lines 5–9), not to replace it as their primary means of investigation.
D   Lines 31–33 reveal that the life stories were edited, not complete.
E   The passage provides no information about such guidelines.

The correct answer is B.

Questions 39–44 refer to the passage on page 36.

39. The primary function of the passage as a whole is to

    (A) account for the popularity of a practice
    (B) evaluate the utility of a practice
    (C) demonstrate how to institute a practice
    (D) weigh the ethics of using a strategy
    (E) explain the reasons for pursuing a strategy

Main idea

This question explicitly requires looking at the passage as a whole in order to determine the author's purpose. The first paragraph explains the practice of offering guarantees and lists circumstances in which an unconditional guarantee may be an appropriate marketing tool. The second paragraph begins with *However*, implying that a contradiction is about to follow. The serious drawbacks to guarantees are examined, and the passage closes with a warning.

A The passage does not discuss the popularity of guarantees.
B **Correct.** The passage examines and judges the advantages and disadvantages of a business practice.
C The passage does not show how to put guarantees into place.
D The passage does not discuss ethics.
E The first paragraph does explain the reasons for offering guarantees, but that is only a portion of the passage, not the passage as a whole.

The correct answer is B.

40. All of the following are mentioned in the passage as circumstances in which professional service firms can benefit from offering an unconditional guarantee EXCEPT:

    (A) The firm is having difficulty retaining its clients of long standing.
    (B) The firm is having difficulty getting business through client recommendations.
    (C) The firm charges substantial fees for its services.
    (D) The adverse effects of poor performance by the firm are significant for the client.
    (E) The client is reluctant to incur risk.

Supporting ideas

The phrase *mentioned in the passage* indicates that the necessary information is explicitly stated. To answer this question, use the process of elimination to find the one example that is NOT mentioned in the passage. The question refers to lines 8–13, where the circumstances in which an unconditional guarantee might be beneficial to a firm are listed. Check each of the responses to the question against the list; the one that does not appear in the list is the correct answer.

A **Correct.** The sentence begins by noting that unconditional guarantees are particularly important with new clients; clients of long standing are not discussed.
B Lines 12–13 include the difficulty of getting business through referrals and word-of-mouth.
C Line 10 cites high fees as such a circumstance.
D Lines 10–11 include the severe repercussions of bad service.
E Lines 9–10 cite the cautiousness of the client.

The correct answer is A.

41. Which of the following is cited in the passage as a goal of some professional service firms in offering unconditional guarantees of satisfaction?

    (A) A limit on the firm's liability
    (B) Successful competition against other firms
    (C) Ability to justify fee increases
    (D) Attainment of an outstanding reputation in a field
    (E) Improvement in the quality of the firm's service

Supporting ideas

When the question says to find an answer *cited* in the passage, the answer will be explicitly stated information. The passage opens with an explanation of why some firms want to offer unconditional guarantees: *Seeking a competitive advantage* explains their rationale. Firms offer the guarantees to compete more effectively against firms that do not offer guarantees.

A   The passage does not mention liability limits.
B   **Correct.** Some firms offer unconditional guarantees as a way to compete successfully against firms that do not offer them.
C   Line 10 mentions that high fees would be a reason to offer guarantees, but fee increases are not discussed.
D   The second paragraph suggests the reverse: offering a guarantee may hurt a firm's reputation.
E   Improving the quality of service is not mentioned as a reason to offer guarantees.

The correct answer is B.

42. The passage's description of the issue raised by unconditional guarantees for health care or legal services most clearly implies that which of the following is true?

    (A) The legal and medical professions have standards of practice that would be violated by attempts to fulfill such unconditional guarantees.
    (B) The result of a lawsuit or medical procedure cannot necessarily be determined in advance by the professionals handling a client's case.
    (C) The dignity of the legal and medical professions is undermined by any attempts at marketing of professional services, including unconditional guarantees.
    (D) Clients whose lawsuits or medical procedures have unsatisfactory outcomes cannot be adequately compensated by financial settlements alone.
    (E) Predicting the monetary cost of legal or health care services is more difficult than predicting the monetary cost of other types of professional services.

Inference

The question's use of the word *implies* means that the answer depends on making an inference. This question refers to one sentence in the passage (lines 21–24), so it is essential to review what that sentence says in order to understand what it implies. An unconditional guarantee of satisfaction may have a particular disadvantage in the case of health care and legal services because clients may be misled into believing that lawsuits or medical procedures have guaranteed outcomes when they do not. Since an inference may be drawn only from explicitly stated information, the correct response must be about the problem of guarantees and outcomes.

A   Although this statement may be true, it cannot be derived from the cited reference.
B   **Correct.** Legal and medical professionals cannot guarantee the outcomes of their work.
C   This statement cannot be drawn from the description of the issue.
D   Compensation is not discussed in the reference.
E   Predicting costs is not discussed in the reference.

The correct answer is B.

43. Which of the following hypothetical situations best exemplifies the potential problem noted in the second sentence of the second paragraph (lines 15–19)?

    (A) A physician's unconditional guarantee of satisfaction encourages patients to sue for malpractice if they are unhappy with the treatment they receive.

    (B) A lawyer's unconditional guarantee of satisfaction makes clients suspect that the lawyer needs to find new clients quickly to increase the firm's income.

    (C) A business consultant's unconditional guarantee of satisfaction is undermined when the consultant fails to provide all of the services that are promised.

    (D) An architect's unconditional guarantee of satisfaction makes clients wonder how often the architect's buildings fail to please clients.

    (E) An accountant's unconditional guarantee of satisfaction leads clients to believe that tax returns prepared by the accountant are certain to be accurate.

Application

This question involves taking the problem identified in lines 15–19 and applying it to the hypothetical situation that best fits it. Offering an unconditional guarantee may not work as a marketing strategy because potential clients may *doubt* the *firm's ability to deliver the promised level of service.* This strategy may actually introduce doubts or reservations on the part of potential clients and in fact discourage them from ever hiring the firm or the individual providing the service.

A   In this case, the problem occurs after, not before, the service is rendered.

B   This situation exemplifies another problem of unconditional guarantees, the suggestion that a *firm is begging for business* (line 21).

C   The problem occurs after, not before, the service is rendered.

D   Correct. The architect's apparent need to offer an unconditional guarantee makes potential clients question the outcome of the architect's work by suggesting the likelihood of their dissatisfaction with the architectural services.

E   This situation contradicts the problem.

The correct answer is D.

44. The passage most clearly implies which of the following about the professional service firms mentioned in lines 24–27?

    (A) They are unlikely to have offered unconditional guarantees of satisfaction in the past.

    (B) They are usually profitable enough to be able to compensate clients according to the terms of an unconditional guarantee.

    (C) They usually practice in fields in which the outcomes are predictable.

    (D) Their fees are usually more affordable than those charged by other professional service firms.

    (E) Their clients are usually already satisfied with the quality of service that is delivered.

Inference

The question asks for the implications of the statement in lines 24–27: *professional service firms with outstanding reputations and performance to match have little to gain from offering unconditional guarantees.* Why is it logical to infer that these firms have little to gain from this strategy? If their performance and reputation are both outstanding, it is likely that their clients are already satisfied with the quality of the work they provide and that offering such guarantees would provide no competitive advantage.

A   The statement in the passage concerns the present; nothing is implied about what may have been true in the past.

B   The statement includes no information about profitability, so no inference may be drawn.

C   No information is provided about specific fields or likely outcomes.

D   Fees are not discussed in this statement.

E   Correct. No guarantee is needed when clients are already satisfied with the quality of work provided.

The correct answer is E.

Questions 45–49 refer to the passage on page 38.

45. The passage is primarily concerned with

    (A) identifying historical circumstances that led Du Bois to alter his long-term goals

    (B) defining "accommodationism" and showing how Du Bois used this strategy to achieve certain goals

    (C) accounting for a particular position adopted by Du Bois during the First World War

    (D) contesting the view that Du Bois was significantly influenced by either Washington or Trotter

    (E) assessing the effectiveness of a strategy that Du Bois urged African Americans to adopt

Main idea

This question asks what the passage as a whole is attempting to do. The passage opens by indicating that many African Americans were surprised by a political position taken by Du Bois in 1918, which seemed more accommodationist than expected. The passage then goes on to demonstrate that Du Bois often *shifted positions* (line 9) and states that Du Bois's 1918 position was pragmatic in that it responded to real social pressure. The passage then indicates that Du Bois's accommodationist stance *did not last* (line 31), and that he returned to a more confrontationist stance upon learning of the treatment of African Americans in the military.

A   The passage indicates that Du Bois did not change his long-term goals (lines 22–24).

B   *Accomodationism* is not defined in the passage but is associated with certain actions (community improvement), ideologies (solidarity), and leaders (Washington); the passage does not indicate if Du Bois was successful in achieving the accommodationist goals of 1895 (lines 11–15).

C   **Correct.** The passage explains why Du Bois took his accommodationist position and why he eventually rejected it.

D   The passage offers no judgment as to how much Du Bois was influenced by Washington or Trotter.

E   The passage does not indicate that there was widespread adoption of any of the strategies Du Bois recommended.

The correct answer is C.

46. The passage indicates which of the following about Du Bois's attitude toward Washington?

    (A) It underwent a shift during the First World War as Du Bois became more sympathetic with Trotter's views.

    (B) It underwent a shift in 1903 for reasons other than Du Bois's disagreement with Washington's accommodationist views.

    (C) It underwent a shift as Du Bois made a long-term commitment to the strategy of accommodation.

    (D) It remained consistently positive even though Du Bois disagreed with Washington's efforts to control the African American press.

    (E) It was shaped primarily by Du Bois's appreciation of Washington's pragmatic approach to the advancement of the interests of African Americans.

Supporting ideas

Answering this question involves recognizing what the passage indicates about a particular point of view it describes. In line 15, the passage indicates that Du Bois praised Washington's ideas, but that in 1903 Du Bois aligned himself with *Washington's militant opponent* (lines 16–17), a shift the passage describes as being due less to *ideological reasons* (lines 17–21) than to political reasons.

A   The passage indicates that the shift described occurred in 1903, not during the First World War.

B   **Correct.** The passage indicates Du Bois's shift was not due to differences he had with Washington's ideas or views.

C   The passage indicates that Du Bois accommodationist stance *did not last* (lines 30–31) and therefore was not a long-term commitment.

D   The passage indicates in lines 16–17 that Du Bois at one point aligned himself with Washington's militant opponent.

E   The passage indicates that Du Bois eventually rejected the accommodationist views of Washington.

The correct answer is B.

47. The passage suggests which of the following about the contributions of African Americans to the United States war effort during the First World War?

    (A) The contributions were made largely in response to Du Bois's 1918 editorial.

    (B) The contributions had much the same effect as African Americans' contributions to previous wars.

    (C) The contributions did not end discrimination against African Americans in the military.

    (D) The contributions were made in protest against Trotter's confrontationist tactics.

    (E) The contributions were made primarily by civil rights activists who returned to activism after the war.

Inference

This question requires making an inference from information given in the passage. The passage begins by indicating that Du Bois called on African Americans to suspend their fight for equality and to help with the war effort during the First World War. The final sentence of the passage, however, indicates that Du Bois learned that African Americans were experiencing *systematic discrimination* in the military during this time.

A   The passage does not indicate how African Americans responded to Du Bois's editorial other than that many African Americans were surprised by it.

B   The passage indicates that African Americans' participation in previous wars brought legal and political advances but that African Americans experienced discrimination in the First World War.

C   **Correct.** The passage indicates that African Americans experienced systematic discrimination in the military during the First World War.

D   The passage does not describe how African Americans responded to Trotter's tactics during the First World War.

E   The passage does not indicate whether African Americans involved in the war effort were primarily civil rights activists.

The correct answer is C.

48. The author of the passage refers to Washington's call to African Americans in 1895 primarily in order to

    (A) identify Du Bois's characteristic position on the continuum between accommodationism and confrontationism

    (B) explain why Du Bois was sympathetic with Washington's views in 1895

    (C) clarify how Trotter's views differed from those of Washington in 1895

    (D) support an assertion about Du Bois's tendency to shift his political positions

    (E) dismiss the claim that Du Bois's position in his 1918 editorial was consistent with his previous views

Evaluation

This question requires understanding how a part of the passage functions within the passage as a whole. The passage begins by indicating that many African Americans were surprised by Du Bois's views in his 1918 editorial. The passage then explains that Du Bois *often shifted positions along the continuum* (lines 9–10). To demonstrate this, the passage indicates that Du Bois praised Washington's 1895 speech directed to African Americans, but that by 1903, Du Bois had aligned himself with Washington's *militant opponent* (lines 16–17).

A   The passage indicates that Du Bois *shifted positions* (line 9) along the accommodationist-confrontationist continuum.

B   The passage does not indicate why Du Bois praised Washington's 1895 speech.

C   The passage does not indicate what Trotter's views of Washington's 1895 speech were.

D   **Correct.** The passage uses Du Bois's praise for Washington's 1895 speech and subsequent support of Trotter to illustrate Du Bois's tendency to shift positions.

E   The passage does not include any claims that Du Bois's 1918 editorial was consistent with his previous views.

The correct answer is D.

49. According to the passage, which of the following is true of the strategy that Du Bois's 1918 editorial urged African Americans to adopt during the First World War?

   (A) It was a strategy that Du Bois had consistently rejected in the past.

   (B) It represented a compromise between Du Bois's own views and those of Trotter.

   (C) It represented a significant redefinition of the long-term goals Du Bois held prior to the war.

   (D) It was advocated by Du Bois in response to his recognition of the discrimination faced by African Americans during the war.

   (E) It was advocated by Du Bois in part because of his historical knowledge of gains African Americans had made during past wars.

Supporting ideas

This question requires recognizing how a part of the passage functions within the passage as a whole. The passage begins by indicating that Du Bois's 1918 editorial called on African Americans to abandon political and social activism and help with the war effort in the First World War. In the second paragraph, the passage indicates that Du Bois's wartime position, expressed in his 1918 speech, was at least partly motivated by his belief that *African Americans' contributions to past war efforts had brought them some legal and political advances* (lines 28–30).

A   The passage does not discuss whether Du Bois recommended this strategy prior to 1918.

B   The passage does not indicate that Du Bois consciously compromised with Trotter's views.

C   The passage indicates that his 1918 wartime views were *not a change in his long-term goals* (lines 22–23).

D   The passage indicates that Du Bois's recognition of discrimination in the military caused him to reject his own 1918 wartime views.

E   **Correct.** The passage indicates that Du Bois's 1918 views were influenced partly by a belief that past war efforts helped African Americans both legally and politically.

The correct answer is E.

Questions 50–55 refer to the passage on page 40.

50. The primary purpose of the passage is to

   (A) contrast possible outcomes of a type of business investment

   (B) suggest more careful evaluation of a type of business investment

   (C) illustrate various ways in which a type of business investment could fail to enhance revenues

   (D) trace the general problems of a company to a certain type of business investment

   (E) criticize the way in which managers tend to analyze the costs and benefits of business investments

Main idea

Look at the passage as a whole to find the primary purpose. This passage uses an example, described in the second paragraph, to illustrate the principle of business practice explained in the first paragraph. The author begins by saying that efforts to improve service do not always result in a *competitive advantage* for a company. Thus, an investment in service must be carefully evaluated to determine if it will reduce costs or increase revenues (lines 4–8).

A   Only one outcome, failure to gain a competitive advantage, is examined.

B   **Correct.** Investments in service must be carefully evaluated for the returns they will bring.

C   Only one way, an unnecessary investment in improved service, is discussed.

D   The example of the bank is used only to illustrate a general business principle; the bank itself is not the focus of the passage.

E   The passage criticizes the absence of such an analysis, not the way it is conducted.

The correct answer is B.

51. According to the passage, investments in service are comparable to investments in production and distribution in terms of the

    (A) tangibility of the benefits that they tend to confer
    (B) increased revenues that they ultimately produce
    (C) basis on which they need to be weighed
    (D) insufficient analysis that managers devote to them
    (E) degree of competitive advantage that they are likely to provide

Supporting ideas

The phrase *according to the passage* indicates that the question covers material that is explicitly stated in the passage. The answer to this question demands a careful reading of the second sentence (lines 4–8). Investments in service are like investments in production and distribution because they *must be balanced against other types of investments on the basis of direct, tangible benefits.* Thus, these investments should be weighed on the same basis.

A   The author is not equating the tangible benefits the different kinds of investments reap, but rather the basis on which decisions to make investments are made.
B   Revenues generated from investing in service are not said to be comparable to revenues generated from investing in production and distribution.
C   **Correct.** An evaluation of whether or not to make these investments must be made on the same basis.
D   How managers analyze investments in production and distribution is not discussed.
E   The competitive advantage of superior service is acknowledged, but not the degree of it; it is not mentioned at all in the context of production and distribution.

The correct answer is C.

52. The passage suggests which of the following about service provided by the regional bank prior to its investment in enhancing that service?

    (A) It enabled the bank to retain customers at an acceptable rate.
    (B) It threatened to weaken the bank's competitive position with respect to other regional banks.
    (C) It had already been improved after having caused damage to the bank's reputation in the past.
    (D) It was slightly superior to that of the bank's regional competitors.
    (E) It needed to be improved to attain parity with the service provided by competing banks.

Inference

Because the question uses the word *suggests*, finding the answer depends on making an inference about service at the bank. The paragraph that discusses the bank begins with the transitional expression, *this truth*, which refers to the previous sentence (lines 8–15). The *truth* is that investing in improved service is a waste *if a company is already effectively on a par with its competitors because it provides service that avoids a damaging reputation and keeps customers from leaving at an unacceptable rate.* Because of the way the author has linked this generalization to the description of the bank after investment, it is reasonable to infer that the hypothetical company's situation describes the bank prior to its investment in improved service.

A   **Correct.** The bank's service would have been good enough to avoid a damaging reputation and to retain customers at an acceptable rate.
B   The passage does not suggest that the bank's service was either poor or deficient to that of its competitors.
C   The passage implies that the bank's service avoided *a damaging reputation*.
D   The bank would have been *on a par with its competitors*, not superior to them.
E   The bank would have been *on a par with its competitors*, not inferior to them.

The correct answer is A.

53. The passage suggests that bank managers failed to consider whether or not the service improvement mentioned in lines 18–20

(A) was too complicated to be easily described to prospective customers

(B) made a measurable change in the experiences of customers in the bank's offices

(C) could be sustained if the number of customers increased significantly

(D) was an innovation that competing banks could have imitated

(E) was adequate to bring the bank's general level of service to a level that was comparable with that of its competitors

Inference

The question's use of the word *suggests* means that the answer depends on making an inference. To answer this question, look at the entire second paragraph. Managers failed to think ahead. Would the service improvement attract new customers because other banks would find it difficult to copy? Or would the service improvement be easily imitated by competitors? The managers should have investigated this area before investing in improved service.

A The passage states the improvement *could easily be described to customers* (lines 28–29).

B No evidence in the passage shows that the managers failed to think about their customers' experience in the bank.

C The passage does not imply that managers failed to consider an increase in clients.

D Correct. The managers did not wonder if other banks would copy their service improvement.

E Lines 8–12 imply that the bank enjoyed a comparable level of service before investing in service improvement.

The correct answer is D.

54. The discussion of the regional bank in the second paragraph serves which of the following functions within the passage as a whole?

(A) It describes an exceptional case in which investment in service actually failed to produce a competitive advantage.

(B) It illustrates the pitfalls of choosing to invest in service at a time when investment is needed more urgently in another area.

(C) It demonstrates the kind of analysis that managers apply when they choose one kind of service investment over another.

(D) It supports the argument that investments in certain aspects of service are more advantageous than investments in other aspects of service.

(E) It provides an example of the point about investment in service made in the first paragraph.

Logical structure

This question requires thinking about what the second paragraph contributes to the whole passage. The first paragraph makes a generalization about investing in improvements in service; in certain conditions, such improvements do not result in the *competitive advantage* a company hopes for. The second paragraph offers the bank as an example of this generalization.

A The first sentence of the passage explains that improving service does not necessarily bring a *competitive advantage*, so the bank is not exceptional.

B The bank illustrates the pitfall of not evaluating a service improvement on the basis of tangible benefits; other areas of the bank are not mentioned.

C The passage does not discuss how managers analyze and choose different service investments.

D Investments in different aspects of service are not evaluated in the passage.

E Correct. The bank is an example of the position stated in the first paragraph that investing in improved service can be a waste if the investment is not evaluated carefully.

The correct answer is E.

55. The author uses the word "only" in line 27 most likely in order to

(A) highlight the oddity of the service improvement

(B) emphasize the relatively low value of the investment in service improvement

(C) distinguish the primary attribute of the service improvement from secondary attributes

(D) single out a certain merit of the service improvement from other merits

(E) point out the limited duration of the actual service improvement

Logical structure

The question asks you to consider the logic of the author's word choice. The previous two sentences discuss why the service improvement was a wasted investment. In contrast, the final sentence turns to the sole advantage of the service improvement, which is trivial by comparison. The author uses *only* to modify *merit* in order to emphasize the minimal nature of this advantage.

A The passage does not indicate that the service improvement is somehow strange or peculiar.

B Correct. *Only* emphasizes the low value attached to the single benefit.

C No attributes of the service improvement are mentioned.

D *Only* signifies that there was one sole merit of the service improvement.

E The duration of the benefit is not discussed in the passage.

The correct answer is B.

Questions 56–60 refer to the passage on page 42.

56. According to the passage, before the final results of the study were known, which of the following seemed likely?

(A) That workers with the highest productivity would also be the most accurate

(B) That workers who initially achieved high productivity ratings would continue to do so consistently

(C) That the highest performance ratings would be achieved by workers with the highest productivity

(D) That the most productive workers would be those whose supervisors claimed to value productivity

(E) That supervisors who claimed to value productivity would place equal value on customer satisfaction

Supporting ideas

The phrase *according to the passage* indicates that the answer is stated in the passage. Only lines 17–20 refer to the expected outcome of the study: *there should have been a strong correlation between a monitored worker's productivity and the overall rating the worker received.*

A The passage does not state a prediction linking productivity with accuracy.

B No prediction is stated that workers rated highly productive would remain so.

C Correct. It was expected that the most productive workers would be the most highly rated.

D The passage does not state such a prediction.

E The passage makes no such prediction.

The correct answer is C.

57. It can be inferred that the author of the passage discusses "unmonitored workers" (line 11) primarily in order to

(A) compare the ratings of these workers with the ratings of monitored workers

(B) provide an example of a case in which monitoring might be effective

(C) provide evidence of an inappropriate use of CPMCS

(D) emphasize the effect that CPMCS may have on workers' perceptions of their jobs

(E) illustrate the effect that CPMCS may have on workers' ratings

Inference

An inference is drawn from stated information. Go to the specific line reference in the question to find the reason that the author included the detail about unmonitored workers. Unmonitored workers are compared with monitored workers on a single point: what they believe to be the most important element of their job (and thus of their ratings). While unmonitored workers believe it is customer service, monitored workers point to productivity. The logical inference from the information given is that the author is using this contrast to show that CPMCS affect how workers think about their jobs.

A   Unmonitored workers' ratings are not discussed in the passage.
B   The passage does not link unmonitored workers with a potentially effective use of monitoring.
C   The passage does not connect unmonitored workers with inappropriate uses of CPMCS.
D   **Correct.** The contrast in the workers' responses demonstrates that CPMCS may influence how workers think about their jobs.
E   The passage does not connect unmonitored workers with the effect of CPMCS on workers' ratings.

The correct answer is D.

58. Which of the following, if true, would most clearly have supported the conclusion referred to in lines 22–25?

(A) Ratings of productivity correlated highly with ratings of both accuracy and attendance.

(B) Electronic monitoring greatly increased productivity.

(C) Most supervisors based overall ratings of performance on measures of productivity alone.

(D) Overall ratings of performance correlated more highly with measures of productivity than the researchers expected.

(E) Overall ratings of performance correlated more highly with measures of accuracy than with measures of productivity.

Logical structure

To answer this question, look at the actual conclusion of the study: in rating workers' performances, *supervisors gave considerable weight to . . . attendance, accuracy, and indications of customer satisfaction.* What additional piece of information would support this conclusion? If one of these three criteria mattered as much as or more than productivity in assessing workers' performances, then the conclusion would be strengthened. Thus, the supervisors' overall performance ratings should correlate with measures of attendance, accuracy, or customer service to at least the same extent that they correlate with measures of productivity.

A   The conclusion is about the value supervisors place on criteria other than productivity, so a finding about productivity is irrelevant to the conclusion.
B   Increased productivity is not relevant to the conclusion, which concerns other criteria in performance assessment.
C   This statement contradicts the conclusion that supervisors value other criteria.
D   This statement contradicts the conclusion stated in lines 22–25.
E   **Correct.** The conclusion is strengthened when measures of accuracy, one of the three criteria supervisors consider other than productivity, correlate with overall performance ratings more highly than measures of productivity do.

The correct answer is E.

59. According to the passage, a "hygiene factor" (line 27) is an aspect of a worker's performance that

    (A) has no effect on the rating of a worker's performance

    (B) is so basic to performance that it is assumed to be adequate for all workers

    (C) is given less importance than it deserves in rating a worker's performance

    (D) is not likely to affect a worker's rating unless it is judged to be inadequate

    (E) is important primarily because of the effect it has on a worker's rating

Supporting ideas

The phrase *according to the passage* indicates that the answer is explicitly stated in the passage. By putting *hygiene factor* in quotation marks, the author is calling attention to the expression, which is explained in lines 27–31. A *"hygiene factor"* is a criterion in assessing job performance that hurts the overall rating if it is too low, but that does not improve the rating beyond a certain point.

A   If too low, a *"hygiene factor"* affects the rating negatively (lines 27–28).

B   Because the *"hygiene factor"* can affect the rating, it is not assumed to be uniformly adequate.

C   The passage does not provide enough information to make this determination.

D   Correct. When low, the *"hygiene factor"* may affect workers' overall ratings negatively, but when high, it does not affect the ratings beyond a certain point.

E   The passage does not assert that the primary importance of the *"hygiene factor"* is its effect on ratings.

The correct answer is D.

60. The primary purpose of the passage is to

    (A) explain the need for the introduction of an innovative strategy

    (B) discuss a study of the use of a particular method

    (C) recommend a course of action

    (D) resolve a difference of opinion

    (E) suggest an alternative approach

Main idea

To answer this question, look at the entire passage. What is its main point? It begins by explaining the use of CPMCS in some companies, and then it shows that a study of employees being monitored by CPMCS revealed unexpected results. The rest of the passage discusses the study.

A   The passage reports rather than argues; it does not explain the need for a strategy.

B   Correct. The passage presents a method of recording workers' activities, CPMCS, and then reports the findings of a study of this method.

C   The passage describes a study of a method; it does not recommend a course of action.

D   The passage provides study results, not conflicting opinions.

E   No alternative to CPMCS is discussed in the passage.

The correct answer is B.

Questions 61–63 refer to the passage on page 44.

61. The primary purpose of the passage is to

(A) refute the idea that the zonation exhibited in mangrove forests is caused by adaptation to salinity

(B) describe the pattern of zonation typically found in Florida mangrove forests

(C) argue that Davis' succession paradigm cannot be successfully applied to Florida mangrove forests

(D) discuss hypotheses that attempt to explain the zonation of coastal mangrove forests

(E) establish that plants that do well in saline forest environments require salt to achieve maximum metabolic efficiency

Main idea

Look at the passage as a whole in order to find the passage's primary purpose. The first paragraph discusses zonation and species distribution in mangrove forests. The second paragraph presents Davis' theory that zonation is caused by plant succession. The third paragraph discusses a challenge to Davis' theory. The final paragraph presents research on salinity tolerance and zonation in mangrove forests. The passage as a whole is concerned with different explanations of zonation in mangrove forests.

A The fourth paragraph discusses the relation of salinity and zonation, but the passage does not refute this idea. Since this idea is only discussed in one paragraph, it cannot be the primary concern of the whole passage.

B Zonation is described in the first paragraph, but the passage's primary interest is in the possible causes of zonation.

C The third paragraph shows that Davis' paradigm applies to some mangrove forests but not to those on stable coastlines.

D **Correct.** The passage's primary purpose, as expressed throughout, is looking at different explanations of the causes of zonation in mangrove forests.

E Salinity is discussed in the final paragraph, but the passage states that salt is not required. The brief discussion of this point shows that it is not the primary concern of the passage.

The correct answer is D.

62. According to the passage, the earliest research on mangrove forests produced which of the following?

(A) Data that implied random patterns of mangrove species distribution

(B) Descriptions of species distributions suggesting zonation

(C) Descriptions of the development of mangrove forests over time

(D) Reclassification of species formerly thought to be identical

(E) Data that confirmed the "land-building" role of mangroves

Supporting ideas

As indicated by the phrase *according to the passage*, this question is based on factual information stated in the passage. Lines 5–8 describe the *earliest research on mangrove forests*. This research *produced descriptions of species distribution from shore to land*. This shore-to-land pattern is described as *"zonal"* in the first sentence.

A The passage suggests that the distribution was not random.

B **Correct.** The description of the species distribution goes from shore to land, fitting the definition of *"zonal"* in the first sentence.

C The passage does not indicate that the earliest research looked at mangrove forest development over time.

D There is no evidence that the earliest research involved reclassification.

E The earliest research produced only descriptions; the land-building theory came later.

The correct answer is B.

63. It can be inferred from the passage that Davis' paradigm does NOT apply to which of the following?

    (A)   The shoreline of Florida mangrove forests first studied by Davis

    (B)   A shoreline in an area with weak currents

    (C)   A shoreline in an area with weak tidal energy

    (D)   A shoreline extended by "land-building" species of mangroves

    (E)   A shoreline in which few sediments can accumulate

Application

To answer this question, apply Davis' paradigm to the situations in the answer choices. One situation will NOT fit the paradigm. According to Davis, the shoreline is extended seaward because of *the "land-building" role of mangroves* (lines 12–14). The third paragraph describes the circumstances favorable to the land-building process: weak currents, weak tidal energies, and the accumulation of sediments. In the absence of these conditions, land-building would not occur.

A   Since this is the area from which Davis drew his conclusions, it obviously fits the paradigm.

B   Weak currents favor the land-building paradigm.

C   Weak tidal energies favor the land-building paradigm.

D   If land-building has occurred, then the paradigm describing that land-building applies.

E   **Correct.** If few sediments can accumulate, land-building is NOT able to occur.

The correct answer is E.

Questions 64–70 refer to the passage on page 46.

64. The primary purpose of the passage is to

    (A)   review research demonstrating the benefits of corporate mergers and acquisitions and examine some of the drawbacks that acquisition behavior entails

    (B)   contrast the effects of corporate mergers and acquisitions on acquiring firms and on firms that are acquired

    (C)   report findings that raise questions about a reason for corporate mergers and acquisitions and suggest possible alternative reasons

    (D)   explain changes in attitude on the part of acquiring firms toward corporate mergers and acquisitions

    (E)   account for a recent decline in the rate of corporate mergers and acquisitions

Main idea

This question requires understanding what the passage as a whole is trying to do. The passage begins by citing three studies that demonstrate that when firms acquire other firms, there is not necessarily a worthwhile economic gain. The passage then cites economic interests as the reason given by firms when they acquire other firms but calls into question the veracity of this reasoning. The passage then goes on to speculate as to why mergers and acquisitions occur.

A   The research cited in the passage calls into question whether mergers and acquisitions are beneficial to firms.

B   The passage is not concerned with comparing the relative effects of mergers and acquisitions on the acquired and acquiring firms.

C   **Correct.** The passage surveys reports that question the reasons given by firms when they acquire other firms and suggests other reasons for these acquisitions.

D   The passage does not indicate that there has been a change in the attitude of acquiring firms toward mergers and acquisitions.

E   The passage does not indicate that there has been a decline in the rate of mergers and acquisitions.

The correct answer is C.

65. The findings cited in the passage suggest which of the following about the outcomes of corporate mergers and acquisitions with respect to acquiring firms?

   (A) They include a decrease in value of many acquiring firms' stocks.
   (B) They tend to be more beneficial for small firms than for large firms.
   (C) They do not fulfill the professed goals of most acquiring firms.
   (D) They tend to be beneficial to such firms in the long term even though apparently detrimental in the short term.
   (E) They discourage many such firms from attempting to make subsequent bids and acquisitions.

Inference

Answering this question requires recognizing what is inferable from information given in the passage. The passage begins by citing three studies that show that mergers and acquisitions often harm the economic goals of acquiring firms. The passage also indicates that, nonetheless, acquiring firms *continue to assert that their objectives are economic ones* (lines 15–16), suggesting that the goals of these firms are not met by acquiring other firms.

A   The passage suggests that the stock of acquiring firms *tends to increase in value* (lines 12–13), albeit less than the firm it acquires.
B   The three studies cited in the passage do contrast the effects of corporate mergers on acquiring firms and on acquired firms, but the effects in question are significant only insofar as they contribute to the wider investigation into why mergers take place at all.
C   **Correct.** The passage indicates that even while acquiring firms cite economic goals, the results of the studies indicate that these goals are not being met.
D   The passage makes no comparison between the long-term and short-term gains of acquiring firms.
E   The passage does not indicate that firms have been affected by the results of the studies cited.

The correct answer is C.

66. It can be inferred from the passage that the author would be most likely to agree with which of the following statements about corporate acquisitions?

   (A) Their known benefits to national economies explain their appeal to individual firms during the 1970s and 1980s.
   (B) Despite their adverse impact on some firms, they are the best way to channel resources from less to more productive sectors of a nation's economy.
   (C) They are as likely to occur because of poor monitoring by boards of directors as to be caused by incentive compensation for managers.
   (D) They will be less prevalent in the future, since their actual effects will gain wider recognition.
   (E) Factors other than economic benefit to the acquiring firm help to explain the frequency with which they occur.

Inference

This question requires understanding what view the author has about a particular issue. The three studies cited by the passage all suggest that mergers and acquisitions do not necessarily bring economic benefit to the acquiring firms. The author concludes therefore that *factors having little to do with corporate economic interests explain acquisitions* (lines 23–24) and then goes on to speculate as to what the reasons may actually be.

A   The passage indicates that while mergers and acquisitions may benefit the national economy, the appeal of mergers and acquisitions must be tied to companies' *private economic interests* (lines 19–22).
B   The passage makes no judgment as to the best way for firms to help channel resources from less to more efficient economic sectors.
C   The passage makes no comparison between the influence of poor monitoring by boards and that of executive incentives.
D   The passage makes no prediction as to future trends in the market for mergers and acquisitions.
E   **Correct.** The passage states that factors other than economic interests drive mergers and acquisitions.

The correct answer is E.

67. The author of the passage mentions the effect of acquisitions on national economies most probably in order to

(A) provide an explanation for the mergers and acquisitions of the 1970s and 1980s overlooked by the findings discussed in the passage

(B) suggest that national economic interests played an important role in the mergers and acquisitions of the 1970s and 1980s

(C) support a noneconomic explanation for the mergers and acquisitions of the 1970s and 1980s that was cited earlier in the passage

(D) cite and point out the inadequacy of one possible explanation for the prevalence of mergers and acquisitions during the 1970s and 1980s

(E) explain how modeling affected the decisions made by managers involved in mergers and acquisitions during the 1970s and 1980s

Evaluation

This question requires understanding why a piece of information is included in the passage. After the passage cites the results of the three studies on mergers and acquisitions, which call into question the economic benefits of acquisitions, it indicates that firms nonetheless claim that their objectives are economic. The passage then states that while acquisitions *may well have* a desirable effect on national economies (lines 17–19), the results of the studies suggest that factors other than economic interest must drive executives to arrange mergers and acquisitions.

A   The passage does not mention national economies as part of an explanation for the occurrence of mergers and acquisitions.

B   The passage suggests that the effect of acquisitions on national economies is not tied to any explanations for why acquisitions occur.

C   The effect of acquisitions on national economies is not mentioned in the passage as an explanation for why acquisitions occur.

D   **Correct.** The passage uses the mention of national economies as part of a larger point questioning the stated motivations behind firms' efforts to acquire other firms.

E   In the passage, modeling is unrelated to the idea that acquisitions may have a desirable effect on national economies.

The correct answer is D.

68. According to the passage, during the 1970s and 1980s bidding firms differed from the firms for which they bid in that bidding firms

(A) tended to be more profitable before a merger than after a merger

(B) were more often concerned about the impact of acquisitions on national economies

(C) were run by managers whose actions were modeled on those of other managers

(D) anticipated greater economic advantages from prospective mergers

(E) experienced less of an increase in stock value when a prospective merger was announced

Supporting ideas

This question requires recognizing information contained in the passage. In lines 10–14, the passage describes the findings of the third study of mergers and acquisitions in the 1970s and 1980s. This study found that, after the announcement of a possible merger, the stock value of an acquiring, or bidding, firm increases much less than the stock value of the firm for which it is in the process of bidding.

A   The passage does not indicate whether the profitability of acquiring firms tended to be greater or less after a merger.

B   The passage does not indicate that acquiring firms were concerned about the impact of their actions on national economies.

C   The passage does not mention the actions of managers at firms that are being acquired.

D   The passage does not discuss whether acquiring firms tended to expect greater overall economic gains than actually occurred.

E   **Correct.** The passage indicates that the stock value of acquiring firms grew less than that of the firms they were attempting to acquire.

The correct answer is E.

69. According to the passage, which of the following was true of corporate acquisitions that occurred during the 1970s and 1980s?

(A) Few of the acquisitions that firms made were subsequently divested.

(B) Most such acquisitions produced only small increases in acquired firms' levels of profitability.

(C) Most such acquisitions were based on an overestimation of the value of target firms.

(D) The gains realized by most acquiring firms did not equal the amounts expended in acquiring target firms.

(E) About half of such acquisitions led to long-term increases in the value of acquiring firms' stocks.

Supporting ideas

This question requires recognizing information contained in the passage. The passage reports on three studies of mergers and acquisitions in the 1970s and 1980s. In lines 7–10, the passage indicates that the second study found that the postacquisition gains to most of the acquiring firms did not offset, or at least equal, the price paid to acquire the firms.

A   The passage does not discuss post-acquisition divesting.

B   The passage indicates that on average, the profitability of acquired firms fell after being acquired (lines 5–7).

C   The passage does not indicate whether most acquiring firms overestimated the value of the firms they acquired.

D   Correct. The passage states that for most acquiring firms the costs of buying the acquired firm were greater than the gains derived from acquiring it.

E   The passage does not indicate what percentage of acquiring firms, if any, experienced long-term gains in their stock value.

The correct answer is D.

70. The author of the passage implies that which of the following is a possible partial explanation for acquisition behavior during the 1970s and 1980s?

(A) Managers wished to imitate other managers primarily because they saw how financially beneficial other firms' acquisitions were.

(B) Managers miscalculated the value of firms that were to be acquired.

(C) Lack of consensus within boards of directors resulted in their imposing conflicting goals on managers.

(D) Total compensation packages for managers increased during that period.

(E) The value of bidding firms' stock increased significantly when prospective mergers were announced.

Inference

This question requires recognizing what can be inferred from the information in the passage. After providing the results of the studies of mergers and acquisitions, the author concludes that even though acquiring firms state that their objectives are economic, factors having little to do with corporate economic interests explain acquisitions (lines 22–24). Among alternative explanations, the author points to managerial error in estimating the value of firms targeted for acquisition (lines 27–28) as possibly contributing to acquisition behavior in the 1970s and 1980s.

A   While the passage indicates that managers may have modeled their behavior on other managers, it does not provide a reason for why this would be so.

B   Correct. The author states that one explanation for acquisition behavior may be that managers erred when they estimated the value of firms being acquired.

C   The author discusses a lack of monitoring by boards of directors but makes no mention of consensus within these boards.

D   The author does not discuss compensation packages for managers.

E   The passage does not state how significantly the value of the bidding firm's stock increased upon announcing a merger but only that it increased less in value than did the stock of the prospective firm being acquired.

The correct answer is B.

Questions 71–76 refer to the passage on page 48.

71. The primary purpose of the passage is to

   (A) discuss a plan for investigation of a phenomenon that is not yet fully understood

   (B) present two explanations of a phenomenon and reconcile the differences between them

   (C) summarize two theories and suggest a third theory that overcomes the problems encountered in the first two

   (D) describe an alternative hypothesis and provide evidence and arguments that support it

   (E) challenge the validity of a theory by exposing the inconsistencies and contradictions in it

Main idea

Examining the structure of the whole passage helps to identify the passage's primary purpose or main idea. The first two paragraphs introduce a recent hypothesis about how caffeine affects behavior. The third paragraph looks at an earlier, widely accepted theory and then presents the objections to it made by the scientists proposing the more recent hypothesis. The fourth and fifth paragraphs provide evidence to support the newer hypothesis. Since most of the passage is devoted to the recent hypothesis, clearly the primary purpose must be to present that hypothesis to readers.

A The passage discusses a current investigation, not one planned for the future.

B The passage examines two explanations, but the earlier theory is discussed only to expose its weakness and the differences between the explanations are not reconciled. Most of the passage is devoted to the more recent hypothesis.

C Only two theories are presented in the passage.

D **Correct.** The recent hypothesis provides an alternative to an earlier one and is supported by evidence and arguments.

E Lines 32–37 do pose such a challenge to the earlier theory; however, the challenge is a small part of the whole passage. Similarly, in the final paragraph, an exception to the more recent theory is introduced, only to be dismissed as an unimportant concern.

The correct answer is D.

72. According to Snyder et al., caffeine differs from adenosine in that caffeine

   (A) stimulates behavior in the mouse and in humans, whereas adenosine stimulates behavior in humans only

   (B) has mixed effects in the brain, whereas adenosine has only a stimulatory effect

   (C) increases cyclic AMP concentrations in target neurons, whereas adenosine decreases such concentrations

   (D) permits release of neurotransmitters when it is bound to adenosine receptors, whereas adenosine inhibits such release

   (E) inhibits both neuron firing and the production of phosphodiesterase when there is a sufficient concentration in the brain, whereas adenosine inhibits only neuron firing

Supporting ideas

To answer this question, look for the section in the passage that discusses adenosine and caffeine. The first paragraph leads the reader through how adenosine (lines 7–11) and caffeine (lines 4–7) work in the brain, according to Snyder et al. Adenosine *depresses neuron firing* by *inhibiting the release of neurotransmitters*; it is able to achieve this by binding to *specific receptors on neuronal membranes*. Caffeine interrupts this process by binding to the receptors, which prevents adenosine from attaching to them, and the neurons then *fire more readily than they otherwise would* (lines 17–21).

A The passage does not suggest that adenosine stimulates behavior.

B While the final paragraph reveals that caffeine displays mixed effects, the passage does not state that adenosine has a stimulatory effect.

C Increasing cyclic AMP concentrations is part of the earlier theory, not that of Snyder et al.

D **Correct.** Lines 17–21 explain that caffeine binds to the receptors, releasing neurotransmitters, whereas adenosine hinders that release.

E Inhibiting the production of phosphodiesterase is discussed in the earlier theory, not in the work of Snyder et al.

The correct answer is D.

73. In response to experimental results concerning IBMX, Snyder et al. contended that it is not uncommon for psychoactive drugs to have

(A) mixed effects in the brain
(B) inhibitory effects on enzymes in the brain
(C) close structural relationships with caffeine
(D) depressive effects on mouse locomotion
(E) the ability to dislodge caffeine from receptors in the brain

Supporting ideas

To answer this question, look at the last paragraph, which discusses the effects of IBMX. This compound binds to the adenosine receptors, but instead of acting as a stimulant as other caffeine derivatives do, it was found to depress locomotion in mice. Snyder et al. explain that IBMX *has mixed effects in the brain, a not unusual occurrence with psychoactive drugs* (lines 58–60).

A **Correct.** The results of one experiment can be explained by *mixed effects in the brain*, which Snyder et al. say may occur with psychoactive drugs.
B This response refers back to the earlier theory, not to Snyder et al.'s response concerning IBMX experiment results.
C Caffeine is only included within the broad category of psychoactive drugs.
D This effect is attributed to one compound, IBMX, not to all psychoactive drugs.
E This ability is not discussed in the passage.

The correct answer is A.

74. According to Snyder et al., all of the following compounds can bind to specific receptors in the brain EXCEPT

(A) IBMX
(B) caffeine
(C) adenosine
(D) theophylline
(E) phosphodiesterase

Supporting ideas

This question asks the reader to rule out all the possibilities discussed in the text, leaving the single exception. The first paragraph explains that

both adenosine and caffeine bind to receptors in the brain. The third paragraph attests to the ability of theophylline to bind to the receptors. The last paragraph describes IBMX as a compound that binds to adenosine receptors. Thus, the exception has to be the enzyme phosphodiesterase.

A Lines 54–55 state that IBMX binds to receptors.
B Lines 17–19 state that caffeine binds to receptors.
C Lines 13–14 state that adenosine binds to receptors.
D Lines 46–50 state that theophylline binds to receptors.
E **Correct.** The passage includes no evidence that phosphodiesterase binds to receptors.

The correct answer is E.

75. Snyder et al. suggest that caffeine's ability to bind to A_1 and A_2 receptors can be at least partially attributed to which of the following?

(A) The chemical relationship between caffeine and phosphodiesterase
(B) The structural relationship between caffeine and adenosine
(C) The structural similarity between caffeine and neurotransmitters
(D) The ability of caffeine to stimulate behavior
(E) The natural occurrence of caffeine and adenosine in the brain

Supporting ideas

This question asks the reader to find information that is suggested but not directly stated in the passage. The A_1 and A_2 receptors are mentioned in line 16, so look at the surrounding material. Snyder et al. propose that caffeine, *which is structurally similar to adenosine*, binds to both types of receptors, just as adenosine does. Caffeine's ability to bind to these receptors may be due to this structural similarity to adenosine.

A Phosphodiesterase is discussed in an entirely different context in lines 22–25.
B **Correct.** Lines 17–19 suggest that caffeine's structural similarity to adenosine may be responsible for its ability to bind to A_1 and A_2 receptors.

C   Caffeine acts on neurotransmitters; it is not structurally similar to them.
D   Caffeine's ability to stimulate behavior results from, rather than causes, this process.
E   The passage does not discuss the natural occurrence of these compounds.

The correct answer is B.

76. The author quotes Snyder et al. in lines 43–48 most probably in order to

(A)   reveal some of the assumptions underlying their theory
(B)   summarize a major finding of their experiments
(C)   point out that their experiments were limited to the mouse
(D)   indicate that their experiments resulted only in general correlations
(E)   refute the objections made by supporters of the older theory

Logical structure

To find the reason that the author quotes Snyder et al., examine the fourth paragraph, where the quotation appears. The paragraph starts with evidence supporting the new hypothesis on the basis of experiments with mice. The quotation then begins with the phrase *in general*, which implies a summary of the results of the work with mice. The quoted material explains that the more the compounds were able to bind to the receptors, the greater the stimulatory effect. This major finding supports the hypothesis.

A   The quotation explains results of an experiment, not assumptions about a theory.
B   **Correct.** The quotation summarizes the experiment with mice and reports a major finding in support of the hypothesis.
C   The quotation generalizes on the basis of the experiment; it does not limit the finding to mice.
D   Specific, not general, correlations were made between the ability to bind to receptors and to stimulate locomotion.
E   The passage includes no such objections; therefore no refutations are needed.

The correct answer is B.

Questions 77–84 refer to the passage on page 50.

77.   According to the passage, job segregation by sex in the United States was

(A)   greatly diminished by labor mobilization during the Second World War
(B)   perpetuated by those textile-mill owners who argued in favor of women's employment in wage labor
(C)   one means by which women achieved greater job security
(D)   reluctantly challenged by employers except when the economic advantages were obvious
(E)   a constant source of labor unrest in the young textile industry

Supporting ideas

The question uses the phrase *according to the passage*, indicating that the answer is based on information stated in the passage. The second paragraph explains that *a prevailing definition of femininity* often dictates what jobs are given to women. For example, textile-mill owners used *hoary stereotypes associated with . . . homemaking activities* in order to justify their employment of women, claiming that *women were by nature skillful at detailed tasks and patient in carrying out repetitive chores.*

A   Just the reverse is true: Although some women were permitted to take "male" jobs during the Second World War, lines 45–47 show that *job segregation by sex characterized even the most important war industries.*
B   **Correct.** Textile-mill owners exploited stereotypes about women and the work suited to them in order to justify employing them as wage laborers.
C   Many "*female*" jobs were *less secure* (lines 35–36).
D   No information in the passage leads to this conclusion; in fact, employers showed little interest in challenging job segregation *even when higher profits beckoned* (lines 40–42).
E   Labor unrest among textile-mill workers is not discussed.

The correct answer is B.

78. According to the passage, historians of women's labor focused on factory work as a more promising area of research than service-sector work because factory work

    (A) involved the payment of higher wages

    (B) required skill in detailed tasks

    (C) was assumed to be less characterized by sex segregation

    (D) was more readily accepted by women than by men

    (E) fit the economic dynamic of industrialism better

Supporting ideas

The phrase *according to the passage* indicates that the answer is stated in the passage. Look at the first paragraph, which discusses historians of women's labor. These historians disregarded service work in favor of factory work not only because factory work differed from traditional *"women's work,"* but also because the *forces of industrialism were presumed to be gender-blind* (lines 8–10).

A   The passage does not indicate that historians studied factory workers because of higher wages.

B   The passage gives no evidence that historians chose this research area for this reason.

C   Correct. The passage indicates that the historians chose this research area because they assumed that sex segregation was less prevalent in factory work than in service-sector work.

D   Although the passage states that women accepted factory work more readily than did men, this difference is not cited in the passage as the reason historians focused on factory work.

E   Factory work may have fit the dynamic of industrialism better, but this is not the reason the passage gives for the historians' choice.

The correct answer is C.

79. It can be inferred from the passage that early historians of women's labor in the United States paid little attention to women's employment in the service sector of the economy because

    (A) the extreme variety of these occupations made it very difficult to assemble meaningful statistics about them

    (B) fewer women found employment in the service sector than in factory work

    (C) the wages paid to workers in the service sector were much lower than those paid in the industrial sector

    (D) women's employment in the service sector tended to be much more short-term than in factory work

    (E) employment in the service sector seemed to have much in common with the unpaid work associated with homemaking

Inference

Since this question asks for an inference, the answer is not directly stated in the passage; it must instead be derived from the information given. To answer this question, look at what the first paragraph says about the historians' focus on factory work. The historians *disregarded* service work and *focused instead on factory work* in part because *it seemed so different from traditional, unpaid "women's work" in the home* (lines 5–8). Since the two kinds of work are explicitly contrasted, it is reasonable to infer that what is not true of factory work is true of service work; service work is similar to *traditional, unpaid "women's work" in the home*.

A   No mention of statistics is made in the passage and service-sector jobs are not characterized as extremely various.

B   The numbers of women in each kind of work are not compared.

C   Wages earned in the two kinds of work are not compared.

D   Duration of employment in the two kinds of work is not compared.

E   Correct. Historians disregarded service work because it was similar to unpaid *"women's work"* in the home.

The correct answer is E.

80. The passage supports which of the following statements about the early mill owners mentioned in the second paragraph?

(A) They hoped that by creating relatively unattractive "female" jobs they would discourage women from losing interest in marriage and family life.

(B) They sought to increase the size of the available labor force as a means to keep men's wages low.

(C) They argued that women were inherently suited to do well in particular kinds of factory work.

(D) They thought that factory work bettered the condition of women by emancipating them from dependence on income earned by men.

(E) They felt guilty about disturbing the traditional division of labor in the family.

Supporting ideas

The second paragraph discusses the assumptions and actions of the mill owners. To answer this question, look for a perspective or action that the paragraph explicitly supports. The mill owners accepted and perpetuated the stereotypes of women, including their supposed greater attention to detail and patience with repetitive tasks, and thus argued that women were inherently (*by nature*) suited to the work in a textile mill.

A The passage states that the mill owners *assumed that women's "real" aspirations were for marriage and family life*, which they used as an excuse to pay women less.

B The passage does not say that mill owners tried to keep men's wages low.

C **Correct.** The mill owners contended that certain factory work was suitable to a woman's alleged patient, detail-oriented nature.

D The passage does not credit mill owners with trying to emancipate women.

E There is no indication in the passage that the mill owners felt any guilt.

The correct answer is C.

81. It can be inferred from the passage that the "unfinished revolution" the author mentions in line 15 refers to the

(A) entry of women into the industrial labor market

(B) recognition that work done by women as homemakers should be compensated at rates comparable to those prevailing in the service sector of the economy

(C) development of a new definition of femininity unrelated to the economic forces of industrialism

(D) introduction of equal pay for equal work in all professions

(E) emancipation of women wage earners from gender-determined job allocation

Inference

An inference requires going beyond the material explicitly stated in the passage to the author's ideas that underlie that material. To understand this reference, it is first necessary to analyze its context. The first paragraph explains that historians focused on factory work on the assumption that it was *gender-blind* and *emancipatory in effect*. However, the paragraph concludes, *emancipation has been less profound than expected, for not even industrial wage labor has escaped continued sex segregation in the workplace* (lines 11–14). The phrase *this unfinished revolution* occurs in the next sentence, and it refers back to *continued sex segregation in the workplace*. Here the passage implies that the author believes the revolution is unfinished because jobs are still allocated to women on the basis of their sex.

A The first paragraph has established that women are already in the industrial workforce; this is not unfinished, even if women were excluded from some jobs during the Second World War.

B Compensation for work at home is not discussed in the passage.

C The only definition of femininity referred to in the passage is said to determine the kinds of jobs available to women.

D Equal pay for equal work is not addressed in the passage.

E **Correct.** The *unfinished revolution* refers to an emancipation that is incomplete because job segregation on the basis of sex continues.

The correct answer is E.

82. The passage supports which of the following statements about hiring policies in the United States?

    (A) After a crisis many formerly "male" jobs are reclassified as "female" jobs.

    (B) Industrial employers generally prefer to hire women with previous experience as homemakers.

    (C) Post–Second World War hiring policies caused women to lose many of their wartime gains in employment opportunity.

    (D) Even war industries during the Second World War were reluctant to hire women for factory work.

    (E) The service sector of the economy has proved more nearly gender-blind in its hiring policies than has the manufacturing sector.

Supporting ideas

Review each answer choice to see if it is explicitly supported by information in the passage. The last sentence of the passage states that, once the Second World War was over, men returned to take the "*male*" jobs that women had been temporarily allowed to master. Thus, the gains women had been allowed to make during the war (despite continued job segregation) were lost to them after men returned to work.

A   The last paragraph shows that after the Second World War, "*male*" jobs that had been held by women during the war were returned to men.

B   The passage does not mention industrial employers' preferences for women with homemaking experience.

C   **Correct.** After the Second World War, women lost many employment opportunities that had been available to them during the war.

D   The passage says that job segregation persisted during the Second World War, but it does not indicate that those industries were reluctant to hire women.

E   No comparison is made in the passage to support this conclusion.

The correct answer is C.

83. Which of the following words best expresses the opinion of the author of the passage concerning the notion that women are more skillful than men in carrying out detailed tasks?

    (A) "patient" (line 24)

    (B) "repetitive" (line 24)

    (C) "hoary" (line 26)

    (D) "homemaking" (line 27)

    (E) "purview" (line 28)

Inference

This question asks the reader to make an inference about the author's attitude. Word choice may reveal attitude, as it does here when the author describes the *hoary stereotypes* about women that mill owners perpetuated. *Hoary* means old—literally white with age—and so the stereotypes are being dismissed by the author as old-fashioned, even obsolete.

A   The mill owners stereotyped women as *patient*; this does not express the author's opinion.

B   Mill owners claimed that women were suited to *repetitive* work; this does not express the author's opinion.

C   **Correct.** *Hoary* carries with it a judgment, suggesting that the mill owners' stereotypes are impossibly antiquated.

D   *Homemaking* describes activities but does not reveal the author's opinion.

E   *Purview* simply means a range or a scope; it does not reveal an opinion.

The correct answer is C.

84. Which of the following best describes the relationship of the final paragraph to the passage as a whole?

(A) The central idea is reinforced by the citation of evidence drawn from twentieth-century history.

(B) The central idea is restated in such a way as to form a transition to a new topic for discussion.

(C) The central idea is restated and juxtaposed with evidence that might appear to contradict it.

(D) A partial exception to the generalizations of the central idea is dismissed as unimportant.

(E) Recent history is cited to suggest that the central idea's validity is gradually diminishing.

Logical structure

Consider the final paragraph in the context of the whole passage to evaluate its relationship to the whole. The first two paragraphs examine job segregation in an unspecified but earlier time. The final paragraph brings the reader into the twentieth century, when, as the example drawn from the Second World War shows, job segregation persisted. Thus, the final paragraph updates and reinforces the author's thesis about the persistence of job segregation.

A **Correct.** The central idea that sex segregation continued in the twentieth-century workplace is reinforced with an example from the Second World War.

B The central idea is the persistence of job segregation, which is the only topic in the paragraph.

C The last paragraph supports the passage; no apparently contradictory evidence is introduced.

D The last paragraph supports the central idea with a twentieth-century example; no exceptions are either entertained or dismissed.

E Twentieth-century history is cited to support the central idea, not to show that its validity is diminishing.

The correct answer is A.

Questions 85–90 refer to the passage on page 52.

85. The author of the passage alludes to the well-established nature of the concept of individual rights in the Anglo-Saxon legal and political tradition in order to

(A) illustrate the influence of individualist feminist thought on more general intellectual trends in English history

(B) argue that feminism was already a part of the larger Anglo-Saxon intellectual tradition, even though this has often gone unnoticed by critics of women's emancipation

(C) explain the decline in individualist thinking among feminists in non-English-speaking countries

(D) help account for an increasing shift toward individualist feminism among feminists in English-speaking countries

(E) account for the philosophical differences between individualist and relational feminists in English-speaking countries

Logical structure

This question asks for the reason that the author has chosen to include the information about the Anglo-Saxon tradition in lines 24–28. The concept of individual rights was *well established* in this tradition, and that is the reason that *individualist feminism came to predominate in English-speaking countries.* Thus, this detail explains why feminists in English-speaking countries turned to individualist, rather than relational, feminism.

A This statement reverses the order: the more general intellectual trends in English history influenced individualist feminism.

B Feminism is not said to be a part of the Anglo-Saxon tradition.

C While relational feminism is said to predominate among European and non-Western feminists, the passage offers no evidence of a decline in individualist feminism among these groups.

D **Correct.** The author uses the information about individual rights and the Anglo-Saxon tradition to explain why individualist feminism predominated in English-speaking countries.

E   The Anglo-Saxon tradition is not said to account for all the philosophical differences between the two feminist traditions in English-speaking countries, but only for the fact that individualist feminism became predominant there.

The correct answer is D.

86. The passage suggests that the author of the passage believes which of the following?

(A)   The predominance of individualist feminism in English-speaking countries is a historical phenomenon, the causes of which have not yet been investigated.

(B)   The individualist and relational feminist views are irreconcilable, given their theoretical differences concerning the foundations of society.

(C)   A consensus concerning the direction of future feminist politics will probably soon emerge, given the awareness among feminists of the need for cooperation among women.

(D)   Political adversaries of feminism often misuse arguments predicated on differences between the sexes to argue that the existing social system should be maintained.

(E)   Relational feminism provides the best theoretical framework for contemporary feminist politics, but individualist feminism could contribute much toward refining and strengthening modern feminist thought.

Supporting ideas

To answer this question, look for an idea that the author explicitly supports in the passage. The first sentence of the last paragraph (lines 41–45) states that the relational feminists' argument—that women's biological role gives them a special (and undervalued) place in society—may be used by opponents of feminism to reinforce the existing dominance of men.

A   In lines 19–24, the author identifies one cause for the situation.

B   In lines 51–55, the author implies that a reconciliation might be possible, making this an overstatement.

C   The author does not suggest that consensus is likely to happen soon; cooperation is not discussed.

D   **Correct.** This statement is consistent with the view the author expressed in the third paragraph.

E   The last paragraph discusses the problems of both feminist traditions, but the author does not say one is better for contemporary feminist politics than the other.

The correct answer is D.

87. It can be inferred from the passage that the individualist feminist tradition denies the validity of which of the following causal statements?

(A)   A division of labor in a social group can result in increased efficiency with regard to the performance of group tasks.

(B)   A division of labor in a social group causes inequities in the distribution of opportunities and benefits among group members.

(C)   A division of labor on the basis of gender in a social group is necessitated by the existence of sex-linked biological differences between male and female members of the group.

(D)   Culturally determined distinctions based on gender in a social group foster the existence of differing attitudes and opinions among group members.

(E)   Educational programs aimed at reducing inequalities based on gender among members of a social group can result in a sense of greater well-being for all members of the group.

Inference

To make an inference about the individualist feminist tradition, begin by rereading the first paragraph, which sets forth the differing *modes of argumentation*. Relational feminism holds that the biological differences of the sexes must result in a division of labor based on those differences (lines 6–11). *By contrast*, individualist feminism downplays the importance of gender roles and attaches little importance to the biological function of childbearing (lines 11–16). Thus, it can be inferred that individualist feminists would disagree with the statement that biological differences should determine a gender-based division of labor in society.

A   The passage neither discusses increased efficiency nor implies that individualist feminists would reject it.

B   The passage does not indicate that individualist feminists would disagree with this statement.

C   Correct. This statement reflects the position of the relational feminists that the individualist feminists oppose; individualist feminists instead stress individual rights and personal autonomy.

D   The passage offers no evidence that individualist feminists would disagree with this statement.

E   Nothing in the passage indicates that individualist feminists would disagree with this statement.

The correct answer is C.

88. According to the passage, relational feminists and individualist feminists agree that

(A) individual human rights take precedence over most other social claims

(B) the gender-based division of labor in society should be eliminated

(C) laws guaranteeing equal treatment for all citizens regardless of gender should be passed

(D) a greater degree of social awareness concerning the importance of motherhood would be beneficial to society

(E) the same educational and economic opportunities should be available to both sexes

Supporting ideas

This question asks for information that is explicitly stated in the passage in slightly different language. While the passage is largely devoted to the differences between the two feminist traditions, lines 30–34 indicate a point of convergence. Individualist feminists believe in *equal rights for all*. Relational feminists believe that *equal educational and economic opportunities* should be available to women.

A   Only individualist feminists believe that individual human rights are most important (lines 11–13).

B   Relational feminists do believe in a gender-based division of labor (lines 6–8).

C   Lines 30–37 show that relational feminists do not believe in gender-blind equal rights laws.

D   Only relational feminists believe in the importance of women's *special contributions to society* (lines 35–36).

E   Correct. Practitioners of both feminist traditions believe that equal educational and economic opportunities should be available to both sexes.

The correct answer is E.

89. According to the author, which of the following was true of feminist thought in Western societies before 1890?

(A) Individualist feminist arguments were not found in the thought or writing of non-English-speaking feminists.

(B) Individualist feminism was a strain in feminist thought, but another strain, relational feminism, predominated.

(C) Relational and individualist approaches were equally prevalent in feminist thought and writing.

(D) The predominant view among feminists held that the welfare of women was ultimately less important than the welfare of children.

(E) The predominant view among feminists held that the sexes should receive equal treatment under the law.

Supporting ideas

To answer this question, look at what the author states in lines 17–24, where the years before and after 1890 are discussed. The second paragraph begins by explaining that the two feminist traditions *coexisted* up until the late nineteenth century, although relational feminism *had been the dominant strain in feminist thought*.

A   The passage states that relational feminism was *the dominant strain* of the two views that *coexisted*; thus, the individualist arguments existed before 1890.

B   Correct. Lines 20–21 explicitly state that relational feminism *had been the dominant strain in feminist thought* before 1890.

C   The passage shows that the two feminist traditions were not equally prevalent; relational feminism predominated.

D   No evidence in the passage supports this statement.

E   The passage does not show that most feminists before 1890 took this position.

The correct answer is B.

103

90. The author implies that which of the following was true of most feminist thinkers in England and the United States after 1920?

(A) They were less concerned with politics than with intellectual issues.

(B) They began to reach a broader audience and their programs began to be adopted by mainstream political parties.

(C) They called repeatedly for international cooperation among women's groups to achieve their goals.

(D) They moderated their initial criticism of the economic systems that characterized their societies.

(E) They did not attempt to unite the two different feminist approaches in their thought.

Inference

Answering this question involves making an inference. Before 1890, the two feminist traditions *coexisted*. After 1920, *the goals of the two approaches began to seem increasingly irreconcilable* (lines 28–30). Lines 30–40 provide details on the differing and even opposing priorities of the relational feminists and individualist feminists. It is reasonable to infer that both feminist traditions pursued their own goals and did not try to reconcile the two different approaches in their work. The final paragraph reveals that the two feminist traditions continue to remain separate, although the author offers a possibility for their harmonization.

A Individualist feminists advocated a *system with equal rights*, and relational feminists sought *protective legislation*, so it is clear both groups were politically active; the author does not imply that they were more interested in intellectual issues.

B The passage offers no evidence to show broader or growing support for feminist ideas.

C International cooperation is not discussed in the passage.

D No information in the passage supports this statement.

E **Correct.** As the goals of the two feminist traditions grew *increasingly irreconcilable*, feminists in England and the United States did not try to harmonize the two strains in their thinking.

The correct answer is E.

Questions 91–97 refer to the passage on page 54.

91. According to the passage, conventional spiral galaxies differ from low-surface-brightness galaxies in which of the following ways?

(A) They have fewer stars than do low-surface-brightness galaxies.

(B) They evolve more quickly than low-surface-brightness galaxies.

(C) They are more diffuse than low-surface-brightness galaxies.

(D) They contain less helium than do low-surface-brightness galaxies.

(E) They are larger than low-surface-brightness galaxies.

Supporting ideas

This question requires recognizing information that is provided in the passage. The first paragraph describes and compares two types of galaxies: conventional galaxies and dim, or low-surface-brightness, galaxies. It states that dim galaxies have the same approximate number of stars as a common type of conventional galaxy but tend to be larger and more diffuse because their mass is spread over wider areas (lines 4–10). The passage also indicates that dim galaxies take longer than conventional galaxies to convert their primordial gases into stars, meaning that dim galaxies evolve much more slowly than conventional galaxies (lines 10–14), which entails that conventional galaxies evolve more quickly than dim galaxies.

A The passage states that dim galaxies have approximately the same numbers of stars as a common type of conventional galaxy.

B **Correct.** The passage indicates that dim galaxies evolve much more slowly than conventional galaxies, which entails that conventional galaxies evolve more quickly.

C The passage states that dim galaxies are more spread out, and therefore more diffuse, than conventional galaxies.

D The passage does not mention the relative amounts of helium in the two types of galaxies under discussion.

E The passage states that dim galaxies tend to be much larger than conventional galaxies.

The correct answer is B.

92. It can be inferred from the passage that which of the following is an accurate physical description of typical low-surface-brightness galaxies?

    (A) They are large spiral galaxies containing fewer stars than do conventional galaxies.

    (B) They are compact but very dim spiral galaxies.

    (C) They are diffuse spiral galaxies that occupy a large volume of space.

    (D) They are small, young spiral galaxies that contain a high proportion of primordial gas.

    (E) They are large, dense spirals with low luminosity.

Inference

This question requires drawing an inference from information given in the passage. The first paragraph compares dim galaxies and conventional galaxies. Dim galaxies are described as having the same general shape (lines 4–5) as a common type of conventional galaxy, the spiral galaxy, suggesting that dim galaxies are, themselves, spiral shaped. The passage also indicates that, although both types of galaxies tend to have approximately the same number of stars, dim galaxies tend to be much larger and spread out over larger areas of space (lines 4–10) than conventional galaxies.

A   The passage states that the two types of galaxies have approximately the same number of stars.

B   The passage indicates that dim galaxies are relatively large and spread out.

C   Correct. The passage indicates that dim galaxies have the same general shape as spiral galaxies and that their mass is spread out over large areas of space.

D   The passage indicates that dim galaxies are relatively large and spread out.

E   The passage states that dim galaxies have few stars per unit of volume, suggesting that they are not dense but diffuse.

The correct answer is C.

93. It can be inferred from the passage that the "long-standing puzzle" refers to which of the following?

    (A) The difference between the rate at which conventional galaxies evolve and the rate at which low-surface-brightness galaxies evolve

    (B) The discrepancy between estimates of total baryonic mass derived from measuring helium and estimates based on measuring galactic luminosity

    (C) The inconsistency between the observed amount of helium in the universe and the number of stars in typical low-surface-brightness galaxies

    (D) Uncertainties regarding what proportion of baryonic mass is contained in intergalactic space and what proportion in conventional galaxies

    (E) Difficulties involved in detecting very distant galaxies and in investigating their luminosity

Inference

This question requires drawing an inference from information given in the passage. The second paragraph describes *the long-standing puzzle of the missing baryonic mass in the universe*. The passage states that baryons are the source of galactic luminosity, and so scientists can estimate the amount of baryonic mass in the universe by measuring the luminosity of galaxies (lines 17–21). The puzzle is that spectroscopic measures of helium in the universe suggest that the baryonic mass in the universe is much higher than measures of luminosity would indicate (21–25).

A   The differences between the rates of evolution of the two types of galaxies is not treated as being controversial in the passage.

B   Correct. The passage indicates that measurements using spectroscopy and measurements using luminosity result in puzzling differences in estimates of the universe's baryonic mass.

C   The passage does not suggest how helium might relate to the numbers of stars in dim galaxies.

D   The passage indicates that astronomers have speculated that the missing baryonic mass might be discovered in intergalactic space or hard-to-detect galaxies, but does not suggest that these speculations are constituents of the long-standing puzzle.

E   The passage does not mention how the distance to galaxies affects scientists' ability to detect these galaxies.

The correct answer is B.

94.   The author implies that low-surface-brightness galaxies could constitute an answer to the puzzle discussed in the second paragraph primarily because

(A)   they contain baryonic mass that was not taken into account by researchers using galactic luminosity to estimate the number of baryons in the universe

(B)   they, like conventional galaxies that contain many baryons, have evolved from massive, primordial gas clouds

(C)   they may contain relatively more helium, and hence more baryons, than do galaxies whose helium content has been studied using spectroscopy

(D)   they have recently been discovered to contain more baryonic mass than scientists had thought when low-surface-brightness galaxies were first observed

(E)   they contain stars that are significantly more luminous than would have been predicted on the basis of initial studies of luminosity in low-surface-brightness galaxies

Inference

This question requires drawing an inference from information given in the passage. The puzzle is that estimates of the baryonic mass of the universe based on luminosity are lower than those based on spectroscopy (lines 21–25). The passage states that astronomers did not notice dim galaxies until recently (lines 2–3), and that these galaxies may help account for the missing baryonic mass in the universe (lines 15–17). The passage also suggests that astronomers measure the luminosity of specific galaxies (lines 19–21). Thus it can be inferred that, prior to their being noticed by astronomers, the luminosity of these dim galaxies was not measured, and their baryonic mass was not taken into account in the estimates of luminosity that led to the long-standing puzzle.

A   **Correct.** The passage states that the missing baryonic mass in the universe may be discovered in the dim galaxies that have only recently been noticed by astronomers.

B   The passage does not suggest that dim and conventional galaxies both originating from primordial gas clouds help solve the long-standing puzzle of the missing baryonic mass in the universe.

C   The passage does not suggest that dim galaxies might contain more helium than do conventional galaxies, or that measures of baryonic mass using spectroscopy do not take some dim galaxies into account.

D   The passage does not suggest that dim galaxies contain more baryonic mass than scientists originally believed upon discovering these galaxies.

E   The passage suggests that scientists measured the luminosity of galaxies, not of individual stars.

The correct answer is A.

95.   The author mentions the fact that baryons are the source of stars' luminosity primarily in order to explain

(A)   how astronomers determine that some galaxies contain fewer stars per unit volume than do others

(B)   how astronomers are able to calculate the total luminosity of a galaxy

(C)   why astronomers can use galactic luminosity to estimate baryonic mass

(D)   why astronomers' estimates of baryonic mass based on galactic luminosity are more reliable than those based on spectroscopic studies of helium

(E)   how astronomers know bright galaxies contain more baryons than do dim galaxies

Evaluation

This question requires understanding how one aspect of the passage relates to the reasoning in a larger portion of the passage. The second paragraph explains that scientists have been puzzled over missing baryonic mass in the universe as measured by luminosity (lines 21–25). Given that baryons are the source of luminosity in the galaxy (lines 17–19), astronomers can estimate the baryonic mass of a galaxy by measuring its luminosity.

A   The passage discussion of baryons does not address the number of stars in individual galaxies.

B   The passage discusses how the luminosity of galaxies can be used to estimate baryonic mass, but does not address how total luminosity is measured.

C   **Correct.** The passage indicates that because baryons are the source of galactic luminosity, measuring luminosity can be used to estimate baryonic mass of galaxies.

D   The passage suggests that estimates based on luminosity may have been less accurate, not more accurate, than those based on spectroscopy.

E   The passage does not indicate that bright galaxies contain more baryons than do dim galaxies.

The correct answer is C.

96. The author of the passage would be most likely to disagree with which of the following statements?

(A) Low-surface-brightness galaxies are more difficult to detect than are conventional galaxies.

(B) Low-surface-brightness galaxies are often spiral in shape.

(C) Astronomers have advanced plausible ideas about where missing baryonic mass might be found.

(D) Astronomers have devised a useful way of estimating the total baryonic mass in the universe.

(E) Astronomers have discovered a substantial amount of baryonic mass in intergalactic space.

Inference

This question involves identifying which answer option potentially conflicts with the information the author has provided in the passage. The second paragraph indicates that astronomers' estimates of the baryonic mass of the universe is lower when measured using luminosity than it is when measured using spectroscopy (lines 21–25). The final sentence states that astronomers have speculated that the missing baryonic mass might be discovered in intergalactic space or in hard-to-detect galaxies (lines 25–29). Although the passage does indicate that the discovery of dim, low-surface-brightness galaxies might help account for the missing baryonic mass (lines 15–17), the passage provides no support for the possibility that baryonic mass has been discovered in intergalactic space

A   The passage indicates that low-surface-brightness galaxies went unnoticed until recently, unlike conventional galaxies.

B   The passage indicates that low-surface-brightness galaxies have the same general shape as spiral galaxies.

C   The passage describes two possible explanations astronomers have given for the missing baryonic mass, one of which was made more plausible by the discovery of low-surface-brightness galaxies.

D   The passage indicates that astronomers have used spectroscopy to estimate baryonic mass and gives no reason to suspect that this method is not useful.

E   **Correct.** The passage does not indicate that astronomers have found any baryonic mass in intergalactic space.

The correct answer is E.

97. The primary purpose of the passage is to

   (A) describe a phenomenon and consider its scientific significance

   (B) contrast two phenomena and discuss a puzzling difference between them

   (C) identify a newly discovered phenomenon and explain its origins

   (D) compare two classes of objects and discuss the physical properties of each

   (E) discuss a discovery and point out its inconsistency with existing theory

Main idea

This question requires understanding, in broad terms, the purpose of the passage as a whole. The first paragraph describes a phenomenon: the discovery of dim galaxies and some of their general attributes. The second paragraph describes how this discovery may help astronomers to solve a long-standing puzzle about the baryonic mass of the universe.

A **Correct.** The passage describes the phenomenon of dim galaxies and describes their significance in solving the long-standing puzzle of the missing baryonic mass in the universe.

B Although the passage discusses the puzzling difference between the two estimates of baryonic mass, this option does not account for the broader topic of dim galaxies.

C While the passage identifies the newly discovered phenomenon of dim galaxies, it does not offer a significant explanation for these galaxies' origins.

D Although the passage compares dim and conventional galaxies in the first paragraph, this option does not account for the important detail that dim galaxies may help solve a long-standing puzzle.

E The discovery of dim galaxies discussed in the passage is not said to be inconsistent with any existing scientific theory.

The correct answer is A.

Questions 98–104 refer to the passage on page 56.

98. According to the passage, all of the following were benefits of privatizing state-owned industries in the United Kingdom EXCEPT:

   (A) Privatized industries paid taxes to the government.

   (B) The government gained revenue from selling state-owned industries.

   (C) The government repaid some of its national debt.

   (D) Profits from industries that were still state-owned increased.

   (E) Total borrowings and losses of state-owned industries decreased.

Supporting ideas

This question begins with the phrase *according to the passage*, indicating that it can be answered using facts stated in the passage. The first paragraph lists the benefits of privatization. Use the process of elimination and check the five possible answer choices against the benefits described in lines 8–16. The point that is NOT discussed in the passage is the correct answer.

A Lines 11–12 discuss tax revenues.
B Lines 10–11 discuss revenue from the sales.
C Lines 14–16 discuss debt repayment.
D **Correct.** Profits from state-owned industries are not discussed.
E Lines 9–10 discuss decreased borrowings and losses.

The correct answer is D.

99. According to the passage, which of the following resulted in increased productivity in companies that have been privatized?

   (A) A large number of employees chose to purchase shares in their companies.

   (B) Free shares were widely distributed to individual shareholders.

   (C) The government ceased to regulate major industries.

   (D) Unions conducted wage negotiations for employees.

   (E) Employee-owners agreed to have their wages lowered.

Supporting ideas

This question is based on information explicitly stated in the passage. The second paragraph describes the increased productivity, and the third paragraph begins by stating one reason for it: *employees of privatized industries were given the opportunity to buy shares in their own companies* (lines 28–31). The paragraph also cites the high percentage of employees buying shares in three privatized companies, supporting the idea that many employees bought shares.

A **Correct.** Productivity increased after employees became shareholders in their companies.
B The theoretical advantages and disadvantages of free shares are discussed (lines 43–52), but the passage does not say that any were given away.
C The passage does not examine governmental regulation.
D Although wages are discussed in lines 38–42, the passage does not analyze the relation between wages and productivity.
E Lines 38–42 cite one example of employee-owner willingness to accept lower wages, but this is not said to have resulted in increased productivity.

The correct answer is A.

100. It can be inferred from the passage that the author considers labor disruptions to be

(A) an inevitable problem in a weak national economy
(B) a positive sign of employee concern about a company
(C) a predictor of employee reactions to a company's offer to sell shares to them
(D) a phenomenon found more often in state-owned industries than in private companies
(E) a deterrence to high performance levels in an industry

Inference

This question states that an inference is required; this inference is based on material presented in the second paragraph. To demonstrate that privatization has *raised the level of performance in every area*, the author gives three examples (lines 19–27). One example is the disappearance of labor disruptions, once common. If the absence of labor disruptions raises the level of performance, then the author must believe that the presence of labor disruptions impedes an increase in performance levels.

A The author does not link labor disruptions with a weak national economy.
B The author does not present labor disruptions in a positive light.
C The author does not identify labor disruptions as a predictor of employees' responses to opportunities to buy a company's shares.
D Labor disruptions in state-owned and private industries are not compared.
E **Correct.** The author implies that labor disruptions interfere with high levels of performance in industry.

The correct answer is E.

101. The passage supports which of the following statements about employees buying shares in their own companies?

(A) At three different companies, approximately nine out of ten of the workers were eligible to buy shares in their companies.
(B) Approximately 90 percent of the eligible workers at three different companies chose to buy shares in their companies.
(C) The opportunity to buy shares was discouraged by at least some labor unions.
(D) Companies that demonstrated the highest productivity were the first to allow their employees the opportunity to buy shares.
(E) Eligibility to buy shares was contingent on employees' agreeing to increased work loads.

Supporting ideas

Check each statement by comparing it to the information presented in the passage. Only one statement is supported. The third paragraph presents the percentages of the eligible employees who purchased shares in their companies: 89 percent at one company, 90 percent at a second, and 92 percent at a third (lines 32–35). Thus, it is true that roughly 90 percent of the eligible work force at three different companies bought shares in their companies once they were given the opportunity to do so.

A   The passage cites the percentages of the eligible employees who bought shares, not the percentages of the total workforce that were eligible.
B   **Correct.** The passage shows that roughly 90 percent of the eligible employees at three different companies bought shares in their companies.
C   The passage does not address the attitude of labor unions toward employee share buying.
D   The passage offers no evidence that companies with high productivity were the first to offer shares to their employees.
E   The passage does not show eligibility to be dependent on increased workload.

The correct answer is B.

102. Which of the following statements is most consistent with the principle described in lines 35–38?

(A)   A democratic government that decides it is inappropriate to own a particular industry has in no way abdicated its responsibilities as guardian of the public interest.

(B)   The ideal way for a government to protect employee interests is to force companies to maintain their share of a competitive market without government subsidies.

(C)   The failure to harness the power of self-interest is an important reason that state-owned industries perform poorly.

(D)   Governments that want to implement privatization programs must try to eliminate all resistance to the free-market system.

(E)   The individual shareholder will reap only a minute share of the gains from whatever sacrifices he or she makes to achieve these gains.

Application

To answer this question, first identify the principle involved, and then find the statement that is most compatible with that principle. Lines 35–38 argue that having *a personal stake* in a business makes employees *work to make it prosper*. When there is no personal stake, or self-interest, involved, employees do not have the same incentive to work hard to make their industry *prosper*. Thus, the poor performance of state-owned industries can be ascribed in part to employees' lack of motivation when they have no personal stake in the business.

A   The principle involves a personal, rather than governmental, relationship.
B   According to the principle, self-interest may inspire people to do more; government coercion is not consistent with this principle.
C   **Correct.** State-owned industries perform poorly in part because employees do not have the powerful motivation of self-interest.
D   The principle has to do with the motivation of individuals, not governments; eliminating all resistance to the free-market system is not discussed.
E   Lines 35–38 describe the principle of self-interest, not self-sacrifice.

The correct answer is C.

3.6 Reading Comprehension Answer Explanations

103. Which of the following can be inferred from the passage about the privatization process in the United Kingdom?

(A) It depends to a potentially dangerous degree on individual ownership of shares.

(B) It conforms in its most general outlines to Thomas Paine's prescription for business ownership.

(C) It was originally conceived to include some giving away of free shares.

(D) It has been successful, even though privatization has failed in other countries.

(E) It is taking place more slowly than some economists suggest is necessary.

Inference

Answering this question requires looking at each possible inference to see if it is supported somewhere in the passage. Support for the inference about the pace of privatization is provided by the suggestion of some economists that *giving away free shares would provide a needed acceleration of the privatization process* (lines 43–45). If some economists think privatization needs to be accelerated, then it must be going too slowly, at least according to these economists.

A The passage does not allude to any danger in individual ownership of shares.

B Paine is quoted only in reference to employees' receiving free shares as opposed to buying shares; also, the process of privatization had occurred before employees bought shares in the newly privatized companies.

C No evidence supports the distribution of free shares as part of the United Kingdom's plan to privatize.

D A phrase in line 4, *one approach that works*, suggests that perhaps there were other approaches that did not work; however, nowhere does the passage indicate that privatization has not worked in other countries.

E **Correct.** The economists' suggestion comes from what they see as the need to speed up a process that is currently taking too long.

The correct answer is E.

104. The quotation in lines 46–47 is most probably used to

(A) counter a position that the author of the passage believes is incorrect

(B) state a solution to a problem described in the previous sentence

(C) show how opponents of the viewpoint of the author of the passage have supported their arguments

(D) point out a paradox contained in a controversial viewpoint

(E) present a historical maxim to challenge the principle introduced in the third paragraph

Logical structure

Looking at the quotation's context leads to an understanding of why the quotation was used. Paine's quotation offers a concise and time-honored counterargument to the view voiced in the preceding sentence. The economists suggest giving away free shares, but the author notes that these economists are forgetting that, according to Paine, people do not value what they get too cheaply. The author uses the quotation to show the basic error in the economists' thinking.

A **Correct.** The author uses Paine's quotation as an apt counter to the economists' suggestion.

B The quotation challenges the solution posed in the previous sentence.

C The author agrees with Paine, as is evident in the final lines of the passage.

D The author implies that a viewpoint is ill advised, but does not say it is controversial.

E Paine's maxim does not challenge the principle of self-interest.

The correct answer is A.

4.0   Critical Reasoning

4.0 Critical Reasoning

Critical reasoning questions appear in the Verbal section of the GMAT® test. The Verbal section uses multiple-choice questions to measure your ability to read and comprehend written material, to reason and to evaluate arguments, and to correct written material to conform to standard written English. Because the Verbal section includes content from a variety of topics, you may be generally familiar with some of the material; however, neither the passages nor the questions assume knowledge of the topics discussed. Critical reasoning questions are intermingled with reading comprehension and sentence correction questions throughout the Verbal section of the test.

You will have 75 minutes to complete the Verbal section, or about 1¾ minutes to answer each question. Although critical reasoning questions are based on written passages, these passages are shorter than reading comprehension passages. They tend to be less than 100 words in length and generally are followed by one or two questions. For these questions, you will see a split computer screen. The written passage will remain visible as each question associated with that passage appears in turn on the screen. You will see only one question at a time.

Critical reasoning questions are designed to test the reasoning skills involved in (1) making arguments, (2) evaluating arguments, and (3) formulating or evaluating a plan of action. The materials on which questions are based are drawn from a variety of sources. The GMAT test does not suppose any familiarity with the subject matter of those materials.

In these questions, you are to analyze the situation on which each question is based, and then select the answer choice that most appropriately answers the question. Begin by reading the passages carefully, then reading the five answer choices. If the correct answer is not immediately obvious to you, see whether you can eliminate some of the wrong answers. Reading the passage a second time may be helpful in illuminating subtleties that were not immediately evident.

Answering critical reasoning questions requires no specialized knowledge of any particular field; you don't have to have knowledge of the terminology and conventions of formal logic. The sample critical reasoning questions in this chapter illustrate the variety of topics the test may cover, the kinds of questions it may ask, and the level of analysis it requires.

The following pages describe what critical reasoning questions are designed to measure and present the directions that will precede questions of this type. Sample questions and explanations of the correct answers follow.

4.1 What Is Measured

Critical reasoning questions are designed to provide one measure of your ability to reason effectively in the following areas:

- **Argument construction**
  Questions in this category may ask you to recognize such things as the basic structure of an argument, properly drawn conclusions, underlying assumptions, well-supported explanatory hypotheses, and parallels between structurally similar arguments.

- **Argument evaluation**
  These questions may ask you to analyze a given argument and to recognize such things as factors that would strengthen or weaken the given argument; reasoning errors committed in making that argument; and aspects of the method by which the argument proceeds.

- **Formulating and evaluating a plan of action**
  This type of question may ask you to recognize such things as the relative appropriateness, effectiveness, or efficiency of different plans of action; factors that would strengthen or weaken the prospects of success of a proposed plan of action; and assumptions underlying a proposed plan of action.

4.2 Test-Taking Strategies

1. **Read very carefully the set of statements on which a question is based.**
    Pay close attention to

    - what is put forward as factual information

    - what is not said but necessarily follows from what is said

    - what is claimed to follow from facts that have been put forward

    - how well substantiated are any claims that a particular conclusion follows from the facts that have been put forward

    In reading the arguments, it is important to pay attention to the logical reasoning used; the actual truth of statements portrayed as fact is not important.

2. **Identify the conclusion.**
    The conclusion does not necessarily come at the end of the text; it may come somewhere in the middle or even at the beginning. Be alert to clues in the text that an argument follows logically from another statement or statements in the text.

3. **Determine exactly what each question asks.**
    You might find it helpful to read the question first, before reading the material on which it is based; don't assume that you know what you will be asked about an argument. An argument may have obvious flaws, and one question may ask you to detect them. But another question may direct you to select the one answer choice that does NOT describe a flaw in the argument.

4. **Read all the answer choices carefully.**
    Do not assume that a given answer is the best without first reading all the choices.

4.3 The Directions

These are the directions you will see for critical reasoning questions when you take the GMAT test. If you read them carefully and understand them clearly before going to sit for the test, you will not need to spend too much time reviewing them when you are at the test center and the test is under way.

For these questions, select the best of the answer choices given.

4.4 Sample Questions

Each of the <u>critical reasoning</u> questions is based on a short argument, a set of statements, or a plan of action. For each question, select the best answer of the choices given.

1. Which of the following, if true, most logically completes the argument below?

    Manufacturers are now required to make all cigarette lighters child-resistant by equipping them with safety levers. But this change is unlikely to result in a significant reduction in the number of fires caused by children playing with lighters, because children given the opportunity can figure out how to work the safety levers and _____.

    (A) the addition of the safety levers has made lighters more expensive than they were before the requirement was instituted

    (B) adults are more likely to leave child-resistant lighters than non-child-resistant lighters in places that are accessible to children

    (C) many of the fires started by young children are quickly detected and extinguished by their parents

    (D) unlike child-resistant lighters, lighters that are not child-resistant can be operated by children as young as two years old

    (E) approximately 5,000 fires per year have been attributed to children playing with lighters before the safety levers were required

2. A cost-effective solution to the problem of airport congestion is to provide high-speed ground transportation between major cities lying 200 to 500 miles apart. The successful implementation of this plan would cost far less than expanding existing airports and would also reduce the number of airplanes clogging both airports and airways.

    Which of the following, if true, could proponents of the plan above most appropriately cite as a piece of evidence for the soundness of their plan?

    (A) An effective high-speed ground-transportation system would require major repairs to many highways and mass-transit improvements.

    (B) One-half of all departing flights in the nation's busiest airport head for a destination in a major city 225 miles away.

    (C) The majority of travelers departing from rural airports are flying to destinations in cities over 600 miles away.

    (D) Many new airports are being built in areas that are presently served by high-speed ground-transportation systems.

    (E) A large proportion of air travelers are vacationers who are taking long-distance flights.

3. People's television-viewing habits could be monitored by having television sets, when on, send out low-level electromagnetic waves that are reflected back to the sets. The reflected waves could then be analyzed to determine how many persons are within the viewing area of the sets. Critics fear adverse health effects of such a monitoring system, but a proponent responds, "The average dose of radiation is less than one chest x-ray. As they watch, viewers won't feel a thing."

    Which of the following issues would it be most important to resolve in evaluating the dispute concerning the health effects of the proposed system?

    (A) Whether the proposed method of monitoring viewership can distinguish between people and pets

    (B) Whether radar speed monitors also operate on the principle of analyzing reflected waves of electromagnetic radiation

    (C) Whether the proposed system has been tried out in various areas of the country or in a single area only

    (D) What uses are foreseen for the viewership data

    (E) Whether the average dose that the proponent describes is a short-term dose or a lifetime cumulative dose

4. The price the government pays for standard weapons purchased from military contractors is determined by a pricing method called "historical costing." Historical costing allows contractors to protect their profits by adding a percentage increase, based on the current rate of inflation, to the previous year's contractual price.

    Which of the following statements, if true, is the best basis for a criticism of historical costing as an economically sound pricing method for military contracts?

    (A) The government might continue to pay for past inefficient use of funds.

    (B) The rate of inflation has varied considerably over the past twenty years.

    (C) The contractual price will be greatly affected by the cost of materials used for the products.

    (D) Many taxpayers question the amount of money the government spends on military contracts.

    (E) The pricing method based on historical costing might not encourage the development of innovative weapons.

5. Since the mayor's publicity campaign for Greenville's bus service began six months ago, morning automobile traffic into the midtown area of the city has decreased 7 percent. During the same period, there has been an equivalent rise in the number of persons riding buses into the midtown area. Obviously, the mayor's publicity campaign has convinced many people to leave their cars at home and ride the bus to work.

    Which of the following, if true, casts the most serious doubt on the conclusion drawn above?

    (A) Fares for all bus routes in Greenville have risen an average of 5 percent during the past six months.

    (B) The mayor of Greenville rides the bus to City Hall in the city's midtown area.

    (C) Road reconstruction has greatly reduced the number of lanes available to commuters in major streets leading to the midtown area during the past six months.

    (D) The number of buses entering the midtown area of Greenville during the morning hours is exactly the same now as it was one year ago.

    (E) Surveys show that longtime bus riders are no more satisfied with the Greenville bus service than they were before the mayor's publicity campaign began.

6. Patrick usually provides child care for six children. Parents leave their children at Patrick's house in the morning and pick them up after work. At the end of each workweek, the parents pay Patrick at an hourly rate for the child care provided that week. The weekly income Patrick receives is usually adequate but not always uniform, particularly in the winter, when children are likely to get sick and be unpredictably absent.

    Which of the following plans, if put into effect, has the best prospect of making Patrick's weekly income both uniform and adequate?

    (A) Pool resources with a neighbor who provides child care under similar arrangements, so that the two of them cooperate in caring for twice as many children as Patrick currently does.

    (B) Replace payment by actual hours of child care provided with a fixed weekly fee based upon the number of hours of child care that Patrick would typically be expected to provide.

    (C) Hire a full-time helper and invest in facilities for providing child care to sick children.

    (D) Increase the hourly rate to a level that would provide adequate income even in a week when half of the children Patrick usually cares for are absent.

    (E) Increase the number of hours made available for child care each day, so that parents can leave their children in Patrick's care for a longer period each day at the current hourly rate.

7. A researcher discovered that people who have low levels of immune-system activity tend to score much lower on tests of mental health than do people with normal or high immune-system activity. The researcher concluded from this experiment that the immune system protects against mental illness as well as against physical disease.

    The researcher's conclusion depends on which of the following assumptions?

    (A) High immune-system activity protects against mental illness better than normal immune-system activity does.

    (B) Mental illness is similar to physical disease in its effects on body systems.

    (C) People with high immune-system activity cannot develop mental illness.

    (D) Mental illness does not cause people's immune-system activity to decrease.

    (E) Psychological treatment of mental illness is not as effective as is medical treatment.

8. Extinction is a process that can depend on a variety of ecological, geographical, and physiological variables. These variables affect different species of organisms in different ways, and should, therefore, yield a random pattern of extinctions. However, the fossil record shows that extinction occurs in a surprisingly definite pattern, with many species vanishing at the same time.

    Which of the following, if true, forms the best basis for at least a partial explanation of the patterned extinctions revealed by the fossil record?

    (A) Major episodes of extinction can result from widespread environmental disturbances that affect numerous different species.

    (B) Certain extinction episodes selectively affect organisms with particular sets of characteristics unique to their species.

    (C) Some species become extinct because of accumulated gradual changes in their local environments.

    (D) In geologically recent times, for which there is no fossil record, human intervention has changed the pattern of extinctions.

    (E) Species that are widely dispersed are the least likely to become extinct.

9. In parts of South America, vitamin-A deficiency is a serious health problem, especially among children. In one region, agriculturists are attempting to improve nutrition by encouraging farmers to plant a new variety of sweet potato called SPK004 that is rich in beta-carotene, which the body converts into vitamin A. The plan has good chances of success, since sweet potato is a staple of the region's diet and agriculture, and the varieties currently grown contain little beta-carotene.

Which of the following, if true, most strongly supports the prediction that the plan will succeed?

(A) The growing conditions required by the varieties of sweet potato currently cultivated in the region are conditions in which SPK004 can flourish.

(B) The flesh of SPK004 differs from that of the currently cultivated sweet potatoes in color and texture, so traditional foods would look somewhat different when prepared from SPK004.

(C) There are no other varieties of sweet potato that are significantly richer in beta-carotene than SPK004 is.

(D) The varieties of sweet potato currently cultivated in the region contain some important nutrients that are lacking in SPK004.

(E) There are other vegetables currently grown in the region that contain more beta-carotene than the currently cultivated varieties of sweet potato do.

10. Which of the following best completes the passage below?

At a recent conference on environmental threats to the North Sea, most participating countries favored uniform controls on the quality of effluents, whether or not specific environmental damage could be attributed to a particular source of effluent. What must, of course, be shown, in order to avoid excessively restrictive controls, is that _____.

(A) any uniform controls that are adopted are likely to be implemented without delay

(B) any substance to be made subject to controls can actually cause environmental damage

(C) the countries favoring uniform controls are those generating the largest quantities of effluents

(D) all of any given pollutant that is to be controlled actually reaches the North Sea at present

(E) environmental damage already inflicted on the North Sea is reversible

11. Shelby Industries manufactures and sells the same gauges as Jones Industries. Employee wages account for 40 percent of the cost of manufacturing gauges at both Shelby Industries and Jones Industries. Shelby Industries is seeking a competitive advantage over Jones Industries. Therefore, to promote this end, Shelby Industries should lower employee wages.

Which of the following, if true, would most weaken the argument above?

(A) Because they make a small number of precision instruments, gauge manufacturers cannot receive volume discounts on raw materials.

(B) Lowering wages would reduce the quality of employee work, and this reduced quality would lead to lowered sales.

(C) Jones Industries has taken away 20 percent of Shelby Industries' business over the last year.

(D) Shelby Industries pays its employees, on average, 10 percent more than does Jones Industries.

(E) Many people who work for manufacturing plants live in areas in which the manufacturing plant they work for is the only industry.

12. Large national budget deficits do not cause large trade deficits. If they did, countries with the largest budget deficits would also have the largest trade deficits. In fact, when deficit figures are adjusted so that different countries are reliably comparable to each other, there is no such correlation.

   If the statements above are all true, which of the following can properly be inferred on the basis of them?

   (A) Countries with large national budget deficits tend to restrict foreign trade.

   (B) Reliable comparisons of the deficit figures of one country with those of another are impossible.

   (C) Reducing a country's national budget deficit will not necessarily result in a lowering of any trade deficit that country may have.

   (D) When countries are ordered from largest to smallest in terms of population, the smallest countries generally have the smallest budget and trade deficits.

   (E) Countries with the largest trade deficits never have similarly large national budget deficits.

13. Which of the following most logically completes the argument?

   The last members of a now-extinct species of a European wild deer called the giant deer lived in Ireland about 16,000 years ago. Prehistoric cave paintings in France depict this animal as having a large hump on its back. Fossils of this animal, however, do not show any hump. Nevertheless, there is no reason to conclude that the cave paintings are therefore inaccurate in this regard, since _____.

   (A) some prehistoric cave paintings in France also depict other animals as having a hump

   (B) fossils of the giant deer are much more common in Ireland than in France

   (C) animal humps are composed of fatty tissue, which does not fossilize

   (D) the cave paintings of the giant deer were painted well before 16,000 years ago

   (E) only one currently existing species of deer has any anatomical feature that even remotely resembles a hump

14. The sustained massive use of pesticides in farming has two effects that are especially pernicious. First, it often kills off the pests' natural enemies in the area. Second, it often unintentionally gives rise to insecticide-resistant pests, since those insects that survive a particular insecticide will be the ones most resistant to it, and they are the ones left to breed.

   From the passage above, it can be properly inferred that the effectiveness of the sustained massive use of pesticides can be extended by doing which of the following, assuming that each is a realistic possibility?

   (A) Using only chemically stable insecticides

   (B) Periodically switching the type of insecticide used

   (C) Gradually increasing the quantities of pesticides used

   (D) Leaving a few fields fallow every year

   (E) Breeding higher-yielding varieties of crop plants

15. In an attempt to promote the widespread use of paper rather than plastic, and thus reduce nonbiodegradable waste, the council of a small town plans to ban the sale of disposable plastic goods for which substitutes made of paper exist. The council argues that since most paper is entirely biodegradable, paper goods are environmentally preferable.

   Which of the following, if true, indicates that the plan to ban the sale of disposable plastic goods is ill suited to the town council's environmental goals?

   (A) Although biodegradable plastic goods are now available, members of the town council believe biodegradable paper goods to be safer for the environment.

   (B) The paper factory at which most of the townspeople are employed plans to increase production of biodegradable paper goods.

   (C) After other towns enacted similar bans on the sale of plastic goods, the environmental benefits were not discernible for several years.

   (D) Since most townspeople prefer plastic goods to paper goods in many instances, they are likely to purchase them in neighboring towns where plastic goods are available for sale.

   (E) Products other than those derived from wood pulp are often used in the manufacture of paper goods that are entirely biodegradable.

16. Since the deregulation of airlines, delays at the nation's increasingly busy airports have increased by 25 percent. To combat this problem, more of the takeoff and landing slots at the busiest airports must be allocated to commercial airlines.

    Which of the following, if true, casts the most doubt on the effectiveness of the solution proposed above?

    (A) The major causes of delays at the nation's busiest airports are bad weather and overtaxed air traffic control equipment.

    (B) Since airline deregulation began, the number of airplanes in operation has increased by 25 percent.

    (C) Over 60 percent of the takeoff and landing slots at the nation's busiest airports are reserved for commercial airlines.

    (D) After a small Midwestern airport doubled its allocation of takeoff and landing slots, the number of delays that were reported decreased by 50 percent.

    (E) Since deregulation the average length of delay at the nation's busiest airports has doubled.

17. A major health insurance company in Lagolia pays for special procedures prescribed by physicians only if the procedure is first approved as "medically necessary" by a company-appointed review panel. The rule is intended to save the company the money it might otherwise spend on medically unnecessary procedures. The company has recently announced that in order to reduce its costs, it will abandon this rule.

    Which of the following, if true, provides the strongest justification for the company's decision?

    (A) Patients often register dissatisfaction with physicians who prescribe nothing for their ailments.

    (B) Physicians often prescribe special procedures that are helpful but not altogether necessary for the health of the patient.

    (C) The review process is expensive and practically always results in approval of the prescribed procedure.

    (D) The company's review process does not interfere with the prerogative of physicians, in cases where more than one effective procedure is available, to select the one they personally prefer.

    (E) The number of members of the company-appointed review panel who review a given procedure depends on the cost of the procedure.

18. Unlike the wholesale price of raw wool, the wholesale price of raw cotton has fallen considerably in the last year. Thus, although the retail price of cotton clothing at retail clothing stores has not yet fallen, it will inevitably fall.

Which of the following, if true, most seriously weakens the argument above?

(A) The cost of processing raw cotton for cloth has increased during the last year.

(B) The wholesale price of raw wool is typically higher than that of the same volume of raw cotton.

(C) The operating costs of the average retail clothing store have remained constant during the last year.

(D) Changes in retail prices always lag behind changes in wholesale prices.

(E) The cost of harvesting raw cotton has increased in the last year.

19. A computer equipped with signature-recognition software, which restricts access to a computer to those people whose signatures are on file, identifies a person's signature by analyzing not only the form of the signature but also such characteristics as pen pressure and signing speed. Even the most adept forgers cannot duplicate all of the characteristics the program analyzes.

Which of the following can be logically concluded from the passage above?

(A) The time it takes to record and analyze a signature makes the software impractical for everyday use.

(B) Computers equipped with the software will soon be installed in most banks.

(C) Nobody can gain access to a computer equipped with the software solely by virtue of skill at forging signatures.

(D) Signature-recognition software has taken many years to develop and perfect.

(E) In many cases even authorized users are denied legitimate access to computers equipped with the software.

20. Start-up companies financed by venture capitalists have a much lower failure rate than companies financed by other means. Source of financing, therefore, must be a more important causative factor in the success of a start-up company than are such factors as the personal characteristics of the entrepreneur, the quality of strategic planning, or the management structure of the company.

Which of the following, if true, most seriously weakens the argument above?

(A) Venture capitalists tend to be more responsive than other sources of financing to changes in a start-up company's financial needs.

(B) The strategic planning of a start-up company is a less important factor in the long-term success of the company than are the personal characteristics of the entrepreneur.

(C) More than half of all new companies fail within five years.

(D) The management structures of start-up companies are generally less formal than the management structures of ongoing businesses.

(E) Venture capitalists base their decisions to fund start-up companies on such factors as the characteristics of the entrepreneur and quality of strategic planning of the company.

21. Aphasia, an impairment of the capacity to use language, often occurs when a stroke damages the left half of the brain. Many people with stroke-related aphasia recover at least some capacity to use language within a year. One proposed explanation for such recoveries is that the right side of the brain, which is not usually the major language center, develops its latent language capabilities to compensate for the damage to the left side.

Which of the following, if true, most strongly supports the explanation?

(A) In a study of local brain activity in people performing a language task, people with stroke-related aphasia showed higher activity levels in the right half of the brain than people who did not have aphasia.

(B) A blow to the head injuring the left half of the brain can result in impairment of the capacity to use language indistinguishable from that produced by a stroke.

(C) Among people with stroke-related aphasia, recovering lost capacity to use language does not lead to any impairment of those capacities normally controlled by the right half of the brain.

(D) A stroke that damages the left half of the brain often causes physical impairments of the right side of the body that lessen over time.

(E) Studies of numerous people with aphasia have indicated that the functions that govern language production and those that govern language comprehension are located in separate areas of the brain.

22. In the arid land along the Colorado River, use of the river's water supply is strictly controlled: farms along the river each have a limited allocation that they are allowed to use for irrigation. But the trees that grow in narrow strips along the river's banks also use its water. Clearly, therefore, if farmers were to remove those trees, more water would be available for crop irrigation.

Which of the following, if true, most seriously weakens the argument?

(A) The trees along the river's banks shelter it from the sun and wind, thereby greatly reducing the amount of water lost through evaporation.

(B) Owners of farms along the river will probably not undertake the expense of cutting down trees along the banks unless they are granted a greater allocation of water in return.

(C) Many of the tree species currently found along the river's banks are specifically adapted to growing in places where tree roots remain constantly wet.

(D) The strip of land where trees grow along the river's banks would not be suitable for growing crops if the trees were removed.

(E) The distribution of water allocations for irrigation is intended to prevent farms farther upstream from using water needed by farms farther downstream.

23. Near Chicago a newly built hydroponic spinach "factory," a completely controlled environment for growing spinach, produces on 1 acre of floor space what it takes 100 acres of fields to produce. Expenses, especially for electricity, are high, however, and the spinach produced costs about four times as much as washed California field spinach, the spinach commonly sold throughout the United States.

Which of the following, if true, best supports a projection that the spinach-growing facility near Chicago will be profitable?

(A) Once the operators of the facility are experienced, they will be able to cut operating expenses by about 25 percent.

(B) There is virtually no scope for any further reduction in the cost per pound for California field spinach.

(C) Unlike washed field spinach, the hydroponically grown spinach is untainted by any pesticides or herbicides and thus will sell at exceptionally high prices to such customers as health food restaurants.

(D) Since spinach is a crop that ships relatively well, the market for the hydroponically grown spinach is no more limited to the Chicago area than the market for California field spinach is to California.

(E) A second hydroponic facility is being built in Canada, taking advantage of inexpensive electricity and high vegetable prices.

24. Automobile Dealer's Advertisement:

The Highway Traffic Safety Institute reports that the PZ 1000 has the fewest injuries per accident of any car in its class. This shows that the PZ 1000 is one of the safest cars available today.

Which of the following, if true, most seriously weakens the argument in the advertisement?

(A) The Highway Traffic Safety Institute report listed many cars in other classes that had more injuries per accident than did the PZ 1000.

(B) In recent years many more PZ 1000s have been sold than have any other kind of car in its class.

(C) Cars in the class to which the PZ 1000 belongs are more likely to be involved in accidents than are other types of cars.

(D) The difference between the number of injuries per accident for the PZ 1000 and that for other cars in its class is quite pronounced.

(E) The Highway Traffic Safety Institute issues reports only once a year.

25. Which of the following most logically completes the reasoning?

Either food scarcity or excessive hunting can threaten a population of animals. If the group faces food scarcity, individuals in the group will reach reproductive maturity later than otherwise. If the group faces excessive hunting, individuals that reach reproductive maturity earlier will come to predominate. Therefore, it should be possible to determine whether prehistoric mastodons became extinct because of food scarcity or human hunting, since there are fossilized mastodon remains from both before and after mastodon populations declined, and _____.

(A) there are more fossilized mastodon remains from the period before mastodon populations began to decline than from after that period

(B) the average age at which mastodons from a given period reached reproductive maturity can be established from their fossilized remains

(C) it can be accurately estimated from fossilized remains when mastodons became extinct

(D) it is not known when humans first began hunting mastodons

(E) climate changes may have gradually reduced the food available to mastodons

26. Editorial: The mayor plans to deactivate the city's fire alarm boxes, because most calls received from them are false alarms. The mayor claims that the alarm boxes are no longer necessary, since most people now have access to either public or private telephones. But the city's commercial district, where there is the greatest risk of fire, has few residents and few public telephones, so some alarm boxes are still necessary.

Which of the following, if true, most seriously weakens the editorial's argument?

(A) Maintaining the fire alarm boxes costs the city more than five million dollars annually.

(B) Commercial buildings have automatic fire alarm systems that are linked directly to the fire department.

(C) The fire department gets less information from an alarm box than it does from a telephone call.

(D) The city's fire department is located much closer to the residential areas than to the commercial district.

(E) On average, almost 25 percent of the public telephones in the city are out of order.

27. State spokesperson: Many businesspeople who have not been to our state believe that we have an inadequate road system. Those people are mistaken, as is obvious from the fact that in each of the past six years, our state has spent more money per mile on road improvements than any other state.

Which of the following, if true, most seriously undermines the reasoning in the spokesperson's argument?

(A) In the spokesperson's state, spending on road improvements has been increasing more slowly over the past six years than it has in several other states.

(B) Adequacy of a state's road system is generally less important to a businessperson considering doing business there than is the availability of qualified employees.

(C) Over the past six years, numerous businesses have left the spokesperson's state, but about as many businesses have moved into the state.

(D) In general, the number of miles of road in a state's road system depends on both the area and the population of the state.

(E) Only states with seriously inadequate road systems need to spend large amounts of money on road improvements.

28. Company Alpha buys free-travel coupons from people who are awarded the coupons by Bravo Airlines for flying frequently on Bravo airplanes. The coupons are sold to people who pay less for the coupons than they would pay by purchasing tickets from Bravo. This marketing of coupons results in lost revenue for Bravo.

To discourage the buying and selling of free-travel coupons, it would be best for Bravo Airlines to restrict the

(A) number of coupons that a person can be awarded in a particular year

(B) use of the coupons to those who were awarded the coupons and members of their immediate families

(C) days that the coupons can be used to Monday through Friday

(D) amount of time that the coupons can be used after they are issued

(E) number of routes on which travelers can use the coupons

29. Pro-Tect Insurance Company has recently been paying out more on car-theft claims than it expected. Cars with special antitheft devices or alarm systems are much less likely to be stolen than are other cars. Consequently Pro-Tect, as part of an effort to reduce its annual payouts, will offer a discount to holders of car-theft policies if their cars have antitheft devices or alarm systems.

Which of the following, if true, provides the strongest indication that the plan is likely to achieve its goal?

(A) The decrease in the risk of car theft conferred by having a car alarm is greatest when only a few cars have such alarms.

(B) The number of policyholders who have filed a claim in the past year is higher for Pro-Tect than for other insurance companies.

(C) In one or two years, the discount that Pro-Tect is offering will amount to more than the cost of buying certain highly effective antitheft devices.

(D) Currently, Pro-Tect cannot legally raise the premiums it charges for a given amount of insurance against car theft.

(E) The amount Pro-Tect has been paying out on car-theft claims has been greater for some models of car than for others.

30. Toughened hiring standards have not been the primary cause of the present staffing shortage in public schools. The shortage of teachers is primarily caused by the fact that in recent years teachers have not experienced any improvements in working conditions and their salaries have not kept pace with salaries in other professions.

Which of the following, if true, would most support the claims above?

(A) Many teachers already in the profession would not have been hired under the new hiring standards.

(B) Today more teachers are entering the profession with a higher educational level than in the past.

(C) Some teachers have cited higher standards for hiring as a reason for the current staffing shortage.

(D) Many teachers have cited low pay and lack of professional freedom as reasons for their leaving the profession.

(E) Many prospective teachers have cited the new hiring standards as a reason for not entering the profession.

31. A proposed ordinance requires the installation in new homes of sprinklers automatically triggered by the presence of a fire. However, a home builder argued that because more than 90 percent of residential fires are extinguished by a household member, residential sprinklers would only marginally decrease property damage caused by residential fires.

Which of the following, if true, would most seriously weaken the home builder's argument?

(A) Most individuals have no formal training in how to extinguish fires.

(B) Since new homes are only a tiny percentage of available housing in the city, the new ordinance would be extremely narrow in scope.

(C) The installation of smoke detectors in new residences costs significantly less than the installation of sprinklers.

(D) In the city where the ordinance was proposed, the average time required by the fire department to respond to a fire was less than the national average.

(E) The largest proportion of property damage that results from residential fires is caused by fires that start when no household member is present.

32. A recent spate of launching and operating mishaps with television satellites led to a corresponding surge in claims against companies underwriting satellite insurance. As a result, insurance premiums shot up, making satellites more expensive to launch and operate. This, in turn, had added to the pressure to squeeze more performance out of currently operating satellites.

Which of the following, if true, taken together with the information above, best supports the conclusion that the cost of television satellites will continue to increase?

(A) Since the risk to insurers of satellites is spread over relatively few units, insurance premiums are necessarily very high.

(B) When satellites reach orbit and then fail, the causes of failure are generally impossible to pinpoint with confidence.

(C) The greater the performance demands placed on satellites, the more frequently those satellites break down.

(D) Most satellites are produced in such small numbers that no economies of scale can be realized.

(E) Since many satellites are built by unwieldy international consortia, inefficiencies are inevitable.

33. Art restorers who have been studying the factors that cause Renaissance oil paintings to deteriorate physically when subject to climatic changes have found that the oil paint used in these paintings actually adjusts to these changes well. The restorers therefore hypothesize that it is a layer of material called gesso, which is under the paint, that causes the deterioration.

    Which of the following, if true, most strongly supports the restorers' hypothesis?

    (A) Renaissance oil paintings with a thin layer of gesso are less likely to show deterioration in response to climatic changes than those with a thicker layer.

    (B) Renaissance oil paintings are often painted on wooden panels, which swell when humidity increases and contract when it declines.

    (C) Oil paint expands and contracts readily in response to changes in temperature, but it absorbs little water and so is little affected by changes in humidity.

    (D) An especially hard and nonabsorbent type of gesso was the raw material for moldings on the frames of Renaissance oil paintings.

    (E) Gesso layers applied by Renaissance painters typically consisted of a coarse base layer onto which several increasingly fine-grained layers were applied.

34. If the airspace around centrally located airports were restricted to commercial airliners and only those private planes equipped with radar, most of the private-plane traffic would be forced to use outlying airfields. Such a reduction in the amount of private-plane traffic would reduce the risk of midair collision around the centrally located airports.

    The conclusion drawn in the first sentence depends on which of the following assumptions?

    (A) Outlying airfields would be as convenient as centrally located airports for most pilots of private planes.

    (B) Most outlying airfields are not equipped to handle commercial-airline traffic.

    (C) Most private planes that use centrally located airports are not equipped with radar.

    (D) Commercial airliners are at greater risk of becoming involved in midair collisions than are private planes.

    (E) A reduction in the risk of midair collision would eventually lead to increases in commercial airline traffic.

35. Two decades after the Emerald River Dam was built, none of the eight fish species native to the Emerald River was still reproducing adequately in the river below the dam. Since the dam reduced the annual range of water temperature in the river below the dam from 50 degrees to 6 degrees, scientists have hypothesized that sharply rising water temperatures must be involved in signaling the native species to begin the reproductive cycle.

   Which of the following statements, if true, would most strengthen the scientists' hypothesis?

   (A) The native fish species were still able to reproduce only in side streams of the river below the dam where the annual temperature range remains approximately 50 degrees.

   (B) Before the dam was built, the Emerald River annually overflowed its banks, creating backwaters that were critical breeding areas for the native species of fish.

   (C) The lowest recorded temperature of the Emerald River before the dam was built was 34 degrees, whereas the lowest recorded temperature of the river after the dam was built has been 43 degrees.

   (D) Nonnative species of fish, introduced into the Emerald River after the dam was built, have begun competing with the declining native fish species for food and space.

   (E) Five of the fish species native to the Emerald River are not native to any other river in North America.

36. Certain messenger molecules fight damage to the lungs from noxious air by telling the muscle cells encircling the lungs' airways to contract. This partially seals off the lungs. An asthma attack occurs when the messenger molecules are activated unnecessarily, in response to harmless things like pollen or household dust.

   Which of the following, if true, points to the most serious flaw of a plan to develop a medication that would prevent asthma attacks by blocking receipt of any messages sent by the messenger molecules referred to above?

   (A) Researchers do not yet know how the body produces the messenger molecules that trigger asthma attacks.

   (B) Researchers do not yet know what makes one person's messenger molecules more easily activated than another's.

   (C) Such a medication would not become available for several years, because of long lead times in both development and manufacture.

   (D) Such a medication would be unable to distinguish between messages triggered by pollen and household dust and messages triggered by noxious air.

   (E) Such a medication would be a preventative only and would be unable to alleviate an asthma attack once it had started.

37. Which of the following most logically completes the argument?

Although the pesticide TDX has been widely used by fruit growers since the early 1960s, a regulation in force since 1960 has prohibited sale of fruit on which any TDX residue can be detected. That regulation is about to be replaced by one that allows sale of fruit on which trace amounts of TDX residue are detected. In fact, however, the change will not allow more TDX on fruit than was allowed in the 1960s, because _____.

(A) pre-1970 techniques for detecting TDX residue could detect it only when it was present on fruit in more than the trace amounts allowed by the new regulations

(B) many more people today than in the 1960s habitually purchase and eat fruit without making an effort to clean residues off the fruit

(C) people today do not individually consume any more pieces of fruit, on average, than did the people in the 1960s

(D) at least a small fraction of the fruit sold each year since the early 1960s has had on it greater levels of TDX than the regulation allows

(E) the presence of TDX on fruit in greater than trace amounts has not been shown to cause any harm even to children who eat large amounts of fruit

38. Which of the following best completes the passage below?

The more worried investors are about losing their money, the more they will demand a high potential return on their investment; great risks must be offset by the chance of great rewards. This principle is the fundamental one in determining interest rates, and it is illustrated by the fact that _____.

(A) successful investors are distinguished by an ability to make very risky investments without worrying about their money

(B) lenders receive higher interest rates on unsecured loans than on loans backed by collateral

(C) in times of high inflation, the interest paid to depositors by banks can actually be below the rate of inflation

(D) at any one time, a commercial bank will have a single rate of interest that it will expect all of its individual borrowers to pay

(E) the potential return on investment in a new company is typically lower than the potential return on investment in a well-established company

39. A certain mayor has proposed a fee of five dollars per day on private vehicles entering the city, claiming that the fee will alleviate the city's traffic congestion. The mayor reasons that, since the fee will exceed the cost of round-trip bus fare from many nearby points, many people will switch from using their cars to using the bus.

Which of the following statements, if true, provides the best evidence that the mayor's reasoning is flawed?

(A) Projected increases in the price of gasoline will increase the cost of taking a private vehicle into the city.

(B) The cost of parking fees already makes it considerably more expensive for most people to take a private vehicle into the city than to take a bus.

(C) Most of the people currently riding the bus do not own private vehicles.

(D) Many commuters opposing the mayor's plan have indicated that they would rather endure traffic congestion than pay a five-dollar-per-day fee.

(E) During the average workday, private vehicles owned and operated by people living within the city account for 20 percent of the city's traffic congestion.

40. Journalist: Well-known businessman Arnold Bergeron has long been popular in the state, and he has often talked about running for governor, but he has never run. However, we have just learned that Bergeron has fulfilled the financial disclosure requirement for candidacy by submitting a detailed list of his current financial holdings to the election commission. So, it is very likely that Bergeron will be a candidate for governor this year.

The answer to which of the following questions would be most useful in evaluating the journalist's argument?

(A) Has anybody else who has fulfilled the financial disclosure requirement for the upcoming election reported greater financial holdings than Bergeron?

(B) Is submitting a list of holdings the only way to fulfill the election commission's financial disclosure requirements?

(C) Did the information recently obtained by the journalist come directly from the election commission?

(D) Have Bergeron's financial holdings increased in value in recent years?

(E) Had Bergeron also fulfilled the financial disclosure requirements for candidacy before any previous gubernatorial elections?

41. Dental researchers recently discovered that toothbrushes can become contaminated with bacteria that cause pneumonia and strep throat. They found that contamination usually occurs after toothbrushes have been used for four weeks. For that reason, people should replace their toothbrushes at least once a month.

    Which of the following, if true, would most weaken the conclusion above?

    (A) The dental researchers could not discover why toothbrush contamination usually occurred only after toothbrushes had been used for four weeks.

    (B) The dental researchers failed to investigate contamination of toothbrushes by viruses, yeasts, and other pathogenic microorganisms.

    (C) The dental researchers found that among people who used toothbrushes contaminated with bacteria that cause pneumonia and strep throat, the incidence of these diseases was no higher than among people who used uncontaminated toothbrushes.

    (D) The dental researchers found that people who rinsed their toothbrushes thoroughly in hot water after each use were as likely to have contaminated toothbrushes as were people who only rinsed their toothbrushes hurriedly in cold water after each use.

    (E) The dental researchers found that, after six weeks of use, greater length of use of a toothbrush did not correlate with a higher number of bacteria being present.

42. Leaders of a miners' union on strike against Coalco are contemplating additional measures to pressure the company to accept the union's contract proposal. The union leaders are considering as their principal new tactic a consumer boycott against Gasco gas stations, which are owned by Energy Incorporated, the same corporation that owns Coalco.

    The answer to which of the following questions is LEAST directly relevant to the union leaders' consideration of whether attempting a boycott of Gasco will lead to acceptance of their contract proposal?

    (A) Would revenue losses by Gasco seriously affect Energy Incorporated?

    (B) Can current Gasco customers easily obtain gasoline elsewhere?

    (C) Have other miners' unions won contracts similar to the one proposed by this union?

    (D) Have other unions that have employed a similar tactic achieved their goals with it?

    (E) Do other corporations that own coal companies also own gas stations?

43. Laws requiring the use of headlights during daylight hours can prevent automobile collisions. However, since daylight visibility is worse in countries farther from the equator, any such laws would obviously be more effective in preventing collisions in those countries. In fact, the only countries that actually have such laws are farther from the equator than is the continental United States.

    Which of the following conclusions could be most properly drawn from the information given above?

    (A) Drivers in the continental United States who used their headlights during the day would be just as likely to become involved in a collision as would drivers who did not use their headlights.

    (B) In many countries that are farther from the equator than is the continental United States, poor daylight visibility is the single most important factor in automobile collisions.

    (C) The proportion of automobile collisions that occur in the daytime is greater in the continental United States than in the countries that have daytime headlight laws.

    (D) Fewer automobile collisions probably occur each year in countries that have daytime headlight laws than occur within the continental United States.

    (E) Daytime headlight laws would probably do less to prevent automobile collisions in the continental United States than they do in the countries that have the laws.

44. Bank depositors in the United States are all financially protected against bank failure because the government insures all individuals' bank deposits. An economist argues that this insurance is partly responsible for the high rate of bank failures, since it removes from depositors any financial incentive to find out whether the bank that holds their money is secure against failure. If depositors were more selective, then banks would need to be secure in order to compete for depositors' money.

    The economist's argument makes which of the following assumptions?

    (A) Bank failures are caused when big borrowers default on loan repayments.

    (B) A significant proportion of depositors maintain accounts at several different banks.

    (C) The more a depositor has to deposit, the more careful he or she tends to be in selecting a bank.

    (D) The difference in the interest rates paid to depositors by different banks is not a significant factor in bank failures.

    (E) Potential depositors are able to determine which banks are secure against failure.

45. Often patients with ankle fractures that are stable, and thus do not require surgery, are given follow-up x-rays because their orthopedists are concerned about possibly having misjudged the stability of the fracture. When a number of follow-up x-rays were reviewed, however, all the fractures that had initially been judged stable were found to have healed correctly. Therefore, it is a waste of money to order follow-up x-rays of ankle fractures initially judged stable.

Which of the following, if true, most strengthens the argument?

(A) Doctors who are general practitioners rather than orthopedists are less likely than orthopedists to judge the stability of an ankle fracture correctly.

(B) Many ankle injuries for which an initial x-ray is ordered are revealed by the x-ray not to involve any fracture of the ankle.

(C) X-rays of patients of many different orthopedists working in several hospitals were reviewed.

(D) The healing of ankle fractures that have been surgically repaired is always checked by means of a follow-up x-ray.

(E) Orthopedists routinely order follow-up x-rays for fractures of bones other than ankle bones.

46. A study of marital relationships in which one partner's sleeping and waking cycles differ from those of the other partner reveals that such couples share fewer activities with each other and have more violent arguments than do couples in a relationship in which both partners follow the same sleeping and waking patterns. Thus, mismatched sleeping and waking cycles can seriously jeopardize a marriage.

Which of the following, if true, most seriously weakens the argument above?

(A) Married couples in which both spouses follow the same sleeping and waking patterns also occasionally have arguments that can jeopardize the couple's marriage.

(B) The sleeping and waking cycles of individuals tend to vary from season to season.

(C) The individuals who have sleeping and waking cycles that differ significantly from those of their spouses tend to argue little with colleagues at work.

(D) People in unhappy marriages have been found to express hostility by adopting a different sleeping and waking cycle from that of their spouses.

(E) According to a recent study, most people's sleeping and waking cycles can be controlled and modified easily.

47. In the past most airline companies minimized aircraft weight to minimize fuel costs. The safest airline seats were heavy, and airlines equipped their planes with few of these seats. This year the seat that has sold best to airlines has been the safest one—a clear indication that airlines are assigning a higher priority to safe seating than to minimizing fuel costs.

Which of the following, if true, most seriously weakens the argument above?

(A) Last year's best-selling airline seat was not the safest airline seat on the market.

(B) No airline company has announced that it would be making safe seating a higher priority this year.

(C) The price of fuel was higher this year than it had been in most of the years when the safest airline seats sold poorly.

(D) Because of increases in the cost of materials, all airline seats were more expensive to manufacture this year than in any previous year.

(E) Because of technological innovations, the safest airline seat on the market this year weighed less than most other airline seats on the market.

48. Editorial: An arrest made by a Midville police officer is provisional until the officer has taken the suspect to the police station and the watch commander has officially approved the arrest. Such approval is denied if the commander judges that the evidence on which the provisional arrest is based is insufficient. A government efficiency expert has observed that **almost all provisional arrests meet the standards for adequacy of evidence that the watch commanders enforce**. The expert has therefore recommended that, because **the officers' time spent obtaining approval is largely wasted**, the watch commander's approval no longer be required. This recommendation should be rejected as dangerous, however, since there is no assurance that the watch commanders' standards will continue to be observed once approval is no longer required.

In the editorial, the two portions in **boldface** play which of the following roles?

(A) The first is a claim, the accuracy of which is disputed by the editorial; the second is a conclusion drawn in order to support the main conclusion of the editorial.

(B) The first is an observation that the editorial disputes; the second is a conclusion that was drawn from that observation.

(C) The first is a finding that was used in support of a proposal that the editorial opposes; the second is a judgment that was based on that finding and in turn was used to support the proposal.

(D) The first is a finding introduced to support the main conclusion of the editorial; the second is that main conclusion.

(E) The first is a conclusion, the evidence for which the editorial evaluates; the second is part of the evidence cited in favor of that conclusion.

49. Division manager: I want to replace the Microton computers in my division with Vitech computers.

    General manager: Why?

    Division manager: It costs 28 percent less to train new staff on the Vitech.

    General manager: But that is not a good enough reason. We can simply hire only people who already know how to use the Microton computer.

    Which of the following, if true, most seriously undermines the general manager's objection to the replacement of Microton computers with Vitechs?

    (A) Currently all employees in the company are required to attend workshops on how to use Microton computers in new applications.

    (B) Once employees learn how to use a computer, they tend to change employers more readily than before.

    (C) Experienced users of Microton computers command much higher salaries than do prospective employees who have no experience in the use of computers.

    (D) The average productivity of employees in the general manager's company is below the average productivity of the employees of its competitors.

    (E) The high costs of replacement parts make Vitech computers more expensive to maintain than Microton computers.

50. Crops can be traded on the futures market before they are harvested. If a poor corn harvest is predicted, prices of corn futures rise; if a bountiful corn harvest is predicted, prices of corn futures fall. This morning meteorologists are predicting much-needed rain for the corn-growing region starting tomorrow. Therefore, since adequate moisture is essential for the current crop's survival, prices of corn futures will fall sharply today.

    Which of the following, if true, most weakens the argument above?

    (A) Corn that does not receive adequate moisture during its critical pollination stage will not produce a bountiful harvest.

    (B) Futures prices for corn have been fluctuating more dramatically this season than last season.

    (C) The rain that meteorologists predicted for tomorrow is expected to extend well beyond the corn-growing region.

    (D) Agriculture experts announced today that a disease that has devastated some of the corn crop will spread widely before the end of the growing season.

    (E) Most people who trade in corn futures rarely take physical possession of the corn they trade.

51. A company plans to develop a prototype weeding machine that uses cutting blades with optical sensors and microprocessors that distinguish weeds from crop plants by differences in shade of color. The inventor of the machine claims that it will reduce labor costs by virtually eliminating the need for manual weeding.

    Which of the following is a consideration in favor of the company's implementing its plan to develop the prototype?

    (A) There is a considerable degree of variation in shade of color between weeds of different species.

    (B) The shade of color of some plants tends to change appreciably over the course of their growing season.

    (C) When crops are weeded manually, overall size and leaf shape are taken into account in distinguishing crop plants from weeds.

    (D) Selection and genetic manipulation allow plants of virtually any species to be economically bred to have a distinctive shade of color without altering their other characteristics.

    (E) Farm laborers who are responsible for the manual weeding of crops carry out other agricultural duties at times in the growing season when extensive weeding is not necessary.

52. The interview is an essential part of a successful hiring program because, with it, job applicants who have personalities that are unsuited to the requirements of the job will be eliminated from consideration.

    The argument above logically depends on which of the following assumptions?

    (A) A hiring program will be successful if it includes interviews.

    (B) The interview is a more important part of a successful hiring program than is the development of a job description.

    (C) Interviewers can accurately identify applicants whose personalities are unsuited to the requirements of the job.

    (D) The only purpose of an interview is to evaluate whether job applicants' personalities are suited to the requirements of the job.

    (E) The fit of job applicants' personalities to the requirements of the job was once the most important factor in making hiring decisions.

53. Useful protein drugs, such as insulin, must still be administered by the cumbersome procedure of injection under the skin. If proteins are taken orally, they are digested and cannot reach their target cells. Certain nonprotein drugs, however, contain chemical bonds that are not broken down by the digestive system. They can, thus, be taken orally.

    The statements above most strongly support a claim that a research procedure that successfully accomplishes which of the following would be beneficial to users of protein drugs?

    (A) Coating insulin with compounds that are broken down by target cells, but whose chemical bonds are resistant to digestion

    (B) Converting into protein compounds, by procedures that work in the laboratory, the nonprotein drugs that resist digestion

    (C) Removing permanently from the digestive system any substances that digest proteins

    (D) Determining, in a systematic way, what enzymes and bacteria are present in the normal digestive system and whether they tend to be broken down within the body

    (E) Determining the amount of time each nonprotein drug takes to reach its target cells

54. Tanco, a leather manufacturer, uses large quantities of common salt to preserve animal hides. New environmental regulations have significantly increased the cost of disposing of salt water that results from this use, and, in consequence, Tanco is considering a plan to use potassium chloride in place of common salt. Research has shown that Tanco could reprocess the by-product of potassium chloride use to yield a crop fertilizer, leaving a relatively small volume of waste for disposal.

   In determining the impact on company profits of using potassium chloride in place of common salt, it would be important for Tanco to research all of the following EXCEPT:

   (A) What difference, if any, is there between the cost of the common salt needed to preserve a given quantity of animal hides and the cost of the potassium chloride needed to preserve the same quantity of hides?

   (B) To what extent is the equipment involved in preserving animal hides using common salt suitable for preserving animal hides using potassium chloride?

   (C) What environmental regulations, if any, constrain the disposal of the waste generated in reprocessing the by-product of potassium chloride?

   (D) How closely does leather that results when common salt is used to preserve hides resemble that which results when potassium chloride is used?

   (E) Are the chemical properties that make potassium chloride an effective means for preserving animal hides the same as those that make common salt an effective means for doing so?

55. There is a great deal of geographical variation in the frequency of many surgical procedures—up to tenfold variation per hundred thousand people between different areas in the numbers of hysterectomies, prostatectomies, and tonsillectomies.

   To support a conclusion that much of the variation is due to unnecessary surgical procedures, it would be most important to establish which of the following?

   (A) A local board of review at each hospital examines the records of every operation to determine whether the surgical procedure was necessary.

   (B) The variation is unrelated to factors (other than the surgical procedures themselves) that influence the incidence of diseases for which surgery might be considered.

   (C) There are several categories of surgical procedure (other than hysterectomies, prostatectomies, and tonsillectomies) that are often performed unnecessarily.

   (D) For certain surgical procedures, it is difficult to determine after the operation whether the procedures were necessary or whether alternative treatment would have succeeded.

   (E) With respect to how often they are performed unnecessarily, hysterectomies, prostatectomies, and tonsillectomies are representative of surgical procedures in general.

56. Gortland has long been narrowly self-sufficient in both grain and meat. However, as per capita income in Gortland has risen toward the world average, per capita consumption of meat has also risen toward the world average, and it takes several pounds of grain to produce one pound of meat. Therefore, since per capita income continues to rise, whereas domestic grain production will not increase, Gortland will soon have to import either grain or meat or both.

Which of the following is an assumption on which the argument depends?

(A) The total acreage devoted to grain production in Gortland will not decrease substantially.

(B) The population of Gortland has remained relatively constant during the country's years of growing prosperity.

(C) The per capita consumption of meat in Gortland is roughly the same across all income levels.

(D) In Gortland, neither meat nor grain is subject to government price controls.

(E) People in Gortland who increase their consumption of meat will not radically decrease their consumption of grain.

57. Meteorite explosions in the Earth's atmosphere as large as the one that destroyed forests in Siberia, with approximately the force of a twelve-megaton nuclear blast, occur about once a century.

The response of highly automated systems controlled by complex computer programs to unexpected circumstances is unpredictable.

Which of the following conclusions can most properly be drawn, if the statements above are true, about a highly automated nuclear-missile defense system controlled by a complex computer program?

(A) Within a century after its construction, the system would react inappropriately and might accidentally start a nuclear war.

(B) The system would be destroyed if an explosion of a large meteorite occurred in the Earth's atmosphere.

(C) It would be impossible for the system to distinguish the explosion of a large meteorite from the explosion of a nuclear weapon.

(D) Whether the system would respond inappropriately to the explosion of a large meteorite would depend on the location of the blast.

(E) It is not certain what the system's response to the explosion of a large meteorite would be, if its designers did not plan for such a contingency.

58. If there is an oil-supply disruption resulting in higher international oil prices, domestic oil prices in open-market countries such as the United States will rise as well, whether such countries import all or none of their oil.

If the statement above concerning oil-supply disruptions is true, which of the following policies in an open-market nation is most likely to reduce the long-term economic impact on that nation of sharp and unexpected increases in international oil prices?

(A) Maintaining the quantity of oil imported at constant yearly levels

(B) Increasing the number of oil tankers in its fleet

(C) Suspending diplomatic relations with major oil-producing nations

(D) Decreasing oil consumption through conservation

(E) Decreasing domestic production of oil

59. Boreal owls range over a much larger area than do other owls of similar size. The reason for this behavior is probably that the small mammals on which owls feed are especially scarce in the forests where boreal owls live, and the relative scarcity of prey requires the owls to range more extensively to find sufficient food.

Which of the following, if true, most helps to confirm the explanation above?

(A) Some boreal owls range over an area eight times larger than the area over which any other owl of similar size ranges.

(B) Boreal owls range over larger areas in regions where food of the sort eaten by small mammals is sparse than they do in regions where such food is abundant.

(C) After their young hatch, boreal owls must hunt more often than before in order to feed both themselves and their newly hatched young.

(D) Sometimes individual boreal owls hunt near a single location for many weeks at a time and do not range farther than a few hundred yards.

(E) The boreal owl requires less food, relative to its weight, than is required by members of other owl species.

60. The tobacco industry is still profitable and projections are that it will remain so. In the United States this year, the total amount of tobacco sold by tobacco farmers has increased, even though the number of adults who smoke has decreased.

Each of the following, if true, could explain the simultaneous increase in tobacco sales and decrease in the number of adults who smoke EXCEPT:

(A) During this year, the number of women who have begun to smoke is greater than the number of men who have quit smoking.

(B) The number of teenage children who have begun to smoke this year is greater than the number of adults who have quit smoking during the same period.

(C) During this year, the number of nonsmokers who have begun to use chewing tobacco or snuff is greater than the number of people who have quit smoking.

(D) The people who have continued to smoke consume more tobacco per person than they did in the past.

(E) More of the cigarettes made in the United States this year were exported to other countries than was the case last year.

61. A milepost on the towpath read "21" on the side facing the hiker as she approached it and "23" on its back. She reasoned that the next milepost forward on the path would indicate that she was halfway between one end of the path and the other. However, the milepost one mile further on read "20" facing her and "24" behind.

Which of the following, if true, would explain the discrepancy described above?

(A) The numbers on the next milepost had been reversed.

(B) The numbers on the mileposts indicate kilometers, not miles.

(C) The facing numbers indicate miles to the end of the path, not miles from the beginning.

(D) A milepost was missing between the two the hiker encountered.

(E) The mileposts had originally been put in place for the use of mountain bikers, not for hikers.

62. In response to viral infection, the immune systems of mice typically produce antibodies that destroy the virus by binding to proteins on its surface. Mice infected with a herpesvirus generally develop keratitis, a degenerative disease affecting part of the eye. Since proteins on the surface of cells in this part of the eye closely resemble those on the herpesvirus surface, scientists hypothesize that these cases of keratitis are caused by antibodies to herpesvirus.

   Which of the following, if true, gives the greatest additional support to the scientists' hypothesis?

   (A) Other types of virus have surface proteins that closely resemble proteins found in various organs of mice.

   (B) There are mice that are unable to form antibodies in response to herpes infections, and these mice contract herpes at roughly the same rate as other mice.

   (C) Mice that are infected with a herpesvirus but do not develop keratitis produce as many antibodies as infected mice that do develop keratitis.

   (D) There are mice that are unable to form antibodies in response to herpes infections, and these mice survive these infections without ever developing keratitis.

   (E) Mice that have never been infected with a herpesvirus can sometimes develop keratitis.

63. Traditionally, decision making by managers that is reasoned step-by-step has been considered preferable to intuitive decision making. However, a recent study found that top managers used intuition significantly more than did most middle- or lower-level managers. This confirms the alternative view that intuition is actually more effective than careful, methodical reasoning.

   The conclusion above is based on which of the following assumptions?

   (A) Methodical, step-by-step reasoning is inappropriate for making many real-life management decisions.

   (B) Top managers have the ability to use either intuitive reasoning or methodical, step-by-step reasoning in making decisions.

   (C) The decisions made by middle- and lower-level managers can be made as easily by using methodical reasoning as by using intuitive reasoning.

   (D) Top managers use intuitive reasoning in making the majority of their decisions.

   (E) Top managers are more effective at decision making than middle- or lower-level managers.

64. High levels of fertilizer and pesticides, needed when farmers try to produce high yields of the same crop year after year, pollute water supplies. Experts therefore urge farmers to diversify their crops and to rotate their plantings yearly.

To receive governmental price-support benefits for a crop, farmers must have produced that same crop for the past several years.

The statements above, if true, best support which of the following conclusions?

(A) The rules for governmental support of farm prices work against efforts to reduce water pollution.

(B) The only solution to the problem of water pollution from fertilizers and pesticides is to take farmland out of production.

(C) Farmers can continue to make a profit by rotating diverse crops, thus reducing costs for chemicals, but not by planting the same crop each year.

(D) New farming techniques will be developed to make it possible for farmers to reduce the application of fertilizers and pesticides.

(E) Governmental price supports for farm products are set at levels that are not high enough to allow farmers to get out of debt.

65. Which of the following most logically completes the argument?

Utrania was formerly a major petroleum exporter, but in recent decades economic stagnation and restrictive regulations inhibited investment in new oil fields. In consequence, Utranian oil exports dropped steadily as old fields became depleted. Utrania's currently improving economic situation, together with less-restrictive regulations, will undoubtedly result in the rapid development of new fields. However, it would be premature to conclude that the rapid development of new fields will result in higher oil exports, because

_____ .

(A) the price of oil is expected to remain relatively stable over the next several years

(B) the improvement in the economic situation in Utrania is expected to result in a dramatic increase in the proportion of Utranians who own automobiles

(C) most of the investment in new oil fields in Utrania is expected to come from foreign sources

(D) new technology is available to recover oil from old oil fields formerly regarded as depleted

(E) many of the new oil fields in Utrania are likely to be as productive as those that were developed during the period when Utrania was a major oil exporter

66. Hardin argued that grazing land held in common (that is, open to any user) would always be used less carefully than private grazing land. Each rancher would be tempted to overuse common land because the benefits would accrue to the individual, while the costs of reduced land quality that results from overuse would be spread among all users. But a study comparing 217 million acres of common grazing land with 433 million acres of private grazing land showed that the common land was in better condition.

The answer to which of the following questions would be most useful in evaluating the significance, in relation to Hardin's claim, of the study described above?

(A) Did any of the ranchers whose land was studied use both common and private land?

(B) Did the ranchers whose land was studied tend to prefer using common land over using private land for grazing?

(C) Was the private land that was studied of comparable quality to the common land before either was used for grazing?

(D) Were the users of the common land that was studied at least as prosperous as the users of the private land?

(E) Were there any owners of herds who used only common land, and no private land, for grazing?

67. A compelling optical illusion called the illusion of velocity and size makes objects appear to be moving more slowly the larger the objects are. Therefore, a motorist's estimate of the time available for crossing a highway with a small car approaching is bound to be lower than it would be with a large truck approaching.

The conclusion above would be more properly drawn if it were made clear that the

(A) truck's speed is assumed to be lower than the car's

(B) truck's speed is assumed to be the same as the car's

(C) truck's speed is assumed to be higher than the car's

(D) motorist's estimate of time available is assumed to be more accurate with cars approaching than with trucks approaching

(E) motorist's estimate of time available is assumed to be more accurate with trucks approaching than with cars approaching

68. Manufacturers sometimes discount the price of a product to retailers for a promotion period when the product is advertised to consumers. Such promotions often result in a dramatic increase in amount of product sold by the manufacturers to retailers. Nevertheless, the manufacturers could often make more profit by not holding the promotions.

Which of the following, if true, most strongly supports the claim above about the manufacturers' profit?

(A) The amount of discount generally offered by manufacturers to retailers is carefully calculated to represent the minimum needed to draw consumers' attention to the product.

(B) For many consumer products the period of advertising discounted prices to consumers is about a week, not sufficiently long for consumers to become used to the sale price.

(C) For products that are not newly introduced, the purpose of such promotions is to keep the products in the minds of consumers and to attract consumers who are currently using competing products.

(D) During such a promotion retailers tend to accumulate in their warehouses inventory bought at discount; they then sell much of it later at their regular price.

(E) If a manufacturer fails to offer such promotions but its competitor offers them, that competitor will tend to attract consumers away from the manufacturer's product.

69. When people evade income taxes by not declaring taxable income, a vicious cycle results. Tax evasion forces lawmakers to raise income tax rates, which causes the tax burden on nonevading taxpayers to become heavier. This, in turn, encourages even more taxpayers to evade income taxes by hiding taxable income.

The vicious cycle described above could not result unless which of the following were true?

(A) An increase in tax rates tends to function as an incentive for taxpayers to try to increase their pretax incomes.

(B) Some methods for detecting tax evaders, and thus recovering some tax revenue lost through evasion, bring in more than they cost, but their success rate varies from year to year.

(C) When lawmakers establish income tax rates in order to generate a certain level of revenue, they do not allow adequately for revenue that will be lost through evasion.

(D) No one who routinely hides some taxable income can be induced by a lowering of tax rates to stop hiding such income unless fines for evaders are raised at the same time.

(E) Taxpayers do not differ from each other with respect to the rate of taxation that will cause them to evade taxes.

70. Plantings of cotton bioengineered to produce its own insecticide against bollworms, a major cause of crop failure, sustained little bollworm damage until this year. This year the plantings are being seriously damaged by bollworms. Bollworms, however, are not necessarily developing resistance to the cotton's insecticide. Bollworms breed on corn, and last year more corn than usual was planted throughout cotton-growing regions. So it is likely that the cotton is simply being overwhelmed by corn-bred bollworms.

In evaluating the argument, which of the following would it be most useful to establish?

(A) Whether corn could be bioengineered to produce the insecticide

(B) Whether plantings of cotton that does not produce the insecticide are suffering unusually extensive damage from bollworms this year

(C) Whether other crops that have been bioengineered to produce their own insecticide successfully resist the pests against which the insecticide was to protect them

(D) Whether plantings of bioengineered cotton are frequently damaged by insect pests other than bollworms

(E) Whether there are insecticides that can be used against bollworms that have developed resistance to the insecticide produced by the bioengineered cotton

71. Because postage rates are rising, *Home Decorator* magazine plans to maximize its profits by reducing by one-half the number of issues it publishes each year. The quality of articles, the number of articles published per year, and the subscription price will not change. Market research shows that neither subscribers nor advertisers will be lost if the magazine's plan is instituted.

Which of the following, if true, provides the strongest evidence that the magazine's profits are likely to decline if the plan is instituted?

(A) With the new postage rates, a typical issue under the proposed plan would cost about one-third more to mail than a typical current issue would.

(B) The majority of the magazine's subscribers are less concerned about a possible reduction in the quantity of the magazine's articles than about a possible loss of the current high quality of its articles.

(C) Many of the magazine's long-time subscribers would continue their subscriptions even if the subscription price were increased.

(D) Most of the advertisers that purchase advertising space in the magazine will continue to spend the same amount on advertising per issue as they have in the past.

(E) Production costs for the magazine are expected to remain stable.

72. A discount retailer of basic household necessities employs thousands of people and pays most of them at the minimum wage rate. Yet following a federally mandated increase of the minimum wage rate that increased the retailer's operating costs considerably, the retailer's profits increased markedly.

Which of the following, if true, most helps to resolve the apparent paradox?

(A) Over half of the retailer's operating costs consist of payroll expenditures; yet only a small percentage of those expenditures go to pay management salaries.

(B) The retailer's customer base is made up primarily of people who earn, or who depend on the earnings of others who earn, the minimum wage.

(C) The retailer's operating costs, other than wages, increased substantially after the increase in the minimum wage rate went into effect.

(D) When the increase in the minimum wage rate went into effect, the retailer also raised the wage rate for employees who had been earning just above minimum wage.

(E) The majority of the retailer's employees work as cashiers, and most cashiers are paid the minimum wage.

73. The cotton farms of Country Q became so productive that the market could not absorb all that they produced. Consequently, cotton prices fell. The government tried to boost cotton prices by offering farmers who took 25 percent of their cotton acreage out of production direct support payments up to a specified maximum per farm.

The government's program, if successful, will not be a net burden on the budget. Which of the following, if true, is the best basis for an explanation of how this could be so?

(A) Depressed cotton prices meant operating losses for cotton farms, and the government lost revenue from taxes on farm profits.

(B) Cotton production in several countries other than Q declined slightly the year that the support-payment program went into effect in Q.

(C) The first year that the support-payment program was in effect, cotton acreage in Q was 5 percent below its level in the base year for the program.

(D) The specified maximum per farm meant that for very large cotton farms the support payments were less per acre for those acres that were withdrawn from production than they were for smaller farms.

(E) Farmers who wished to qualify for support payments could not use the cotton acreage that was withdrawn from production to grow any other crop.

74. A product that represents a clear technological advance over competing products can generally command a high price. Because **technological advances tend to be quickly surpassed** and companies want to make large profits while they still can, **many companies charge the maximum possible price for such a product**. But large profits on the new product will give competitors a strong incentive to quickly match the new product's capabilities. Consequently, the strategy to maximize overall profit from a new product is to charge less than the greatest possible price.

In the argument above, the two portions in **boldface** play which of the following roles?

(A) The first is a consideration raised to argue that a certain strategy is counterproductive; the second presents that strategy.

(B) The first is a consideration raised to support the strategy that the argument recommends; the second presents that strategy.

(C) The first is a consideration raised to help explain the popularity of a certain strategy; the second presents that strategy.

(D) The first is an assumption, rejected by the argument, that has been used to justify a course of action; the second presents that course of action.

(E) The first is a consideration that has been used to justify adopting a certain strategy; the second presents the intended outcome of that strategy.

75. United States hospitals have traditionally relied primarily on revenues from paying patients to offset losses from unreimbursed care. Almost all paying patients now rely on governmental or private health insurance to pay hospital bills. Recently, insurers have been strictly limiting what they pay hospitals for the care of insured patients to amounts at or below actual costs.

Which of the following conclusions is best supported by the information above?

(A) Although the advance of technology has made expensive medical procedures available to the wealthy, such procedures are out of the reach of low-income patients.

(B) If hospitals do not find ways of raising additional income for unreimbursed care, they must either deny some of that care or suffer losses if they give it.

(C) Some patients have incomes too high for eligibility for governmental health insurance but are unable to afford private insurance for hospital care.

(D) If the hospitals reduce their costs in providing care, insurance companies will maintain the current level of reimbursement, thereby providing more funds for unreimbursed care.

(E) Even though philanthropic donations have traditionally provided some support for the hospitals, such donations are at present declining.

76. Generally scientists enter their field with the goal of doing important new research and accept as their colleagues those with similar motivation. Therefore, when any scientist wins renown as an expounder of science to general audiences, most other scientists conclude that this popularizer should no longer be regarded as a true colleague.

The explanation offered above for the low esteem in which scientific popularizers are held by research scientists assumes that

(A) serious scientific research is not a solitary activity, but relies on active cooperation among a group of colleagues

(B) research scientists tend not to regard as colleagues those scientists whose renown they envy

(C) a scientist can become a famous popularizer without having completed any important research

(D) research scientists believe that those who are well known as popularizers of science are not motivated to do important new research

(E) no important new research can be accessible to or accurately assessed by those who are not themselves scientists

77. Country Y uses its scarce foreign-exchange reserves to buy scrap iron for recycling into steel. Although the steel thus produced earns more foreign exchange than it costs, that policy is foolish. Country Y's own territory has vast deposits of iron ore, which can be mined with minimal expenditure of foreign exchange.

Which of the following, if true, provides the strongest support for Country Y's policy of buying scrap iron abroad?

(A) The price of scrap iron on international markets rose significantly in 1987.

(B) Country Y's foreign-exchange reserves dropped significantly in 1987.

(C) There is virtually no difference in quality between steel produced from scrap iron and that produced from iron ore.

(D) Scrap iron is now used in the production of roughly half the steel used in the world today, and experts predict that scrap iron will be used even more extensively in the future.

(E) Furnaces that process scrap iron can be built and operated in Country Y with substantially less foreign exchange than can furnaces that process iron ore.

78. Which of the following most logically completes the passage?

The figures in portraits by the Spanish painter El Greco (1541–1614) are systematically elongated. In El Greco's time, the intentional distortion of human figures was unprecedented in European painting. Consequently, some critics have suggested that El Greco had an astigmatism, a type of visual impairment, that resulted in people appearing to him in the distorted way that is characteristic of his paintings. However, this suggestion cannot be the explanation, because _____.

(A) several twentieth-century artists have consciously adopted from El Greco's paintings the systematic elongation of the human form

(B) some people do have elongated bodies somewhat like those depicted in El Greco's portraits

(C) if El Greco had an astigmatism, then, relative to how people looked to him, the elongated figures in his paintings would have appeared to him to be distorted

(D) even if El Greco had an astigmatism, there would have been no correction for it available in the period in which he lived

(E) there were non-European artists, even in El Greco's time, who included in their works human figures that were intentionally distorted

79. Consumer health advocate: Your candy company adds caffeine to your chocolate candy bars so that each one delivers a specified amount of caffeine. Since caffeine is highly addictive, this indicates that you intend to keep your customers addicted.

Candy manufacturer: Our manufacturing process results in there being less caffeine in each chocolate candy bar than in the unprocessed cacao beans from which the chocolate is made.

The candy manufacturer's response is flawed as a refutation of the consumer health advocate's argument because it

(A) fails to address the issue of whether the level of caffeine in the candy bars sold by the manufacturer is enough to keep people addicted

(B) assumes without warrant that all unprocessed cacao beans contain a uniform amount of caffeine

(C) does not specify exactly how caffeine is lost in the manufacturing process

(D) treats the consumer health advocate's argument as though it were about each candy bar rather than about the manufacturer's candy in general

(E) merely contradicts the consumer health advocate's conclusion without giving any reason to believe that the advocate's reasoning is unsound

80. To evaluate a plan to save money on office-space expenditures by having its employees work at home, XYZ Company asked volunteers from its staff to try the arrangement for six months. During this period, the productivity of these employees was as high as or higher than before.

Which of the following, if true, would argue most strongly against deciding, on the basis of the trial results, to implement the company's plan?

(A) The employees who agreed to participate in the test of the plan were among the company's most self-motivated and independent workers.

(B) The savings that would accrue from reduced office-space expenditures alone would be sufficient to justify the arrangement for the company, apart from any productivity increases.

(C) Other companies that have achieved successful results from work-at-home plans have workforces that are substantially larger than that of XYZ.

(D) The volunteers who worked at home were able to communicate with other employees as necessary for performing the work.

(E) Minor changes in the way office work is organized at XYZ would yield increases in employee productivity similar to those achieved in the trial.

81. Political Advertisement:

Mayor Delmont's critics complain about the jobs that were lost in the city under Delmont's leadership. Yet the fact is that not only were more jobs created than were eliminated, but each year since Delmont took office the average pay for the new jobs created has been higher than that year's average pay for jobs citywide. So it stands to reason that throughout Delmont's tenure the average paycheck in this city has been getting steadily bigger.

Which of the following, if true, most seriously weakens the argument in the advertisement?

(A) The unemployment rate in the city is higher today than it was when Mayor Delmont took office.

(B) The average pay for jobs in the city was at a ten-year low when Mayor Delmont took office.

(C) Each year during Mayor Delmont's tenure, the average pay for jobs that were eliminated has been higher than the average pay for jobs citywide.

(D) Most of the jobs eliminated during Mayor Delmont's tenure were in declining industries.

(E) The average pay for jobs in the city is currently lower than it is for jobs in the suburbs surrounding the city.

82. Vitacorp, a manufacturer, wishes to make its information booth at an industry convention more productive in terms of boosting sales. The booth offers information introducing the company's new products and services. To achieve the desired result, Vitacorp's marketing department will attempt to attract more people to the booth. The marketing director's first measure was to instruct each salesperson to call his or her five best customers and personally invite them to visit the booth.

Which of the following, if true, most strongly supports the prediction that the marketing director's first measure will contribute to meeting the goal of boosting sales?

(A) Vitacorp's salespeople routinely inform each important customer about new products and services as soon as the decision to launch them has been made.

(B) Many of Vitacorp's competitors have made plans for making their own information booths more productive in increasing sales.

(C) An information booth that is well attended tends to attract visitors who would not otherwise have attended the booth.

(D) Most of Vitacorp's best customers also have business dealings with Vitacorp's competitors.

(E) Vitacorp has fewer new products and services available this year than it had in previous years.

83. An eyeglass manufacturer tried to boost sales for the summer quarter by offering its distributors a special discount if their orders for that quarter exceeded those for last year's summer quarter by at least 20 percent. Many distributors qualified for this discount. Even with much merchandise discounted, sales increased enough to produce a healthy gain in net profits. The manufacturer plans to repeat this success by offering the same sort of discount for the fall quarter.

    Which of the following, if true, most clearly points to a flaw in the manufacturer's plan to repeat the successful performance of the summer quarter?

    (A) In general, a distributor's orders for the summer quarter are no higher than those for the spring quarter.

    (B) Along with offering special discounts to qualifying distributors, the manufacturer increased newspaper and radio advertising in those distributors' sales areas.

    (C) The distributors most likely to qualify for the manufacturer's special discount are those whose orders were unusually low a year earlier.

    (D) The distributors who qualified for the manufacturer's special discount were free to decide how much of that discount to pass on to their own customers.

    (E) The distributors' ordering more goods in the summer quarter left them overstocked for the fall quarter.

4.5 Answer Key

1.	B	22.	A	43.	E	64.	A
2.	B	23.	C	44.	E	65.	B
3.	E	24.	C	45.	C	66.	C
4.	A	25.	B	46.	D	67.	B
5.	C	26.	B	47.	E	68.	D
6.	B	27.	E	48.	C	69.	C
7.	D	28.	B	49.	C	70.	B
8.	A	29.	C	50.	D	71.	D
9.	A	30.	D	51.	D	72.	B
10.	B	31.	E	52.	C	73.	A
11.	B	32.	C	53.	A	74.	C
12.	C	33.	A	54.	E	75.	B
13.	C	34.	C	55.	B	76.	D
14.	B	35.	A	56.	E	77.	E
15.	D	36.	D	57.	E	78.	C
16.	A	37.	A	58.	D	79.	A
17.	C	38.	B	59.	B	80.	A
18.	A	39.	B	60.	A	81.	C
19.	C	40.	E	61.	C	82.	C
20.	E	41.	C	62.	D	83.	E
21.	A	42.	E	63.	E		

4.6 Answer Explanations

The following discussion is intended to familiarize you with the most efficient and effective approaches to critical reasoning questions. The particular questions in this chapter are generally representative of the kinds of critical reasoning questions you will encounter on the GMAT. Remember that it is the problem solving strategy that is important, not the specific details of a particular question.

1.   Which of the following, if true, most logically completes the argument below?

Manufacturers are now required to make all cigarette lighters child-resistant by equipping them with safety levers. But this change is unlikely to result in a significant reduction in the number of fires caused by children playing with lighters, because children given the opportunity can figure out how to work the safety levers and _____.

(A)   the addition of the safety levers has made lighters more expensive than they were before the requirement was instituted

(B)   adults are more likely to leave child-resistant lighters than non-child-resistant lighters in places that are accessible to children

(C)   many of the fires started by young children are quickly detected and extinguished by their parents

(D)   unlike child-resistant lighters, lighters that are not child-resistant can be operated by children as young as two years old

(E)   approximately 5,000 fires per year have been attributed to children playing with lighters before the safety levers were required

Argument Construction

Situation   Manufacturers must equip all cigarette lighters with child-resistant safety levers, but children can figure out how to circumvent the safety levers and thereby often start fires.

Reasoning   *What point would most logically complete the argument?* What would make it likely that the number of fires caused by children playing with lighters would remain the same? In order for children to start fires using lighters equipped with safety levers, they must be given the opportunity to figure out how the safety levers work and then to use them. They must, that is, have access to the lighters.

A   If safety-lever-equipped lighters are more expensive than lighters that are not so equipped, fewer lighters might be sold. This would most likely afford children less access to lighters, thus giving them less opportunity to start fires with them.

B   **Correct.** This statement properly identifies a point that logically completes the argument: it explains why children are likely to have access to lighters equipped with safety levers.

C   The speed with which fires are extinguished does not have any bearing on the number of fires that are started.

D   This provides a reason to believe that the number of fires started by children will most likely decrease, rather than stay the same: fewer children will be able to operate the lighters, and thus fewer fires are likely to be started.

E   This information about how many fires were started by children before safety levers were required does not have any bearing on the question of how many fires are likely to be started by children now that the safety levers are required.

The correct answer is B.

2. A cost-effective solution to the problem of airport congestion is to provide high-speed ground transportation between major cities lying 200 to 500 miles apart. The successful implementation of this plan would cost far less than expanding existing airports and would also reduce the number of airplanes clogging both airports and airways.

Which of the following, if true, could proponents of the plan above most appropriately cite as a piece of evidence for the soundness of their plan?

(A) An effective high-speed ground-transportation system would require major repairs to many highways and mass-transit improvements.

(B) One-half of all departing flights in the nation's busiest airport head for a destination in a major city 225 miles away.

(C) The majority of travelers departing from rural airports are flying to destinations in cities over 600 miles away.

(D) Many new airports are being built in areas that are presently served by high-speed ground-transportation systems.

(E) A large proportion of air travelers are vacationers who are taking long-distance flights.

Evaluation of a Plan

Situation   Providing high-speed ground transportation between cities 200 to 500 miles apart is a more cost-effective and efficient way to reduce airport congestion than expanding existing airports.

Reasoning   *What evidence supports the plan?* The transportation plan will work only if people are likely to use the high-speed ground transportation. If half the flights leaving the busiest airport fly to destinations within range (200–500 miles) of ground transportation, then many people might choose high-speed ground transportation over air travel. Then, fewer flights would be needed and airport congestion would decrease.

A   Expensive repairs are an argument against, not for, ground transportation.

B   **Correct.** This statement properly identifies evidence that supports the plan.

C   Rural travelers are not included in this proposal, which addresses travel between major cities.

D   New airports covering the same routes are a threat to the plan.

E   The information that the airports are congested because of long-distance travelers, rather than those heading to destinations within 500 miles, argues against the proposal.

The correct answer is B.

3. People's television-viewing habits could be monitored by having television sets, when on, send out low-level electromagnetic waves that are reflected back to the sets. The reflected waves could then be analyzed to determine how many persons are within the viewing area of the sets. Critics fear adverse health effects of such a monitoring system, but a proponent responds, "The average dose of radiation is less than one chest x-ray. As they watch, viewers won't feel a thing."

Which of the following issues would it be most important to resolve in evaluating the dispute concerning the health effects of the proposed system?

(A) Whether the proposed method of monitoring viewership can distinguish between people and pets
(B) Whether radar speed monitors also operate on the principle of analyzing reflected waves of electromagnetic radiation
(C) Whether the proposed system has been tried out in various areas of the country or in a single area only
(D) What uses are foreseen for the viewership data
(E) Whether the average dose that the proponent describes is a short-term dose or a lifetime cumulative dose

Evaluation of a Plan

Situation People's television habits could be tracked using electromagnetic waves. Critics of this plan are concerned that the electromagnetic waves would prove detrimental to people's health, but proponents say that viewers will feel nothing, for the average dose of radiation is less than one chest x-ray.

Reasoning *What would it be most useful to know in order to resolve the dispute?* The dispute centers on the potential dangers of the radiation directed at those around the television. If the proponent's claim is accurate, then presumably people have nothing to worry about. But there is a significant ambiguity in the proponent's claim: what *"average"* is the proponent talking about? Over what length of time is this *"average"* dose of radiation administered by the television—a day, a year, a lifetime? Resolving this question would go a long way toward establishing whether the critics of the plan are justified in their concerns.

A This speaks to whether the data obtained from the radiation plan will be useful to those who wish to monitor people's television habits, not to whether the monitoring system will produce adverse health effects.

B This is tangentially related to the dispute, for it could be said that if reflected waves of radiomagnetic radiation were in fact dangerous, radar speed monitors would never have been approved for use. But since no information is given about whether the amount of radiation to which people are exposed by radar speed monitors is comparable to the amount to which they would be exposed by the proposed television system, the information given would not help to resolve the dispute.

C It would be useful to know whether the health effects of the proposed system have been investigated through trials of the system. But merely knowing whether the system has been tried out in various areas of the country or in only a single area would not in itself help in determining how likely the system is to produce adverse health effects.

D The uses to which the viewership data will be put are unrelated to the question of whether the proposed system will have adverse health effects.

E **Correct.** This statement properly identifies an issue that, if resolved, would help to determine the health effects of the proposed system.

The correct answer is E.

4. The price the government pays for standard weapons purchased from military contractors is determined by a pricing method called "historical costing." Historical costing allows contractors to protect their profits by adding a percentage increase, based on the current rate of inflation, to the previous year's contractual price.

Which of the following statements, if true, is the best basis for a criticism of historical costing as an economically sound pricing method for military contracts?

(A) The government might continue to pay for past inefficient use of funds.

(B) The rate of inflation has varied considerably over the past twenty years.

(C) The contractual price will be greatly affected by the cost of materials used for the products.

(D) Many taxpayers question the amount of money the government spends on military contracts.

(E) The pricing method based on historical costing might not encourage the development of innovative weapons.

Argument Evaluation

Situation   Military contractors add a percentage increase, based on the rate of inflation, to prices specified in previous contracts for standard weapons.

Reasoning   *What could be wrong in simply adding a percentage increase each year?* If the original contract price accommodated the contractors' inefficiencies, the government's overpayments for these inefficiencies are simply perpetuated, and money continues to be wasted. Additionally, historical costing assumes costs only go up, never down.

A   **Correct.** This statement properly identifies a serious problem with historical costing.

B   Because historical costing involves making a price adjustment based on the most recent inflation rate, the fact that inflation rates have varied is not a weakness of the method.

C   Presumably the cost of materials was factored into the previous year's contractual price, and the percentage increase allowed by historical costing will likely reflect any increases in the cost of materials.

D   Taxpayers may question the amount spent on military contracts even if the contracts are priced using an economically sound method.

E   The contract is for standard weapons only; innovative weapons are not discussed.

The correct answer is A.

5. Since the mayor's publicity campaign for Greenville's bus service began six months ago, morning automobile traffic into the midtown area of the city has decreased 7 percent. During the same period, there has been an equivalent rise in the number of persons riding buses into the midtown area. Obviously, the mayor's publicity campaign has convinced many people to leave their cars at home and ride the bus to work.

Which of the following, if true, casts the most serious doubt on the conclusion drawn above?

(A)   Fares for all bus routes in Greenville have risen an average of 5 percent during the past six months.

(B)   The mayor of Greenville rides the bus to City Hall in the city's midtown area.

(C)   Road reconstruction has greatly reduced the number of lanes available to commuters in major streets leading to the midtown area during the past six months.

(D)   The number of buses entering the midtown area of Greenville during the morning hours is exactly the same now as it was one year ago.

(E)   Surveys show that longtime bus riders are no more satisfied with the Greenville bus service than they were before the mayor's publicity campaign began.

Argument Evaluation

Situation   Traffic into midtown has decreased by 7 percent, and bus ridership has increased by an equivalent amount. The mayor's publicity campaign is responsible for this change.

Reasoning   *What casts doubt on this conclusion?* Another reasonable explanation of what caused the decrease in automobile traffic and the increase in bus ridership would make this conclusion suspect. Road construction impeding access to midtown over the same period of time is a reasonable alternative explanation. The road construction projects would likely have discouraged people from driving to midtown; many of these people have probably taken the bus.

A   An increase in fares might be a reasonable explanation for a decrease in ridership, but not for an increase.

B   The mayor's decision to ride the bus sets a good example for citizens, so this would tend to strengthen rather than weaken support for the conclusion.

C   **Correct.** This statement properly identifies an explanation that weakens support for the conclusion.

D   If more buses were running, then more seats would be available for people traveling into midtown. Ruling out this scenario helps strengthen, not weaken, support for the conclusion.

E   Passengers perceive bus service to be the same, so better service can be eliminated as a possible cause of the increased ridership.

The correct answer is C.

6. Patrick usually provides child care for six children. Parents leave their children at Patrick's house in the morning and pick them up after work. At the end of each workweek, the parents pay Patrick at an hourly rate for the child care provided that week. The weekly income Patrick receives is usually adequate but not always uniform, particularly in the winter, when children are likely to get sick and be unpredictably absent.

Which of the following plans, if put into effect, has the best prospect of making Patrick's weekly income both uniform and adequate?

(A) Pool resources with a neighbor who provides child care under similar arrangements, so that the two of them cooperate in caring for twice as many children as Patrick currently does.

(B) Replace payment by actual hours of child care provided with a fixed weekly fee based upon the number of hours of child care that Patrick would typically be expected to provide.

(C) Hire a full-time helper and invest in facilities for providing child care to sick children.

(D) Increase the hourly rate to a level that would provide adequate income even in a week when half of the children Patrick usually cares for are absent.

(E) Increase the number of hours made available for child care each day, so that parents can leave their children in Patrick's care for a longer period each day at the current hourly rate.

Evaluation of a Plan

Situation   At the end of the workweek Patrick is paid a certain amount for each hour of child care he has provided. Patrick usually receives adequate weekly income under this arrangement, but in the winter Patrick's income fluctuates, because children are unpredictably absent due to illness.

Reasoning   *Which plan would be most likely to meet the two goals of uniform weekly income and adequate weekly income?* Patrick must find a way to ensure that his weekly income is both adequate—that is, not reduced significantly from current levels—and uniform—that is, not subject to seasonal or other fluctuations. A successful plan would thus most likely be one that does not increase Patrick's costs. Further, the plan need not increase Patrick's weekly income; it must merely ensure that that income is more reliable. It should therefore also provide some way to mitigate the unexpected loss of income from children's absences.

A   This plan might raise Patrick's income slightly, because he and the neighbor might pay out less in costs if they pool their resources. But this plan would have no effect on the problem that unpredictable absences pose for Patrick's weekly income.

B   Correct. This statement properly identifies a plan that would most likely keep Patrick's income adequate (he would probably receive approximately the same amount of money per child as he does now) and uniform (he would receive the money regardless of whether a child was present or absent).

C   While this plan might somewhat mitigate the unpredictability in Patrick's income that results from sick children's absences—because parents would be less likely to keep sick children at home—it would increase Patrick's costs. Paying a helper and investing in different facilities would reduce Patrick's income and might thus result in that income being inadequate.

D   Under this plan, if we assume that parents did not balk at the increase in Patrick's hourly rate and find alternative child care, Patrick's income would most likely be adequate. But this plan would not help make Patrick's weekly income uniform. His income would continue to fluctuate when children are absent. Remember, there are two goals with regard to Patrick's income: adequacy and uniformity.

E   This plan might increase Patrick's income, in that he might be paid for more hours of child care each week. The goals here, however, are to make Patrick's weekly income both adequate and uniform, and this plan does not address the issue of uniformity.

The correct answer is B.

7. A researcher discovered that people who have low levels of immune-system activity tend to score much lower on tests of mental health than do people with normal or high immune-system activity. The researcher concluded from this experiment that the immune system protects against mental illness as well as against physical disease.

   The researcher's conclusion depends on which of the following assumptions?

   (A) High immune-system activity protects against mental illness better than normal immune-system activity does.

   (B) Mental illness is similar to physical disease in its effects on body systems.

   (C) People with high immune-system activity cannot develop mental illness.

   (D) Mental illness does not cause people's immune-system activity to decrease.

   (E) Psychological treatment of mental illness is not as effective as is medical treatment.

Argument Construction

Situation   Finding that people with low immune-system activity score lower on mental health tests than people with normal or high levels of immune-system activity, a researcher concludes that the immune system protects mental as well as physical health.

Reasoning   *What assumption does the researcher make?* The researcher asserts that immune-system activity can inhibit mental illness as it does physical illness. While it is possible that mental illness might itself depress immune-system activity, the researcher assumes that this is not the case. If mental illness caused a decline in immune-system activity, then lower levels of immune-system activity would be expected as a result, and the higher levels would merely indicate the absence of illness rather than any effect on illness.

A   The researcher does not distinguish between high and normal levels of immune-system activity, so this assumption is not needed.

B   The researcher's inference is not related to the effects of mental illness.

C   Immune-system activity could protect mental health without offering total prevention of mental illness; this assumption is not needed.

D   **Correct.** This statement properly identifies the researcher's underlying assumption that mental illness does not decrease immune system activity.

E   Since different treatments are not discussed, any assumption about them is unnecessary.

The correct answer is D.

8. Extinction is a process that can depend on a variety of ecological, geographical, and physiological variables. These variables affect different species of organisms in different ways, and should, therefore, yield a random pattern of extinctions. However, the fossil record shows that extinction occurs in a surprisingly definite pattern, with many species vanishing at the same time.

Which of the following, if true, forms the best basis for at least a partial explanation of the patterned extinctions revealed by the fossil record?

(A) Major episodes of extinction can result from widespread environmental disturbances that affect numerous different species.

(B) Certain extinction episodes selectively affect organisms with particular sets of characteristics unique to their species.

(C) Some species become extinct because of accumulated gradual changes in their local environments.

(D) In geologically recent times, for which there is no fossil record, human intervention has changed the pattern of extinctions.

(E) Species that are widely dispersed are the least likely to become extinct.

Argument Construction

Situation   The fossil record reveals that species become extinct in a surprisingly definite pattern, with multiple species vanishing simultaneously.

Reasoning   *Which point provides a basis for explaining the pattern?* The passage states that the process of extinction depends on so many variables—in the ecology and geography of the environment and in the physiology of the species—that the expected outcome would be a random pattern of extinctions. Yet a definite pattern is found instead. What could explain the disappearance of multiple species at the same time? If there were significant widespread changes in the environment, multiple species could be affected simultaneously, causing their extinction.

A   **Correct.** This statement properly identifies a basis for explaining the pattern of many species becoming extinct simultaneously.

B   This explanation of selective extinction does not explain how many species become extinct at the same time.

C   This explanation addresses only some species, not *many species*.

D   The passage is based on what the fossil record suggests; more recent times, having no fossil record, are outside the consideration of the passage.

E   Indicating which species are least likely to become extinct does not explain a pattern of simultaneous extinction of many species.

The correct answer is A.

4.6 Critical Reasoning Answer Explanations

9. In parts of South America, vitamin-A deficiency is a serious health problem, especially among children. In one region, agriculturists are attempting to improve nutrition by encouraging farmers to plant a new variety of sweet potato called SPK004 that is rich in beta-carotene, which the body converts into vitamin A. The plan has good chances of success, since sweet potato is a staple of the region's diet and agriculture, and the varieties currently grown contain little beta-carotene.

Which of the following, if true, most strongly supports the prediction that the plan will succeed?

(A) The growing conditions required by the varieties of sweet potato currently cultivated in the region are conditions in which SPK004 can flourish.

(B) The flesh of SPK004 differs from that of the currently cultivated sweet potatoes in color and texture, so traditional foods would look somewhat different when prepared from SPK004.

(C) There are no other varieties of sweet potato that are significantly richer in beta-carotene than SPK004 is.

(D) The varieties of sweet potato currently cultivated in the region contain some important nutrients that are lacking in SPK004.

(E) There are other vegetables currently grown in the region that contain more beta-carotene than the currently cultivated varieties of sweet potato do.

Evaluation of a Plan

Situation Agriculturists believe that if farmers in a particular South American region plant a new beta-carotene-rich variety of sweet potato, SPK004, the vitamin-A deficiency suffered in that region can be alleviated. Even though sweet potatoes are a staple of the region and the body can convert a sweet potato's beta-carotene into vitamin A, the varieties currently grown there contain little beta-carotene.

Reasoning *What would most support the success of the plan to improve nutrition by encouraging farmers to plant SPK004?* What, that is, would make farmers respond positively to encouragement to plant SPK004? Farmers in the region would probably be inclined to substitute SPK004 for the varieties of sweet potato they currently grow if they could be assured that SPK004 would grow as well as those other varieties do. This would in turn most likely lead to SPK004 being substituted for current varieties of sweet potato in staple dishes, and thus to an improvement in nutrition in the region.

A **Correct.** This statement properly identifies a factor that would support a prediction of the plan's success.

B If dishes made with SPK004 look different than traditional sweet potato dishes in the region do, people might be less likely to eat those dishes; in such a situation, the plan's success would be less likely, rather than more likely.

C It is SPK004's beta-carotene content relative to the beta-carotene content of the sweet potatoes currently grown in the region that is relevant here, so it does not matter if there are other varieties of sweet potato that are richer in beta-carotene than SPK004 is.

D This suggests that switching from currently grown sweet potatoes to SPK004 could negatively affect nutrition in the region; this undermines, rather than supports, the prediction that the plan to improve nutrition will succeed.

E These other vegetables, despite their beta-carotene content being higher than that of the currently cultivated varieties of sweet potato, are clearly not sufficient to prevent a vitamin-A deficiency in the region. This information does nothing to support the prediction that encouraging farmers to plant SPK004 will help to meet those beta-carotene needs.

The correct answer is A.

10. Which of the following best completes the passage below?

At a recent conference on environmental threats to the North Sea, most participating countries favored uniform controls on the quality of effluents, whether or not specific environmental damage could be attributed to a particular source of effluent. What must, of course, be shown, in order to avoid excessively restrictive controls, is that _____.

(A) any uniform controls that are adopted are likely to be implemented without delay

(B) any substance to be made subject to controls can actually cause environmental damage

(C) the countries favoring uniform controls are those generating the largest quantities of effluents

(D) all of any given pollutant that is to be controlled actually reaches the North Sea at present

(E) environmental damage already inflicted on the North Sea is reversible

Argument Construction

Situation   In the face of environmental threats to the North Sea, restrictions on effluents are considered.

Reasoning   *How can excessively restrictive controls be avoided?* To prevent pollutants from entering the North Sea, countries decide to control the quality of effluents. They need to control only those effluents that cause environmental damage. There is no need to restrict harmless effluents.

A   The immediacy of adopting controls does not prevent the controls from being overly restrictive.

B   **Correct.** This statement properly identifies the fact that controls on harmless effluents would be excessively restrictive and so should be avoided.

C   Avoiding unnecessary restrictions involves analyzing the quality of the effluents, not the composition of the countries favoring the restrictions.

D   It is not necessary to prove that all of a pollutant reaches the North Sea. It is necessary to prove only that some of it does.

E   The environmental damage that has already been caused is outside the scope of the restrictions. Finding that the damage is reversible will do nothing to prevent unnecessary restrictions.

The correct answer is B.

11. Shelby Industries manufactures and sells the same gauges as Jones Industries. Employee wages account for 40 percent of the cost of manufacturing gauges at both Shelby Industries and Jones Industries. Shelby Industries is seeking a competitive advantage over Jones Industries. Therefore, to promote this end, Shelby Industries should lower employee wages.

    Which of the following, if true, would most weaken the argument above?

    (A) Because they make a small number of precision instruments, gauge manufacturers cannot receive volume discounts on raw materials.

    (B) Lowering wages would reduce the quality of employee work, and this reduced quality would lead to lowered sales.

    (C) Jones Industries has taken away 20 percent of Shelby Industries' business over the last year.

    (D) Shelby Industries pays its employees, on average, 10 percent more than does Jones Industries.

    (E) Many people who work for manufacturing plants live in areas in which the manufacturing plant they work for is the only industry.

Evaluation of a Plan

Situation   Two companies manufacture the same product, and employee wages at both companies account for the same percentage of the manufacturing cost. One company seeks a competitive edge by lowering employee wages.

Reasoning   *What point weakens the argument in favor of lowering wages?* The company anticipates that the result of lowering wages will be a competitive edge, presumably gained through offering its products at lower prices as the result of having lower production costs. If evidence can be shown that lowering wages will not result in gaining a competitive advantage, the argument is weakened. If instead the result of lowered wages is lowered employee morale, and thus a lower quality of work and products, the declining quality could lead to a competitive disadvantage, lowering sales.

A   Because the company is unable to get lower costs on its raw materials, it is more likely to seek other ways of lowering its costs, such as reducing wages. This statement tends to support the argument.

B   **Correct.** This statement properly identifies a factor that weakens the argument.

C   The loss of business would only help explain why Shelby Industries is in need of a competitive edge; it indicates nothing about whether cutting employee wages is a good way to do so.

D   Its relatively higher employee wages show only why the company might reduce wages; the support for the conclusion about gaining a competitive advantage is strengthened rather than weakened.

E   We do not know whether this applies to either of the companies.

The correct answer is B.

12. Large national budget deficits do not cause large trade deficits. If they did, countries with the largest budget deficits would also have the largest trade deficits. In fact, when deficit figures are adjusted so that different countries are reliably comparable to each other, there is no such correlation.

If the statements above are all true, which of the following can properly be inferred on the basis of them?

(A) Countries with large national budget deficits tend to restrict foreign trade.

(B) Reliable comparisons of the deficit figures of one country with those of another are impossible.

(C) Reducing a country's national budget deficit will not necessarily result in a lowering of any trade deficit that country may have.

(D) When countries are ordered from largest to smallest in terms of population, the smallest countries generally have the smallest budget and trade deficits.

(E) Countries with the largest trade deficits never have similarly large national budget deficits.

Argument Construction

Situation   No correlation is found between large national budget deficits and large trade deficits.

Reasoning   *What inference can be drawn from this information?* Since the passage states that national budget deficits do not correlate with trade deficits, it is logical to anticipate an inference about the independent nature of the relationship between the two kinds of deficits. One possible inference is that reducing one deficit need not result in a reduction of the other.

A   This would receive some support if there were information indicating that there was a correlation between large budget deficits and small trade deficits, but no such information is given.

B   The passage states that reliable comparisons have been developed.

C   **Correct.** This statement properly identifies an inference that can be drawn from the given information.

D   The passage gives no indication as to whether either type of deficit correlates in any way with the population size of a country.

E   Though there is no general correlation between the two kinds of deficits, it cannot be inferred that there are no countries in which both kinds of deficits are large.

The correct answer is C.

13. Which of the following most logically completes the argument?

    The last members of a now-extinct species of a European wild deer called the giant deer lived in Ireland about 16,000 years ago. Prehistoric cave paintings in France depict this animal as having a large hump on its back. Fossils of this animal, however, do not show any hump. Nevertheless, there is no reason to conclude that the cave paintings are therefore inaccurate in this regard, since _____.

    (A) some prehistoric cave paintings in France also depict other animals as having a hump

    (B) fossils of the giant deer are much more common in Ireland than in France

    (C) animal humps are composed of fatty tissue, which does not fossilize

    (D) the cave paintings of the giant deer were painted well before 16,000 years ago

    (E) only one currently existing species of deer has any anatomical feature that even remotely resembles a hump

Argument Construction

Situation   Representations found in prehistoric cave paintings in France of the now-extinct giant deer species—the last members of which lived in Ireland about 16,000 years ago—depict the deer as having a hump on its back. Fossils of the deer, however, do not feature a hump.

Reasoning   *What point would most logically complete the argument? That is, what would show that the cave paintings are not inaccurate even though fossils of the giant deer show no hump?* How could it be the case that the paintings show a hump while the fossils do not? One way in which this could be so is if the humps are not part of the fossils—that is, if there is some reason why a hump would not be preserved with the rest of an animal's remains.

A   We do not know whether these other cave paintings accurately depict the animals as having humps, so this provides no reason to think that the depictions of giant deer are accurate.

B   Where giant deer fossils are found has no bearing on whether cave paintings of giant deer that show a hump on the animal's back are inaccurate. It could be that this suggests that the painters responsible for the representations would not be very familiar with the species; if this were so, it would give some reason to conclude that the representations *were* inaccurate.

C   **Correct.** This statement properly identifies a point that logically completes the argument. A hump would not be found as part of a giant deer's fossilized remains if the humps were fatty tissue that would not be fossilized.

D   That the cave paintings were painted well before 16,000 years ago shows that they were executed before the giant deer became extinct, but this does not help to explain the discrepancy between the paintings' depiction of a hump on the deer's back and the fossil record's lack of such a hump. It could be that even though the cave painters coexisted with the giant deer, they were not sufficiently familiar with them to depict them accurately.

E   That currently existing species of deer lack humps, or even that one species does have a feature resembling a hump, has little bearing on whether cave paintings in France accurately depict the giant deer as having a hump.

The correct answer is C.

14. The sustained massive use of pesticides in farming has two effects that are especially pernicious. First, it often kills off the pests' natural enemies in the area. Second, it often unintentionally gives rise to insecticide-resistant pests, since those insects that survive a particular insecticide will be the ones most resistant to it, and they are the ones left to breed.

From the passage above, it can be properly inferred that the effectiveness of the sustained massive use of pesticides can be extended by doing which of the following, assuming that each is a realistic possibility?

(A) Using only chemically stable insecticides

(B) Periodically switching the type of insecticide used

(C) Gradually increasing the quantities of pesticides used

(D) Leaving a few fields fallow every year

(E) Breeding higher-yielding varieties of crop plants

Evaluation of a Plan

Situation	Continued high-level pesticide use often kills off the targeted pests' natural enemies. In addition, the pests that survive the application of the pesticide may become resistant to it, and these pesticide-resistant pests will continue breeding.
Reasoning	*What can be done to prolong the effectiveness of pesticide use?* It can be inferred that the ongoing use of a particular pesticide will not continue to be effective against the future generations of pests with an inherent resistance to that pesticide. What would be effective against these future generations? If farmers periodically change the particular pesticide they use, then pests resistant to one kind of pesticide might be killed by another. This would continue, with pests being killed off in cycles as the pesticides are changed. It is also possible that this rotation might allow some of the pests' natural enemies to survive, at least until the next cycle.

A Not enough information about chemically stable insecticides is given to make a sound inference.

B Correct. This statement properly identifies an action that could extend the effectiveness of pesticide use.

C Gradually increasing the amount of the pesticides being used will not help the situation since the pests are already resistant to it.

D Continued use of pesticides is assumed as part of the argument. Since pesticides would be unnecessary for fallow fields, this suggestion is irrelevant.

E Breeding higher-yielding varieties of crops does nothing to extend the effectiveness of the use of pesticides.

The correct answer is B.

15. In an attempt to promote the widespread use of paper rather than plastic, and thus reduce nonbiodegradable waste, the council of a small town plans to ban the sale of disposable plastic goods for which substitutes made of paper exist. The council argues that since most paper is entirely biodegradable, paper goods are environmentally preferable.

    Which of the following, if true, indicates that the plan to ban the sale of disposable plastic goods is ill suited to the town council's environmental goals?

    (A) Although biodegradable plastic goods are now available, members of the town council believe biodegradable paper goods to be safer for the environment.

    (B) The paper factory at which most of the townspeople are employed plans to increase production of biodegradable paper goods.

    (C) After other towns enacted similar bans on the sale of plastic goods, the environmental benefits were not discernible for several years.

    (D) Since most townspeople prefer plastic goods to paper goods in many instances, they are likely to purchase them in neighboring towns where plastic goods are available for sale.

    (E) Products other than those derived from wood pulp are often used in the manufacture of paper goods that are entirely biodegradable.

Evaluation of a Plan

Situation   A town council considers banning the sale of disposable plastic goods for which there are paper substitutes because paper is biodegradable and therefore environmentally preferable.

Reasoning   *What problem might there be in the council's plan?* The plan is intended to reduce the amount of plastic used by the citizens of the town. The town council's plan is, however, only as effective as the support it has from the town's citizens. If the citizens prefer disposable plastic goods and if the goods are also readily available in neighboring towns, there is nothing to stop them from buying the plastic goods elsewhere if that is their preference.

A   The existence of biodegradable plastic does not make the town's plan to ban disposable plastic goods unsuitable to its environmental goal, which is to reduce nonbiodegradable waste.

B   That the local factory will increase production of biodegradable paper goods makes it more likely that a sufficient amount of such products will be available for townspeople who wish to switch from disposable plastic goods, so this does not indicate that the council's plan is ill suited for its goals.

C   Environmental benefits need not be immediate. Even though benefits were not perceived *for several years* after similar bans, the benefits did occur.

D   Correct. This statement properly identifies the problem with the council's plan.

E   The specific materials that go into making nonbiodegradable paper are not in question. This statement is irrelevant to the plan.

The correct answer is D.

16. Since the deregulation of airlines, delays at the nation's increasingly busy airports have increased by 25 percent. To combat this problem, more of the takeoff and landing slots at the busiest airports must be allocated to commercial airlines.

Which of the following, if true, casts the most doubt on the effectiveness of the solution proposed above?

(A) The major causes of delays at the nation's busiest airports are bad weather and overtaxed air traffic control equipment.

(B) Since airline deregulation began, the number of airplanes in operation has increased by 25 percent.

(C) Over 60 percent of the takeoff and landing slots at the nation's busiest airports are reserved for commercial airlines.

(D) After a small Midwestern airport doubled its allocation of takeoff and landing slots, the number of delays that were reported decreased by 50 percent.

(E) Since deregulation the average length of delay at the nation's busiest airports has doubled.

Evaluation of a Plan

Situation   To reduce delays, more takeoff and landing slots at the busiest airports should go to commercial airlines.

Reasoning   *What point casts the most doubt on the proposed solution?* Evaluating the effectiveness of this solution means examining the relation between the problem, an increase in delays, and the solution, an increase in available takeoff and landing slots. Could the delays be caused by other factors that the solution fails to address? If the major causes for delays are related to weather and air traffic control equipment, not to the number of slots for takeoff and landing, then the proposed solution of changing the allocations of the slots is bound to be less effective.

A   **Correct.** This statement properly identifies a weakness in the proposed solution.

B   The increasing number of planes shows why airports are busier. Since there is no information about whether these planes are private or commercial, this statement neither casts doubt on the solution nor supports it.

C   This statement suggests that there are additional slots that could be allocable to commercial airlines and thus offers at least some support for the proposed solution.

D   The example of one airport shows that the solution may work.

E   The increase in length of delay shows the scope of the problem; this fact does not cast doubt on the solution.

The correct answer is A.

17. A major health insurance company in Lagolia pays for special procedures prescribed by physicians only if the procedure is first approved as "medically necessary" by a company-appointed review panel. The rule is intended to save the company the money it might otherwise spend on medically unnecessary procedures. The company has recently announced that in order to reduce its costs, it will abandon this rule.

    Which of the following, if true, provides the strongest justification for the company's decision?

    (A) Patients often register dissatisfaction with physicians who prescribe nothing for their ailments.

    (B) Physicians often prescribe special procedures that are helpful but not altogether necessary for the health of the patient.

    (C) The review process is expensive and practically always results in approval of the prescribed procedure.

    (D) The company's review process does not interfere with the prerogative of physicians, in cases where more than one effective procedure is available, to select the one they personally prefer.

    (E) The number of members of the company-appointed review panel who review a given procedure depends on the cost of the procedure.

Evaluation of a Plan

Situation   In order to cut costs, a major health insurance company is abandoning a rule stating that it will pay for special procedures only if the procedure is approved as medically necessary by a review panel.

Reasoning   *What piece of information would most help to justify the company's decision?* For the company to save money, it would need to be in some way cutting its costs by abandoning the rule. Under what circumstances might the rule cost, rather than save, the company money? The panel itself might be expensive to convene, for example. Further, the cost savings achieved by the panel might be minimal if the panel did not deny significant numbers of procedures.

A   This suggests that patients might be pressuring their physicians to prescribe certain unnecessary procedures for their ailments, which in turn suggests that the panel is reviewing these procedures and denying them. But if so, then the panel is probably saving the insurance company money, so abandoning the panel's review would not reduce the company's costs.

B   This suggests that certain procedures that are being prescribed by physicians are not medically necessary, which in turn suggests that the panel reviewing these procedures may be denying them. If this is the case, then the panel is probably saving the insurance company a significant amount of money, so abandoning the panel's review may well increase rather than decrease the company's costs.

C   **Correct.** This statement properly identifies information that would help to justify the company's decision.

D   Even if the panel does not interfere with physicians' choices when more than one medically effective procedure is available, the panel may still be denying pay for many procedures that are not medically necessary. In such cases the panel may be saving the insurance company money, and abandoning the review process would not reduce the company's costs.

E   This suggests that the more expensive the procedure under review, the more expensive the panel itself is. Even so, if the panel denies payment for very expensive procedures, it may nonetheless save the company significantly more than the company has to pay to convene the panel, so abandoning the review process would not reduce the company's costs.

The correct answer is C.

18. Unlike the wholesale price of raw wool, the wholesale price of raw cotton has fallen considerably in the last year. Thus, although the retail price of cotton clothing at retail clothing stores has not yet fallen, it will inevitably fall.

Which of the following, if true, most seriously weakens the argument above?

(A) The cost of processing raw cotton for cloth has increased during the last year.

(B) The wholesale price of raw wool is typically higher than that of the same volume of raw cotton.

(C) The operating costs of the average retail clothing store have remained constant during the last year.

(D) Changes in retail prices always lag behind changes in wholesale prices.

(E) The cost of harvesting raw cotton has increased in the last year.

Argument Evaluation

Situation   Since the wholesale price of raw cotton has fallen significantly, the retail price of cotton clothing in stores will inevitably fall.

Reasoning   *What point weakens this argument?* Consider carefully the difference between the two products for which costs are being compared: cotton and cloth. This argument assumes that lower wholesale prices for a raw product must necessarily result in lower retail prices for a processed product. What other factors could have an impact on the final retail prices of cotton clothing? If any of the costs of transforming the raw product into a processed product increase, then the retail prices of cotton clothing will not necessarily fall.

A   **Correct.** This statement properly identifies a weakness in the argument.

B   The relative prices of raw wool and raw cotton are irrelevant to price changes in raw cotton and processed cotton.

C   One step between wholesale and retail prices is the operating cost of the retail store. If that operating cost has been constant rather than rising, it is possible that the retail prices could follow the lower wholesale prices. Thus the argument is not weakened.

D   The argument notes that the wholesale price has fallen *in the last year* and that though the retail price *has not yet fallen, it will inevitably fall.* The argument has already taken the lag into account and is not weakened by this statement.

E   Harvesting costs are part of the assumed increased price of raw cotton and do not affect current retail prices.

The correct answer is A.

4.6 Critical Reasoning Answer Explanations

19. A computer equipped with signature-recognition software, which restricts access to a computer to those people whose signatures are on file, identifies a person's signature by analyzing not only the form of the signature but also such characteristics as pen pressure and signing speed. Even the most adept forgers cannot duplicate all of the characteristics the program analyzes.

    Which of the following can be logically concluded from the passage above?

    (A) The time it takes to record and analyze a signature makes the software impractical for everyday use.
    (B) Computers equipped with the software will soon be installed in most banks.
    (C) Nobody can gain access to a computer equipped with the software solely by virtue of skill at forging signatures.
    (D) Signature-recognition software has taken many years to develop and perfect.
    (E) In many cases even authorized users are denied legitimate access to computers equipped with the software.

Argument Construction

Situation Forgers cannot duplicate all the characteristics that signature-recognition software analyzes, including the form of a signature, pen pressure, and signing speed. Computers equipped with this software restrict access to those whose signatures are on file.

Reasoning *What conclusion can be reached about computers equipped with this software?* The passage states that the software detects more characteristics in a signature than the most accomplished forger can possibly reproduce. Thus, skill at forging signatures is not enough to allow someone to gain access to a computer equipped with the software.

A   No information about the speed of the analysis is given, so no such conclusion can be drawn.
B   Although the software would likely be of benefit to banks, we cannot conclude that it will be installed in most banks because the passage doesn't rule out, e.g., that the software may be too costly or that there may be proprietary constraints.
C   **Correct.** This statement properly identifies a conclusion that can be drawn from the passage.
D   Although it seems reasonable to think that the software took a long time to develop, nothing in the passage justifies the claim that it took years.
E   Nothing in the passage rules out the possibility that the software functions so well that authorized users will never be denied legitimate access to computers equipped with the software.

The correct answer is C.

20. Start-up companies financed by venture capitalists have a much lower failure rate than companies financed by other means. Source of financing, therefore, must be a more important causative factor in the success of a start-up company than are such factors as the personal characteristics of the entrepreneur, the quality of strategic planning, or the management structure of the company.

Which of the following, if true, most seriously weakens the argument above?

(A) Venture capitalists tend to be more responsive than other sources of financing to changes in a start-up company's financial needs.

(B) The strategic planning of a start-up company is a less important factor in the long-term success of the company than are the personal characteristics of the entrepreneur.

(C) More than half of all new companies fail within five years.

(D) The management structures of start-up companies are generally less formal than the management structures of ongoing businesses.

(E) Venture capitalists base their decisions to fund start-up companies on such factors as the characteristics of the entrepreneur and quality of strategic planning of the company.

Argument Evaluation

Situation   When venture capitalists fund start-up companies, the failure rate is much lower than when the companies are funded by other means. The success of start-up companies, then, may be attributed more to their source of funding than to any other factor.

Reasoning   *What point weakens the argument?* The argument concludes that the source of funding is the single most important factor in determining the success of a start-up company. But what if the source of that funding, venture capitalists, considers other factors before making its investment? Venture capitalists may evaluate the characteristics of the entrepreneur as well as the company's strategic plan and management structure before deciding to fund the start-up company. If this is the case, then the most important causative factor in the success of the company cannot be said to be the source of the funding.

A   The responsiveness of venture capitalists is a point in favor of the argument, not against it.

B   This statement about the relative importance of strategic planning and the personality of the entrepreneur does not weaken the argument because it does not address the importance of these factors in relation to financial backing.

C   The argument concerns only successful start-up companies, so high failure rates are irrelevant.

D   The argument deals with the success rates of start-up companies based on their sources of funding. A comparison of start-up companies in general with ongoing businesses has no bearing on the argument.

E   **Correct.** This statement properly identifies evidence that weakens the argument.

The correct answer is E.

21. Aphasia, an impairment of the capacity to use language, often occurs when a stroke damages the left half of the brain. Many people with stroke-related aphasia recover at least some capacity to use language within a year. One proposed explanation for such recoveries is that the right side of the brain, which is not usually the major language center, develops its latent language capabilities to compensate for the damage to the left side.

Which of the following, if true, most strongly supports the explanation?

(A) In a study of local brain activity in people performing a language task, people with stroke-related aphasia showed higher activity levels in the right half of the brain than people who did not have aphasia.

(B) A blow to the head injuring the left half of the brain can result in impairment of the capacity to use language indistinguishable from that produced by a stroke.

(C) Among people with stroke-related aphasia, recovering lost capacity to use language does not lead to any impairment of those capacities normally controlled by the right half of the brain.

(D) A stroke that damages the left half of the brain often causes physical impairments of the right side of the body that lessen over time.

(E) Studies of numerous people with aphasia have indicated that the functions that govern language production and those that govern language comprehension are located in separate areas of the brain.

Argument Evaluation

Situation Strokes that damage the left half of the brain can cause aphasia, or an impaired capacity to use language. This impairment is often at least partially mitigated within a year of a stroke, which may be explained by the right side of the brain—which is usually not the major language center—developing latent language capabilities to compensate for damage to the left side of the brain.

Reasoning *What evidence supports the explanation that the right side of the brain develops language capabilities to compensate for damage to the left side?* The explanation would be supported by evidence that when performing a language task, people who have suffered damage to the left half of their brain have more activity in the right side of their brain than do people who have not suffered such damage.

A **Correct.** This statement properly identifies evidence supporting the explanation.

B That a blow to the head can result in aphasia just as a stroke can is irrelevant to the argument. The argument is concerned with finding an explanation for the recovery of the capacity to use language, not with what other than strokes causes the loss of this capacity.

C This provides no evidence about whether it is the right half of the brain's developing its latent language capabilities that alleviates aphasia. It could be these patients experience no impairment of capacities controlled by the right half of the brain because the right half of the brain is completely uninvolved in stroke patients' recovery of language-use capability.

D Any effect that a stroke may have on the body beyond aphasia is irrelevant to the argument.

E That language production and language comprehension are governed by different parts of the brain indicates nothing about whether the recovery of language capabilities by stroke-related aphasia patients is explained by the right side of the brain developing those capabilities.

The correct answer is A.

22. In the arid land along the Colorado River, use of the river's water supply is strictly controlled: farms along the river each have a limited allocation that they are allowed to use for irrigation. But the trees that grow in narrow strips along the river's banks also use its water. Clearly, therefore, if farmers were to remove those trees, more water would be available for crop irrigation.

Which of the following, if true, most seriously weakens the argument?

(A) The trees along the river's banks shelter it from the sun and wind, thereby greatly reducing the amount of water lost through evaporation.

(B) Owners of farms along the river will probably not undertake the expense of cutting down trees along the banks unless they are granted a greater allocation of water in return.

(C) Many of the tree species currently found along the river's banks are specifically adapted to growing in places where tree roots remain constantly wet.

(D) The strip of land where trees grow along the river's banks would not be suitable for growing crops if the trees were removed.

(E) The distribution of water allocations for irrigation is intended to prevent farms farther upstream from using water needed by farms farther downstream.

Argument Evaluation

Situation   Water is scarce and precious in the land along the Colorado River, and the amount allocated for irrigating farmland is strictly controlled. Farmers would have more water available for crop irrigation if the riverside trees, which also use the water, were removed.

Reasoning   *What point weakens the argument?* The reason given for removing the trees is to make more water available for crops. What if the trees actually conserve water rather than simply consume it? If the trees protect the river from sun and wind, their presence can greatly reduce the amount of river water lost to evaporation. Thus, the farmers would lose water, not gain it, by cutting down the trees.

A   **Correct.** This statement properly identifies a weakness in the argument.

B   The argument is about the greater availability of water *if* the trees are removed; it is not about what conditions are necessary for the farmers to agree to remove them. This statement does not weaken the argument.

C   This statement suggests that certain tree species along the river tend to remove more water from the river than is typical of trees, which strengthens rather than weakens the argument.

D   The argument concerns the greater availability of water, not the greater availability of arable land.

E   The reason for the water allocation does not have any bearing on whether removing the trees will provide more water for irrigation.

The correct answer is A.

23. Near Chicago a newly built hydroponic spinach "factory," a completely controlled environment for growing spinach, produces on 1 acre of floor space what it takes 100 acres of fields to produce. Expenses, especially for electricity, are high, however, and the spinach produced costs about four times as much as washed California field spinach, the spinach commonly sold throughout the United States.

   Which of the following, if true, best supports a projection that the spinach-growing facility near Chicago will be profitable?

   (A) Once the operators of the facility are experienced, they will be able to cut operating expenses by about 25 percent.

   (B) There is virtually no scope for any further reduction in the cost per pound for California field spinach.

   (C) Unlike washed field spinach, the hydroponically grown spinach is untainted by any pesticides or herbicides and thus will sell at exceptionally high prices to such customers as health food restaurants.

   (D) Since spinach is a crop that ships relatively well, the market for the hydroponically grown spinach is no more limited to the Chicago area than the market for California field spinach is to California.

   (E) A second hydroponic facility is being built in Canada, taking advantage of inexpensive electricity and high vegetable prices.

Argument Evaluation

Situation   Spinach grown hydroponically in a controlled environment at a facility near Chicago is four times as expensive as the popular washed field spinach grown in California.

Reasoning   *What point best supports the projection of profitability for the hydroponic spinach?* The hydroponic spinach cannot compete with the California spinach in price. What might be another way for the hydroponic spinach to compete successfully against the field washed spinach? That is, what feature of the hydroponic spinach is the California spinach unable to match? If the California spinach is tainted with pesticides or herbicides, health-conscious consumers could be willing to pay much higher prices for hydroponic spinach that is grown in pristine conditions without herbicides or pesticides.

A   The 25 percent reduction in operating costs cannot compensate for the much larger price difference, so this statement does not support the projection.

B   Knowing that the price of California spinach can go no lower does not help to explain how the hydroponic spinach can possibly compensate for the huge price difference between the two products.

C   **Correct.** This statement properly identifies a value that allows the high-priced hydroponic spinach to compete successfully with the less expensive California spinach.

D   The ease of shipping is an advantage shared equally by the two types of spinach.

E   The existence of a facility in Canada would make it less likely that the Chicago facility will be profitable, because the Canadian facility would be in competition with the Chicago facility.

The correct answer is C.

24. Automobile Dealer's Advertisement:

The Highway Traffic Safety Institute reports that the PZ 1000 has the fewest injuries per accident of any car in its class. This shows that the PZ 1000 is one of the safest cars available today.

Which of the following, if true, most seriously weakens the argument in the advertisement?

(A) The Highway Traffic Safety Institute report listed many cars in other classes that had more injuries per accident than did the PZ 1000.

(B) In recent years many more PZ 1000s have been sold than have any other kind of car in its class.

(C) Cars in the class to which the PZ 1000 belongs are more likely to be involved in accidents than are other types of cars.

(D) The difference between the number of injuries per accident for the PZ 1000 and that for other cars in its class is quite pronounced.

(E) The Highway Traffic Safety Institute issues reports only once a year.

Argument Evaluation

Situation   An advertisement claims that the PZ 1000 is one of the safest cars available; it bases this claim on the Highway Traffic Safety Institute's report that this model had the fewest injuries per accident of any car in its class.

Reasoning   *What point weakens the advertisement's claim?* Examine closely the difference between the report and the conclusion the advertisement draws from it. While the Highway Traffic Safety Institute compares the PZ 1000 to other cars *in its class,* the advertisement compares the PZ 1000 to *all cars available today.* What if the class of cars to which the PZ 1000 belongs is a more dangerous class of cars? In that case, while the PZ 1000 may the safest car of a dangerous class, it cannot be said to be one of the safest cars available.

A   The higher incidence of injuries per accident in other classes of cars supports rather than weakens the advertisement's argument.

B   The fact that the PZ 1000 is the best selling car in its class might be explained by the fact that it is the safest car in its class, but if this has any effect on the argument at all, it would be to strengthen rather than weaken it.

C   **Correct.** This statement properly identifies a weakness in the advertisement's argument.

D   This slightly strengthens, rather than weakens, the argument.

E   The frequency of the reports is irrelevant to the advertisement's claim.

The correct answer is C.

25. Which of the following most logically completes the reasoning?

    Either food scarcity or excessive hunting can threaten a population of animals. If the group faces food scarcity, individuals in the group will reach reproductive maturity later than otherwise. If the group faces excessive hunting, individuals that reach reproductive maturity earlier will come to predominate. Therefore, it should be possible to determine whether prehistoric mastodons became extinct because of food scarcity or human hunting, since there are fossilized mastodon remains from both before and after mastodon populations declined, and _____.

    (A) there are more fossilized mastodon remains from the period before mastodon populations began to decline than from after that period

    (B) the average age at which mastodons from a given period reached reproductive maturity can be established from their fossilized remains

    (C) it can be accurately estimated from fossilized remains when mastodons became extinct

    (D) it is not known when humans first began hunting mastodons

    (E) climate changes may have gradually reduced the food available to mastodons

Argument Construction

Situation   In a population of animals, food scarcity causes later reproductive maturity; if that population is hunted excessively, earlier-maturing animals will be more numerous in the population.

Reasoning   *What point would most logically complete the argument?* For the information given to be of use in determining what caused mastodons' extinction, mastodon fossils would need to indicate the age at which mastodons reached reproductive maturity, since that is what the argument suggests can indicate cause of extinction. If fossilized remains exist from before and after mastodon populations began to decline, and if the age at which those fossilized mastodons reached reproductive maturity can be determined, then we will have a good idea of what caused their extinction: if they reached reproductive maturity late, it was probably food scarcity, but if they matured earlier, it was most likely hunting.

A This fact only helps indicate that there was a decline; it tells us nothing about what caused the decline.

B **Correct.** This statement properly identifies a point that logically completes the argument: it explains how the fossilized mastodon remains could be used to help determine what caused mastodons' extinction.

C The point at which mastodons became extinct is not part of this argument, which is concerned with the cause of their extinction. The only way in which this could be relevant to the issue at hand is if mastodons became extinct before humans took up hunting mastodons—but the argument includes no information on whether this was so.

D Not knowing when humans began hunting mastodons would have no effect on the argument, which is concerned with how mastodon fossils, combined with knowledge about how food scarcity and hunting affect mastodon reproductive maturity, can help determine how mastodons became extinct.

E This fact only shows that food scarcity *may* have led to mastodon's decline. It tells us nothing about whether fossilized remains can help determine whether it was food scarcity or human hunting that actually led to the decline.

The correct answer is B.

26. Editorial: The mayor plans to deactivate the city's fire alarm boxes, because most calls received from them are false alarms. The mayor claims that the alarm boxes are no longer necessary, since most people now have access to either public or private telephones. But the city's commercial district, where there is the greatest risk of fire, has few residents and few public telephones, so some alarm boxes are still necessary.

Which of the following, if true, most seriously weakens the editorial's argument?

(A) Maintaining the fire alarm boxes costs the city more than five million dollars annually.

(B) Commercial buildings have automatic fire alarm systems that are linked directly to the fire department.

(C) The fire department gets less information from an alarm box than it does from a telephone call.

(D) The city's fire department is located much closer to the residential areas than to the commercial district.

(E) On average, almost 25 percent of the public telephones in the city are out of order.

Argument Evaluation

Situation   The mayor considers fire alarm boxes unnecessary since most people have access to public or private phones. An editorial argues that some boxes should be kept in the commercial district since the district has few residents and few public phones.

Reasoning   *What point weakens the editorial's argument?* Even if there are few private or public telephones available in the commercial district, it may be that alarm boxes are not necessary. What if alternative systems to notify the fire department are already in place in the commercial district? If the commercial buildings are already using automatic fire alarm systems that are directly linked to the fire department and provide automated notifications, then the alarm boxes are indeed unnecessary.

A   The editorial's argument is about the necessity of alarm boxes in the commercial district. This statement only tells us how costly those boxes are; it does not indicate that they are not necessary.

B   **Correct.** This statement properly identifies a weakness in the editorial's argument.

C   This statement is beside the point, since the argument indicates that it is not likely that the fire department will receive a telephone call regarding a fire in the commercial district.

D   The greater distance that the fire department must travel to the commercial district addresses the importance of response time; this point does not weaken the argument.

E   Alarm boxes would be more necessary, not less, if public telephones were frequently out of order, so this statement supports the editorial.

The correct answer is B.

27. State spokesperson: Many businesspeople who have not been to our state believe that we have an inadequate road system. Those people are mistaken, as is obvious from the fact that in each of the past six years, our state has spent more money per mile on road improvements than any other state.

    Which of the following, if true, most seriously undermines the reasoning in the spokesperson's argument?

    (A) In the spokesperson's state, spending on road improvements has been increasing more slowly over the past six years than it has in several other states.

    (B) Adequacy of a state's road system is generally less important to a businessperson considering doing business there than is the availability of qualified employees.

    (C) Over the past six years, numerous businesses have left the spokesperson's state, but about as many businesses have moved into the state.

    (D) In general, the number of miles of road in a state's road system depends on both the area and the population of the state.

    (E) Only states with seriously inadequate road systems need to spend large amounts of money on road improvements.

Argument Evaluation

Situation   A state spokesperson responds to the criticism that the road system is inadequate by observing that the state has spent more money per mile on road improvements than any other state has spent.

Reasoning   *What point undermines the spokesperson's reasoning?* When might heavy spending on road improvements *not* result in an adequate road system? If the state has needed to spend more money on road improvements than any other state, it suggests that its roads have needed more improving than those in any other state. The high level of state spending on road improvements provides evidence only that the road system was in dire need of improvement and not that it has yet achieved adequacy.

A   A slower rate of increases in spending does not contradict the spokesperson's statement that the state has spent more than others, and it offers no information on the adequacy of the road system.

B   The argument is about the adequacy of the road system, not about finding employees, so this point does not undermine the argument.

C   Since the road system is not mentioned as a reason that businesses left the state or came to it, this point is irrelevant to the argument.

D   This background information about area and population does not affect the argument about the adequacy of the road system.

E   **Correct.** This statement properly identifies a point that undermines the spokesperson's reasoning.

The correct answer is E.

28. Company Alpha buys free-travel coupons from people who are awarded the coupons by Bravo Airlines for flying frequently on Bravo airplanes. The coupons are sold to people who pay less for the coupons than they would pay by purchasing tickets from Bravo. This marketing of coupons results in lost revenue for Bravo.

To discourage the buying and selling of free-travel coupons, it would be best for Bravo Airlines to restrict the

(A) number of coupons that a person can be awarded in a particular year

(B) use of the coupons to those who were awarded the coupons and members of their immediate families

(C) days that the coupons can be used to Monday through Friday

(D) amount of time that the coupons can be used after they are issued

(E) number of routes on which travelers can use the coupons

Evaluation of a Plan

Situation   A company that buys and sells travel coupons reduces the revenue of an airline. The airline wants to discourage the trade in coupons.

Reasoning   *How can the airline discourage its customers from selling their coupons?* Limiting the use of the coupons to those who earned them and their immediate families rewards passengers for flying the airline and encourages them to continue to do so while at the same time making the sale of the coupons useless.

A   Limiting the number of coupons awarded a year does nothing to discourage their resale.

B   **Correct.** This statement properly identifies a limitation that makes the sale of coupons useless while maintaining the coupons' value as a reward.

C   Limiting the time of use to weekdays does not discourage resale and makes the coupons less valuable to the airline's customers.

D   Imposing a date by which the coupons must be used does not discourage resale and diminishes the coupons' value as a reward.

E   Restricting the routes available does not discourage resale but does reduce the coupons' value as a reward.

The correct answer is B.

29. Pro-Tect Insurance Company has recently been paying out more on car-theft claims than it expected. Cars with special antitheft devices or alarm systems are much less likely to be stolen than are other cars. Consequently Pro-Tect, as part of an effort to reduce its annual payouts, will offer a discount to holders of car-theft policies if their cars have antitheft devices or alarm systems.

Which of the following, if true, provides the strongest indication that the plan is likely to achieve its goal?

(A) The decrease in the risk of car theft conferred by having a car alarm is greatest when only a few cars have such alarms.

(B) The number of policyholders who have filed a claim in the past year is higher for Pro-Tect than for other insurance companies.

(C) In one or two years, the discount that Pro-Tect is offering will amount to more than the cost of buying certain highly effective antitheft devices.

(D) Currently, Pro-Tect cannot legally raise the premiums it charges for a given amount of insurance against car theft.

(E) The amount Pro-Tect has been paying out on car-theft claims has been greater for some models of car than for others.

Evaluation of a Plan

Situation   An insurance company is paying more money on car-theft claims than anticipated. To reduce these payments, the company is planning to offer discounts to customers whose cars have antitheft devices or alarm systems, because such cars are less likely to be stolen.

Reasoning   *What piece of information would indicate that the plan is likely to succeed?* Pro-Tect wishes to reduce its annual payouts, and one way for that to happen is for fewer cars insured by Pro-Tect to be stolen. To help accomplish this, Pro-Tect is offering discounts to policyholders whose cars are so equipped, because cars equipped with antitheft devices or alarm systems are less likely to be stolen than are cars without such devices. What would interfere with the success of Pro-Tect's plan? Car owners would probably resist investing in antitheft devices or alarm systems if the cost of such systems is higher than the discount they will receive. So if Pro-Tect sets the discount at a level that makes installing antitheft devices seem like a bargain to car owners, the plan will most likely succeed.

A   Pro-Tect's plan is designed to increase the number of cars equipped with car alarms. If having more cars equipped with car alarms reduces those alarms' effectivity in preventing thefts, then Pro-Tect's plan is unlikely to achieve its goal.

B   Pro-Tect's claims in relation to those of other insurance companies are not relevant to whether Pro-Tect's plan to reduce its own car-theft claims will achieve its goal.

C   **Correct.** This statement suggests that Pro-Tect's plan will provide an effective incentive for car owners to install antitheft devices; this statement therefore properly identifies information that indicates the plan is likely to achieve its goal.

D   Because Pro-Tect's plan does not involve raising the premiums it charges, restrictions on its ability to do so are irrelevant to whether that plan will achieve its goal.

E   Pro-Tect's plan does not distinguish among different models of car, so this statement indicates nothing about whether the proposed plan will succeed.

The correct answer is C.

30. Toughened hiring standards have not been the primary cause of the present staffing shortage in public schools. The shortage of teachers is primarily caused by the fact that in recent years teachers have not experienced any improvements in working conditions and their salaries have not kept pace with salaries in other professions.

    Which of the following, if true, would most support the claims above?

    (A) Many teachers already in the profession would not have been hired under the new hiring standards.

    (B) Today more teachers are entering the profession with a higher educational level than in the past.

    (C) Some teachers have cited higher standards for hiring as a reason for the current staffing shortage.

    (D) Many teachers have cited low pay and lack of professional freedom as reasons for their leaving the profession.

    (E) Many prospective teachers have cited the new hiring standards as a reason for not entering the profession.

Argument Evaluation

Situation   The teacher shortage can be explained by poor working conditions and poor salaries rather than by stricter hiring practices.

Reasoning   *Which statement supports this point of view?* This argument about the cause of the teacher shortage dismisses one possibility—obstacles created by higher standards in hiring—and endorses another—the failure to improve working conditions and salaries. A response that gives information suggesting that working conditions and salaries are in fact why there is a shortage of teachers would support the claims.

A   This statement modestly undermines the claims made—because it suggests that the toughened hiring standards might in fact be the primary cause of the shortage—rather than supports them.

B   This statement modestly undermines the claims, because it is odd that more teachers with a higher educational level are entering the profession if working conditions for teachers have not improved and salaries for teachers have not kept up with those of other professions.

C   This statement modestly undermines the first claim made in the passage.

D   Correct. This statement properly identifies evidence that pay and working conditions have caused teachers to leave the profession and thus supports the claim that these factors are causes of the teacher shortage.

E   This statement undermines the first claim made in the passage.

The correct answer is D.

31. A proposed ordinance requires the installation in new homes of sprinklers automatically triggered by the presence of a fire. However, a home builder argued that because more than 90 percent of residential fires are extinguished by a household member, residential sprinklers would only marginally decrease property damage caused by residential fires.

Which of the following, if true, would most seriously weaken the home builder's argument?

(A) Most individuals have no formal training in how to extinguish fires.
(B) Since new homes are only a tiny percentage of available housing in the city, the new ordinance would be extremely narrow in scope.
(C) The installation of smoke detectors in new residences costs significantly less than the installation of sprinklers.
(D) In the city where the ordinance was proposed, the average time required by the fire department to respond to a fire was less than the national average.
(E) The largest proportion of property damage that results from residential fires is caused by fires that start when no household member is present.

Argument Evaluation

Situation   A home builder claims that requiring automatic sprinklers in new homes will not significantly decrease property damage from residential fires because more than 90 percent of home fires are put out by a household member.

Reasoning   *Which point weakens the argument?* The home builder's argument implicitly recognizes that there are some residential fires that are not extinguished by household members. For instance, fires may occur when no one is home to put out the fire—a situation that automatic sprinklers would remedy. If such fires lead to considerable damage, then the home builder's conclusion is not justified.

A   If more than 90 percent of residential fires are successfully extinguished by the individuals who live there, then no formal training appears to be necessary.
B   The small percentage of new homes supports the builder's position; it does not weaken the argument.
C   The argument is about sprinkler systems, not smoke detection devices.
D   The argument is not about a comparison between fire departments and sprinkler systems.
E   **Correct.** This statement properly identifies a weakness in the home builder's argument by showing that the most damage occurs when no household member is present to put out the fire.

The correct answer is E.

32. A recent spate of launching and operating mishaps with television satellites led to a corresponding surge in claims against companies underwriting satellite insurance. As a result, insurance premiums shot up, making satellites more expensive to launch and operate. This, in turn, had added to the pressure to squeeze more performance out of currently operating satellites.

Which of the following, if true, taken together with the information above, best supports the conclusion that the cost of television satellites will continue to increase?

(A) Since the risk to insurers of satellites is spread over relatively few units, insurance premiums are necessarily very high.

(B) When satellites reach orbit and then fail, the causes of failure are generally impossible to pinpoint with confidence.

(C) The greater the performance demands placed on satellites, the more frequently those satellites break down.

(D) Most satellites are produced in such small numbers that no economies of scale can be realized.

(E) Since many satellites are built by unwieldy international consortia, inefficiencies are inevitable.

Argument Evaluation

Situation   A rise in the number of claims after a series of accidents has forced insurance companies to raise prices for coverage of television satellites. Consequently, new satellites are more expensive, and existing satellites must perform more. The cost of television satellites will continue to increase.

Reasoning   *Why might the cost continue to increase?* The passage says that the existing satellites are being asked to work harder than previously. If that increase in workload brings with it an increased number of breakdowns, growing satellite repair and replacement costs will add to the already increased cost of insurance premiums.

A   The high rate of premiums is a given; nothing in this statement reflects why the costs would increase further.

B   The difficulty of diagnosing the causes of satellite failure shows one reason the costs are high; it does not show why they are increasing.

C   **Correct.** This statement properly identifies a factor that explains why costs will continue to increase.

D   The small number of satellites shows one reason they are expensive; it does not explain why costs would continue to increase.

E   The inefficiencies may partially account for initial high costs; nothing in this statement explains an increase in costs.

The correct answer is C.

33. Art restorers who have been studying the factors that cause Renaissance oil paintings to deteriorate physically when subject to climatic changes have found that the oil paint used in these paintings actually adjusts to these changes well. The restorers therefore hypothesize that it is a layer of material called gesso, which is under the paint, that causes the deterioration.

Which of the following, if true, most strongly supports the restorers' hypothesis?

(A) Renaissance oil paintings with a thin layer of gesso are less likely to show deterioration in response to climatic changes than those with a thicker layer.

(B) Renaissance oil paintings are often painted on wooden panels, which swell when humidity increases and contract when it declines.

(C) Oil paint expands and contracts readily in response to changes in temperature, but it absorbs little water and so is little affected by changes in humidity.

(D) An especially hard and nonabsorbent type of gesso was the raw material for moldings on the frames of Renaissance oil paintings.

(E) Gesso layers applied by Renaissance painters typically consisted of a coarse base layer onto which several increasingly fine-grained layers were applied.

Argument Evaluation

Situation　　Renaissance paintings are subject to deterioration due to changes in climate, but their actual paint is not a factor in this deterioration. Instead, restorers hypothesize, it is gesso, the material under the paint, that causes problems for the paintings.

Reasoning　　*What would most strongly support the hypothesis that gesso is causing the deterioration?* An indication that gesso is affected by climatic changes would be most helpful in supporting the hypothesis. What could show that gesso is affected in this way? If the extent of a painting's deterioration is directly related to the amount of gesso used under that painting, then the gesso clearly plays some part in that deterioration.

A　**Correct.** This statement properly identifies a point supporting the hypothesis.

B　This suggests that another factor—the wood of the panels—has a role in the paintings' deterioration. Thus it weakens the hypothesis that gesso causes the deterioration.

C　This merely reinforces given information, that the paint itself is not responsible for the paintings' deterioration.

D　Because this gives no information about any connection between this especially hard and nonabsorbent type of gesso and the type of gesso used under the paint in Renaissance paintings, the properties and usage of the former type of gesso are irrelevant to the question of whether gesso is responsible for the paintings' deterioration.

E　Because we are told nothing about whether this technique of gesso application increases or decreases the likelihood that gesso will be affected by climatic change, it does not support the restorers' hypothesis.

The correct answer is A.

34. If the airspace around centrally located airports were restricted to commercial airliners and only those private planes equipped with radar, most of the private-plane traffic would be forced to use outlying airfields. Such a reduction in the amount of private-plane traffic would reduce the risk of midair collision around the centrally located airports.

The conclusion drawn in the first sentence depends on which of the following assumptions?

(A) Outlying airfields would be as convenient as centrally located airports for most pilots of private planes.

(B) Most outlying airfields are not equipped to handle commercial-airline traffic.

(C) Most private planes that use centrally located airports are not equipped with radar.

(D) Commercial airliners are at greater risk of becoming involved in midair collisions than are private planes.

(E) A reduction in the risk of midair collision would eventually lead to increases in commercial airline traffic.

Argument Construction

Situation   Only commercial airliners and private planes with radar would be allowed to use the airspace around centrally located airports; most private-plane traffic would use outlying airfields instead. The result would be fewer midair collisions around centrally located airports.

Reasoning   *What assumption underlies the conclusion that most private planes would be forced to use outlying airfields?* The argument assumes that if the proposed restriction were put in place, most private-plane traffic would be rerouted to outlying airports. Because the restriction allows private planes that have radar to land at the centrally located airports, it must be assumed that the planes involved in most private-plane traffic at those airports are not equipped with radar.

A   Convenience is not at issue.

B   The capacity of outlying airfields to handle commercial airlines is outside the scope of the question.

C   **Correct.** This statement properly identifies the assumption that most of these private planes lack radar and would no longer be allowed to land at the centrally located airports.

D   Private-plane traffic could be diverted to outlying airfields even if this statement were not true.

E   The future of commercial airline traffic is beyond the scope of the question.

The correct answer is C.

35. Two decades after the Emerald River Dam was built, none of the eight fish species native to the Emerald River was still reproducing adequately in the river below the dam. Since the dam reduced the annual range of water temperature in the river below the dam from 50 degrees to 6 degrees, scientists have hypothesized that sharply rising water temperatures must be involved in signaling the native species to begin the reproductive cycle.

Which of the following statements, if true, would most strengthen the scientists' hypothesis?

(A) The native fish species were still able to reproduce only in side streams of the river below the dam where the annual temperature range remains approximately 50 degrees.

(B) Before the dam was built, the Emerald River annually overflowed its banks, creating backwaters that were critical breeding areas for the native species of fish.

(C) The lowest recorded temperature of the Emerald River before the dam was built was 34 degrees, whereas the lowest recorded temperature of the river after the dam was built has been 43 degrees.

(D) Nonnative species of fish, introduced into the Emerald River after the dam was built, have begun competing with the declining native fish species for food and space.

(E) Five of the fish species native to the Emerald River are not native to any other river in North America.

Argument Evaluation

Situation   The construction of a dam has significantly reduced the range of water temperatures in the river below the dam. Scientists have implicated this change in the failure of native fish species to reproduce adequately.

Reasoning   *What evidence would strengthen the hypothesis?* To test the hypothesis, scientists need to study the same fish in the same river, but with only one variable changed: the temperature range of the water. If the same species of fish successfully reproduce in water that retains the same temperature range that the river had had before the dam was built, then the scientists have likely found the cause of the problem.

A   Correct. This statement properly identifies evidence that strengthens the scientists' hypothesis.

B   The overflow's creation of breeding areas offers an alternative hypothesis; it rivals rather than strengthens the hypothesis about temperature range.

C   These differences in lowest recorded temperatures are simply specific data-points related to the proposed cause; they do nothing to support the hypothesis.

D   The introduction of nonnative species competing for food and space is an additional variable, and thus offers an alternative hypothesis.

E   The rareness of certain species points to the severity of the problem, not to its cause.

The correct answer is A.

36. Certain messenger molecules fight damage to the lungs from noxious air by telling the muscle cells encircling the lungs' airways to contract. This partially seals off the lungs. An asthma attack occurs when the messenger molecules are activated unnecessarily, in response to harmless things like pollen or household dust.

    Which of the following, if true, points to the most serious flaw of a plan to develop a medication that would prevent asthma attacks by blocking receipt of any messages sent by the messenger molecules referred to above?

    (A) Researchers do not yet know how the body produces the messenger molecules that trigger asthma attacks.

    (B) Researchers do not yet know what makes one person's messenger molecules more easily activated than another's.

    (C) Such a medication would not become available for several years, because of long lead times in both development and manufacture.

    (D) Such a medication would be unable to distinguish between messages triggered by pollen and household dust and messages triggered by noxious air.

    (E) Such a medication would be a preventative only and would be unable to alleviate an asthma attack once it had started.

Evaluation of a Plan

Situation   The lungs are partially sealed off when certain molecules signal the muscle cells of the airway to contract. While this process prevents damage to the lungs from noxious air, harmless substances can trigger the process in asthma patients. A medication to block this process is considered.

Reasoning   *Why is the plan to develop the medication flawed?* Consider the action that the medication is intended to perform. How might that action be problematic? The process initiated by the messenger molecules has the useful and necessary purpose of protecting the lungs against harmful agents in the air. A medication to block the process completely would not distinguish between when the process is unnecessary, in the presence of harmless substances, and when that process is entirely necessary, in the presence of noxious air. Thus the medication would leave asthma patients unprotected from potential damage to their lungs.

A   Although it might be useful to know how the body produces these messenger molecules, it isn't necessary for the development of the proposed medication; many medications have been developed in cases where the relevant physiology is not very well understood.

B   The greater sensitivity of some people's messenger molecules is not the issue.

C   Pointing out long lead times does not explain a flaw in the medication itself.

D   **Correct.** This statement properly identifies the fact that the medication is flawed because it could do harm by preventing a necessary process.

E   The proposed medication makes no claim to alleviate asthma attacks once they have begun.

The correct answer is D.

37. Which of the following most logically completes the argument?

Although the pesticide TDX has been widely used by fruit growers since the early 1960s, a regulation in force since 1960 has prohibited sale of fruit on which any TDX residue can be detected. That regulation is about to be replaced by one that allows sale of fruit on which trace amounts of TDX residue are detected. In fact, however, the change will not allow more TDX on fruit than was allowed in the 1960s, because _____.

(A) pre-1970 techniques for detecting TDX residue could detect it only when it was present on fruit in more than the trace amounts allowed by the new regulations

(B) many more people today than in the 1960s habitually purchase and eat fruit without making an effort to clean residues off the fruit

(C) people today do not individually consume any more pieces of fruit, on average, than did the people in the 1960s

(D) at least a small fraction of the fruit sold each year since the early 1960s has had on it greater levels of TDX than the regulation allows

(E) the presence of TDX on fruit in greater than trace amounts has not been shown to cause any harm even to children who eat large amounts of fruit

Argument Construction

Situation   A regulation that will allow the sale of fruit with trace amounts of TDX residue, a pesticide in use since the 1960s, is soon to be adopted. This regulation will replace the regulation, in place since 1960, that prohibited the sale of fruit on which trace amounts of TDX residue has been detected.

Reasoning   *What point would most logically complete the argument?* How could it be the case that the new regulation will not allow more TDX on fruit now than was allowed in the 1960s? The most important thing to note is that the 1960 regulation prohibited sale of fruit on which TDX residue could be *detected*. Detection techniques in the 1960s might not have been particularly sensitive, which would have allowed some TDX to be present—though undetected—on fruit. If those techniques could not have detected the trace amounts of TDX that are now allowed, then it could be the case that TDX amounts allowed on fruit will not be different under the new regulation.

A   **Correct.** This statement properly identifies a point that logically completes the argument.

B   This statement indicates that *if* the new regulation does allow more TDX on fruit that is sold, then people may end up consuming more TDX. However, it indicates nothing as to whether the regulation will in fact allow more TDX on fruit that is sold.

C   People's consumption of fruit is irrelevant to the question of what the regulations governing the sale of that fruit allow.

D   The question is about allowances expressed in the two regulations. The information in this statement only suggests that the older regulation was not always fully enforced; but the same may end up being true of the new regulation.

E   This might show that the new regulation will not be harmful to consumers, even if the new regulation were to allow more TDX on fruit sold than was allowed in the 1960s. But that is irrelevant to the question at hand, which is whether the new regulation will allow more TDX on fruit than was allowed in the 1960s.

The correct answer is A.

38. Which of the following best completes the passage below?

The more worried investors are about losing their money, the more they will demand a high potential return on their investment; great risks must be offset by the chance of great rewards. This principle is the fundamental one in determining interest rates, and it is illustrated by the fact that _____.

(A) successful investors are distinguished by an ability to make very risky investments without worrying about their money

(B) lenders receive higher interest rates on unsecured loans than on loans backed by collateral

(C) in times of high inflation, the interest paid to depositors by banks can actually be below the rate of inflation

(D) at any one time, a commercial bank will have a single rate of interest that it will expect all of its individual borrowers to pay

(E) the potential return on investment in a new company is typically lower than the potential return on investment in a well-established company

Argument Construction

Situation   The principle of determining interest rates is related to the risk involved in making the investment of a loan. Potentially greater rewards will lead lenders (investors) to accept greater risks.

Reasoning   *Which example illustrates the principle that greater risks should produce greater rewards?* The example must be about the relationship of risk to benefit. Lenders take a greater risk when loans are unsecured (not backed by collateral) because there is a chance they could lose their money entirely. The principle indicates that the lenders—who by definition are investors—would demand the reward of higher interest rates.

A   The freedom from anxiety enjoyed by some investors is not relevant. While risky investments are mentioned, this statement does not mention their return.

B   **Correct.** This statement properly identifies an example that shows that riskier loans—those not backed by collateral—receive the benefit of higher interest rates.

C   This discussion of interest rates in times of inflation does not mention potential risk or potential benefit.

D   A single rate of interest for all investments, no matter the level of risk, contradicts the principle and so cannot possibly be an example of it.

E   New companies are generally riskier than established ones. A lower rate of return for such riskier new companies contradicts the principle.

The correct answer is B.

39. A certain mayor has proposed a fee of five dollars per day on private vehicles entering the city, claiming that the fee will alleviate the city's traffic congestion. The mayor reasons that, since the fee will exceed the cost of round-trip bus fare from many nearby points, many people will switch from using their cars to using the bus.

    Which of the following statements, if true, provides the best evidence that the mayor's reasoning is flawed?

    (A) Projected increases in the price of gasoline will increase the cost of taking a private vehicle into the city.

    (B) The cost of parking fees already makes it considerably more expensive for most people to take a private vehicle into the city than to take a bus.

    (C) Most of the people currently riding the bus do not own private vehicles.

    (D) Many commuters opposing the mayor's plan have indicated that they would rather endure traffic congestion than pay a five-dollar-per-day fee.

    (E) During the average workday, private vehicles owned and operated by people living within the city account for 20 percent of the city's traffic congestion.

Evaluation of a Plan

Situation   In order to alleviate traffic congestion, the mayor proposes a five-dollar daily fee on private vehicles entering the city. Since the fee is more than the round-trip bus fare, the mayor believes many drivers will switch to buses.

Reasoning   *What flaw exists in the mayor's reasoning?* The mayor apparently believes that saving money is the decisive issue for drivers. If, however, drivers are already paying considerably more in parking fees than they would in fares as bus commuters, then saving money is not the primary reason they are choosing to drive their cars rather than take the bus. This suggests that drivers may not change their behavior simply to save money.

A   This statement does not indicate whether the increased cost will dissuade people from taking private vehicles into the city, and therefore does not indicate whether the mayor's reasoning is flawed.

B   **Correct.** This statement properly identifies a flaw in the mayor's reasoning.

C   Current bus riders are not relevant to the mayor's plan, which anticipates only that people currently driving private vehicles into the city will become bus riders.

D   Many drivers may continue to commute in their private vehicles, but others might switch to buses. The mayor's plan does not anticipate a switch by all drivers.

E   The 20 percent figure shows that most congestion is caused by vehicles entering from outside the city; this does not point out a weakness in the mayor's plan.

The correct answer is B.

40. Journalist: Well-known businessman Arnold Bergeron has long been popular in the state, and he has often talked about running for governor, but he has never run. However, we have just learned that Bergeron has fulfilled the financial disclosure requirement for candidacy by submitting a detailed list of his current financial holdings to the election commission. So, it is very likely that Bergeron will be a candidate for governor this year.

The answer to which of the following questions would be most useful in evaluating the journalist's argument?

(A) Has anybody else who has fulfilled the financial disclosure requirement for the upcoming election reported greater financial holdings than Bergeron?

(B) Is submitting a list of holdings the only way to fulfill the election commission's financial disclosure requirements?

(C) Did the information recently obtained by the journalist come directly from the election commission?

(D) Have Bergeron's financial holdings increased in value in recent years?

(E) Had Bergeron also fulfilled the financial disclosure requirements for candidacy before any previous gubernatorial elections?

Argument Evaluation

Situation   The journalist states that Bergeron, a popular businessman, has often talked about running for governor but has never done so. Bergeron recently disclosed his finances to the election commission, and such disclosure is required of candidates. So, the journalist concludes, Bergeron will probably run for governor this year.

Reasoning   *What would it be most useful to know in evaluating the journalist's argument?* What might suggest, contrary to what the journalist concludes, that Bergeron is *not*, in fact, likely to run? The journalist is relying on Bergeron's financial disclosure as an indicator of his intentions. But what if Bergeron has filed this financial paperwork before and then not run? In that case, his disclosure would not be nearly as strong an indicator of his intentions, and the journalist's argument would be much weaker.

A   Bergeron's holdings relative to other potential candidates are not relevant to the journalist's argument regarding the likelihood of Bergeron's running for governor.

B   Whether Bergeron could have fulfilled the disclosure requirements in some other way is irrelevant to the journalist's argument, which is based on the fact that Bergeron *did* fulfill the disclosure requirements.

C   It would be somewhat useful to know whether the journalist's information is reliable, but there is no way to determine whether the journalist's actual source, if it was not the election commission, is more or less reliable than the election commission. So this is not the best answer.

D   Any changes in Bergeron's financial holdings are irrelevant to the journalist's argument, which is based on Bergeron's having fulfilled the financial disclosure requirements.

E   **Correct.** It would be useful in evaluating the journalist's argument to know the answer to this question.

The correct answer is E.

41. Dental researchers recently discovered that toothbrushes can become contaminated with bacteria that cause pneumonia and strep throat. They found that contamination usually occurs after toothbrushes have been used for four weeks. For that reason, people should replace their toothbrushes at least once a month.

Which of the following, if true, would most weaken the conclusion above?

(A) The dental researchers could not discover why toothbrush contamination usually occurred only after toothbrushes had been used for four weeks.

(B) The dental researchers failed to investigate contamination of toothbrushes by viruses, yeasts, and other pathogenic microorganisms.

(C) The dental researchers found that among people who used toothbrushes contaminated with bacteria that cause pneumonia and strep throat, the incidence of these diseases was no higher than among people who used uncontaminated toothbrushes.

(D) The dental researchers found that people who rinsed their toothbrushes thoroughly in hot water after each use were as likely to have contaminated toothbrushes as were people who only rinsed their toothbrushes hurriedly in cold water after each use.

(E) The dental researchers found that, after six weeks of use, greater length of use of a toothbrush did not correlate with a higher number of bacteria being present.

Argument Evaluation

Situation   Researchers have found that, after four weeks of use, toothbrushes may become contaminated with disease bacteria. Therefore, toothbrushes should be replaced once a month.

Reasoning   *What information weakens the conclusion?* The passage concludes that contaminated toothbrushes should be replaced monthly. Clearly, the assumption underlying this conclusion is that such replacement is necessary because the bacterial contamination is potentially harmful to the user of the toothbrush. Do people actually become ill because of their use of contaminated toothbrushes? If a comparison of disease rates for people using uncontaminated toothbrushes and for people using contaminated toothbrushes shows no difference between the groups, then the assumption about the potential harm is proven wrong and support for the conclusion is thereby weakened.

A   The recommendation to change every four weeks is not weakened simply because researchers cannot explain why it takes that long for contamination to occur.

B   The failure to investigate other possible contaminants of toothbrushes does not weaken the recommendation.

C   **Correct.** This statement properly identifies the information that weakens the conclusion: using contaminated toothbrushes is no more likely to result in disease than using uncontaminated ones, and thus changing toothbrushes every month is unnecessary.

D   Since even careful maintenance of toothbrushes does not reduce contamination, the recommendation is strengthened.

E   If the contamination still remains at six weeks, even if it is not worse, the recommendation based on the bacteria existing at four weeks is not weakened.

The correct answer is C.

42. Leaders of a miners' union on strike against Coalco are contemplating additional measures to pressure the company to accept the union's contract proposal. The union leaders are considering as their principal new tactic a consumer boycott against Gasco gas stations, which are owned by Energy Incorporated, the same corporation that owns Coalco.

The answer to which of the following questions is LEAST directly relevant to the union leaders' consideration of whether attempting a boycott of Gasco will lead to acceptance of their contract proposal?

(A) Would revenue losses by Gasco seriously affect Energy Incorporated?

(B) Can current Gasco customers easily obtain gasoline elsewhere?

(C) Have other miners' unions won contracts similar to the one proposed by this union?

(D) Have other unions that have employed a similar tactic achieved their goals with it?

(E) Do other corporations that own coal companies also own gas stations?

Evaluation of a Plan

Situation   In an effort to pressure Coalco to accept their contract proposal, union leaders consider organizing a consumer boycott of gas stations owned by Coalco's parent company.

Reasoning   *Which question is LEAST relevant to the boycott decision?* Union leaders have a number of questions to consider in deciding what to do. This problem requires finding the one question that is NOT relevant to deciding if a boycott would be an effective tactic. Examine each in turn. Whether other corporations that own coal companies also own gas stations is NOT directly relevant to whether a boycott of Gasco gas stations will coerce Coalco to accept a proposal.

A   Knowing how seriously the parent corporation would be hurt by revenue losses from the boycott is relevant.

B   If consumers cannot easily get gas elsewhere, the boycott is likely to fail, so this question is relevant.

C   If other miners' unions have won similar contracts, then the union's proposal is reasonable. This question is relevant.

D   If other unions have succeeded (or failed) with a similar plan, that information is relevant to the likely success (or failure) of this plan.

E   **Correct.** This question is the only one that does not clearly bear upon the plan; an answer to it is the one least directly relevant to the boycott decision.

The correct answer is E.

43. Laws requiring the use of headlights during daylight hours can prevent automobile collisions. However, since daylight visibility is worse in countries farther from the equator, any such laws would obviously be more effective in preventing collisions in those countries. In fact, the only countries that actually have such laws are farther from the equator than is the continental United States.

    Which of the following conclusions could be most properly drawn from the information given above?

    (A)   Drivers in the continental United States who used their headlights during the day would be just as likely to become involved in a collision as would drivers who did not use their headlights.
    (B)   In many countries that are farther from the equator than is the continental United States, poor daylight visibility is the single most important factor in automobile collisions.
    (C)   The proportion of automobile collisions that occur in the daytime is greater in the continental United States than in the countries that have daytime headlight laws.
    (D)   Fewer automobile collisions probably occur each year in countries that have daytime headlight laws than occur within the continental United States.
    (E)   Daytime headlight laws would probably do less to prevent automobile collisions in the continental United States than they do in the countries that have the laws.

    Argument Construction

    Situation   Laws requiring the use of headlights during the daytime are more effective at preventing car collisions in countries with lower daylight visibility, that is, in countries at greater distances from the equator. The only countries having these laws are those located farther from the equator than is the continental United States.

    Reasoning   *What conclusion can be drawn from this information?* Countries with daytime headlight laws are all farther from the equator than is the continental United States. The location is significant because daytime visibility is worse in those countries than it is in the continental United States. How effective at preventing collisions would such laws be in the continental United States with its greater proximity to the equator? It is reasonable to conclude that such laws would be less effective at preventing collisions there than they are in the countries farther from the equator.

    A   Although daytime headlight use may be less effective in countries with more daylight, it cannot be concluded that U.S. drivers using daytime headlights would gain no benefit from them and would be just as likely to have collisions as those who do not use them.

    B   The passage offers no evidence for the conclusion that poor visibility is the *greatest* cause for collisions in these countries.

    C   Many factors besides use of headlights during daylight hours influence accident rates, and these factors may vary widely from one country to another. We are given no information about these other factors or about their relative impact in various countries.

    D   Without specific data, no conclusion can be drawn about the relative number of accidents that occur.

    E   **Correct.** This statement properly identifies a conclusion to be drawn from the given information.

    The correct answer is E.

44. Bank depositors in the United States are all financially protected against bank failure because the government insures all individuals' bank deposits. An economist argues that this insurance is partly responsible for the high rate of bank failures, since it removes from depositors any financial incentive to find out whether the bank that holds their money is secure against failure. If depositors were more selective, then banks would need to be secure in order to compete for depositors' money.

The economist's argument makes which of the following assumptions?

(A) Bank failures are caused when big borrowers default on loan repayments.

(B) A significant proportion of depositors maintain accounts at several different banks.

(C) The more a depositor has to deposit, the more careful he or she tends to be in selecting a bank.

(D) The difference in the interest rates paid to depositors by different banks is not a significant factor in bank failures.

(E) Potential depositors are able to determine which banks are secure against failure.

Argument Construction

Situation An economist contends that the high rate of bank failures can partly be blamed on federal insurance of bank deposits. The insurance removes any financial incentive for depositors to seek those banks that are the most secure against failure. In the absence of more selective depositors, the banks need not be secure to compete for deposits.

Reasoning *What assumption underlies the economist's argument?* The economist argues that banks would have to be more secure in a competitive environment with more discriminating depositors. The economist encourages potential depositors to be *more selective* in choosing a bank and therefore must believe that many depositors have sufficiently sound ideas about what makes a bank secure against failure and can often apply those ideas in determining which banks are secure.

A Although this statement explains how a bank failure may occur, it is not a necessary assumption for the economist's argument about how depositors choose a bank.

B The argument never discusses multiple accounts, so this statement cannot be assumed.

C The economist argues that depositors are not careful in selecting banks; this statement contradicts that position, at least for some depositors, so it cannot be assumed.

D In arguing about choosing banks, the economist mentions nothing about the relation of interest rates to bank failures, so this statement is not assumed.

E **Correct.** This statement properly identifies the economist's underlying assumption that potential depositors are able to determine which banks are more secure.

The correct answer is E.

45. Often patients with ankle fractures that are stable, and thus do not require surgery, are given follow-up x-rays because their orthopedists are concerned about possibly having misjudged the stability of the fracture. When a number of follow-up x-rays were reviewed, however, all the fractures that had initially been judged stable were found to have healed correctly. Therefore, it is a waste of money to order follow-up x-rays of ankle fractures initially judged stable.

Which of the following, if true, most strengthens the argument?

(A) Doctors who are general practitioners rather than orthopedists are less likely than orthopedists to judge the stability of an ankle fracture correctly.

(B) Many ankle injuries for which an initial x-ray is ordered are revealed by the x-ray not to involve any fracture of the ankle.

(C) X-rays of patients of many different orthopedists working in several hospitals were reviewed.

(D) The healing of ankle fractures that have been surgically repaired is always checked by means of a follow-up x-ray.

(E) Orthopedists routinely order follow-up x-rays for fractures of bones other than ankle bones.

Argument Evaluation

Situation Often patients with ankle fractures that their orthopedists have judged not to require surgery are given follow-up x-rays to check whether the fracture healed correctly. An examination of a sample of those x-rays found that the ankle had, in each case, healed properly.

Reasoning *The question is which of the options, if true, would most strengthen the argument.* The argument is based on data concerning follow-up x-rays, each of which revealed no problem with the orthopedist's initial judgment that the ankle fracture was stable (and would heal without surgery). This invites the question whether the follow-up x-rays are really needed. The argument concludes that they are a waste of money. But was the x-ray data truly representative of orthopedists generally? After all, some orthopedists—perhaps more experienced, better-trained, or employed at a facility with better staff or facilities—may be much better than others at judging ankle fractures. If we add the information that the data for the conclusion comes from many orthopedists working at many different hospitals, we have greater assurance that the x-ray data is representative, and the argument will be made much stronger.

A Neither the study nor the conclusion that is drawn from it concerns general practitioners, so this point is irrelevant.

B Naturally many ankle injuries do not involve fractures—x-rays may sometimes be used to determine this—but the argument concerns only cases where there have been ankle fractures.

C **Correct.** This shows that the sample of x-ray data examined was probably sufficiently representative of cases of ankle fracture judged to be stable by orthopedists.

D The argument does not concern cases of ankle fracture that have been surgically repaired.

E The argument concerns only x-rays of ankles. From the information given here, we cannot infer that orthopedists are generally wasteful in routinely ordering follow-up x-rays.

The correct answer is C.

46. A study of marital relationships in which one partner's sleeping and waking cycles differ from those of the other partner reveals that such couples share fewer activities with each other and have more violent arguments than do couples in a relationship in which both partners follow the same sleeping and waking patterns. Thus, mismatched sleeping and waking cycles can seriously jeopardize a marriage.

    Which of the following, if true, most seriously weakens the argument above?

    (A) Married couples in which both spouses follow the same sleeping and waking patterns also occasionally have arguments that can jeopardize the couple's marriage.

    (B) The sleeping and waking cycles of individuals tend to vary from season to season.

    (C) The individuals who have sleeping and waking cycles that differ significantly from those of their spouses tend to argue little with colleagues at work.

    (D) People in unhappy marriages have been found to express hostility by adopting a different sleeping and waking cycle from that of their spouses.

    (E) According to a recent study, most people's sleeping and waking cycles can be controlled and modified easily.

Argument Evaluation

Situation   A study of married couples reveals that spouses with different sleeping and waking cycles tend to have fewer activities in common and more intense arguments than spouses with similar sleeping and waking cycles. Thus, different sleep-wake cycles may severely endanger a marriage.

Reasoning   *Which of the options, if added to the argument's premises, would most undermine the argument's support for the conclusion?* The given premises in the passage provide information that different sleep-wake cycles tend to be accompanied by marital discord. The conclusion then asserts that the different sleep-wake cycles cause the marital problems. But what if the different sleep-wake cycles result from preexisting marital problems? The argument would be weakened if data shows that unhappily married spouses express hostility by deliberately adopting cycles different from those of their spouses.

A   The argument does not say that mismatched cycles are the *only* cause of the arguments jeopardizing a marriage or that only couples with such a mismatch have such arguments.

B   This statement does not relate seasonal variability to mismatched cycles in marriage, and so it is irrelevant.

C   The argument is about the effect of mismatched cycles on a marriage, and the relationship with colleagues is not directly relevant to that issue.

D   **Correct.** This information provides a new perspective on the situation: instead of blaming the different sleep patterns for the hostility, it blames the hostility for those different patterns. This alternative explanation of the study's findings weakens the argument.

E   While suggesting that sleep-wake behaviors can be modified, this statement still does not provide evidence that weakens the argument.

The correct answer is D.

47. In the past most airline companies minimized aircraft weight to minimize fuel costs. The safest airline seats were heavy, and airlines equipped their planes with few of these seats. This year the seat that has sold best to airlines has been the safest one—a clear indication that airlines are assigning a higher priority to safe seating than to minimizing fuel costs.

    Which of the following, if true, most seriously weakens the argument above?

    (A) Last year's best-selling airline seat was not the safest airline seat on the market.
    (B) No airline company has announced that it would be making safe seating a higher priority this year.
    (C) The price of fuel was higher this year than it had been in most of the years when the safest airline seats sold poorly.
    (D) Because of increases in the cost of materials, all airline seats were more expensive to manufacture this year than in any previous year.
    (E) Because of technological innovations, the safest airline seat on the market this year weighed less than most other airline seats on the market.

Argument Evaluation

Situation   The safest airline seats were heavy, but since additional weight meant higher fuel costs, airlines had bought few of these seats. Because the best-selling seats this year are the safest ones, the airlines have clearly reset their priorities, choosing safe seating over minimizing fuel costs.

Reasoning   *What information weakens this argument?* Previously, the safest seats were heavy, so the airlines purchased lighter—and less safe—seats to minimize fuel costs. But if the safest seat this year is among the lightest, the airlines may simply be pursuing their previous priority of minimizing fuel costs by reducing weight.

A   The new information does little more than corroborate information already provided in the premises.

B   This weakens the argument only if the argument assumes that if such a change in priorities *had* occurred, it *would have* been announced. But this is not assumed.

C   This tends to strengthen rather than weaken the argument. In a time of high fuel costs, if an airline chooses the safest seat regardless of weight, that choice suggests that the airline is making safety a greater priority than fuel economy.

D   This information does not weaken the argument, since it suggests no reason for purchasing one type of seat as opposed to another.

E   **Correct.** This statement disconfirms a critically important assumption made by the argument—namely that the currently safest seat would also be heavier than the less safe seats.

The correct answer is E.

48. Editorial: An arrest made by a Midville police officer is provisional until the officer has taken the suspect to the police station and the watch commander has officially approved the arrest. Such approval is denied if the commander judges that the evidence on which the provisional arrest is based is insufficient. A government efficiency expert has observed that **almost all provisional arrests meet the standards for adequacy of evidence that the watch commanders enforce**. The expert has therefore recommended that, because **the officers' time spent obtaining approval is largely wasted**, the watch commander's approval no longer be required. This recommendation should be rejected as dangerous, however, since there is no assurance that the watch commanders' standards will continue to be observed once approval is no longer required.

In the editorial, the two portions in **boldface** play which of the following roles?

(A) The first is a claim, the accuracy of which is disputed by the editorial; the second is a conclusion drawn in order to support the main conclusion of the editorial.

(B) The first is an observation that the editorial disputes; the second is a conclusion that was drawn from that observation.

(C) The first is a finding that was used in support of a proposal that the editorial opposes; the second is a judgment that was based on that finding and in turn was used to support the proposal.

(D) The first is a finding introduced to support the main conclusion of the editorial; the second is that main conclusion.

(E) The first is a conclusion, the evidence for which the editorial evaluates; the second is part of the evidence cited in favor of that conclusion.

Argument Construction

Situation   Arrests by Midville police officers are provisional until approved by the watch commander. Because almost all such arrests meet that standard, a government efficiency expert recommends that this requirement be dropped. The editorial opposes this recommendation, on the grounds that without the approval requirement the evidence standard for arrest might not continue to be satisfied by the arresting officers.

Reasoning   *What roles do the two portions in boldface play in the editorial?* The first boldface portion asserts that provisional arrests almost always meet the standards for evidence that watch commanders enforce. The second boldface portion states that officers' time obtaining such approval is largely wasted. This is what the efficiency expert infers from the first boldface portion; and from this the efficiency expert, in turn, concludes that the watch commander's approval should no longer be required. But the editorial opposes this position.

A   The editorial does not dispute that almost all provisional arrests meet the standard for adequacy of evidence. The editorial implicitly rejects the second boldface portion, and rejects the conclusion that the efficiency expert draws from it.

B   The editorial does not dispute that the first boldface portion is true.

C   **Correct.** This is the only choice that accords with the analysis of the reasoning given above.

D   The role of the first boldface portion is not to support the editorial's main conclusion but to provide support for the efficiency expert's conclusion. The role of the second boldface portion is not as the main conclusion of the editorial but as support for the efficiency expert's conclusion.

E   The first boldface portion is not inferred or concluded from some other statement in the passage, nor is it challenged by the editorial. The direction of the efficiency expert's inference is from the first portion, not to it.

The correct answer is C.

49. Division manager: I want to replace the Microton computers in my division with Vitech computers.

    General manager: Why?

    Division manager: It costs 28 percent less to train new staff on the Vitech.

    General manager: But that is not a good enough reason. We can simply hire only people who already know how to use the Microton computer.

    Which of the following, if true, most seriously undermines the general manager's objection to the replacement of Microton computers with Vitechs?

    (A) Currently all employees in the company are required to attend workshops on how to use Microton computers in new applications.
    (B) Once employees learn how to use a computer, they tend to change employers more readily than before.
    (C) Experienced users of Microton computers command much higher salaries than do prospective employees who have no experience in the use of computers.
    (D) The average productivity of employees in the general manager's company is below the average productivity of the employees of its competitors.
    (E) The high costs of replacement parts make Vitech computers more expensive to maintain than Microton computers.

Argument Evaluation

Situation A division manager wants to replace Microton computers with Vitech computers in order to reduce training costs for new staff. The general manager objects to this reasoning, arguing that the company can hire only those people who already know how to use the Microton computers.

Reasoning *What point weakens the general manager's argument?* The division manager's preference for Vitech equipment is based on reduced training costs for newly hired staff. The general manager rejects this cost-reduction rationale and counters by suggesting a way to avoid these costs altogether. Both managers thus accept costs as the basis for making the decision between the two brands. Any evidence that overall costs would be higher when using the Microton computers weakens the general manager's argument. If the costs associated with employing experienced Microton users are greater, then hiring exclusively from this pool and paying their *much higher* salaries may result in higher overall costs for the company than the costs for training new staff on the Vitechs.

A This information about Microton suggests that even staff who have Microton skills when hired would still have to be trained with all other staff in new applications. Does this undermine the general manager's reply? No—because the information given about training costs by the division manager refers only to the costs of training newly hired staff.

B The information that computer-skilled staff move easily to a new job suggests that it might be possible to do what the general manager recommends. Obviously that does not undermine the general manager's recommendation.

C **Correct.** This statement properly identifies evidence that undermines the general manager's argument.

D Productivity at the company and at its competitors is not at issue.

E Only staff-related costs, not the cost of maintaining the computers, are being discussed in the argument.

The correct answer is C.

50. Crops can be traded on the futures market before they are harvested. If a poor corn harvest is predicted, prices of corn futures rise; if a bountiful corn harvest is predicted, prices of corn futures fall. This morning meteorologists are predicting much-needed rain for the corn-growing region starting tomorrow. Therefore, since adequate moisture is essential for the current crop's survival, prices of corn futures will fall sharply today.

Which of the following, if true, most weakens the argument above?

(A) Corn that does not receive adequate moisture during its critical pollination stage will not produce a bountiful harvest.

(B) Futures prices for corn have been fluctuating more dramatically this season than last season.

(C) The rain that meteorologists predicted for tomorrow is expected to extend well beyond the corn-growing region.

(D) Agriculture experts announced today that a disease that has devastated some of the corn crop will spread widely before the end of the growing season.

(E) Most people who trade in corn futures rarely take physical possession of the corn they trade.

Argument Evaluation

Situation   Crop futures rise when a harvest is expected to be small and drop when a harvest is expected to be large. Today's weather forecast for the corn-growing area predicts much-needed rain, so corn futures will fall today.

Reasoning   *What information weakens the argument that corn futures will fall?* The prediction that corn futures will drop sharply today is made solely on the basis of the forecast of rain, which would lead futures buyers to expect an abundant crop. However, if it becomes known that some harmful circumstance such as a devastating disease will severely affect the corn crop before the end of the growing season, this knowledge may lead buyers of futures to expect a smaller harvest, causing prices of futures to rise rather than fall.

A   This statement tells at what exact point in the growing cycle rain is critical to a good harvest, but it gives no information about this year's harvest.

B   This comparison of past price fluctuations does not affect what will happen to today's corn futures on account of the predicted rain. The argument is not weakened.

C   The only rain that matters is the rain that affects the corn-growing region, not areas beyond it; this statement is irrelevant to the prediction.

D   **Correct.** This statement properly identifies information that weakens the argument.

E   Physical possession of the corn is irrelevant to the price of corn futures.

The correct answer is D.

51. A company plans to develop a prototype weeding machine that uses cutting blades with optical sensors and microprocessors that distinguish weeds from crop plants by differences in shade of color. The inventor of the machine claims that it will reduce labor costs by virtually eliminating the need for manual weeding.

    Which of the following is a consideration in favor of the company's implementing its plan to develop the prototype?

    (A) There is a considerable degree of variation in shade of color between weeds of different species.

    (B) The shade of color of some plants tends to change appreciably over the course of their growing season.

    (C) When crops are weeded manually, overall size and leaf shape are taken into account in distinguishing crop plants from weeds.

    (D) Selection and genetic manipulation allow plants of virtually any species to be economically bred to have a distinctive shade of color without altering their other characteristics.

    (E) Farm laborers who are responsible for the manual weeding of crops carry out other agricultural duties at times in the growing season when extensive weeding is not necessary.

Evaluation of a Plan

Situation   A company plans to develop an automated weeding machine that would distinguish weeds from crop plants by differences in shade of color. It is supposed to reduce labor costs by eliminating the need for manual weeding.

Reasoning   *Which option describes a consideration that would favor the company's plan?* The passage supports the plan by claiming that the machine would reduce labor costs by virtually eliminating weeding by hand. The correct option will be one that adds to this support. Labor costs will be reduced only if the machine works well. The machine relies on shade of color to distinguish between weeds and crop plants. If crop plants can be bred to have distinctive color without sacrificing other qualities, it would be more likely that the machine could be used effectively.

A   Greater variation among weed plants would make it more difficult for the machine to distinguish between weeds and crop plants, and this would make it less likely that the machine would be effective.

B   This option tends to disfavor the effectiveness of the machine. The more changeable the colors of the plants to be distinguished, the more complex the task of distinguishing between weeds and crop plants based on their color.

C   This option tends to disfavor the likely benefits of the machine because it indicates that manual weeding distinguishes weeds from crop plants by using criteria that the machine does not take into account. If the machine does not distinguish weeds from crop plants as accurately and reliably as manual weeding does, then the machine is less apt to make manual weeding unnecessary.

D   **Correct.** Making crop plants easily distinguishable from weeds would facilitate the effective use of the weeding machine.

E   This does not favor the company's implementing the plan to develop the machine. There would still be tasks other than weeding that would require hiring staff. Thus there would still be labor costs even if the need for manual weeding were eliminated.

The correct answer is D.

52. The interview is an essential part of a successful hiring program because, with it, job applicants who have personalities that are unsuited to the requirements of the job will be eliminated from consideration.

    The argument above logically depends on which of the following assumptions?

    (A) A hiring program will be successful if it includes interviews.

    (B) The interview is a more important part of a successful hiring program than is the development of a job description.

    (C) Interviewers can accurately identify applicants whose personalities are unsuited to the requirements of the job.

    (D) The only purpose of an interview is to evaluate whether job applicants' personalities are suited to the requirements of the job.

    (E) The fit of job applicants' personalities to the requirements of the job was once the most important factor in making hiring decisions.

Argument Construction

Situation   The interview is a necessary part of hiring because candidates with unsuitable personalities are eliminated from consideration.

Reasoning   *What is being assumed in this argument?* The argument puts forth one reason that the interview is important: it eliminates candidates with unsuitable personalities. This presupposes that interviewers can, with a fair degree of accuracy, rule out those candidates whose personalities do not fit the needs of the job.

A   The argument does not go so far as to say that interviews guarantee a successful hiring program.

B   The argument does not prioritize the parts of a hiring program.

C   **Correct.** This statement properly identifies the assumption underlying the argument.

D   The argument gives one reason that the interview is important, but it does not say it is the *only* reason.

E   This concerns past practices in hiring, and is irrelevant to the argument.

The correct answer is C.

53. Useful protein drugs, such as insulin, must still be administered by the cumbersome procedure of injection under the skin. If proteins are taken orally, they are digested and cannot reach their target cells. Certain nonprotein drugs, however, contain chemical bonds that are not broken down by the digestive system. They can, thus, be taken orally.

    The statements above most strongly support a claim that a research procedure that successfully accomplishes which of the following would be beneficial to users of protein drugs?

    (A) Coating insulin with compounds that are broken down by target cells, but whose chemical bonds are resistant to digestion
    (B) Converting into protein compounds, by procedures that work in the laboratory, the nonprotein drugs that resist digestion
    (C) Removing permanently from the digestive system any substances that digest proteins
    (D) Determining, in a systematic way, what enzymes and bacteria are present in the normal digestive system and whether they tend to be broken down within the body
    (E) Determining the amount of time each nonprotein drug takes to reach its target cells

Argument Construction

Situation   Since protein drugs taken orally are digested and do not reach their target cells, they must be injected under the skin. Some nonprotein drugs have chemical bonds resistant to digestion and may be taken orally.

Reasoning   *What procedure might be beneficial for users of protein drugs?* Clearly it would be beneficial for users if protein drugs could be administered orally rather than by injection. Digestion has been the obstacle to the oral use of such drugs. Some nonprotein drugs have chemical bonds that resist digestion. If protein drugs such as insulin could use similar chemical bonds to resist digestion, thus allowing the protein to reach its target cells, then the protein drugs could be taken orally, a clear benefit to the users of those drugs.

A   **Correct.** This statement properly identifies a procedure that would be beneficial for users of protein drugs: coating a protein drug (such as insulin) so that it is resistant to digestion but able to reach its target cells would allow users to take it orally rather than by injection.

B   No benefit for users of protein drugs is gained by converting nonprotein drugs into protein compounds because then they too would need to be injected rather than taken orally.

C   The digestive system needs the substances that digest protein in order to function normally, so this procedure would do more harm than good.

D   Determining whether normally present enzymes and bacteria are broken down in the body does not offer any specific benefits for users of protein drugs.

E   The time required by nonprotein drugs to reach target cells is irrelevant to the question of benefits to users of protein drugs.

The correct answer is A.

54. Tanco, a leather manufacturer, uses large quantities of common salt to preserve animal hides. New environmental regulations have significantly increased the cost of disposing of salt water that results from this use, and, in consequence, Tanco is considering a plan to use potassium chloride in place of common salt. Research has shown that Tanco could reprocess the by-product of potassium chloride use to yield a crop fertilizer, leaving a relatively small volume of waste for disposal.

In determining the impact on company profits of using potassium chloride in place of common salt, it would be important for Tanco to research all of the following EXCEPT:

(A) What difference, if any, is there between the cost of the common salt needed to preserve a given quantity of animal hides and the cost of the potassium chloride needed to preserve the same quantity of hides?

(B) To what extent is the equipment involved in preserving animal hides using common salt suitable for preserving animal hides using potassium chloride?

(C) What environmental regulations, if any, constrain the disposal of the waste generated in reprocessing the by-product of potassium chloride?

(D) How closely does leather that results when common salt is used to preserve hides resemble that which results when potassium chloride is used?

(E) Are the chemical properties that make potassium chloride an effective means for preserving animal hides the same as those that make common salt an effective means for doing so?

Evaluation of a Plan

Situation New environmental regulations will increase the costs of disposing of the salt water that results from the use of large amounts of common salt in leather manufacturing. The manufacturer is considering switching from common salt to potassium chloride, because the by-product of the latter could be reprocessed to yield a crop fertilizer, with little waste left over to be disposed.

Reasoning *In order to determine whether it would be profitable to switch from using common salt to using potassium chloride, which of the five questions does the manufacturer NOT need to answer?* The chemical properties making potassium chloride an effective means of preserving animal hides might be quite different from those that make common salt effective, but there is no particular reason for thinking that this would impact the profitability of switching to potassium chloride. The relevant effects on the preserved hides might be the same even if the properties that brought about those effects were quite different. Thus, without more information than is provided in the passage, this question is irrelevant.

A The savings in waste disposal costs that would be gained by switching to potassium chloride could be cancelled out if the cost of potassium chloride needed far exceeded that for common salt.

B If switching to potassium chloride would force the manufacturer to replace the equipment it uses for preserving hides, then it might be less profitable to switch.

C Even though there is said to be relatively little waste associated with using potassium chloride in the process, if the costs of this disposal are very high due to environmental regulations, it might be less profitable to switch.

D If the leather that results from the use of potassium chloride looks substantially different from that which results when common salt has been used, then the leather might be less attractive to consumers, which would adversely affect the economics of switching to potassium chloride.

E **Correct.** Note that the question as stated here presupposes that potassium chloride and salt are both effective means for preserving animal hides—so it does not raise any issue as to whether potassium chloride is adequately effective or as effective as salt (clearly, an issue of effectiveness *would* be relevant to profitability).

The correct answer is E.

55. There is a great deal of geographical variation in the frequency of many surgical procedures—up to tenfold variation per hundred thousand people between different areas in the numbers of hysterectomies, prostatectomies, and tonsillectomies.

To support a conclusion that much of the variation is due to unnecessary surgical procedures, it would be most important to establish which of the following?

(A) A local board of review at each hospital examines the records of every operation to determine whether the surgical procedure was necessary.

(B) The variation is unrelated to factors (other than the surgical procedures themselves) that influence the incidence of diseases for which surgery might be considered.

(C) There are several categories of surgical procedure (other than hysterectomies, prostatectomies, and tonsillectomies) that are often performed unnecessarily.

(D) For certain surgical procedures, it is difficult to determine after the operation whether the procedures were necessary or whether alternative treatment would have succeeded.

(E) With respect to how often they are performed unnecessarily, hysterectomies, prostatectomies, and tonsillectomies are representative of surgical procedures in general.

Argument Construction

Situation   The frequency of certain surgical procedures, e.g., hysterectomies, prostatectomies, and tonsillectomies, varies dramatically by geographical region. It may be possible to conclude that the disparity is to a large extent the result of the performance of unnecessary surgeries.

Reasoning   *What additional information must be true for this conclusion to hold?* Is it possible that different factors in different regions might reasonably account for the variation? Diseases or medical conditions for which these surgical procedures are appropriate might be more common in one geographical area than another. Unless the possibility of such geographical variations in the incidence of pertinent medical conditions is ruled out, it would be risky to conclude that the variation is attributable to unnecessary surgical procedures.

A   This statement undermines such a conclusion since it cites a process in place for preventing or reducing unnecessary procedures.

B   **Correct.** This statement suggests the geographical variation is not due to variations in incidence of certain diseases—and by eliminating this possibility, it helps to support the claim that unnecessary surgeries are being performed in some places.

C   The argument is concerned only with hysterectomies, prostatectomies, and tonsillectomies; other surgical procedures are irrelevant.

D   This information indicates that there is a fuzzy line dividing necessary from unnecessary surgeries—but this would apply in every place, not just in some; so it provides no support for the intended conclusion.

E   The argument involves only the three kinds of surgery cited in the passage, so this statement is irrelevant to the conclusion.

The correct answer is B.

56. Gortland has long been narrowly self-sufficient in both grain and meat. However, as per capita income in Gortland has risen toward the world average, per capita consumption of meat has also risen toward the world average, and it takes several pounds of grain to produce one pound of meat. Therefore, since per capita income continues to rise, whereas domestic grain production will not increase, Gortland will soon have to import either grain or meat or both.

Which of the following is an assumption on which the argument depends?

(A) The total acreage devoted to grain production in Gortland will not decrease substantially.

(B) The population of Gortland has remained relatively constant during the country's years of growing prosperity.

(C) The per capita consumption of meat in Gortland is roughly the same across all income levels.

(D) In Gortland, neither meat nor grain is subject to government price controls.

(E) People in Gortland who increase their consumption of meat will not radically decrease their consumption of grain.

Argument Construction

Situation   A country previously self-sufficient in grain and meat will soon have to import one or the other or both because its consumption of meat has risen as per capita income has risen. It takes several pounds of grain to produce one pound of meat.

Reasoning   *What conditions must be true for the conclusion to be true?* Meat consumption is rising. What about grain consumption? A sharp reduction in the amount of grain directly consumed by meat eaters could compensate for increased meat consumption, making the conclusion false. If people did radically decrease their grain consumption, it might not be necessary to import grain or meat. Since the argument concludes that the imports are necessary, it assumes that direct consumption of grain by those who begin to eat meat will not plunge.

A   The argument makes no assumptions about the acreage devoted to grain; it assumes only that the demand for grain will rise.

B   The argument is based on rising per capita income, not population levels.

C   The argument involves only meat consumption in general, not its distribution by income level.

D   Since the argument does not refer to price controls, it cannot depend on an assumption about them.

E   **Correct.** This statement properly identifies the assumption that those who begin to eat meat do not then greatly decrease their direct consumption of grains.

The correct answer is E.

57. Meteorite explosions in the Earth's atmosphere as large as the one that destroyed forests in Siberia, with approximately the force of a twelve-megaton nuclear blast, occur about once a century.

    The response of highly automated systems controlled by complex computer programs to unexpected circumstances is unpredictable.

    Which of the following conclusions can most properly be drawn, if the statements above are true, about a highly automated nuclear-missile defense system controlled by a complex computer program?

    (A) Within a century after its construction, the system would react inappropriately and might accidentally start a nuclear war.
    (B) The system would be destroyed if an explosion of a large meteorite occurred in the Earth's atmosphere.
    (C) It would be impossible for the system to distinguish the explosion of a large meteorite from the explosion of a nuclear weapon.
    (D) Whether the system would respond inappropriately to the explosion of a large meteorite would depend on the location of the blast.
    (E) It is not certain what the system's response to the explosion of a large meteorite would be, if its designers did not plan for such a contingency.

Argument Construction

Situation   A meteorite explosion equivalent to a nuclear blast occurs approximately once a century. Automated systems, controlled by computer programs, respond to unexpected occurrences unpredictably.

Reasoning   *What conclusion can be drawn about such a highly automated defense system?* The response of the system to *unexpected circumstances* is *unpredictable*, which means that no reliable information is available about how the system would respond to such unexpected circumstances, that is, to an event that the system was not designed to handle.

A   The fact that the system's response would be unpredictable does not justify a prediction that such a response would actually be inappropriate; it could just as well be appropriate. Neither are we told whether any particular meteorite event would produce such *unexpected circumstances*.

B   The premises offer no evidence that the system would be destroyed.

C   The given information does not tell us whether a system could be designed to distinguish between a nuclear blast and a meteorite explosion.

D   No information is given in the two premises about how the location of the explosion would affect the system.

E   **Correct.** This statement properly identifies the conclusion that the system's response to a meteorite explosion would be uncertain if the system had not been designed to handle such an event.

The correct answer is E.

58. If there is an oil-supply disruption resulting in higher international oil prices, domestic oil prices in open-market countries such as the United States will rise as well, whether such countries import all or none of their oil.

If the statement above concerning oil-supply disruptions is true, which of the following policies in an open-market nation is most likely to reduce the long-term economic impact on that nation of sharp and unexpected increases in international oil prices?

(A) Maintaining the quantity of oil imported at constant yearly levels

(B) Increasing the number of oil tankers in its fleet

(C) Suspending diplomatic relations with major oil-producing nations

(D) Decreasing oil consumption through conservation

(E) Decreasing domestic production of oil

Evaluation of a Plan

Situation   International oil prices rise when a disruption in the oil supply occurs; in this event, open-market countries experience a rise in domestic oil prices, even if they do not import any oil.

Reasoning   *What policy will reduce the economic impact of oil price increases?* All open-market countries experience a rise in oil prices, even when they do not import oil. Thus importing oil is not the issue. A nation can soften the impact of price hikes by using less oil because decreasing oil consumption would decrease the need to purchase oil at increased prices; conservation is a way to lower consumption.

A   Not all countries import oil; for those that do, maintaining the level of oil imports when prices increase would not soften the economic impact of the price increases.

B   The number of oil tankers is irrelevant to the effect on the economy.

C   The diplomatic relationship between countries is irrelevant to the effect on the economy.

D   Correct. *Conservation* suggests smaller energy consumption and more efficient use of energy—without curtailing necessary economic activity. Such a measure would help reduce the economic impact of increases in oil prices.

E   Decreasing domestic oil production would only make the situation worse.

The correct answer is D.

59. Boreal owls range over a much larger area than do other owls of similar size. The reason for this behavior is probably that the small mammals on which owls feed are especially scarce in the forests where boreal owls live, and the relative scarcity of prey requires the owls to range more extensively to find sufficient food.

Which of the following, if true, most helps to confirm the explanation above?

(A) Some boreal owls range over an area eight times larger than the area over which any other owl of similar size ranges.

(B) Boreal owls range over larger areas in regions where food of the sort eaten by small mammals is sparse than they do in regions where such food is abundant.

(C) After their young hatch, boreal owls must hunt more often than before in order to feed both themselves and their newly hatched young.

(D) Sometimes individual boreal owls hunt near a single location for many weeks at a time and do not range farther than a few hundred yards.

(E) The boreal owl requires less food, relative to its weight, than is required by members of other owl species.

Argument Evaluation

Situation   The small mammals on which owls prey are relatively scarce in the forests where boreal owls live. That is why boreal owls range more extensively than do other, similarly sized owls in search of food.

Reasoning   *Which choice, if true, would most help confirm the proposed explanation?* One way to confirm an explanation is by finding further information that one would expect to be true *if* the explanation is valid. If the explanation in the passage is valid, then one would expect that variations in the population density of available small-animal prey for boreal owls would be accompanied by variations in the ranges of the boreal owls. Naturally the population density of available small-animal prey is likely to be affected by how plentiful food is for those small animals.

A   The comparison between different groups of boreal owls is not relevant to the comparison between boreal owls and other owls.

B   **Correct.** This indicates that abundance of food for the boreal owls' small-animal prey in an area (and therefore abundance of small animals in that area) correlates with a smaller range for the boreal owls there. This strengthens the proposed explanation.

C   This option concerns a correlation between owls' need for food and the frequency with which owls hunt, whereas the phenomenon described in the passage and the proposed explanation have to do with the range over which owls hunt.

D   If one were to assume that boreal owls never hunt near a single location for weeks, that would in no way undermine the proposed explanation.

E   If anything, this option tends to undermine the proposed explanation, because it suggests the possibility that boreal owls need not make up for the relative scarcity of prey in their habitats by ranging over larger areas.

The correct answer is B.

60. The tobacco industry is still profitable and projections are that it will remain so. In the United States this year, the total amount of tobacco sold by tobacco farmers has increased, even though the number of adults who smoke has decreased.

Each of the following, if true, could explain the simultaneous increase in tobacco sales and decrease in the number of adults who smoke EXCEPT:

(A) During this year, the number of women who have begun to smoke is greater than the number of men who have quit smoking.

(B) The number of teenage children who have begun to smoke this year is greater than the number of adults who have quit smoking during the same period.

(C) During this year, the number of nonsmokers who have begun to use chewing tobacco or snuff is greater than the number of people who have quit smoking.

(D) The people who have continued to smoke consume more tobacco per person than they did in the past.

(E) More of the cigarettes made in the United States this year were exported to other countries than was the case last year.

Argument Construction

Situation   The number of adult Americans who smoke has decreased, but the amount of tobacco sold has increased.

Reasoning   *Which point does NOT help explain the apparent discrepancy between the decrease in adult smokers and the increase in tobacco sales?* Many possible explanations exist: an increase in teenage smokers, tobacco's use in products that are not smoked, increased consumption by the remaining smokers, an increase in tobacco exports, and so on. To answer this question, use the process of elimination to find the choice that does NOT provide an explanation.

A   **Correct.** This information is compatible with an overall decrease in adult smokers but also with an overall *increase in adult smokers.* How many new male smokers were there? How many women quit smoking? We are not told—so the information provided in this choice cannot explain the overall decrease in adult smokers. But since it is compatible with an overall decrease, it is not a sufficient explanation of increased tobacco sales.

B   A rise in teenager smokers would offset the decline in adult smokers and so could explain the paradox.

C   Rising tobacco sales despite a decrease in smokers could be explained by an increase in the use of snuff and chewing tobacco by nonsmokers.

D   Even though there are now fewer smokers, if these remaining smokers smoked substantially more, then the rise in tobacco sales could be explained.

E   Rising exports could explain rising tobacco sales at a time when fewer adult Americans smoke.

The correct answer is A.

61. A milepost on the towpath read "21" on the side facing the hiker as she approached it and "23" on its back. She reasoned that the next milepost forward on the path would indicate that she was halfway between one end of the path and the other. However, the milepost one mile further on read "20" facing her and "24" behind.

    Which of the following, if true, would explain the discrepancy described above?

    (A)   The numbers on the next milepost had been reversed.
    (B)   The numbers on the mileposts indicate kilometers, not miles.
    (C)   The facing numbers indicate miles to the end of the path, not miles from the beginning.
    (D)   A milepost was missing between the two the hiker encountered.
    (E)   The mileposts had originally been put in place for the use of mountain bikers, not for hikers.

    Argument Construction

    Situation   A hiker sees a milepost marked 21 on one side and 23 on the other. She expects the next milepost to read 22 on both sides. However, the actual sign says 20 and 24.

    Reasoning   *What explains the discrepancy?* The hiker assumes that the number facing her is the distance she has traveled from her journey's beginning and that the other number is the distance to her journey's end. That is, at the first milepost she believes she has come 21 miles and has 23 miles left to go. In fact, the numbers are actually the reverse of her reasoning. At the second milepost she has 20 miles left to go and has come 24 miles.

    A   Reversing the numbers would not make any difference; according to the hiker's (incorrect) reasoning, both numbers would be 22.
    B   What unit of measurement is used is irrelevant to the hiker's misinterpretation of the mileposts.
    C   **Correct.** This statement resolves the discrepancy between the true meaning of the mileposts and the hiker's expectation about them by showing how the hiker misinterpreted the mileposts.
    D   A missing milepost would not explain the discrepancy. If there had been a missing milepost with 22 on each side, its discrepancy with the 20/24 milepost would also need explanation.
    E   The numbers are measures of distance, not time, so the mode of transportation is irrelevant.

    The correct answer is C.

62. In response to viral infection, the immune systems of mice typically produce antibodies that destroy the virus by binding to proteins on its surface. Mice infected with a herpesvirus generally develop keratitis, a degenerative disease affecting part of the eye. Since proteins on the surface of cells in this part of the eye closely resemble those on the herpesvirus surface, scientists hypothesize that these cases of keratitis are caused by antibodies to herpesvirus.

    Which of the following, if true, gives the greatest additional support to the scientists' hypothesis?

    (A) Other types of virus have surface proteins that closely resemble proteins found in various organs of mice.

    (B) There are mice that are unable to form antibodies in response to herpes infections, and these mice contract herpes at roughly the same rate as other mice.

    (C) Mice that are infected with a herpesvirus but do not develop keratitis produce as many antibodies as infected mice that do develop keratitis.

    (D) There are mice that are unable to form antibodies in response to herpes infections, and these mice survive these infections without ever developing keratitis.

    (E) Mice that have never been infected with a herpesvirus can sometimes develop keratitis.

Argument Evaluation

Situation Scientists hypothesize that the reason most mice infected with a herpesvirus develop keratitis, a degenerative eye disease, is because the antibodies from the mouse's immune system attack proteins on the eye's surface by mistake. This is because proteins in certain eye cells closely resemble the virus proteins that antibodies attack.

Reasoning *Which option, if true, would provide the greatest additional support for the scientists' hypothesis attempting to explain why keratitis occurs?* When *x* is thought to cause *y*, it is important to consider whether *y* occurs even when *x* is absent: if it does not, that strengthens the notion that *x* is causing *y* in those cases where they occur together. If the scientists' hypothesis is correct, and the antibodies produced by the mice's immune systems to combat the herpesvirus are causing the keratitis, we should not expect to find keratitis in herpes-infected mice whose immune systems are not producing those antibodies. Thus, the scientists' hypothesis is supported by the finding that herpes-infected mice that do not produce antibodies do not develop keratitis.

A The issue at hand concerns only the herpesvirus, so this choice is of little, if any, relevance.

B This finding has no bearing on the hypothesis, for it concerns merely the connection between the antibodies and the development of the herpesvirus disease, whereas the hypothesis concerns the connection between the antibodies and the development of keratitis.

C This finding, if anything, undermines the hypothesis, for if antibodies produced in response to the herpesvirus were indeed causing the keratitis, one would expect that at least in some of the cases in which mice with herpesvirus do not develop keratitis it is because they are deficient in antibodies to the virus.

D **Correct.** The fact that herpes-infected mice that are unable to develop antibodies against herpes do not get keratitis confirms the scientists' hypothesis.

E This finding does not support the hypothesis and may in fact mildly weaken it, for it suggests that keratitis in herpes-infected mice may be unrelated to the organism's response to the virus.

The correct answer is D.

63. Traditionally, decision making by managers that is reasoned step-by-step has been considered preferable to intuitive decision making. However, a recent study found that top managers used intuition significantly more than did most middle- or lower-level managers. This confirms the alternative view that intuition is actually more effective than careful, methodical reasoning.

    The conclusion above is based on which of the following assumptions?

    (A) Methodical, step-by-step reasoning is inappropriate for making many real-life management decisions.
    (B) Top managers have the ability to use either intuitive reasoning or methodical, step-by-step reasoning in making decisions.
    (C) The decisions made by middle- and lower-level managers can be made as easily by using methodical reasoning as by using intuitive reasoning.
    (D) Top managers use intuitive reasoning in making the majority of their decisions.
    (E) Top managers are more effective at decision making than middle- or lower-level managers.

Argument Construction

Situation   Intuition, used significantly more by top managers than by middle- or lower-level managers, is found to be more effective than step-by-step reasoning in making decisions.

Reasoning   *What assumption does the argument make?* The study shows that top managers use intuition more in decision making than the other managers do. The conclusion is then drawn that intuition is more effective. But the stated premises on their own provide inadequate support for the conclusion, so it is reasonable to think that the argument must be based on an unstated assumption, such as the assumption that top managers, when employing intuitive decision making, make more effective decisions than middle- and lower-level managers. Without some such assumption, the argument fails.

A   While the argument is consistent with this idea, the inappropriateness of step-by-step reasoning is not assumed.

B   Top managers' ability to switch decision methods does not help to show that one method is better than the other.

C   The effectiveness of decision-making methods, not the ease with which the methods are applied, is the subject of the argument.

D   The argument would not necessarily fail if something incompatible with this statement were assumed—for example, if it were assumed that top managers use intuition only in *half* of their decisions. Thus this statement does not have to be assumed. Moreover, even if this statement were to be added as an assumption to the stated premises, the support for the conclusion would still be inadequate unless some additional assumption were made.

E   **Correct.** This is the best choice for the missing assumption. Without some such assumption, the argument would fail.

The correct answer is E.

64. High levels of fertilizer and pesticides, needed when farmers try to produce high yields of the same crop year after year, pollute water supplies. Experts therefore urge farmers to diversify their crops and to rotate their plantings yearly.

To receive governmental price-support benefits for a crop, farmers must have produced that same crop for the past several years.

The statements above, if true, best support which of the following conclusions?

(A) The rules for governmental support of farm prices work against efforts to reduce water pollution.

(B) The only solution to the problem of water pollution from fertilizers and pesticides is to take farmland out of production.

(C) Farmers can continue to make a profit by rotating diverse crops, thus reducing costs for chemicals, but not by planting the same crop each year.

(D) New farming techniques will be developed to make it possible for farmers to reduce the application of fertilizers and pesticides.

(E) Governmental price supports for farm products are set at levels that are not high enough to allow farmers to get out of debt.

Argument Construction

Situation   Farmers are urged to rotate crops annually because the chemicals they must use when continuing to produce the same crops pollute water supplies. On the other hand, farmers may receive federal price-support benefits only if they have been producing the same crop for the past several years.

Reasoning   *What conclusion can be drawn from this information?* Farmers wish to receive the price-support benefits offered by the government, so they grow the same crop for several years. In order to continue getting good yields, they use the high levels of chemicals necessary when the same crop is grown from year to year. The result is water pollution. The government's rules for price-support benefits work against the efforts to reduce water pollution.

A   **Correct.** This statement properly identifies the conclusion supported by the evidence.

B   The experts cited in the passage believe that the rotation of crops is the solution, not the removal of farmland from production.

C   The conclusion that farmers cannot make a profit by producing the same crop year after year is not justified by the information given in the premises. The information given suggests that this conclusion would actually be false, since these farmers would benefit by price-support measures for such a crop.

D   No information in the passage supports a conclusion about farming techniques other than crop diversification and rotation, which are clearly existing farming techniques and not new or yet to be developed.

E   This conclusion is unwarranted because there is no information in the two statements about the levels of the price supports and of the farmers' debts.

The correct answer is A.

65.   Which of the following most logically completes the argument?

Utrania was formerly a major petroleum exporter, but in recent decades economic stagnation and restrictive regulations inhibited investment in new oil fields. In consequence, Utranian oil exports dropped steadily as old fields became depleted. Utrania's currently improving economic situation, together with less-restrictive regulations, will undoubtedly result in the rapid development of new fields. However, it would be premature to conclude that the rapid development of new fields will result in higher oil exports, because _____.

(A)   the price of oil is expected to remain relatively stable over the next several years

(B)   the improvement in the economic situation in Utrania is expected to result in a dramatic increase in the proportion of Utranians who own automobiles

(C)   most of the investment in new oil fields in Utrania is expected to come from foreign sources

(D)   new technology is available to recover oil from old oil fields formerly regarded as depleted

(E)   many of the new oil fields in Utrania are likely to be as productive as those that were developed during the period when Utrania was a major oil exporter

Argument Construction

Situation   A country that had been a major oil exporter has seen its exports decline in recent decades due to economic stagnation, a failure to invest in new fields, and the steady depletion of its old fields. But looser regulations and an improving economy will bring rapid development of new oil fields in the country.

Reasoning   *Which of the options would most logically complete the argument?* The passage describes the conditions that led to Utrania's no longer being a major oil exporter: a lack of investment in new oil fields due to a stagnant economy and restrictive regulations. The passage then says that due to changed regulatory and economic conditions, there will now be rapid development of new oil fields. Nonetheless, this might not bring about an increase in Utrania's oil exports. To logically complete the argument, one must explain how oil exports might not increase even when the condition that led to decreased oil exports has been removed. Suppose there were an increase in domestic oil consumption. A dramatic increase in the rate of car ownership in Utrania could reasonably be expected to significantly increase domestic oil consumption, which could eat up the added oil production from the new fields.

A   This choice is incorrect. There is no reason why stable oil prices should prevent Utrania's oil exports from increasing.

B   **Correct.** An increase in car ownership would increase Utrania's oil consumption—and this supports the claim that oil exports might not increase.

C   If anything, this suggests that oil exports should increase. So it would not be a good choice for completion of the argument.

D   The advent of new technology allowing oil to be extracted from fields previously thought to be depleted would mean that there is even more reason to think that Utrania's oil exports will increase.

E   This does not help to explain why exports would not increase. On the contrary, it suggests that the new fields will lead to increased exports.

The correct answer is B.

66. Hardin argued that grazing land held in common (that is, open to any user) would always be used less carefully than private grazing land. Each rancher would be tempted to overuse common land because the benefits would accrue to the individual, while the costs of reduced land quality that results from overuse would be spread among all users. But a study comparing 217 million acres of common grazing land with 433 million acres of private grazing land showed that the common land was in better condition.

The answer to which of the following questions would be most useful in evaluating the significance, in relation to Hardin's claim, of the study described above?

(A) Did any of the ranchers whose land was studied use both common and private land?

(B) Did the ranchers whose land was studied tend to prefer using common land over using private land for grazing?

(C) Was the private land that was studied of comparable quality to the common land before either was used for grazing?

(D) Were the users of the common land that was studied at least as prosperous as the users of the private land?

(E) Were there any owners of herds who used only common land, and no private land, for grazing?

Argument Evaluation

Situation   Hardin claims that common grazing land is used less carefully than private grazing land because each rancher tries to get the most benefit from the common land, thus overusing it. Contrary to this claim, a study comparing common grazing land with private grazing land found the common land to be in better condition.

Reasoning   *What other information might be useful in evaluating the study?* The study finds that common grazing land was in better condition than private grazing land, which seems to undermine Hardin's argument. To decide whether the study finding really undermines the argument, we need to ask whether the comparison between the common and the private grazing land was sound. In determining this, we need to know, not just how the lands compared *after* grazing use, but also how the lands compared *before* that use. For example, the private land may have been greatly inferior to the public land even before grazing began. If this were the case, the comparison providing the study finding would have been invalid, and the study finding would not succeed in undermining Hardin's argument.

A   It does not matter whether ranchers used one or both types of lands; only the relative condition of the two kinds of lands matters.

B   The ranchers' preferences are not being questioned.

C   **Correct.** This question raises the issue of whether the study finding was based on a valid comparison of like with like.

D   The prosperity of the ranchers is irrelevant to the condition of the two types of grazing lands.

E   It does not matter if some ranchers used only common lands because it is the relative condition of the lands that is important.

The correct answer is C.

67. A compelling optical illusion called the illusion of velocity and size makes objects appear to be moving more slowly the larger the objects are. Therefore, a motorist's estimate of the time available for crossing a highway with a small car approaching is bound to be lower than it would be with a large truck approaching.

    The conclusion above would be more properly drawn if it were made clear that the

    (A) truck's speed is assumed to be lower than the car's
    (B) truck's speed is assumed to be the same as the car's
    (C) truck's speed is assumed to be higher than the car's
    (D) motorist's estimate of time available is assumed to be more accurate with cars approaching than with trucks approaching
    (E) motorist's estimate of time available is assumed to be more accurate with trucks approaching than with cars approaching

Argument Construction

Situation   An optical illusion makes objects appear to be moving more slowly the larger they are. It is concluded that a driver's estimate of the time available to cross a highway is lower with a small car approaching than with a large truck approaching.

Reasoning   *What underlying assumption is made in the reasoning?* From the given premise about the optical illusion, we can infer that, to a motorist crossing a highway, a car actually approaching at 60 miles an hour seems significantly faster than a large truck that is approaching at the same speed. The motorist's estimate of time available to cross will thus be larger for the truck than for the car. The assumption stated here, but not stated in the passage, is that the car and truck are approaching *at the same speed*.

A   If the truck is moving more slowly than the car, then the driver's perception is accurate, and not affected by the optical illusion.

B   Correct. This statement properly identifies an assumption implicit in the reasoning.

C   If the truck is moving faster than the car, the motorist might judge that the two vehicles were moving at the same speed—or even that the truck was moving faster.

D   It does not matter for which type of vehicle the driver's estimate of lead time is more accurate; this assumption is not helpful in explaining the conclusion that the illusion makes larger objects appear to be moving more slowly than small objects.

E   This contradicts information in the passage indicating that the larger the vehicle, the larger the distortion in the perceived speed.

The correct answer is B.

68. Manufacturers sometimes discount the price of a product to retailers for a promotion period when the product is advertised to consumers. Such promotions often result in a dramatic increase in amount of product sold by the manufacturers to retailers. Nevertheless, the manufacturers could often make more profit by not holding the promotions.

Which of the following, if true, most strongly supports the claim above about the manufacturers' profit?

(A) The amount of discount generally offered by manufacturers to retailers is carefully calculated to represent the minimum needed to draw consumers' attention to the product.

(B) For many consumer products the period of advertising discounted prices to consumers is about a week, not sufficiently long for consumers to become used to the sale price.

(C) For products that are not newly introduced, the purpose of such promotions is to keep the products in the minds of consumers and to attract consumers who are currently using competing products.

(D) During such a promotion retailers tend to accumulate in their warehouses inventory bought at discount; they then sell much of it later at their regular price.

(E) If a manufacturer fails to offer such promotions but its competitor offers them, that competitor will tend to attract consumers away from the manufacturer's product.

Argument Construction

Situation   During promotion periods, manufacturers discount prices and dramatically increase the amount of product sold to retailers. However, manufacturers might make more profit without the promotions.

Reasoning   *How could promotion periods cut profits?* It is stated that promotion periods result in increased product sales to retailers. How could such sales decrease the manufacturers' potential profits? If retailers buy more than they can sell during the promotion period, they will store the surplus in warehouses and sell it later at the regular price. Manufacturers lose their normal profits on these sales; moreover, the manufacturer will not be filling orders while the surplus exists. The resulting losses may be greater than any gains from increasing sales or winning new customers during the brief promotion period.

A   Calculating the minimum amount of discount should lead to greater profit for manufacturers, so this statement does not explain the potential loss of profit.

B   The brevity of the promotion period favors manufacturers because consumers do not become accustomed to the lower price.

C   Attracting customers' attention should contribute to higher, not lower, profit.

D   Correct. This statement properly identifies a factor that strengthens the argument.

E   Since the failure to offer promotions results in loss of customers to competitors, this statement shows that manufacturers gain by promotions.

The correct answer is D.

69. When people evade income taxes by not declaring taxable income, a vicious cycle results. Tax evasion forces lawmakers to raise income tax rates, which causes the tax burden on nonevading taxpayers to become heavier. This, in turn, encourages even more taxpayers to evade income taxes by hiding taxable income.

    The vicious cycle described above could not result unless which of the following were true?

    (A) An increase in tax rates tends to function as an incentive for taxpayers to try to increase their pretax incomes.

    (B) Some methods for detecting tax evaders, and thus recovering some tax revenue lost through evasion, bring in more than they cost, but their success rate varies from year to year.

    (C) When lawmakers establish income tax rates in order to generate a certain level of revenue, they do not allow adequately for revenue that will be lost through evasion.

    (D) No one who routinely hides some taxable income can be induced by a lowering of tax rates to stop hiding such income unless fines for evaders are raised at the same time.

    (E) Taxpayers do not differ from each other with respect to the rate of taxation that will cause them to evade taxes.

Argument Construction

Situation   When some people evade income taxes by hiding taxable income, income tax rates must be raised, placing a heavier tax burden on honest taxpayers. The higher rate, in turn, encourages more people to conceal taxable income.

Reasoning   *What must be true in order for this cycle to occur?* Consider the factors that are assumed to drive this cycle. It is said that tax evasion *forces* legislative increases in tax rates to cover the loss of tax revenues. This would be true only if lawmakers, when considering what income tax rates to establish, had failed to sufficiently take into account the amount of revenue that would inevitably be lost to evasion.

A   Any incentive to increase pretax incomes would counter the reported tendency to conceal income and thus break the cycle.

B   Success in detecting tax evaders, no matter how variable or cost-effective, inhibits tax evasion and breaks the cycle.

C   **Correct.** This statement properly identifies the argument's underlying assumption that lawmakers fail to consider the revenue lost to evasion when they determine tax rates, forcing the increased tax rates that drive the cycle.

D   Higher fines deter evaders and thus break the cycle.

E   This is not an assumption of the argument. If it were true, the cycle could never get started. Either everyone would evade taxes or no one would.

The correct answer is C.

70. Plantings of cotton bioengineered to produce its own insecticide against bollworms, a major cause of crop failure, sustained little bollworm damage until this year. This year the plantings are being seriously damaged by bollworms. Bollworms, however, are not necessarily developing resistance to the cotton's insecticide. Bollworms breed on corn, and last year more corn than usual was planted throughout cotton-growing regions. So it is likely that the cotton is simply being overwhelmed by corn-bred bollworms.

In evaluating the argument, which of the following would it be most useful to establish?

(A) Whether corn could be bioengineered to produce the insecticide

(B) Whether plantings of cotton that does not produce the insecticide are suffering unusually extensive damage from bollworms this year

(C) Whether other crops that have been bioengineered to produce their own insecticide successfully resist the pests against which the insecticide was to protect them

(D) Whether plantings of bioengineered cotton are frequently damaged by insect pests other than bollworms

(E) Whether there are insecticides that can be used against bollworms that have developed resistance to the insecticide produced by the bioengineered cotton

Argument Evaluation

Situation   Although plantings of cotton bioengineered to produce an insecticide to combat bollworms were little damaged by the pests in previous years, they are being severely damaged this year. Since the bollworms breed on corn, and there has been more corn planted this year in cotton-growing areas, the cotton is probably being overwhelmed by the corn-bred bollworms.

Reasoning   *In evaluating the argument, which question would it be most useful to have answered?* The argument states that the bioengineered cotton crop failures this year (1) have likely been due to the increased corn plantings and (2) not due to the pests having developed a resistance to the insecticide. This also implies (3) that the failures are not due to some third factor.

It would be useful to know how the bioengineered cotton is faring in comparison to the rest of this year's cotton crop. If the bioengineered cotton is faring better against the bollworms, that fact would support the argument because it would suggest that the insecticide is still combating bollworms. If, on the other hand, the bioengineered cotton is being more severely ravaged by bollworms than is other cotton, that suggests that there is some third cause that is primarily at fault.

A   This would probably be useful information to those trying to alleviate the bollworm problem in bioengineered cotton. But whether such corn could be developed has no bearing on what is causing the bioengineered cotton to be damaged by bollworms this year.

B   **Correct.** If bollworm damage on non-bioengineered cotton is worse than usual this year, then bollworm infestation in general is simply worse than usual, so pesticide resistance does not need to be invoked to explain the bollworm attacks on the bioengineered cotton.

C   Even if other crops that have been bioengineered to resist pests have not successfully resisted them, that fact would not mean that the same is true of this cotton. Furthermore, the facts already suggest that the bioengineered cotton has resisted bollworms.

D   Whether other types of pests often damage bioengineered cotton has no bearing on why bollworms are damaging this type of cotton more this year than in the past.

E   This, too, might be useful information to those trying to alleviate the bollworm problem in bioengineered cotton, but it is not particularly useful in evaluating the argument. Even if there are pesticides that could be used against bollworms that have developed resistance to the insecticide of the bioengineered cotton, that does not mean that such pesticides are being used this year.

The correct answer is B.

71. Because postage rates are rising, *Home Decorator* magazine plans to maximize its profits by reducing by one-half the number of issues it publishes each year. The quality of articles, the number of articles published per year, and the subscription price will not change. Market research shows that neither subscribers nor advertisers will be lost if the magazine's plan is instituted.

    Which of the following, if true, provides the strongest evidence that the magazine's profits are likely to decline if the plan is instituted?

    (A) With the new postage rates, a typical issue under the proposed plan would cost about one-third more to mail than a typical current issue would.

    (B) The majority of the magazine's subscribers are less concerned about a possible reduction in the quantity of the magazine's articles than about a possible loss of the current high quality of its articles.

    (C) Many of the magazine's long-time subscribers would continue their subscriptions even if the subscription price were increased.

    (D) Most of the advertisers that purchase advertising space in the magazine will continue to spend the same amount on advertising per issue as they have in the past.

    (E) Production costs for the magazine are expected to remain stable.

Evaluation of a Plan

Situation   In the face of rising postage costs, a magazine decides to cut in half the number of issues it publishes a year, though the quality and quantity of the articles as well as the subscription price will remain the same. Market research indicates that this plan will not cost the magazine any subscribers or advertisers.

Reasoning   *How might the plan cause profits to decline?* The magazine plans to maximize profits by reducing costs. What could lead to lower profits despite lower costs? Profits could decline if revenue is lost—and revenue will be lost if advertisers spend the same amount on advertising per issue when the number of issues is reduced by half. Therefore, the advertising revenues will be cut in half and a significant decline in profits is likely to result.

A   If the number of issues is cut in half and the postage rate per issue goes up by a third, then mailing costs still go down. This statement does not suggest that the plan will cause a decline in profits.

B   This statement is irrelevant to the magazine's profitability given the stated point that the quantity and quality of articles will not change.

C   The passage says that the subscription price will not increase under the plan, so this statement provides no useful evidence.

D   Correct. This statement properly identifies evidence of a flaw in the plan. While market research shows that *advertisers* will not be lost, this statement shows that a significant amount of *advertising* will be lost.

E   Stable production costs would not lead to a decline in profits.

The correct answer is D.

72. A discount retailer of basic household necessities employs thousands of people and pays most of them at the minimum wage rate. Yet following a federally mandated increase of the minimum wage rate that increased the retailer's operating costs considerably, the retailer's profits increased markedly.

Which of the following, if true, most helps to resolve the apparent paradox?

(A) Over half of the retailer's operating costs consist of payroll expenditures; yet only a small percentage of those expenditures go to pay management salaries.

(B) The retailer's customer base is made up primarily of people who earn, or who depend on the earnings of others who earn, the minimum wage.

(C) The retailer's operating costs, other than wages, increased substantially after the increase in the minimum wage rate went into effect.

(D) When the increase in the minimum wage rate went into effect, the retailer also raised the wage rate for employees who had been earning just above minimum wage.

(E) The majority of the retailer's employees work as cashiers, and most cashiers are paid the minimum wage.

Argument Evaluation

Situation   A discount retailer of household necessities pays the minimum wage to most of its employees. When the minimum wage rate went up, the retailer's operating costs rose. However, its profits also rose.

Reasoning   *What information helps explain the paradoxical situation that the retailer's profits rose even though its costs rose?* Consider the nature of the cost increase: wages have gone up. If the retailer's customer base includes many people who earn minimum wage, their buying power has risen with the minimum wage and they can spend more. This would explain the rise in profits.

A   This statement helps explain the impact of the wage-rate increase on costs but does not explain how rising costs could lead to profits.

B   **Correct.** This statement properly explains the surprising impact of the wage-rate increase on profits.

C   If the retailer's other costs also rose, then the paradox of the retailer's profits is even more mysterious.

D   Increasing other wages contributes to even higher operating costs; there is no information to explain how higher costs could lead to profits.

E   This detail about minimum-wage jobs does not explain how the retailer could be gaining profits when costs are rising.

The correct answer is B.

73. The cotton farms of Country Q became so productive that the market could not absorb all that they produced. Consequently, cotton prices fell. The government tried to boost cotton prices by offering farmers who took 25 percent of their cotton acreage out of production direct support payments up to a specified maximum per farm.

    The government's program, if successful, will not be a net burden on the budget. Which of the following, if true, is the best basis for an explanation of how this could be so?

    (A) Depressed cotton prices meant operating losses for cotton farms, and the government lost revenue from taxes on farm profits.

    (B) Cotton production in several countries other than Q declined slightly the year that the support-payment program went into effect in Q.

    (C) The first year that the support-payment program was in effect, cotton acreage in Q was 5 percent below its level in the base year for the program.

    (D) The specified maximum per farm meant that for very large cotton farms the support payments were less per acre for those acres that were withdrawn from production than they were for smaller farms.

    (E) Farmers who wished to qualify for support payments could not use the cotton acreage that was withdrawn from production to grow any other crop.

Evaluation of a Plan

Situation   Overproduction of cotton had led to falling prices. To boost prices, the government offered direct support payments to farmers who took 25 percent of their cotton acreage out of production. Surprisingly, this plan, if successful, will not be a net burden on the budget.

Reasoning   *What would explain why the plan will not a net burden?* It will not be a net burden only if as much or more will be added to the budget revenue as the amount paid out in support payments. What government revenues would account for such an increase in receipts? If, when cotton prices were falling, the cotton farmers had lower profits, they were paying lower taxes to the government. When cotton prices increase (because less cotton is offered in the market) and cotton farmers make greater profits, the government is able to tax those profits. In the program, the increased tax revenue compensates for the added expenditure.

A   **Correct.** This statement properly explains how no net budget loss would result from the plan.

B   The decline in cotton production in other countries does not explain why the program will not be a net burden on the budget.

C   The difference in cotton acreage does not explain how the government can recover the costs of the direct-payment plan.

D   This statement spells out an implication of the plan but does not help to explain how the plan would not be a net burden on the budget. The passage states that payments are made *up to* a specified maximum per farm, which suggests that large farms will get less per acre than smaller farms.

E   This does not help to explain how the plan could fail to produce a net budget loss. It suggests that farmers cannot use the idled land for other revenue-producing activities—so the idled land is unlikely to be a revenue source for the government budget.

The correct answer is A.

74. A product that represents a clear technological advance over competing products can generally command a high price. Because **technological advances tend to be quickly surpassed** and companies want to make large profits while they still can, **many companies charge the maximum possible price for such a product**. But large profits on the new product will give competitors a strong incentive to quickly match the new product's capabilities. Consequently, the strategy to maximize overall profit from a new product is to charge less than the greatest possible price.

In the argument above, the two portions in **boldface** play which of the following roles?

(A) The first is a consideration raised to argue that a certain strategy is counterproductive; the second presents that strategy.

(B) The first is a consideration raised to support the strategy that the argument recommends; the second presents that strategy.

(C) The first is a consideration raised to help explain the popularity of a certain strategy; the second presents that strategy.

(D) The first is an assumption, rejected by the argument, that has been used to justify a course of action; the second presents that course of action.

(E) The first is a consideration that has been used to justify adopting a certain strategy; the second presents the intended outcome of that strategy.

Argument Construction

Situation   Often, when a company comes out with an innovative product, it will price the product as high as it can to maximize profits before the competitors quickly catch up. But this is not a good strategy because the very high price of the new product only encourages competitors to match the technological advance more quickly.

Reasoning   *Which option best describes the roles that the boldface portions play in the argument?* This type of item concerns only the argument's structure—the way it is intended to work, not the quality of the argument or what might strengthen or weaken the argument. So even if a boldface portion could be used by the argument in a certain way, all that matters is its actual intended role. The fact that *technological advances tend to be quickly surpassed* serves to partly explain why *many companies charge the maximum possible price for such a product*. In other words, the first boldface portion helps explain the popularity of the strategy presented in the second boldface portion. The conclusion of the argument, however, is that the strategy exemplified in this latter boldface portion is unwise, so the argument as a whole opposes that strategy.

A   Although the first boldface portion could be used as part of an argument that the strategy presented in the second boldface portion is counterproductive, that is not how it is used here. Rather, it immediately follows the word *because* and serves to explain the occurrence of what is described in the second boldface portion.

B   This is clearly wrong because the second boldface portion presents the strategy that the argument opposes.

C   **Correct.** It is the only choice that is consistent with the analysis of the reasoning presented above.

D   The first boldface portion is not an assumption rejected by the argument; rather, it is affirmed in the argument.

E   The argument does not expressly claim that the first boldface portion has been used to justify the strategy of setting the price as high as possible, although it implies that this is part of the justification that those adopting the strategy would give. More clearly, the second boldface portion does not describe the intended outcome of the strategy, but rather the means of bringing about that intended outcome (maximizing profits, by means of high prices).

The correct answer is C.

4.6 Critical Reasoning Answer Explanations

75. United States hospitals have traditionally relied primarily on revenues from paying patients to offset losses from unreimbursed care. Almost all paying patients now rely on governmental or private health insurance to pay hospital bills. Recently, insurers have been strictly limiting what they pay hospitals for the care of insured patients to amounts at or below actual costs.

Which of the following conclusions is best supported by the information above?

(A) Although the advance of technology has made expensive medical procedures available to the wealthy, such procedures are out of the reach of low-income patients.

(B) If hospitals do not find ways of raising additional income for unreimbursed care, they must either deny some of that care or suffer losses if they give it.

(C) Some patients have incomes too high for eligibility for governmental health insurance but are unable to afford private insurance for hospital care.

(D) If the hospitals reduce their costs in providing care, insurance companies will maintain the current level of reimbursement, thereby providing more funds for unreimbursed care.

(E) Even though philanthropic donations have traditionally provided some support for the hospitals, such donations are at present declining.

Argument Construction

Situation Hospitals have historically used the revenues from paying patients to compensate for the costs of unreimbursed care, and most paying patients rely on insurance to pay the hospital bills. However, health insurers have recently begun to strictly limit what is paid to the hospitals to amounts at or below the hospital's actual costs.

Reasoning *What conclusion can be drawn from the information in the passage?* The passage shows that with the recent change, paying patients will no longer be helping to cover the costs of unreimbursed care. What will happen to unreimbursed care? Either the hospitals must figure out a new way to cover the costs, or they must deny care. The only other option is to suffer the losses incurred by unreimbursed care.

A The passage does not examine specific medical procedures, so the conclusion that they are available only to some is not warranted.

B **Correct.** This statement properly identifies a conclusion that can be drawn from the passage.

C The passage does not discuss differences between health insurance plans, so no conclusion about them can be drawn.

D The passage states that insurance companies will only reimburse *amounts at or below actual costs*, so any reductions in the costs of health care delivery will result in lower reimbursements.

E No information is provided about the role of philanthropic donations, so no conclusion about them may be drawn.

The correct answer is B.

76. Generally scientists enter their field with the goal of doing important new research and accept as their colleagues those with similar motivation. Therefore, when any scientist wins renown as an expounder of science to general audiences, most other scientists conclude that this popularizer should no longer be regarded as a true colleague.

The explanation offered above for the low esteem in which scientific popularizers are held by research scientists assumes that

(A) serious scientific research is not a solitary activity, but relies on active cooperation among a group of colleagues

(B) research scientists tend not to regard as colleagues those scientists whose renown they envy

(C) a scientist can become a famous popularizer without having completed any important research

(D) research scientists believe that those who are well known as popularizers of science are not motivated to do important new research

(E) no important new research can be accessible to or accurately assessed by those who are not themselves scientists

Argument Construction

Situation   Research scientists desire to do important new research and treat as colleagues just those who have a similar desire. When a scientist becomes popular among a general audience for explaining principles of science, other scientists have less esteem for this popularizer, no longer regarding such a scientist as a serious colleague.

Reasoning   *What assumption do research scientists make about scientists who become popularizers?* The community of scientists shares a common goal: to do important new research. What would cause this community to disapprove of a popularizer and to cease to regard the popularizer as a colleague? It must be because many scientists believe that becoming a popularizer is incompatible with desiring to do important new research.

A   Many scientists make this assumption, of course—but it is not an assumption on which the explanation specifically depends. The explanation concerns the scientists' motivation, not their style of doing research.

B   This statement gives another reason that scientists may reject a popularizer, but because it is not the reason implied in the passage, it is not assumed.

C   Even if this is true, it does not address the core issue of the argument: what scientists believe about the *motivation* of popularizers.

D   **Correct.** This statement properly identifies an assumption on which the explanation for scientists' rejection of popularizers depends.

E   The passage is not concerned with whether nonscientists can understand new research, but rather with the beliefs and motivations of scientists who reject popularizers as colleagues.

The correct answer is D.

77. Country Y uses its scarce foreign-exchange reserves to buy scrap iron for recycling into steel. Although the steel thus produced earns more foreign exchange than it costs, that policy is foolish. Country Y's own territory has vast deposits of iron ore, which can be mined with minimal expenditure of foreign exchange.

    Which of the following, if true, provides the strongest support for Country Y's policy of buying scrap iron abroad?

    (A) The price of scrap iron on international markets rose significantly in 1987.
    (B) Country Y's foreign-exchange reserves dropped significantly in 1987.
    (C) There is virtually no difference in quality between steel produced from scrap iron and that produced from iron ore.
    (D) Scrap iron is now used in the production of roughly half the steel used in the world today, and experts predict that scrap iron will be used even more extensively in the future.
    (E) Furnaces that process scrap iron can be built and operated in Country Y with substantially less foreign exchange than can furnaces that process iron ore.

    Evaluation of a Plan

    Situation   A country could mine its vast deposits of iron ore with minimal expenditure of foreign exchange. Nevertheless, it uses its scarce foreign-exchange reserves to buy scrap iron for recycling into steel; this steel earns more foreign exchange than it costs to produce.

    Reasoning   *Which statement supports the policy of buying scrap iron abroad?* The country is using scant foreign-exchange reserves to buy scrap iron when it could instead be mining its own iron ore with minimal expenditure of foreign exchange. But if processing the scrap iron involves far less expenditure of foreign exchange than processing the raw iron ore, the policy is justified.

    A   A significant increase in the international price of scrap iron would be a reason against the policy.

    B   A significant drop in foreign-exchange reserves means that conserving the reserves is all the more important, so this statement provides no support for the current policy.

    C   This statement helps to preempt a possible objection to the present policy—namely that steel from scrap iron is inferior to steel from iron ore. But it equally helps to preempt a possible objection to *changing* the present policy—namely that steel from iron ore is inferior to steel from scrap iron. It therefore provides no evidence that would weigh distinctly in favor of maintaining the present policy, as opposed to changing it.

    D   The increasing use of scrap iron for recycling into steel merely suggests that steel from scrap iron is an acceptable alternative to steel from iron ore. This general claim does not address the issue of whether Country Y's policy involves a prudent use of foreign exchange.

    E   **Correct.** This statement properly identifies a factor that supports the policy.

    The correct answer is E.

78. Which of the following most logically completes the passage?

The figures in portraits by the Spanish painter El Greco (1541–1614) are systematically elongated. In El Greco's time, the intentional distortion of human figures was unprecedented in European painting. Consequently, some critics have suggested that El Greco had an astigmatism, a type of visual impairment, that resulted in people appearing to him in the distorted way that is characteristic of his paintings. However, this suggestion cannot be the explanation, because _____.

(A) several twentieth-century artists have consciously adopted from El Greco's paintings the systematic elongation of the human form

(B) some people do have elongated bodies somewhat like those depicted in El Greco's portraits

(C) if El Greco had an astigmatism, then, relative to how people looked to him, the elongated figures in his paintings would have appeared to him to be distorted

(D) even if El Greco had an astigmatism, there would have been no correction for it available in the period in which he lived

(E) there were non-European artists, even in El Greco's time, who included in their works human figures that were intentionally distorted

Argument Construction

Situation   Figures in portraits by the Spanish painter El Greco are elongated. Some critics infer that this was because El Greco suffered from an astigmatism that made people appear elongated to him. But this explanation cannot be correct.

Reasoning   *Which option would most logically complete the argument?* We need something that provides the best reason for thinking that the explanation suggested by critics— astigmatism—cannot be right. The critics' explanation might seem to work because ordinarily an artist would try to paint an image of a person so that the image would have the same proportions as the perceived person. So if people seemed to El Greco to have longer arms and legs than they actually had, the arms and legs of the painted figures should appear to others to be longer than people's arms and legs normally are. This is how the explanation seems to make sense. But if astigmatism were the explanation, then the elongated images in his pictures should have appeared to El Greco to be too long: he would have perceived the images as longer than they actually are—and therefore as inaccurate representations of what he perceived. So astigmatism cannot be a sufficient explanation for the elongated figures in his paintings.

A   Even if subsequent artists intentionally depicted human forms as more elongated than human figures actually are, and they did so to mimic El Greco's painted figures, that does not mean that El Greco's figures were intentionally elongated.

B   Although this option provides another possible explanation for El Greco's elongated figures, it provides no evidence that the people El Greco painted had such elongated figures.

C   **Correct.** El Greco would have perceived the images of people in his paintings as too long, relative to his perception of the people themselves. This means that even if El Greco did have astigmatism, that factor would not provide an answer to the question: Why did El Greco paint images that he knew were distorted?

D   The absence of an ability to correct astigmatism in El Greco's day does not undermine the hypothesis that it was astigmatism that caused El Greco to paint elongated figures.

E   Again, this suggests another possible explanation for the distortion—namely, that El Greco did it deliberately—but it does not provide any reason to think that this is the correct explanation (and that the critics' explanation is actually incorrect).

The correct answer is C.

79. Consumer health advocate: Your candy company adds caffeine to your chocolate candy bars so that each one delivers a specified amount of caffeine. Since caffeine is highly addictive, this indicates that you intend to keep your customers addicted.

    Candy manufacturer: Our manufacturing process results in there being less caffeine in each chocolate candy bar than in the unprocessed cacao beans from which the chocolate is made.

    The candy manufacturer's response is flawed as a refutation of the consumer health advocate's argument because it

    (A) fails to address the issue of whether the level of caffeine in the candy bars sold by the manufacturer is enough to keep people addicted
    (B) assumes without warrant that all unprocessed cacao beans contain a uniform amount of caffeine
    (C) does not specify exactly how caffeine is lost in the manufacturing process
    (D) treats the consumer health advocate's argument as though it were about each candy bar rather than about the manufacturer's candy in general
    (E) merely contradicts the consumer health advocate's conclusion without giving any reason to believe that the advocate's reasoning is unsound

Argument Evaluation

Situation   A candy manufacturer is accused of adding caffeine, an addictive substance, to its chocolate candy bars with the intent of keeping its customers addicted. The candy manufacturer responds to this accusation by saying that there is less caffeine in each chocolate candy bar than in the unprocessed cacao beans from which the chocolate is made.

Reasoning   *What is the flaw in the candy manufacturer's response?* First consider whether the response indeed refutes the advocate's charge. In actuality, instead of focusing on the details of the accusation—adding caffeine to its chocolate bars to keep customers addicted—the manufacturer substitutes an entirely different subject, the amount of caffeine in cacao beans. The manufacturer's response is a diversion, not an answer.

A   **Correct.** This statement properly identifies the flaw in the response. The candy manufacturer does not answer the question whether adding caffeine to candy bars is designed to make them addictive.

B   Even if the manufacturer did make this assumption, the information is not relevant to the accusation, which is not concerned with naturally occurring caffeine in cacao beans.

C   The precise amount of caffeine lost in the manufacturing process is not at issue.

D   The manufacturer does not treat the health advocate's argument this way.

E   The manufacturer does not contradict the accusation, but rather avoids it.

The correct answer is A.

80. To evaluate a plan to save money on office-space expenditures by having its employees work at home, XYZ Company asked volunteers from its staff to try the arrangement for six months. During this period, the productivity of these employees was as high as or higher than before.

Which of the following, if true, would argue most strongly against deciding, on the basis of the trial results, to implement the company's plan?

(A) The employees who agreed to participate in the test of the plan were among the company's most self-motivated and independent workers.

(B) The savings that would accrue from reduced office-space expenditures alone would be sufficient to justify the arrangement for the company, apart from any productivity increases.

(C) Other companies that have achieved successful results from work-at-home plans have workforces that are substantially larger than that of XYZ.

(D) The volunteers who worked at home were able to communicate with other employees as necessary for performing the work.

(E) Minor changes in the way office work is organized at XYZ would yield increases in employee productivity similar to those achieved in the trial.

Evaluation of a Plan

Situation To save money on office space expenditures, a company considers having employees work at home. A six-month trial with employees who have volunteered to test the plan shows their productivity to be as high as or higher than before.

Reasoning *Why would the trial results NOT provide a good reason to implement the plan?* Generalizing from a small sample to the group depends on having a sample that is representative. In this case, the employees who participated in the trial are not representative of all employees. The employees who volunteered for the trial may be the type of employees who would be most likely to work successfully at home. It would not be wise to base a generalization about all employees on this sample.

A **Correct.** This statement properly identifies a flaw in the trial that is the basis for the plan.

B This statement supports the implementation of the plan. Moreover, it is not based on the trial results, so it does not answer the question.

C The passage gives no information about how company size might affect the implementation of the plan or the reliability of the trial results.

D If anything, this would tend to support the plan.

E The goal of the plan is to save money on office space, not to increase productivity, so an alternative plan to increase productivity is irrelevant.

The correct answer is A.

81. Political Advertisement:

    Mayor Delmont's critics complain about the jobs that were lost in the city under Delmont's leadership. Yet the fact is that not only were more jobs created than were eliminated, but each year since Delmont took office the average pay for the new jobs created has been higher than that year's average pay for jobs citywide. So it stands to reason that throughout Delmont's tenure the average paycheck in this city has been getting steadily bigger.

    Which of the following, if true, most seriously weakens the argument in the advertisement?

    (A) The unemployment rate in the city is higher today than it was when Mayor Delmont took office.

    (B) The average pay for jobs in the city was at a ten-year low when Mayor Delmont took office.

    (C) Each year during Mayor Delmont's tenure, the average pay for jobs that were eliminated has been higher than the average pay for jobs citywide.

    (D) Most of the jobs eliminated during Mayor Delmont's tenure were in declining industries.

    (E) The average pay for jobs in the city is currently lower than it is for jobs in the suburbs surrounding the city.

Argument Evaluation

Situation   Every year since Mayor Delmont took office, average pay for new jobs has exceeded average pay for jobs citywide. So, the average paycheck in the city has been increasing since Delmont took office.

Reasoning   *Which option, if true, would most seriously weaken the argument?* If average pay for new jobs continually exceeds that for jobs generally, new jobs pay better (on average) than old jobs that still exist. But suppose the following occurred. Every year all of the highest paying jobs are eliminated and replaced with somewhat lower-paying jobs that still pay more than the average job. The result would be that every year the average pay for a new job would be greater than that for existing jobs, but the average pay for all jobs would nonetheless decrease. Thus, if every year during the mayor's tenure the jobs that were eliminated paid better on average than jobs citywide, that would seriously weaken the argument: the conclusion could be false even if the information on which it is based is true.

A   The percentage of people in the city who have a job has no direct bearing on whether the average pay for jobs citywide is increasing or decreasing.

B   Whether the average pay was low when the mayor took office in comparison to the ten preceding years is immaterial to the comparison addressed in the argument's conclusion.

C   **Correct.** This information weakens the argument because it opens up the possibility that the jobs eliminated had higher average pay than the jobs created during Mayor Delmont's tenure. This in turn would mean that the average pay was not increasing during Mayor Delmont's tenure.

D   This, too, has no bearing on the argument, because we have no information about the average pay for jobs in those declining industries.

E   This is also irrelevant. No comparison is made (or implied) in the argument between jobs in the city and jobs in the suburbs.

The correct answer is C.

82. Vitacorp, a manufacturer, wishes to make its information booth at an industry convention more productive in terms of boosting sales. The booth offers information introducing the company's new products and services. To achieve the desired result, Vitacorp's marketing department will attempt to attract more people to the booth. The marketing director's first measure was to instruct each salesperson to call his or her five best customers and personally invite them to visit the booth.

Which of the following, if true, most strongly supports the prediction that the marketing director's first measure will contribute to meeting the goal of boosting sales?

(A) Vitacorp's salespeople routinely inform each important customer about new products and services as soon as the decision to launch them has been made.

(B) Many of Vitacorp's competitors have made plans for making their own information booths more productive in increasing sales.

(C) An information booth that is well attended tends to attract visitors who would not otherwise have attended the booth.

(D) Most of Vitacorp's best customers also have business dealings with Vitacorp's competitors.

(E) Vitacorp has fewer new products and services available this year than it had in previous years.

Evaluation of a Plan

Situation   A manufacturer wants increased sales from its information booth at an industry convention. To boost sales, the marketing department seeks to attract more people to the booth, and the marketing director tells the salespeople to invite their best customers to visit the booth.

Reasoning   *Which point best supports the marketing director's plan?* First ask what would be a valid reason for inviting faithful customers to visit the booth. Such invitations should assure that the booth will generally be busy with visitors. If people are more attracted to a well-attended booth than to an empty one, then more potential customers are likely to visit the busy booth, and more visitors should produce more sales. The marketing director is operating on the principle that success breeds success. Making sure that the booth is well attended by Vitacorp's current customers is likely to attract more potential customers and thus boost sales.

A   If the best customers already have all available new product and service information, they are unlikely to respond to the invitation to visit the booth; this point is a weakness in the plan.

B   Competitors' efforts toward the same goal may hurt Vitacorp's efforts, so this point does not support the plan.

C   **Correct.** This statement properly identifies a point supporting the marketing director's plan.

D   The plan simply aims to attract more visitors to Vitacorp's booth to encourage more sales and does not address the fact that Vitacorp shares its customers with its competitors.

E   This information, if anything, would suggest that the plan would be less successful.

The correct answer is C.

83. An eyeglass manufacturer tried to boost sales for the summer quarter by offering its distributors a special discount if their orders for that quarter exceeded those for last year's summer quarter by at least 20 percent. Many distributors qualified for this discount. Even with much merchandise discounted, sales increased enough to produce a healthy gain in net profits. The manufacturer plans to repeat this success by offering the same sort of discount for the fall quarter.

Which of the following, if true, most clearly points to a flaw in the manufacturer's plan to repeat the successful performance of the summer quarter?

(A) In general, a distributor's orders for the summer quarter are no higher than those for the spring quarter.

(B) Along with offering special discounts to qualifying distributors, the manufacturer increased newspaper and radio advertising in those distributors' sales areas.

(C) The distributors most likely to qualify for the manufacturer's special discount are those whose orders were unusually low a year earlier.

(D) The distributors who qualified for the manufacturer's special discount were free to decide how much of that discount to pass on to their own customers.

(E) The distributors' ordering more goods in the summer quarter left them overstocked for the fall quarter.

Evaluation of a Plan

Situation	A manufacturer successfully boosted sales and gained net profits for the summer quarter by giving distributors a discount if their orders exceeded the previous summer's orders by 20 percent. The manufacturer plans to repeat the success by offering the discount again in the fall quarter.
Reasoning	*What is the flaw in the manufacturer's plan?* The plan assumes that an action that succeeded once will work a second time. Why might the plan not work this time? If the distributors increased their orders during the summer simply because they were eager to take advantage of the discount, the result may be that they are now overstocked for the fall quarter. If so, they will not need to place orders for more goods, and the plan of continuing the discount will have less chance of success now.

A   This is irrelevant to the plan since relevant quarters—fall and summer—are not being compared.

B   Increased advertising should continue to contribute to the plan's success.

C   Even if the qualifying distributors reached only normal levels of sales, there may be other distributors who will qualify in the fall because they had low sales one year earlier.

D   The distributors' freedom to decide how much of the discount to pass on to customers is equally true in both summer and fall quarters and should not affect the success of the plan.

E   **Correct.** This statement properly identifies a flaw in the plan.

The correct answer is E.

5.0   Sentence Correction

5.0 Sentence Correction

Sentence correction questions appear in the Verbal section of the GMAT® test. The Verbal section uses multiple-choice questions to measure your ability to read and comprehend written material, to reason and evaluate arguments, and to correct written material to conform to standard written English. Because the Verbal section includes passages from several different content areas, you may be generally familiar with some of the material; however, neither the passages nor the questions assume detailed knowledge of the topics discussed. Sentence correction questions are intermingled with critical reasoning and reading comprehension questions throughout the Verbal section of the test. You will have 75 minutes to complete the Verbal section, or about 1¾ minutes to answer each question.

Sentence correction questions present a statement in which words are underlined. The questions ask you to select from the answer options the best expression of the idea or relationship described in the underlined section. The first answer choice always repeats the original phrasing, whereas the other four provide alternatives. In some cases, the original phrasing is the best choice. In other cases, the underlined section has obvious or subtle errors that require correction. These questions require you to be familiar with the stylistic conventions and grammatical rules of standard written English and to demonstrate your ability to improve incorrect or ineffective expressions.

You should begin these questions by reading the sentence carefully. Note whether there are any obvious grammatical errors as you read the underlined section. Then read the five answer choices carefully. If there was a subtle error you did not recognize the first time you read the sentence, it may become apparent after you have read the answer choices. If the error is still unclear, see whether you can eliminate some of the answers as being incorrect. Remember that in some cases, the original selection may be the best answer.

5.1 Basic English Grammar Rules

Sentence correction questions ask you to recognize and potentially correct at least one of the following grammar rules. However, these rules are not exhaustive. If you are interested in learning more about English grammar as a way to prepare for the GMAT test, there are several resources available on the Web.

Agreement

Standard English requires elements within a sentence to be consistent. There are two types of agreement: noun-verb and pronoun.

Noun-verb agreement: Singular subjects take singular verbs, whereas plural subjects take plural verbs.
Examples:
Correct: "I walk to the store." Incorrect: "I walks to the store."
Correct: "We go to school." Incorrect: "We goes to school."
Correct: "The number of residents has grown." Incorrect: "The number of residents have grown."
Correct: "The masses have spoken." Incorrect: "The masses has spoken."

Pronoun agreement: A pronoun must agree with the noun or pronoun it refers to in person, number, and gender.

Examples:

Correct: "When you dream, you are usually asleep." Incorrect: "When one dreams, you are usually asleep."

Correct: "When the kids went to sleep, they slept like logs."

Incorrect: "When the kids went to sleep, he slept like a log."

Diction

Words should be chosen to reflect correctly and effectively the appropriate part of speech. There are several words that are commonly used incorrectly. When answering sentence correction questions, pay attention to the following conventions.

Among/between: Among is used to refer to relationships involving more than two objects. *Between* is used to refer to relationships involving only two objects.

Examples:

Correct: "We divided our winnings among the three of us." Incorrect: "We divided our winnings between the three of us."

Correct: "She and I divided the cake between us." Incorrect: "She and I divided the cake among us."

As/like: As can be a preposition meaning "in the capacity of," but more often is a conjunction of manner and is followed by a verb. *Like* is generally used as a preposition, and therefore is followed by a noun, an object pronoun, or a verb ending in *ing.*

Examples:

Correct: "I work as a librarian." Incorrect: "I work like a librarian."

Correct: "Do as I say, not as I do." Incorrect: "Do like I say, not like I do."

Correct: "It felt like a dream." Incorrect: "It felt as a dream."

Correct: "People like you inspire me." Incorrect: "People as you inspire me."

Correct: "There's nothing like biking on a warm, autumn day." Incorrect: "There's nothing as biking on a warm autumn day."

Mass and count words: Mass words are nouns quantified by an amount rather than by a number. *Count* nouns can be quantified by a number.

Examples:

Correct: "We bought a loaf of bread." Incorrect: "We bought one bread."

Correct: "He wished me much happiness." Incorrect: "He wished me many happinesses."

Correct: "We passed many buildings." Incorrect: "We passed much buildings."

Pronouns: Myself should not be used as a substitute for *I* or *me.*

Examples:

Correct: "Mom and I had to go to the store." Incorrect: "Mom and myself had to go to the store."

Correct: "He gave the present to Dad and me." Incorrect: "He gave the present to Dad and myself."

Grammatical Construction

Good grammar requires complete sentences. Be on the lookout for improperly formed constructions.

Fragments: Parts of a sentence that are disconnected from the main clause are called fragments.
Example:
Correct: "We saw the doctor and his nurse at the party." Incorrect: "We saw the doctor at the party. And his nurse."

Run-on sentences: A run-on sentence is two independent clauses that run together without proper punctuation.
Examples:
Correct: "Jose Canseco is still a feared batter; most pitchers don't want to face him."
Incorrect: "Jose Canseco is still a feared batter most pitchers don't want to face him."

Constructions: Avoid wordy, redundant constructions.
Example:
Correct: "We could not come to the meeting because of a conflict." Incorrect: "The reason we could not come to the meeting is because of a conflict."

Idiom

It is important to avoid nonstandard expressions, although English idioms sometimes do not follow conventional grammatical rules. Be careful to use the correct idiom when using the constructions and parts of speech.

Prepositions: Specific prepositions have specific purposes.
Examples:
Correct: "She likes to jog in the morning." Incorrect: "She likes to jog on the morning."
Correct: "They ranged in age from 10 to 15." Incorrect: "They ranged in age from 10 up to 15."

Correlatives: Word combinations such as "not only . . . but also" should be followed by an element of the same grammatical type.
Examples:
Correct: "I have called not only to thank her but also to tell her about the next meeting."
Incorrect: "I have called not only to thank her but also I told her about the next meeting."

Forms of comparison: Many forms follow precise constructions. *Fewer* refers to a specific number, whereas *less than* refers to a continuous quantity. *Between . . . and* is the correct form to designate a choice. *Farther* refers to distance, whereas *further* refers to degree.
Examples:
Correct: "There were fewer children in my class this year." Incorrect: "There were less children in my class this year."
Correct: "There was less devastation than I was told." Incorrect: "There was fewer devastation than I was told."
Correct: "We had to choose between chocolate and vanilla." Incorrect: "We had to choose between chocolate or vanilla." (It is also correct to say, "We had to choose chocolate or vanilla.")
Correct: "I ran farther than John, but he took his weight training further than I did."
Incorrect: "I ran further than John, but he took his weight training farther than I did."

Logical Predication

Watch out for phrases that detract from the logical argument.

Modification problems: Modifiers should be positioned so it is clear what word or words they are meant to modify. If modifiers are not positioned clearly, they can cause illogical references or comparisons, or distort the meaning of the statement.

Examples:

Correct: "I put the cake that I baked by the door." Incorrect: "I put the cake by the door that I baked."

Correct: "Reading my mind, she gave me the delicious cookie." Incorrect: "Reading my mind, the cookie she gave me was delicious."

Correct: "In the Middle Ages, the world was believed to be flat." Incorrect: "In the Middle Ages, the world was flat."

Parallelism

Constructing a sentence that is parallel in structure depends on making sure that the different elements in the sentence balance each other; this is a little bit like making sure that the two sides of a mathematical equation are balanced. To make sure that a sentence is grammatically correct, check to see that phrases, clauses, verbs, and other sentence elements parallel each other.

Examples:

Correct: "I took a bath, went to sleep, and woke up refreshed." Incorrect: "I took a bath, sleeping, and waking up refreshed."

Correct: "The only way to know is to take the plunge." Incorrect: "The only way to know is taking the plunge."

Rhetorical Construction

Good sentence structure avoids constructions that are awkward, wordy, redundant, imprecise, or unclear, even when they are free of grammatical errors.

Example:

Correct: "Before we left on vacation, we watered the plants, checked to see that the stove was off, and set the burglar alarm." Incorrect: "Before we left to go on our vacation, we watered, checked to be sure that the stove had been turned off, and set it."

Verb Form

In addition to watching for problems of agreement or parallelism, make sure that verbs are used in the correct tense. Be alert to whether a verb should reflect past, present, or future tense.

Example:

Correct: "I went to school yesterday." "I go to school every weekday." "I will go to school tomorrow."

Each tense also has a perfect form (used with the past participle—e.g., walked, ran), a progressive form (used with the present participle—e.g., walking, running), and a perfect progressive form (also used with the present participle—e.g., walking, running).

Present perfect: Used with *has* or *have*, the present perfect tense describes an action that occurred at an indefinite time in the past or that began in the past and continues into the present.

Examples:

Correct: "I have traveled all over the world." (at an indefinite time)

Correct: "He has gone to school since he was five years old." (continues into the present)

Past perfect: This verb form is used with *had* to show the order of two events that took place in the past.

Example:

Correct: "By the time I left for school, the cake had been baked."

Future perfect: Used with *will have*, this verb form describes an event in the future that will precede another event.

Example:

Correct: "By the end of the day, I will have studied for all my tests."

Present progressive: Used with *am*, *is*, or *are*, this verb form describes an ongoing action that is happening now.

Example:

Correct: "I am studying for exams." "The student is studying for exams." "We are studying for exams."

Past progressive: Used with *was* or *were*, this verb form describes something that was happening when another action occurred.

Example:

Correct: "The student was studying when the fire alarm rang." "They were studying when the fire broke out."

Future progressive: Used with *will be* or *shall be*, this verb tense describes an ongoing action that will continue into the future.

Example:

Correct: "The students will be studying for exams throughout the month of December."

Present perfect progressive: Used with *have been* or *has been*, this verb tense describes something that began in the past, continues into the present, and may continue into the future.

Example:

Correct: "The student has been studying hard in the hope of acing the test."

Past perfect progressive: Used with *had been*, this verb form describes an action of some duration that was completed before another past action occurred.

Example:

Correct: "Before the fire alarm rang, the student had been studying."

Future perfect progressive: Used with *will have been*, this verb form describes a future, ongoing action that will occur before a specified time.

Example:

Correct: "By the end of next year, the students will have been studying math for five years."

5.2 Study Suggestions

There are two basic ways you can study for sentence correction questions:

- **Read material that reflects standard usage.**
  One way to gain familiarity with the basic conventions of standard written English is simply to read. Suitable material will usually be found in good magazines and nonfiction books, editorials in outstanding newspapers, and the collections of essays used by many college and university writing courses.

- **Review basic rules of grammar and practice with writing exercises.**
  Begin by reviewing the grammar rules laid out in this chapter. Then, if you have school assignments (such as essays and research papers) that have been carefully evaluated for grammatical errors, it may be helpful to review the comments and corrections.

5.3 What Is Measured

Sentence correction questions test three broad aspects of language proficiency:

- **Correct expression**
  A correct sentence is grammatically and structurally sound. It conforms to all the rules of standard written English, including noun-verb agreement, noun-pronoun agreement, pronoun consistency, pronoun case, and verb tense sequence. A correct sentence will not have dangling, misplaced, or improperly formed modifiers; unidiomatic or inconsistent expressions; or faults in parallel construction.

- **Effective expression**
  An effective sentence expresses an idea or relationship clearly and concisely as well as grammatically. This does not mean that the choice with the fewest and simplest words is necessarily the best answer. It means that there are no superfluous words or needlessly complicated expressions in the best choice.

- **Proper diction**
  An effective sentence also uses proper diction. (Diction refers to the standard dictionary meanings of words and the appropriateness of words in context.) In evaluating the diction of a sentence, you must be able to recognize whether the words are well chosen, accurate, and suitable for the context.

5.4 Test-Taking Strategies

1. **Read the entire sentence carefully.**
   Try to understand the specific idea or relationship that the sentence should express.

2. **Evaluate the underlined passage for errors and possible corrections before reading the answer choices.**
   This strategy will help you discriminate among the answer choices. Remember, in some cases the underlined passage is correct.

3. **Read each answer choice carefully.**

   The first answer choice always repeats the underlined portion of the original sentence. Choose this answer if you think that the sentence is best as originally written, but do so *only after* examining all the other choices.

4. **Try to determine how to correct what you consider to be wrong with the original sentence.**

   Some of the answer choices may change things that are not wrong, whereas others may not change everything that is wrong.

5. **Make sure that you evaluate the sentence and the choices thoroughly.**

   Pay attention to general clarity, grammatical and idiomatic usage, economy and precision of language, and appropriateness of diction.

6. **Read the whole sentence, substituting the choice that you prefer for the underlined passage.**

   A choice may be wrong because it does not fit grammatically or structurally with the rest of the sentence. Remember that some sentences will require no correction. When the given sentence requires no correction, choose the first answer.

5.5 The Directions

These are the directions that you will see for sentence correction questions when you take the GMAT test. If you read them carefully and understand them clearly before going to sit for the test, you will not need to spend too much time reviewing them once you are at the test center and the test is under way.

Sentence correction questions present a sentence, part or all of which is underlined. Beneath the sentence, you will find five ways of phrasing the underlined passage. The first answer choice repeats the original underlined passage; the other four are different. If you think the original phrasing is best, choose the first answer; otherwise choose one of the others.

This type of question tests your ability to recognize the correctness and effectiveness of expression in standard written English. In choosing your answer, follow the requirements of standard written English; that is, pay attention to grammar, choice of words, and sentence construction. Choose the answer that produces the most effective sentence; this answer should be clear and exact, without awkwardness, ambiguity, redundancy, or grammatical error.

5.6 Sample Questions

Each of the <u>sentence correction</u> questions presents a sentence, part of or all of which is underlined. Beneath the sentence you will find five ways of phrasing the underlined part. The first of these repeats the original; the other four are different. Follow the requirements of standard written English to choose your answer, paying attention to grammar, word choice, and sentence construction. Select the answer that produces the most effective sentence; your answer should make the sentence clear, exact, and free of grammatical error. It should also minimize awkwardness, ambiguity, and redundancy.

1. Like ants, termites have an elaborate social structure in which a few individuals reproduce and the rest <u>are serving the colony by tending juveniles, gathering food, building the nest, or they battle</u> intruders.

   (A) are serving the colony by tending juveniles, gathering food, building the nest, or they battle
   (B) are serving the colony in that they tend juveniles, gather food, build the nest, or battle
   (C) serve the colony, tending juveniles, gathering food, building the nest, or by battling
   (D) serve the colony by tending juveniles, gathering food, by building the nest, or by battling
   (E) serve the colony by tending juveniles, gathering food, building the nest, or battling

2. Some bat caves, like honeybee hives, have residents that take on different duties such as defending the entrance, <u>acting as sentinels and to sound</u> a warning at the approach of danger, and scouting outside the cave for new food and roosting sites.

   (A) acting as sentinels and to sound
   (B) acting as sentinels and sounding
   (C) to act as sentinels and sound
   (D) to act as sentinels and to sound
   (E) to act as a sentinel sounding

3. <u>However much United States voters may agree that</u> there is waste in government and that the government as a whole spends beyond its means, it is difficult to find broad support for a movement toward a minimal state.

   (A) However much United States voters may agree that
   (B) Despite the agreement among United States voters to the fact
   (C) Although United States voters agree
   (D) Even though United States voters may agree
   (E) There is agreement among United States voters that

4. The voluminous personal papers of Thomas Alva Edison reveal that his inventions typically <u>sprang to life not in a flash of inspiration but evolved slowly</u> from previous works.

   (A) sprang to life not in a flash of inspiration but evolved slowly
   (B) sprang to life not in a flash of inspiration but were slowly evolved
   (C) did not spring to life in a flash of inspiration but evolved slowly
   (D) did not spring to life in a flash of inspiration but had slowly evolved
   (E) did not spring to life in a flash of inspiration but they were slowly evolved

5.   Hundreds of species of fish generate and discharge electric currents, in bursts or as steady electric fields around their bodies, using their power either to find and attack prey, to defend themselves, or also for communicating and navigating.

   (A)   either to find and attack prey, to defend themselves, or also for communicating and navigating

   (B)   either for finding and attacking prey, defend themselves, or for communication and navigation

   (C)   to find and attack prey, for defense, or communication and navigation

   (D)   for finding and attacking prey, to defend themselves, or also for communication and navigation

   (E)   to find and attack prey, to defend themselves, or to communicate and navigate

6.   A Labor Department study states that the numbers of women employed outside the home grew by more than a thirty-five percent increase in the past decade and accounted for more than sixty-two percent of the total growth in the civilian workforce.

   (A)   numbers of women employed outside the home grew by more than a thirty-five percent increase

   (B)   numbers of women employed outside the home grew more than thirty-five percent

   (C)   numbers of women employed outside the home were raised by more than thirty-five percent

   (D)   number of women employed outside the home increased by more than thirty-five percent

   (E)   number of women employed outside the home was raised by more than a thirty-five percent increase

7.   From the earliest days of the tribe, kinship determined the way in which the Ojibwa society organized its labor, provided access to its resources, and defined rights and obligations involved in the distribution and consumption of those resources.

   (A)   and defined rights and obligations involved in the distribution and consumption of those resources

   (B)   defining rights and obligations involved in their distribution and consumption

   (C)   and defined rights and obligations as they were involved in its distribution and consumption

   (D)   whose rights and obligations were defined in their distribution and consumption

   (E)   the distribution and consumption of them defined by rights and obligations

8.   As the cost of wireless service has steadily dropped over the last year and as mobile phones have become increasingly common, many people are finding that they can avoid toll charges on their home phones, using their mobile phones for making long-distance calls at night or on weekends, at a time which many wireless companies provide unlimited airtime for a small monthly fee.

   (A)   phones, using their mobile phones for making long-distance calls at night or on weekends, at a time which

   (B)   phones, instead using mobile phones to make long-distance calls during the night or weekends, during which

   (C)   phones by using their mobile phones to make long-distance calls at night or on weekends, when

   (D)   phones using mobile phones for making long-distance calls during the night or weekends, when

   (E)   phones when using their mobile phones to make long-distance calls at night or on weekends, a time which

9. Delighted by the reported earnings for the first quarter of the fiscal year, <u>it was decided by the company manager to give her staff a raise</u>.

   (A) it was decided by the company manager to give her staff a raise
   (B) the decision of the company manager was to give her staff a raise
   (C) the company manager decided to give her staff a raise
   (D) the staff was given a raise by the company manager
   (E) a raise was given to the staff by the company manager

10. <u>The rising of costs</u> of data-processing operations at many financial institutions has created a growing opportunity for independent companies to provide these services more efficiently and at lower cost.

    (A) The rising of costs
    (B) Rising costs
    (C) The rising cost
    (D) Because the rising cost
    (E) Because of rising costs

11. Native to South America, <u>when peanuts were introduced to Africa by Portuguese explorers early in the sixteenth century they were quickly adopted into Africa's agriculture, probably because of being</u> so similar to the Bambarra groundnut, a popular indigenous plant.

    (A) when peanuts were introduced to Africa by Portuguese explorers early in the sixteenth century they were quickly adopted into Africa's agriculture, probably because of being
    (B) peanuts having been introduced to Africa by Portuguese explorers early in the sixteenth century and quickly adopted into Africa's agriculture, probably because of being
    (C) peanuts were introduced to Africa by Portuguese explorers early in the sixteenth century and were quickly adopted into Africa's agriculture, probably because they were
    (D) peanuts, introduced to Africa by Portuguese explorers early in the sixteenth century and quickly adopted into Africa's agriculture, probably because they were
    (E) peanuts, introduced to Africa by Portuguese explorers early in the sixteenth century and having been quickly adopted into Africa's agriculture, probably because they were

12. William H. Johnson's artistic debt to Scandinavia is evident in paintings that range from sensitive portraits of citizens in his wife's Danish home, Kerteminde, <u>and</u> awe-inspiring views of fjords and mountain peaks in the western and northern regions of Norway.

    (A) and
    (B) to
    (C) and to
    (D) with
    (E) in addition to

13. Growing competitive pressures may be encouraging auditors to bend the rules in favor of <u>clients; auditors may, for instance, allow</u> a questionable loan to remain on the books in order to maintain a bank's profits on paper.

    (A) clients; auditors may, for instance, allow
    (B) clients, as an instance, to allow
    (C) clients, like to allow
    (D) clients, such as to be allowing
    (E) clients; which might, as an instance, be the allowing of

14. The themes that Rita Dove explores in her poetry <u>is universal, encompassing much of the human condition while occasionally she deals</u> with racial issues.

    (A) is universal, encompassing much of the human condition while occasionally she deals
    (B) is universal, encompassing much of the human condition, also occasionally it deals
    (C) are universal, they encompass much of the human condition and occasionally deals
    (D) are universal, encompassing much of the human condition while occasionally dealing
    (E) are universal, they encompass much of the human condition, also occasionally are dealing

15. It is well known in the supermarket industry that how items are placed on shelves and <u>the frequency of inventory turnovers can be</u> crucial to profits.

    (A) the frequency of inventory turnovers can be
    (B) the frequency of inventory turnovers is often
    (C) the frequency with which the inventory turns over is often
    (D) how frequently is the inventory turned over are often
    (E) how frequently the inventory turns over can be

16. Iguanas have been an important food source in Latin America since prehistoric times, and <u>it is still prized as a game animal</u> by the campesinos, who typically cook the meat in a heavily spiced stew.

    (A) it is still prized as a game animal
    (B) it is still prized as game animals
    (C) they are still prized as game animals
    (D) they are still prized as being a game animal
    (E) being still prized as a game animal

17. Travelers to Mars would have to endure low levels of gravity for long periods of time, avoid large doses of radiation, <u>contend with the chemically reactive Martian soil, and perhaps even having to ward</u> off contamination by Martian life-forms.

    (A) contend with the chemically reactive Martian soil, and perhaps even having to ward
    (B) contend with the chemically reactive Martian soil, and perhaps even warding
    (C) contend with the chemically reactive Martian soil, and perhaps even ward
    (D) contending with the chemically reactive Martian soil, and perhaps even to ward
    (E) contending with the chemically reactive Martian soil, and perhaps even warding

18. <u>Except for a concert performance that the composer himself staged</u> in 1911, Scott Joplin's ragtime opera *Treemonisha* was not produced until 1972, sixty-one years after its completion.

    (A) Except for a concert performance that the composer himself staged
    (B) Except for a concert performance with the composer himself staging it
    (C) Besides a concert performance being staged by the composer himself
    (D) Excepting a concert performance that the composer himself staged
    (E) With the exception of a concert performance with the staging done by the composer himself

19. Chinese, the most ancient of living writing systems, consists of tens of thousands of ideographic characters, each character a miniature calligraphic composition inside its own square frame.

    (A) each character a miniature calligraphic composition inside its

    (B) all the characters a miniature calligraphic composition inside their

    (C) all the characters a miniature calligraphic composition inside its

    (D) every character a miniature calligraphic composition inside their

    (E) each character a miniature calligraphic composition inside their

20. Declining values for farm equipment and land, the collateral against which farmers borrow to get through the harvest season, is going to force many lenders to tighten or deny credit this spring.

    (A) the collateral against which farmers borrow to get through the harvest season, is

    (B) which farmers use as collateral to borrow against to get through the harvest season, is

    (C) the collateral which is borrowed against by farmers to get through the harvest season, is

    (D) which farmers use as collateral to borrow against to get through the harvest season, are

    (E) the collateral against which farmers borrow to get through the harvest season, are

21. While depressed property values can hurt some large investors, they are potentially devastating for homeowners, whose equity—in many cases representing a life's savings—can plunge or even disappear.

    (A) they are potentially devastating for homeowners, whose

    (B) they can potentially devastate homeowners in that their

    (C) for homeowners they are potentially devastating, because their

    (D) for homeowners, it is potentially devastating in that their

    (E) it can potentially devastate homeowners, whose

22. Japanese researchers are producing a series of robots that can identify human facial expressions, to which they will then respond; their goal is primarily creating a robot that will empathize with us.

    (A) expressions, to which they will then respond; their goal is primarily creating

    (B) expressions, then responding to them; primarily to create

    (C) expressions and then respond to them; the researchers' primary goal is to create

    (D) expressions as well as giving a response to them; their primary goal is creation of

    (E) expressions and responding to them; primarily, the researchers' goal is creating

23. Consumers may not think of household cleaning products to be hazardous substances, but many of them can be harmful to health, especially if they are used improperly.

    (A) Consumers may not think of household cleaning products to be

    (B) Consumers may not think of household cleaning products being

    (C) A consumer may not think of their household cleaning products being

    (D) A consumer may not think of household cleaning products as

    (E) Household cleaning products may not be thought of, by consumers, as

24. In recent years cattle breeders have increasingly used crossbreeding, in part that their steers should acquire certain characteristics and partly because crossbreeding is said to provide hybrid vigor.

    (A) in part that their steers should acquire certain characteristics

    (B) in part for the acquisition of certain characteristics in their steers

    (C) partly because of their steers acquiring certain characteristics

    (D) partly because certain characteristics should be acquired by their steers

    (E) partly to acquire certain characteristics in their steers

25. Like Auden, the language of James Merrill is chatty, arch, and conversational—given to complex syntactic flights as well as to prosaic free-verse strolls.

    (A) Like Auden, the language of James Merrill
    (B) Like Auden, James Merrill's language
    (C) Like Auden's, James Merrill's language
    (D) As with Auden, James Merrill's language
    (E) As is Auden's the language of James Merrill

26. The Baldrick Manufacturing Company has for several years followed a policy aimed at decreasing operating costs and improving the efficiency of its distribution system.

    (A) aimed at decreasing operating costs and improving
    (B) aimed at the decreasing of operating costs and to improve
    (C) aiming at the decreasing of operating costs and improving
    (D) the aim of which is the decreasing of operating costs and improving
    (E) with the aim to decrease operating costs and to improve

27. Obtaining an investment-grade rating will keep the county's future borrowing costs low, protect its already-tattered image, and increase its ability to buy bond insurance.

    (A) Obtaining an investment-grade rating will keep the county's future borrowing costs low, protect
    (B) To obtain an investment-grade rating will keep the county's future borrowing costs low, and protect
    (C) Having obtained an investment-grade rating will, in keeping the county's future borrowing costs low, protect
    (D) To obtain an investment-grade rating would keep the county's future borrowing costs low, protecting
    (E) Obtaining an investment-grade rating, keeping the county's borrowing costs low, would be protecting

28. Eating saltwater fish may significantly reduce the risk of heart attacks and also aid for sufferers of rheumatoid arthritis and asthma, according to three research studies published in the *New England Journal of Medicine*.

    (A) significantly reduce the risk of heart attacks and also aid for
    (B) be significant in reducing the risk of heart attacks and aid for
    (C) significantly reduce the risk of heart attacks and aid
    (D) cause a significant reduction in the risk of heart attacks and aid to
    (E) significantly reduce the risk of heart attacks as well as aiding

29. According to some economists, the July decrease in unemployment so that it was the lowest in two years suggests that the gradual improvement in the job market is continuing.

    (A) so that it was the lowest in two years
    (B) so that it was the lowest two-year rate
    (C) to what would be the lowest in two years
    (D) to a two-year low level
    (E) to the lowest level in two years

30. Thomas Eakins' powerful style and his choices of subject—the advances in modern surgery, the discipline of sport, the strains of individuals in tension with society or even with themselves—was as disturbing to his own time as it is compelling for ours.

    (A) was as disturbing to his own time as it is
    (B) were as disturbing to his own time as they are
    (C) has been as disturbing in his own time as they are
    (D) had been as disturbing in his own time as it was
    (E) have been as disturbing in his own time as

31. Nearly two tons of nuclear-reactor fuel have already been put into orbit around the Earth, and the chances of a collision involving such material increase greatly <u>as the amount of both space debris and satellites continue to rise</u>.

    (A) as the amount of both space debris and satellites continue to rise

    (B) as the rise continues in both the amount of satellites and space debris

    (C) as the amount of space debris and the number of satellites continue to rise

    (D) with the continually increasing amount of space debris and the number of satellites

    (E) with the amount of space debris continuing to increase along with the number of satellites

32. <u>Like Rousseau, Tolstoi rebelled</u> against the unnatural complexity of human relations in modern society.

    (A) Like Rousseau, Tolstoi rebelled

    (B) Like Rousseau, Tolstoi's rebellion was

    (C) As Rousseau, Tolstoi rebelled

    (D) As did Rousseau, Tolstoi's rebellion was

    (E) Tolstoi's rebellion, as Rousseau's, was

33. The Wallerstein study indicates that even after a decade young men and women still experience some of the effects of a divorce <u>occurring when a child</u>.

    (A) occurring when a child

    (B) occurring when children

    (C) that occurred when a child

    (D) that occurred when they were children

    (E) that has occurred as each was a child

34. Lacking information about energy use, people tend to overestimate the amount of energy used by <u>equipment, such as lights, that are visible and must be turned on and off and underestimate that</u> used by unobtrusive equipment, such as water heaters.

    (A) equipment, such as lights, that are visible and must be turned on and off and underestimate that

    (B) equipment, such as lights, that are visible and must be turned on and off and underestimate it when

    (C) equipment, such as lights, that is visible and must be turned on and off and underestimate it when

    (D) visible equipment, such as lights, that must be turned on and off and underestimate that

    (E) visible equipment, such as lights, that must be turned on and off and underestimate it when

35. The rise in the Commerce Department's index of leading economic indicators <u>suggest that the economy should continue its expansion into the coming months, but that</u> the mixed performance of the index's individual components indicates that economic growth will proceed at a more moderate pace than in the first quarter of this year.

    (A) suggest that the economy should continue its expansion into the coming months, but that

    (B) suggest that the economy is to continue expansion in the coming months, but

    (C) suggests that the economy will continue its expanding in the coming months, but that

    (D) suggests that the economy is continuing to expand into the coming months, but that

    (E) suggests that the economy will continue to expand in the coming months, but

36. Polio, although it is eradicated in the United States, it continues elsewhere and is able to be brought into the country by visitors.

    (A) Polio, although it is eradicated in the United States, it continues elsewhere and is able to be

    (B) Polio, although eradicated in the United States, it still continues elsewhere and can be

    (C) Although still continuing elsewhere, polio has been eradicated in the United States and could be

    (D) Although having been eradicated in the United States, polio still continues elsewhere and is capable of being

    (E) Although eradicated in the United States, polio continues elsewhere and could be

37. Some buildings that were destroyed and heavily damaged in the earthquake last year were constructed in violation of the city's building code.

    (A) Some buildings that were destroyed and heavily damaged in the earthquake last year were

    (B) Some buildings that were destroyed or heavily damaged in the earthquake last year had been

    (C) Some buildings that the earthquake destroyed and heavily damaged last year have been

    (D) Last year the earthquake destroyed or heavily damaged some buildings that have been

    (E) Last year some of the buildings that were destroyed or heavily damaged in the earthquake had been

38. A study commissioned by the Department of Agriculture showed that if calves exercise and associated with other calves, they will require less medication and gain weight quicker than do those raised in confinement.

    (A) associated with other calves, they will require less medication and gain weight quicker than do

    (B) associated with other calves, they require less medication and gain weight quicker than

    (C) associate with other calves, they required less medication and will gain weight quicker than do

    (D) associate with other calves, they have required less medication and will gain weight more quickly than do

    (E) associate with other calves, they require less medication and gain weight more quickly than

39. A recent study has found that within the past few years, many doctors had elected early retirement rather than face the threats of lawsuits and the rising costs of malpractice insurance.

    (A) had elected early retirement rather than face

    (B) had elected early retirement instead of facing

    (C) have elected retiring early instead of facing

    (D) have elected to retire early rather than facing

    (E) have elected to retire early rather than face

40. The Gorton-Dodd bill requires <u>that a bank disclose to their customers how long they will delay access to funds from deposited checks</u>.

    (A) that a bank disclose to their customers how long they will delay access to funds from deposited checks

    (B) a bank to disclose to their customers how long they will delay access to funds from a deposited check

    (C) that a bank disclose to its customers how long it will delay access to funds from deposited checks

    (D) a bank that it should disclose to its customers how long it will delay access to funds from a deposited check

    (E) that banks disclose to customers how long access to funds from their deposited check is to be delayed

41. Unlike a funded pension system, in which contributions are invested to pay future beneficiaries, <u>a pay-as-you-go approach is the foundation of Social Security</u>.

    (A) a pay-as-you-go approach is the foundation of Social Security

    (B) the foundation of Social Security is a pay-as-you-go approach

    (C) the approach of Social Security is pay-as-you-go

    (D) Social Security's approach is pay-as-you-go

    (E) Social Security is founded on a pay-as-you-go approach

42. Twenty-two feet long and 10 feet in diameter, the AM-1 is one of the many new <u>satellites that is a part of 15 years effort of subjecting the interactions of Earth's atmosphere, oceans, and land surfaces</u> to detailed scrutiny from space.

    (A) satellites that is a part of 15 years effort of subjecting the interactions of Earth's atmosphere, oceans, and land surfaces

    (B) satellites, which is a part of a 15-year effort to subject how Earth's atmosphere, oceans, and land surfaces interact

    (C) satellites, part of 15 years effort of subjecting how Earth's atmosphere, oceans, and land surfaces are interacting

    (D) satellites that are part of an effort for 15 years that has subjected the interactions of Earth's atmosphere, oceans, and land surfaces

    (E) satellites that are part of a 15-year effort to subject the interactions of Earth's atmosphere, oceans, and land surfaces

43. Though the term "graphic design" may <u>suggest laying out corporate brochures and annual reports, they have come to signify widely ranging</u> work, from package designs and company logotypes to signs, book jackets, computer graphics, and film titles.

    (A) suggest laying out corporate brochures and annual reports, they have come to signify widely ranging

    (B) suggest laying out corporate brochures and annual reports, it has come to signify a wide range of

    (C) suggest corporate brochure and annual report layout, it has signified widely ranging

    (D) have suggested corporate brochure and annual report layout, it has signified a wide range of

    (E) have suggested laying out corporate brochures and annual reports, they have come to signify widely ranging

44. In contrast to large steel plants that take iron ore through all the steps needed to produce several different kinds of steel, <u>processing steel scrap into a specialized group of products has enabled small mills to put capital into new technology and remain</u> economically viable.

    (A) processing steel scrap into a specialized group of products has enabled small mills to put capital into new technology and remain

    (B) processing steel scrap into a specialized group of products has enabled small mills to put capital into new technology, remaining

    (C) the processing of steel scrap into a specialized group of products has enabled small mills to put capital into new technology, remaining

    (D) small mills, by processing steel scrap into a specialized group of products, have been able to put capital into new technology and remain

    (E) small mills, by processing steel scrap into a specialized group of products, have been able to put capital into new technology and remained

45. Under high pressure and intense heat, graphite, the most stable form of pure carbon, changes into the substance commonly referred to as diamond and <u>remaining this way whether or not</u> the heat and pressure are removed.

    (A) remaining this way whether or not
    (B) remaining like that even as
    (C) remaining as such whether or not
    (D) remains in this way although
    (E) remains thus even when

46. The psychologist William James believed that facial expressions not only provide a visible sign of an <u>emotion, actually contributing to the feeling itself</u>.

    (A) emotion, actually contributing to the feeling itself

    (B) emotion but also actually contributing to the feeling itself

    (C) emotion but also actually contribute to the feeling itself

    (D) emotion; they also actually contribute to the feeling of it

    (E) emotion; the feeling itself is also actually contributed to by them

47. Wisconsin, Illinois, Florida, and Minnesota have begun to enforce statewide bans <u>prohibiting landfills to accept leaves, brush, and grass clippings</u>.

    (A) prohibiting landfills to accept leaves, brush, and grass clippings

    (B) prohibiting that landfills accept leaves, brush, and grass clippings

    (C) prohibiting landfills from accepting leaves, brush, and grass clippings

    (D) that leaves, brush, and grass clippings cannot be accepted in landfills

    (E) that landfills cannot accept leaves, brush, and grass clippings

48. Reporting that one of <u>its many problems had been the recent</u> extended sales slump in women's apparel, the seven-store retailer said it would start a three-month liquidation sale in all of its stores.

    (A) its many problems had been the recent
    (B) its many problems has been the recently
    (C) its many problems is the recently
    (D) their many problems is the recent
    (E) their many problems had been the recent

49. In developing new facilities for the incineration of solid wastes, we must avoid the danger of shifting environmental problems from <u>landfills polluting the water to polluting the air with incinerators</u>.

 (A) landfills polluting the water to polluting the air with incinerators

 (B) landfills polluting the water to the air being polluted with incinerators

 (C) the pollution of water by landfills to the pollution of air by incinerators

 (D) pollution of the water by landfills to incinerators that pollute the air

 (E) water that is polluted by landfills to incinerators that pollute the air

50. The bank holds $3 billion in loans that are seriously delinquent or in such trouble that <u>they do not expect payments when</u> due.

 (A) they do not expect payments when

 (B) it does not expect payments when it is

 (C) it does not expect payments to be made when they are

 (D) payments are not to be expected to be paid when

 (E) payments are not expected to be paid when they will be

51. In a 5-to-4 decision, the Supreme Court ruled <u>that two upstate New York counties owed restitution to three tribes of Oneida Indians for the unlawful seizure of</u> their ancestral lands in the eighteenth century.

 (A) that two upstate New York counties owed restitution to three tribes of Oneida Indians for the unlawful seizure of

 (B) that two upstate New York counties owed restitution to three tribes of Oneida Indians because of their unlawful seizure of

 (C) two upstate New York counties to owe restitution to three tribes of Oneida Indians for their unlawful seizure of

 (D) on two upstate New York counties that owed restitution to three tribes of Oneida Indians because they unlawfully seized

 (E) on the restitution that two upstate New York counties owed to three tribes of Oneida Indians for the unlawful seizure of

52. Recently discovered fossil remains strongly suggest that the Australian egg-laying mammals of today are a branch of the main stem of mammalian evolution <u>rather than developing independently from</u> a common ancestor of mammals more than 220 million years ago.

 (A) rather than developing independently from

 (B) rather than a type that developed independently from

 (C) rather than a type whose development was independent of

 (D) instead of developing independently from

 (E) instead of a development that was independent of

53. The normative model of strategic decision-making suggests that executives examine a firm's external environment and internal <u>conditions, and in using the set of objective criteria they derive from these analyses, can decide</u> on a strategy.

 (A) conditions, and in using the set of objective criteria they derive from these analyses, can decide

 (B) conditions, and they use the set of objective criteria derived from these analyses in deciding

 (C) conditions and, in using the set of objective criteria derived from these analyses, deciding

 (D) conditions and, using the set of objective criteria derived from these analyses, decide

 (E) conditions and, in their use of the set of objective criteria they derive from these analyses, they decide

54. A patient accusing a doctor of malpractice will find it difficult to prove damage <u>if there is a lack of some other doctor to testify</u> about proper medical procedures.

 (A) if there is a lack of some other doctor to testify

 (B) unless there will be another doctor to testify

 (C) without another doctor's testimony

 (D) should there be no testimony from some other doctor

 (E) lacking another doctor to testify

55. The energy source on *Voyager 2* is not a nuclear reactor, in which atoms are actively broken <u>apart; rather</u> a kind of nuclear battery that uses natural radioactive decay to produce power.

    (A) apart; rather
    (B) apart, but rather
    (C) apart, but rather that of
    (D) apart, but that of
    (E) apart; it is that of

56. Archaeologists in Ireland believe that a recently discovered chalice, which dates from the eighth century, was probably buried <u>to keep from</u> being stolen by invaders.

    (A) to keep from
    (B) to keep it from
    (C) to avoid
    (D) in order that it would avoid
    (E) in order to keep from

57. <u>According to its proponents, a proposed new style of aircraft could, by skimming along the top of the atmosphere, fly between most points on Earth in under two hours.</u>

    (A) According to its proponents, a proposed new style of aircraft could, by skimming along the top of the atmosphere, fly between most points on Earth in under two hours.
    (B) By skimming along the top of the atmosphere, proponents of a proposed new style of aircraft say it could fly between most points on Earth in under two hours.
    (C) A proposed new style of aircraft could fly between most points on Earth in under two hours, according to its proponents, with it skimming along the top of the atmosphere.
    (D) A proposed new style of aircraft, say its proponents, could fly between most points on Earth in under two hours because of its skimming along the top of the atmosphere.
    (E) According to its proponents, skimming along the top of the atmosphere makes it possible that a proposed new style of aircraft could fly between most points on Earth in under two hours.

58. Lawmakers are examining measures that would require banks to disclose all fees and account requirements in writing, <u>provide free cashing of government checks, and to create basic savings accounts to carry</u> minimal fees and require minimal initial deposits.

    (A) provide free cashing of government checks, and to create basic savings accounts to carry
    (B) provide free cashing of government checks, and creating basic savings accounts carrying
    (C) to provide free cashing of government checks, and creating basic savings accounts that carry
    (D) to provide free cashing of government checks, creating basic savings accounts to carry
    (E) to provide free cashing of government checks, and to create basic savings accounts that carry

59. Certain pesticides can become ineffective if used repeatedly in the same place; one reason is suggested by the finding that there are much larger populations of pesticide-degrading microbes in soils with a relatively long history of pesticide use than in soils that are free of such chemicals.

(A) Certain pesticides can become ineffective if used repeatedly in the same place; one reason is suggested by the finding that there are much larger populations of pesticide-degrading microbes in soils with a relatively long history of pesticide use than in soils that are free of such chemicals.

(B) If used repeatedly in the same place, one reason that certain pesticides can become ineffective is suggested by the finding that there are much larger populations of pesticide-degrading microbes in soils with a relatively long history of pesticide use than in soils that are free of such chemicals.

(C) If used repeatedly in the same place, one reason certain pesticides can become ineffective is suggested by the finding that much larger populations of pesticide-degrading microbes are found in soils with a relatively long history of pesticide use than those that are free of such chemicals.

(D) The finding that there are much larger populations of pesticide-degrading microbes in soils with a relatively long history of pesticide use than in soils that are free of such chemicals is suggestive of one reason, if used repeatedly in the same place, certain pesticides can become ineffective.

(E) The finding of much larger populations of pesticide-degrading microbes in soils with a relatively long history of pesticide use than in those that are free of such chemicals suggests one reason certain pesticides can become ineffective if used repeatedly in the same place.

60. In the textbook publishing business, the second quarter is historically weak, because revenues are low and marketing expenses are high as companies prepare for the coming school year.

(A) low and marketing expenses are high as companies prepare

(B) low and their marketing expenses are high as they prepare

(C) low with higher marketing expenses in preparation

(D) low, while marketing expenses are higher to prepare

(E) low, while their marketing expenses are higher in preparation

61. Almost a decade after New York State passed laws to protect patients by reducing the grueling hours worked by medical residents, twelve hospitals have been investigated by state medical officials, finding that all twelve consistently break the laws, many residents work longer than 24 hours straight, and that more than half the surgical residents work more than 95 hours a week.

(A) twelve hospitals have been investigated by state medical officials, finding that all twelve consistently break the laws, many residents work longer than 24 hours straight, and that more than half the surgical residents work

(B) an investigation by state medical officials of twelve hospitals have found all twelve consistently breaking the laws, that many residents work longer than 24 hours straight, with more than half the surgical residents working

(C) an investigation of twelve hospitals by state medical officials has found that all twelve consistently break the laws, that many residents work longer than 24 hours straight, and that more than half the surgical residents work

(D) twelve hospitals were investigated by state medical officials who found all twelve breaking the laws, with many residents working longer than 24 hours straight, and more than half the surgical residents work

(E) an investigation by state medical officials has found that, of twelve hospitals, all twelve consistently break the laws, that many residents work longer than 24 hours straight, with more than half the surgical residents working

62. Parliament did not accord full refugee benefits to twelve of the recent immigrants because it believed that <u>to do it rewards</u> them for entering the country illegally.

    (A) to do it rewards
    (B) doing it rewards
    (C) to do this would reward
    (D) doing so would reward
    (E) to do it would reward

63. Many policy experts say that shifting a portion of health-benefit costs back to the workers <u>helps to control the employer's costs, but also helps</u> to limit medical spending by making patients more careful consumers.

    (A) helps to control the employer's costs, but also helps
    (B) helps the control of the employer's costs, and also
    (C) not only helps to control the employer's costs, but also helps
    (D) helps to control not only the employer's costs, but
    (E) not only helps to control the employer's costs, and also helps

64. Ms. Chambers is among the forecasters who predict that the rate of addition to arable lands will drop while <u>those of loss rise</u>.

    (A) those of loss rise
    (B) it rises for loss
    (C) those of losses rise
    (D) the rate of loss rises
    (E) there are rises for the rate of loss

65. The market for recycled <u>commodities like aluminum and other metals remain</u> strong despite economic changes in the recycling industry.

    (A) commodities like aluminum and other metals remain
    (B) commodities like those of aluminum and other metals are remaining
    (C) commodities such as aluminum and other metals remains
    (D) commodities, such as aluminum and other metals, remain
    (E) commodities, like the commodities of aluminum and other metals, remains

66. <u>Unlike auto insurance, the frequency of claims does not affect the premiums for personal property coverage,</u> but if the insurance company is able to prove excessive loss due to owner negligence, it may decline to renew the policy.

    (A) Unlike auto insurance, the frequency of claims does not affect the premiums for personal property coverage,
    (B) Unlike with auto insurance, the frequency of claims do not affect the premiums for personal property coverage,
    (C) Unlike the frequency of claims for auto insurance, the premiums for personal property coverage are not affected by the frequency of claims,
    (D) Unlike the premiums for auto insurance, the premiums for personal property coverage are not affected by the frequency of claims,
    (E) Unlike with the premiums for auto insurance, the premiums for personal property coverage is not affected by the frequency of claims,

67. Faced with an estimated $2 billion budget gap, the city's mayor <u>proposed a nearly 17 percent reduction in the amount allocated the previous year to maintain the city's major cultural institutions and to subsidize</u> hundreds of local arts groups.

    (A) proposed a nearly 17 percent reduction in the amount allocated the previous year to maintain the city's major cultural institutions and to subsidize
    (B) proposed a reduction from the previous year of nearly 17 percent in the amount it was allocating to maintain the city's major cultural institutions and for subsidizing
    (C) proposed to reduce, by nearly 17 percent, the amount from the previous year that was allocated for the maintenance of the city's major cultural institutions and to subsidize
    (D) has proposed a reduction from the previous year of nearly 17 percent of the amount it was allocating for maintaining the city's major cultural institutions, and to subsidize
    (E) was proposing that the amount they were allocating be reduced by nearly 17 percent from the previous year for maintaining the city's major cultural institutions and for the subsidization

68. By offering lower prices and a menu of personal communications options, such as caller identification and voice mail, the new telecommunications company has not only captured customers from other phone companies but also forced them to offer competitive prices.

   (A) has not only captured customers from other phone companies but also forced them

   (B) has not only captured customers from other phone companies, but it also forced them

   (C) has not only captured customers from other phone companies but also forced these companies

   (D) not only has captured customers from other phone companies but also these companies have been forced

   (E) not only captured customers from other phone companies, but it also has forced them

69. The Anasazi settlements at Chaco Canyon were built on a spectacular scale, with more than 75 carefully engineered structures, of up to 600 rooms each, were connected by a complex regional system of roads.

   (A) scale, with more than 75 carefully engineered structures, of up to 600 rooms each, were

   (B) scale, with more than 75 carefully engineered structures, of up to 600 rooms each,

   (C) scale of more than 75 carefully engineered structures of up to 600 rooms, each that had been

   (D) scale of more than 75 carefully engineered structures of up to 600 rooms and with each

   (E) scale of more than 75 carefully engineered structures of up to 600 rooms, each had been

70. The gyrfalcon, an Arctic bird of prey, has survived a close brush with extinction; its numbers are now five times greater than when the use of DDT was sharply restricted in the early 1970s.

   (A) extinction; its numbers are now five times greater than

   (B) extinction; its numbers are now five times more than

   (C) extinction, their numbers now fivefold what they were

   (D) extinction, now with fivefold the numbers they had

   (E) extinction, now with numbers five times greater than

71. Analysts blamed May's sluggish retail sales on unexciting merchandise as well as the weather, colder and wetter than was usual in some regions, which slowed sales of barbecue grills and lawn furniture.

   (A) colder and wetter than was usual in some regions, which slowed

   (B) which was colder and wetter than usual in some regions, slowing

   (C) since it was colder and wetter than usually in some regions, which slowed

   (D) being colder and wetter than usually in some regions, slowing

   (E) having been colder and wetter than was usual in some regions and slowed

72. State officials report that soaring rates of liability insurance have risen to force cutbacks in the operations of everything from local governments and school districts to day-care centers and recreational facilities.

   (A) rates of liability insurance have risen to force

   (B) rates of liability insurance are a force for

   (C) rates for liability insurance are forcing

   (D) rises in liability insurance rates are forcing

   (E) liability insurance rates have risen to force

73. After suffering $2 billion in losses and 25,000 layoffs, the nation's semiconductor industry, which makes chips that run everything from <u>computers and spy satellites to dishwashers, appears to have</u> made a long-awaited recovery.

    (A) computers and spy satellites to dishwashers, appears to have

    (B) computers, spy satellites, and dishwashers, appears having

    (C) computers, spy satellites, and dishwashers, appears that it has

    (D) computers and spy satellites to dishwashers, appears that it has

    (E) computers and spy satellites as well as dishwashers, appears to have

74. While some academicians believe that business ethics should be integrated into every business course, others say that students will take ethics seriously <u>only if it would be taught as a separately required course</u>.

    (A) only if it would be taught as a separately required course

    (B) only if it is taught as a separate, required course

    (C) if it is taught only as a course required separately

    (D) if it was taught only as a separate and required course

    (E) if it would only be taught as a required course, separately

75. Scientists have observed large concentrations of heavy-metal deposits in the upper twenty centimeters of <u>Baltic Sea sediments, which are consistent with the growth of industrial activity there</u>.

    (A) Baltic Sea sediments, which are consistent with the growth of industrial activity there

    (B) Baltic Sea sediments, where the growth of industrial activity is consistent with these findings

    (C) Baltic Sea sediments, findings consistent with its growth of industrial activity

    (D) sediments from the Baltic Sea, findings consistent with the growth of industrial activity in the area

    (E) sediments from the Baltic Sea, consistent with the growth of industrial activity there

76. Under a provision of the Constitution that <u>was never applied, Congress has been required to call a convention for considering possible amendments to the document when formally asked to do it</u> by the legislatures of two-thirds of the states.

    (A) was never applied, Congress has been required to call a convention for considering possible amendments to the document when formally asked to do it

    (B) was never applied, there has been a requirement that Congress call a convention for consideration of possible amendments to the document when asked to do it formally

    (C) was never applied, whereby Congress is required to call a convention for considering possible amendments to the document when asked to do it formally

    (D) has never been applied, whereby Congress is required to call a convention to consider possible amendments to the document when formally asked to do so

    (E) has never been applied, Congress is required to call a convention to consider possible amendments to the document when formally asked to do so

77. Geologists believe that the warning signs for a major earthquake may include sudden fluctuations in local seismic activity, tilting and other deformations of the Earth's crust, <u>changing the measured strain across a fault zone and varying</u> the electrical properties of underground rocks.

    (A) changing the measured strain across a fault zone and varying

    (B) changing measurements of the strain across a fault zone, and varying

    (C) changing the strain as measured across a fault zone, and variations of

    (D) changes in the measured strain across a fault zone, and variations in

    (E) changes in measurements of the strain across a fault zone, and variations among

78. The root systems of most flowering perennials either become too crowded, <u>which results in loss in vigor, and spread</u> too far outward, producing a bare center.

(A) which results in loss in vigor, and spread

(B) resulting in loss in vigor, or spreading

(C) with the result of loss of vigor, or spreading

(D) resulting in loss of vigor, or spread

(E) with a resulting loss of vigor, and spread

79. The computer company has announced that it will purchase the color-printing division of a rival company for $950 <u>million, which is part of a deal that will make</u> it the largest manufacturer in the office color-printing market.

(A) million, which is part of a deal that will make

(B) million, a part of a deal that makes

(C) million, a part of a deal making

(D) million as a part of a deal to make

(E) million as part of a deal that will make

80. Any medical test will sometimes fail to detect <u>a condition when it is present and indicate that there is one</u> when it is not.

(A) a condition when it is present and indicate that there is one

(B) when a condition is present and indicate that there is one

(C) a condition when it is present and indicate that it is present

(D) when a condition is present and indicate its presence

(E) the presence of a condition when it is there and indicate its presence

81. Since 1986, when the Department of Labor began to allow <u>investment officers' fees to be based on how the funds they manage perform, several corporations began</u> paying their investment advisers a small basic fee, with a contract promising higher fees if the managers perform well.

(A) investment officers' fees to be based on how the funds they manage perform, several corporations began

(B) investment officers' fees to be based on the performance of the funds they manage, several corporations began

(C) that fees of investment officers be based on how the funds they manage perform, several corporations have begun

(D) fees of investment officers to be based on the performance of the funds they manage, several corporations have begun

(E) that investment officers' fees be based on the performance of the funds they manage, several corporations began

82. Downzoning, zoning that typically results in the reduction of housing density, allows for more open space in areas where <u>little water or services exist</u>.

(A) little water or services exist

(B) little water or services exists

(C) few services and little water exists

(D) there is little water or services available

(E) there are few services and little available water

83. In theory, international civil servants at the United Nations are prohibited from continuing to draw salaries from their own governments; in practice, however, some governments merely substitute living allowances <u>for their employees' paychecks, assigned by them</u> to the United Nations.

(A) for their employees' paychecks, assigned by them

(B) for the paychecks of their employees who have been assigned

(C) for the paychecks of their employees, having been assigned

(D) in place of their employees' paychecks, for those of them assigned

(E) in place of the paychecks of their employees to have been assigned by them

84. The computer company's present troubles are a result of technological stagnation, marketing missteps, and managerial blunders so that several attempts to revise corporate strategies have failed to correct it.

    (A) so that several attempts to revise corporate strategies have failed to correct it

    (B) so that several attempts at revising corporate strategies have failed to correct

    (C) in that several attempts at revising corporate strategies have failed to correct them

    (D) that several attempts to revise corporate strategies have failed to correct

    (E) that several attempts at revising corporate strategies have failed to correct them

85. According to a study by the Carnegie Foundation for the Advancement of Teaching, companies in the United States are providing job training and general education for nearly eight million people, about equivalent to the enrollment of the nation's four-year colleges and universities.

    (A) equivalent to the enrollment of

    (B) the equivalent of those enrolled in

    (C) equal to those who are enrolled in

    (D) as many as the enrollment of

    (E) as many as are enrolled in

86. Intar, the oldest Hispanic theater company in New York, has moved away from the Spanish classics and now it draws on the works both of contemporary Hispanic authors who live abroad and of those in the United States.

    (A) now it draws on the works both of contemporary Hispanic authors who live abroad and of those

    (B) now draws on the works of contemporary Hispanic authors, both those who live abroad and those who live

    (C) it draws on the works of contemporary Hispanic authors now, both those living abroad and who live

    (D) draws now on the works both of contemporary Hispanic authors living abroad and who are living

    (E) draws on the works now of both contemporary Hispanic authors living abroad and those

87. Last year, land values in most parts of the pinelands rose almost so fast, and in some parts even faster than what they did outside the pinelands.

    (A) so fast, and in some parts even faster than what they did

    (B) so fast, and in some parts even faster than, those

    (C) as fast, and in some parts even faster than, those

    (D) as fast as, and in some parts even faster than, those

    (E) as fast as, and in some parts even faster than what they did

88. Clouds are formed from the evaporation of the oceans' water that is warmed by the sun and rises high into the atmosphere, condensing in tiny droplets on minute particles of dust.

    (A) Clouds are formed from the evaporation of the oceans' water that is warmed by the sun and rises high into the atmosphere, condensing in tiny droplets on minute particles of dust.

    (B) Clouds form by the sun's warmth evaporating the water in the oceans, which rises high into the atmosphere, condensing in tiny droplets on minute particles of dust.

    (C) Warmed by the sun, ocean water evaporates, rises high into the atmosphere, and condenses in tiny droplets on minute particles of dust to form clouds.

    (D) The water in the oceans evaporates, warmed by the sun, rises high into the atmosphere, and condenses in tiny droplets on minute particles of dust, which forms clouds.

    (E) Ocean water, warmed by the sun, evaporates and rises high into the atmosphere, which then condenses in tiny droplets on minute particles of dust to form as clouds.

89. <u>If Dr. Wade was right, any apparent connection of the eating of</u> highly processed foods and excelling at sports is purely coincidental.

   (A) If Dr. Wade was right, any apparent connection of the eating of

   (B) Should Dr. Wade be right, any apparent connection of eating

   (C) If Dr. Wade is right, any connection that is apparent between eating of

   (D) If Dr. Wade is right, any apparent connection between eating

   (E) Should Dr. Wade have been right, any connection apparent between eating

90. The commission proposed <u>that funding for the park's development, which could be open to the public early next year, is</u> obtained through a local bond issue.

   (A) that funding for the park's development, which could be open to the public early next year, is

   (B) that funding for development of the park, which could be open to the public early next year, be

   (C) funding for the development of the park, perhaps open to the public early next year, to be

   (D) funds for the park's development, perhaps open to the public early next year, be

   (E) development funding for the park, which could be open to the public early next year, is to be

91. Seismologists studying the earthquake that struck northern California in October 1989 are still investigating some of its mysteries: the unexpected power of the seismic waves, <u>the upward thrust that threw one man straight into the air, and the strange electromagnetic signals detected hours before the temblor</u>.

   (A) the upward thrust that threw one man straight into the air, and the strange electromagnetic signals detected hours before the temblor

   (B) the upward thrust that threw one man straight into the air, and strange electromagnetic signals were detected hours before the temblor

   (C) the upward thrust threw one man straight into the air, and hours before the temblor strange electromagnetic signals were detected

   (D) one man was thrown straight into the air by the upward thrust, and hours before the temblor strange electromagnetic signals were detected

   (E) one man who was thrown straight into the air by the upward thrust, and strange electromagnetic signals that were detected hours before the temblor

92. Schistosomiasis, a disease caused by a parasitic worm, is prevalent in hot, humid climates, and it has become more widespread as irrigation projects have enlarged the habitat of <u>the freshwater snails that are the parasite's hosts for part of its life cycle</u>.

   (A) the freshwater snails that are the parasite's hosts for part of its life cycle

   (B) the freshwater snails that are the parasite's hosts in part of their life cycle

   (C) freshwater snails which become the parasite's hosts for part of its life cycles

   (D) freshwater snails which become the hosts of the parasite during the parasite's life cycles

   (E) parasite's hosts, freshwater snails which become their hosts during their life cycles

93. Two new studies indicate that many people become obese more <u>due to the fact that their bodies burn calories too slowly than overeating</u>.

    (A) due to the fact that their bodies burn calories too slowly than overeating

    (B) due to their bodies burning calories too slowly than to eating too much

    (C) because their bodies burn calories too slowly than that they are overeaters

    (D) because their bodies burn calories too slowly than because they eat too much

    (E) because of their bodies burning calories too slowly than because of their eating too much

94. Judge Bonham denied a motion <u>to allow members of the jury to go home at the end of each day instead of to confine them to</u> a hotel.

    (A) to allow members of the jury to go home at the end of each day instead of to confine them to

    (B) that would have allowed members of the jury to go home at the end of each day instead of confined to

    (C) under which members of the jury are allowed to go home at the end of each day instead of confining them in

    (D) that would allow members of the jury to go home at the end of each day rather than confinement in

    (E) to allow members of the jury to go home at the end of each day rather than be confined to

95. Proponents of artificial intelligence say they will be able to make computers that can understand English and other human languages, recognize objects, and reason <u>as an expert does—computers that will be used to diagnose equipment breakdowns, deciding whether to authorize a loan, or other purposes such as these</u>.

    (A) as an expert does—computers that will be used to diagnose equipment breakdowns, deciding whether to authorize a loan, or other purposes such as these

    (B) as an expert does, which may be used for purposes such as diagnosing equipment breakdowns or deciding whether to authorize a loan

    (C) like an expert—computers that will be used for such purposes as diagnosing equipment breakdowns or deciding whether to authorize a loan

    (D) like an expert, the use of which would be for purposes like the diagnosis of equipment breakdowns or the decision whether or not a loan should be authorized

    (E) like an expert, to be used to diagnose equipment breakdowns, deciding whether to authorize a loan or not, or the like

96. Floating in the waters of the equatorial Pacific, an array of buoys collects and transmits data on long-term interactions between the ocean and the <u>atmosphere, interactions that affect</u> global climate.

    (A) atmosphere, interactions that affect

    (B) atmosphere, with interactions affecting

    (C) atmosphere that affects

    (D) atmosphere that is affecting

    (E) atmosphere as affects

97. Unlike the United States, where farmers can usually depend on rain or snow all year long, the rains in most parts of Sri Lanka are concentrated in the monsoon months, June to September, and the skies are generally clear for the rest of the year.

(A) Unlike the United States, where farmers can usually depend on rain or snow all year long, the rains in most parts of Sri Lanka

(B) Unlike the United States farmers who can usually depend on rain or snow all year long, the rains in most parts of Sri Lanka

(C) Unlike those of the United States, where farmers can usually depend on rain or snow all year long, most parts of Sri Lanka's rains

(D) In comparison with the United States, whose farmers can usually depend on rain or snow all year long, the rains in most parts of Sri Lanka

(E) In the United States, farmers can usually depend on rain or snow all year long, but in most parts of Sri Lanka the rains

98. Although Napoleon's army entered Russia with far more supplies than they had in their previous campaigns, it had provisions for only twenty-four days.

(A) they had in their previous campaigns,

(B) their previous campaigns had had,

(C) they had for any previous campaign,

(D) in their previous campaigns,

(E) for any previous campaign,

99. After the Civil War, contemporaries of Harriet Tubman's maintained that she has all of the qualities of a great leader: coolness in the face of danger, an excellent sense of strategy, and an ability to plan in minute detail.

(A) Tubman's maintained that she has

(B) Tubman's maintain that she had

(C) Tubman's have maintained that she had

(D) Tubman maintained that she had

(E) Tubman had maintained that she has

100. Sixty-five million years ago, according to some scientists, an asteroid bigger than Mount Everest slammed into North America, which, causing plant and animal extinctions, marks the end of the geologic era known as the Cretaceous Period.

(A) which, causing plant and animal extinctions, marks

(B) which caused the plant and animal extinctions and marks

(C) and causing plant and animal extinctions that mark

(D) an event that caused plant and animal extinctions, which marks

(E) an event that caused the plant and animal extinctions that mark

101. The Federalist papers, a strong defense of the United States Constitution and important as a body of work in political science as well, represents the handiwork of three different authors.

(A) and important as a body of work in political science as well, represents

(B) as well as an important body of work in political science, represent

(C) and also a body of work of importance in political science is representing

(D) an important body of work in political science and has been representative of

(E) and as political science an important body of work too, represent

102. As business grows more complex, students majoring in specialized areas like those of finance and marketing have been becoming increasingly successful in the job market.

(A) majoring in specialized areas like those of finance and marketing have been becoming increasingly

(B) who major in such specialized areas as finance and marketing are becoming more and more

(C) who majored in specialized areas such as those of finance and marketing are being increasingly

(D) who major in specialized areas like those of finance and marketing have been becoming more and more

(E) having majored in such specialized areas as finance and marketing are being increasingly

103. Inuits of the Bering Sea were <u>in isolation from contact with Europeans longer than</u> Aleuts or Inuits of the North Pacific and northern Alaska.

    (A) in isolation from contact with Europeans longer than

    (B) isolated from contact with Europeans longer than

    (C) in isolation from contact with Europeans longer than were

    (D) isolated from contact with Europeans longer than were

    (E) in isolation and without contacts with Europeans longer than

104. <u>Although the first pulsar, or rapidly spinning collapsed star, to be sighted was in the summer of 1967 by graduate student Jocelyn Bell, it had not been announced until February 1968.</u>

    (A) Although the first pulsar, or rapidly spinning collapsed star, to be sighted was in the summer of 1967 by graduate student Jocelyn Bell, it had not been announced until February 1968.

    (B) Although not announced until February 1968, in the summer of 1967 graduate student Jocelyn Bell observed the first pulsar, or rapidly spinning collapsed star, to be sighted.

    (C) Although observed by graduate student Jocelyn Bell in the summer of 1967, the discovery of the first sighted pulsar, or rapidly spinning collapsed star, had not been announced before February 1968.

    (D) The first pulsar, or rapidly spinning collapsed star, to be sighted was observed in the summer of 1967 by graduate student Jocelyn Bell, but the discovery was not announced until February 1968.

    (E) The first sighted pulsar, or rapidly spinning collapsed star, was not announced until February 1968, while it was observed in the summer of 1967 by graduate student Jocelyn Bell.

105. The physical structure of the human eye enables it to sense light of wavelengths up to 0.0005 millimeters; <u>infrared radiation, however, is invisible because its wavelength—0.1 millimeters—is too long to be registered by the eye</u>.

    (A) infrared radiation, however, is invisible because its wavelength—0.1 millimeters—is too long to be registered by the eye

    (B) however, the wavelength of infrared radiation—0.1 millimeters—is too long to be registered by the eye making it invisible

    (C) infrared radiation, however, is invisible because its wavelength—0.1 millimeters—is too long for the eye to register it

    (D) however, because the wavelength of infrared radiation is 0.1 millimeters, it is too long for the eye to register and thus invisible

    (E) however, infrared radiation has a wavelength of 0.1 millimeters that is too long for the eye to register, thus making it invisible

106. <u>As well as heat and light, the sun is the source of a continuous stream</u> of atomic particles known as the solar wind.

    (A) As well as heat and light, the sun is the source of a continuous stream

    (B) Besides heat and light, also the sun is the source of a continuous stream

    (C) Besides heat and light, the sun is also the source of a continuous streaming

    (D) The sun is the source not only of heat and light, but also of a continuous stream

    (E) The sun is the source of not only heat and light but, as well, of a continuous streaming

107. Bluegrass musician Bill Monroe, whose repertory, views on musical collaboration, and vocal style <u>were influential on generations of bluegrass artists, was also an inspiration to many musicians, that included Elvis Presley and Jerry Garcia, whose music differed significantly from</u> his own.

    (A) were influential on generations of bluegrass artists, was also an inspiration to many musicians, that included Elvis Presley and Jerry Garcia, whose music differed significantly from

    (B) influenced generations of bluegrass artists, also inspired many musicians, including Elvis Presley and Jerry Garcia, whose music differed significantly from

    (C) was influential to generations of bluegrass artists, was also inspirational to many musicians, that included Elvis Presley and Jerry Garcia, whose music was different significantly in comparison to

    (D) was influential to generations of bluegrass artists, also inspired many musicians, who included Elvis Presley and Jerry Garcia, the music of whom differed significantly when compared to

    (E) were an influence on generations of bluegrass artists, was also an inspiration to many musicians, including Elvis Presley and Jerry Garcia, whose music was significantly different from that of

108. Sound can travel through water for enormous distances, <u>prevented from dissipating its acoustic energy as a result of</u> boundaries in the ocean created by water layers of different temperatures and densities.

    (A) prevented from dissipating its acoustic energy as a result of

    (B) prevented from having its acoustic energy dissipated by

    (C) its acoustic energy prevented from dissipating by

    (D) its acoustic energy prevented from being dissipated as a result of

    (E) preventing its acoustic energy from dissipating by

109. <u>The nephew of Pliny the Elder wrote the only eyewitness account of the great eruption of Vesuvius in two letters to the historian Tacitus.</u>

    (A) The nephew of Pliny the Elder wrote the only eyewitness account of the great eruption of Vesuvius in two letters to the historian Tacitus.

    (B) To the historian Tacitus, the nephew of Pliny the Elder wrote two letters, being the only eyewitness accounts of the great eruption of Vesuvius.

    (C) The only eyewitness account is in two letters by the nephew of Pliny the Elder writing to the historian Tacitus an account of the great eruption of Vesuvius.

    (D) Writing the only eyewitness account, Pliny the Elder's nephew accounted for the great eruption of Vesuvius in two letters to the historian Tacitus.

    (E) In two letters to the historian Tacitus, the nephew of Pliny the Elder wrote the only eyewitness account of the great eruption of Vesuvius.

110. <u>Being a United States citizen since 1988 and born in Calcutta in 1940, author Bharati Mukherjee has</u> lived in England and Canada, and first came to the United States in 1961 to study at the Iowa Writers' Workshop.

    (A) Being a United States citizen since 1988 and born in Calcutta in 1940, author Bharati Mukherjee has

    (B) Having been a United States citizen since 1988, she was born in Calcutta in 1940; author Bharati Mukherjee

    (C) Born in Calcutta in 1940, author Bharati Mukherjee became a United States citizen in 1988; she has

    (D) Being born in Calcutta in 1940 and having been a United States citizen since 1988, author Bharati Mukherjee

    (E) Having been born in Calcutta in 1940 and being a United States citizen since 1988, author Bharati Mukherjee

111. Initiated five centuries after Europeans arrived in the New World on Columbus Day 1992, Project SETI pledged a $100 million investment in the search for extraterrestrial intelligence.

    (A) Initiated five centuries after Europeans arrived in the New World on Columbus Day 1992, Project SETI pledged a $100 million investment in the search for extraterrestrial intelligence.

    (B) Initiated on Columbus Day 1992, five centuries after Europeans arrived in the New World, a $100 million investment in the search for extraterrestrial intelligence was pledged by Project SETI.

    (C) Initiated on Columbus Day 1992, five centuries after Europeans arrived in the New World, Project SETI pledged a $100 million investment in the search for extraterrestrial intelligence.

    (D) Pledging a $100 million investment in the search for extraterrestrial intelligence, the initiation of Project SETI five centuries after Europeans arrived in the New World on Columbus Day 1992.

    (E) Pledging a $100 million investment in the search for extraterrestrial intelligence five centuries after Europeans arrived in the New World, on Columbus Day 1992, the initiation of Project SETI took place.

112. In the 1980s the federal government was the largest single provider of day care for children, offering child care, health, and educational services to hundreds of thousands of children from poor households through the Head Start program and which supported private day-care facilities through child-care tax credits, state block grants, and tax breaks for employers who subsidized day-care services.

    (A) In the 1980s the federal government was the largest single provider of day care for children, offering

    (B) The federal government was the largest single provider of day care for children in the 1980s, which offered

    (C) In the 1980s the federal government was the largest single provider of day care for children and offered

    (D) The largest single provider of day care for children in the 1980s was the federal government, offering

    (E) In the 1980s the largest single provider of day care for children was the federal government, which offered

113. In A.D. 391, resulting from the destruction of the largest library of the ancient world at Alexandria, later generations lost all but the *Iliad* and *Odyssey* among Greek epics, most of the poetry of Pindar and Sappho, and dozens of plays by Aeschylus and Euripides.

    (A) resulting from the destruction of the largest library of the ancient world at Alexandria,

    (B) the destroying of the largest library of the ancient world at Alexandria resulted and

    (C) because of the result of the destruction of the library at Alexandria, the largest of the ancient world,

    (D) as a result of the destruction of the library at Alexandria, the largest of the ancient world,

    (E) Alexandria's largest library of the ancient world was destroyed, and the result was

5.7 Answer Key

1.	E	30.	B	59.	A	88.	C
2.	B	31.	C	60.	A	89.	D
3.	A	32.	A	61.	C	90.	B
4.	C	33.	D	62.	D	91.	A
5.	E	34.	D	63.	C	92.	A
6.	D	35.	E	64.	D	93.	D
7.	A	36.	E	65.	C	94.	E
8.	C	37.	B	66.	D	95.	C
9.	C	38.	E	67.	A	96.	A
10.	C	39.	E	68.	C	97.	E
11.	C	40.	C	69.	B	98.	E
12.	B	41.	E	70.	A	99.	D
13.	A	42.	E	71.	B	100.	E
14.	D	43.	B	72.	C	101.	B
15.	E	44.	D	73.	A	102.	B
16.	C	45.	E	74.	B	103.	D
17.	C	46.	C	75.	D	104.	D
18.	A	47.	C	76.	E	105.	A
19.	A	48.	A	77.	D	106.	D
20.	E	49.	C	78.	D	107.	B
21.	A	50.	C	79.	E	108.	C
22.	C	51.	A	80.	C	109.	E
23.	D	52.	B	81.	D	110.	C
24.	E	53.	D	82.	E	111.	C
25.	C	54.	C	83.	B	112.	E
26.	A	55.	B	84.	D	113.	D
27.	A	56.	B	85.	E		
28.	C	57.	A	86.	B		
29.	E	58.	E	87.	D		

5.8 Answer Explanations

The following discussion of sentence correction is intended to familiarize you with the most efficient and effective approaches to these kinds of questions. The particular questions in this chapter are generally representative of the kinds of sentence correction questions you will encounter on the GMAT.

1. Like ants, termites have an elaborate social structure in which a few individuals reproduce and the rest <u>are serving the colony by tending juveniles, gathering food, building the nest, or they battle</u> intruders.

    (A) are serving the colony by tending juveniles, gathering food, building the nest, or they battle
    (B) are serving the colony in that they tend juveniles, gather food, build the nest, or battle
    (C) serve the colony, tending juveniles, gathering food, building the nest, or by battling
    (D) serve the colony by tending juveniles, gathering food, by building the nest, or by battling
    (E) serve the colony by tending juveniles, gathering food, building the nest, or battling

Parallelism; Rhetorical construction

The sentence most effectively uses parallel structure to contrast two types of termites in the social structure of termite colonies: those who reproduce, and those who serve the colony in a number of ways. The progressive verb form *are serving* should be changed to simple present tense *serve* to parallel *reproduce*. In the final list of responsibilities, parallelism demands that all assume the gerund form as objects of the preposition: *by tending . . . gathering . . . building . . . or battling*.

A   The progressive verb form *are serving* is inappropriate for this general claim about termite behavior. It should parallel the previous verb *reproduce*. It is unnecessary to introduce a new clause *or they battle intruders*, because *battling* is another way some termites serve the colony and should therefore be expressed as another object of the preposition *by*.

B   *In that they* is an awkward and wordy construction—a poor substitute for *by* in this context.

C   The preposition *by* clarifies *how* the termites serve their colony and should govern all of the task descriptions, not just the final one.

D   There is no need to repeat the preposition *by*, because all tasks can be described in a series of parallel objects of the same preposition. To violate parallel structure by omitting the preposition before one gerund but repeating it for the rest confuses the reader.

E   **Correct.** The sentence uses proper parallel structure and is clear and concise.

The correct answer is E.

2. Some bat caves, like honeybee hives, have residents that take on different duties such as defending the entrance, <u>acting as sentinels and to sound</u> a warning at the approach of danger, and scouting outside the cave for new food and roosting sites.

    (A) acting as sentinels and to sound
    (B) acting as sentinels and sounding
    (C) to act as sentinels and sound
    (D) to act as sentinels and to sound
    (E) to act as a sentinel sounding

Parallelism; Agreement

The original sentence has an error in parallel structure. It starts by using the *ing* (participial) form to list the bats' duties. *Defending, acting,* and *scouting* all use the same *ing* form. The phrase *to sound* uses the *to* (infinitive) form, and so it is not parallel. The word *sounding* is required in this sentence.

A   *To sound* is not parallel to *defending, acting,* and *scouting.*

B   **Correct.** This sentence has *sounding,* which properly parallels *defending, acting,* and *scouting.*

C   *To act* and *sound* are not parallel to *defending* and *scouting.*

D   *To act* and *to sound* are not parallel to *defending* and *scouting*.

E   The singular *a sentinel* produces an agreement error, and *to act* is not parallel to *scouting*.

The correct answer is B.

3.   <u>However much United States voters may agree that</u> there is waste in government and that the government as a whole spends beyond its means, it is difficult to find broad support for a movement toward a minimal state.

(A)   However much United States voters may agree that

(B)   Despite the agreement among United States voters to the fact

(C)   Although United States voters agree

(D)   Even though United States voters may agree

(E)   There is agreement among United States voters that

Parallelism; Grammatical construction

In this correctly written sentence, parallel subordinate clauses are followed by a main clause. These parallel subordinate clauses are both introduced by *that*: *that there is . . .* and *that the government. . . .*

A   **Correct.** In this sentence, the repetition of *that* to introduce two subordinate clauses makes the construction parallel and correct.

B   *That* is omitted. The sense of the sentence is distorted by the omission of *may*. The phrase *agreement . . . to the fact* is awkward.

C   *That* is omitted, and the sense of the sentence is distorted by the omission of *may*.

D   *That* is omitted.

E   Using two independent clauses separated only by a comma creates a run-on sentence, and the sense of the sentence is distorted by the omission of *may*.

The correct answer is A.

4.   The voluminous personal papers of Thomas Alva Edison reveal that his inventions typically <u>sprang to life not in a flash of inspiration but evolved slowly</u> from previous works.

(A)   sprang to life not in a flash of inspiration but evolved slowly

(B)   sprang to life not in a flash of inspiration but were slowly evolved

(C)   did not spring to life in a flash of inspiration but evolved slowly

(D)   did not spring to life in a flash of inspiration but had slowly evolved

(E)   did not spring to life in a flash of inspiration but they were slowly evolved

Parallelism; Idiom

The construction *not . . . but* shows a contrast. The words following *not* must be parallel in construction to the words following *but*. In the original sentence *not* is followed by a prepositional phrase (*in a flash of inspiration*), while *but* is followed by a verb (*evolved*). To make the two contrasting elements parallel, *not* should be followed by a verb rather than a phrase.

A   The construction following *not* is not parallel to the construction following *but*.

B   The construction following *not* is not parallel to the construction following *but*.

C   **Correct.** In this sentence, *not* is followed by the verb *spring* just as *but* is followed by the verb *evolved*.

D   *Had . . . evolved* introduces an incorrect verb tense.

E   The construction following *not* is not parallel to the construction following *but*.

The correct answer is C.

5.   Hundreds of species of fish generate and discharge electric currents, in bursts or as steady electric fields around their bodies, using their power <u>either to find and attack prey, to defend themselves, or also for communicating and navigating</u>.

(A)   either to find and attack prey, to defend themselves, or also for communicating and navigating

(B) either for finding and attacking prey, defend themselves, or for communication and navigation

(C) to find and attack prey, for defense, or communication and navigation

(D) for finding and attacking prey, to defend themselves, or also for communication and navigation

(E) to find and attack prey, to defend themselves, or to communicate and navigate

Idiom; Verb form

The sentence explains that fish discharge electric currents for several purposes, which are most efficiently and effectively described in a parallel structure: *to find and attack*, *to defend*, or *to communicate and navigate*. The use of *either* is inappropriate in this sentence because more than two uses of electric currents are listed; idiomatic usage requires *either* to be followed by *or* to identify alternatives, not by *also*.

A   *Either* inappropriately introduces a list of more than two alternatives, and it should not be followed by *or also*; parallelism requires that *for communicating and navigating* be changed to *to communicate and navigate*.

B   *Defend* is not parallel with the list of gerunds, leaving the reader to wonder how to make sense of *defend themselves*.

C   The lack of parallelism obscures the relationships among the items in the series; it is especially confusing to list an infinitive phrase (*to find* . . .), an object of a preposition (*for defense*), and nouns with no grammatical connection to the verb phrase (*communication and navigation*).

D   This answer choice also violates parallelism by mixing an infinitive with objects of the preposition *for*. *Or also* is an unidiomatic, contradictory expression.

E   **Correct.** The different ways in which the various species of fish use their electric power are correctly expressed in a series of parallel infinitives.

The correct answer is E.

6.   A Labor Department study states that the <u>numbers of women employed outside the home grew by more than a thirty-five percent increase</u> in the past decade and accounted for more than sixty-two percent of the total growth in the civilian workforce.

(A) numbers of women employed outside the home grew by more than a thirty-five percent increase

(B) numbers of women employed outside the home grew more than thirty-five percent

(C) numbers of women employed outside the home were raised by more than thirty-five percent

(D) number of women employed outside the home increased by more than thirty-five percent

(E) number of women employed outside the home was raised by more than a thirty-five percent increase

Diction; Rhetorical construction

The sentence misuses the word *numbers* and contains the redundant word *increase*. The plural *numbers* means a large crowd or multitude, while the singular *number* refers to a specific quantity of individuals. The count of women here should be expressed as *the number*. The noun *increase* repeats the meaning already present in the verb *grew*; only one of the two words is necessary to the sentence.

A   *Numbers* should be *number*. *Grew* and *increase* repeat the same idea.

B   *Numbers* should be the singular *number*.

C   *Numbers* should be *number*. The passive-voice verb *were raised by* is unclear and wordy.

D   **Correct.** In this sentence, *number* correctly replaces *numbers*, and redundancy is eliminated with the use of the verb *increased*.

E   The passive-voice verb *was raised by* is unclear and wordy. *Increase* is redundant.

The correct answer is D.

7. From the earliest days of the tribe, kinship determined the way in which the Ojibwa society organized its labor, provided access to its resources, <u>and defined rights and obligations involved in the distribution and consumption of those resources</u>.

    (A) and defined rights and obligations involved in the distribution and consumption of those resources

    (B) defining rights and obligations involved in their distribution and consumption

    (C) and defined rights and obligations as they were involved in its distribution and consumption

    (D) whose rights and obligations were defined in their distribution and consumption

    (E) the distribution and consumption of them defined by rights and obligations

Parallelism; Logical predication; Grammatical construction

This correctly written sentence uses a series of three parallel constructions to describe how the Ojibwa society *organized* . . . , *provided* . . . , *and defined*. The three verbs match each other, an example of correct parallelism.

A Correct. The three verbs are parallel in this sentence.

B *Defining* is not parallel to *organized* and *provided*.

C *As they were* is wordy and imprecise, and *its* has no clear referent.

D *Whose rights and obligations* illogically refers to *resources*.

E This construction breaks the parallel structure and is illogical and ungrammatical.

The correct answer is A.

8. As the cost of wireless service has steadily dropped over the last year and as mobile phones have become increasingly common, many people are finding that they can avoid toll charges on their home <u>phones, using their mobile phones for making long-distance calls at night or on weekends, at a time which</u> many wireless companies provide unlimited airtime for a small monthly fee.

    (A) phones, using their mobile phones for making long-distance calls at night or on weekends, at a time which

    (B) phones, instead using mobile phones to make long-distance calls during the night or weekends, during which

    (C) phones by using their mobile phones to make long-distance calls at night or on weekends, when

    (D) phones using mobile phones for making long-distance calls during the night or weekends, when

    (E) phones when using their mobile phones to make long-distance calls at night or on weekends, a time which

Rhetorical construction; Grammatical construction

This sentence explains *how* people avoid toll charges on their home phones, and this purpose is best clarified by using the preposition *by* to connect the phrase *can avoid* . . . with the explanatory *using their mobile phones*. The phrase *at a time which* is confusing because it seems to suggest a time other than *at night or on weekends*. *Which* is the wrong relative pronoun for referring to time; substituting *when* for the entire phrase streamlines the sentence and makes its meaning clear.

A *By* is needed between *phones* and *using* to clarify that this sentence explains *how* people avoid charges. *At a time which* should be replaced by *when*.

B *Instead* nonsensically contrasts avoiding toll charges with the method for accomplishing this. *During which* is awkward and unclear, especially as *during* appears twice in the same phrase.

C Correct. The sentence is clear, concise, and grammatically correct.

D *By* is needed between *phones* and *using* to clarify the explanation of *how* people avoid charges.

E *When* inappropriately takes the place of *by*, obscuring the fact that using mobile phones at night and on weekends is a method for avoiding toll charges.

The correct answer is C.

9.   Delighted by the reported earnings for the first quarter of the fiscal year, <u>it was decided by the company manager to give her staff a raise</u>.

(A)   it was decided by the company manager to give her staff a raise

(B)   the decision of the company manager was to give her staff a raise

(C)   the company manager decided to give her staff a raise

(D)   the staff was given a raise by the company manager

(E)   a raise was given to the staff by the company manager

Logical predication; Verb form

Who was *delighted*? The *company manager* was *delighted*. The long modifying phrase that introduces the sentence describes a person, not *it*, so the delighted person must be the subject of the sentence. Correcting the modification error also changes the construction from the wordy passive voice, *it was decided by x*, to the more concise active voice, *x decided*; the active voice is generally preferred.

A   The modifier illogically describes *it*, not the *company manager*. The passive voice is wordy.

B   The modifier illogically describes *the decision*. The construction *decision of the . . . was . . .* is wordy.

C   **Correct.** The modifying phrase correctly modifies the *company manager*; using the active voice creates a more concise sentence.

D   The modifier describes *the staff* rather than *the company manager*; the passive voice is wordy.

E   The modifier illogically describes *a raise*; the passive voice is wordy.

The correct answer is C.

10.   <u>The rising of costs</u> of data-processing operations at many financial institutions has created a growing opportunity for independent companies to provide these services more efficiently and at lower cost.

(A)   The rising of costs

(B)   Rising costs

(C)   The rising cost

(D)   Because the rising cost

(E)   Because of rising costs

Idiom; Agreement; Grammatical construction

The rising of costs is wordy and awkward. The correct idiom is the more concise *the rising cost*. The main verb of the sentence, *has created*, requires a singular subject to maintain subject-verb agreement.

A   *The rising of costs* is not the correct idiom.

B   *Rising costs* does not agree with singular verb, *has created*.

C   **Correct.** *The rising cost* is the correct idiom, and it agrees with the singular verb in this sentence.

D   *Because* introduces a subordinate clause, creating a sentence fragment.

E   *Because* introduces a subordinate clause, creating a sentence fragment.

The correct answer is C.

11.   Native to South America, <u>when peanuts were introduced to Africa by Portuguese explorers early in the sixteenth century they were quickly adopted into Africa's agriculture, probably because of being</u> so similar to the Bambarra groundnut, a popular indigenous plant.

(A)   when peanuts were introduced to Africa by Portuguese explorers early in the sixteenth century they were quickly adopted into Africa's agriculture, probably because of being

(B)   peanuts having been introduced to Africa by Portuguese explorers early in the sixteenth century and quickly adopted into Africa's agriculture, probably because of being

(C)   peanuts were introduced to Africa by Portuguese explorers early in the sixteenth century and were quickly adopted into Africa's agriculture, probably because they were

(D)   peanuts, introduced to Africa by Portuguese explorers early in the sixteenth century and quickly adopted into Africa's agriculture, probably because they were

(E)   peanuts, introduced to Africa by Portuguese explorers early in the sixteenth century and having been quickly adopted into Africa's agriculture, probably because they were

Grammatical construction; Logical predication

The opening adjectival phrase *Native to South America* must be followed immediately by the noun it modifies: *peanuts*. The sentence makes two main points about peanuts—they were introduced to Africa and they were quickly adopted there. The most efficient way to make these points is to make *peanuts* the subject of two main verbs: *were introduced* and *were . . . adopted*.

A   *When* incorrectly intervenes between the opening adjectival phrase and the noun it modifies, and it is also unnecessary because *early in the sixteenth century* explains when. *Because of being* is wordy and indirect.

B   This version of the sentence has no main verb, since *having been introduced* and *quickly adopted* both introduce adjectival phrases.

C   **Correct.** The sentence is properly structured and grammatically correct.

D   This version of the sentence has no main verb because *introduced* and *adopted* both function as adjectives.

E   This version of the sentence has no main verb because *introduced* and *having been . . . adopted* function as adjectives.

The correct answer is C.

12. William H. Johnson's artistic debt to Scandinavia is evident in paintings that range from sensitive portraits of citizens in his wife's Danish home, Kerteminde, <u>and</u> awe-inspiring views of fjords and mountain peaks in the western and northern regions of Norway.

(A)   and
(B)   to
(C)   and to
(D)   with
(E)   in addition to

Idiom; Logical predication

The correct idiom is *range from x to y*. In this sentence, the correct idiom is *paintings that range from sensitive portraits . . . to awe-inspiring views.*

A   *And* does not complete the idiomatic expression correctly.

B   **Correct.** In this sentence, *to* correctly completes the idiomatic construction *range from x to y.*

C   *And to* does not complete the idiomatic expression correctly.

D   *With* does not complete the idiomatic expression correctly.

E   *In addition to* does not complete the idiomatic expression correctly.

The correct answer is B.

13. Growing competitive pressures may be encouraging auditors to bend the rules in favor of <u>clients; auditors may, for instance, allow</u> a questionable loan to remain on the books in order to maintain a bank's profits on paper.

(A)   clients; auditors may, for instance, allow
(B)   clients, as an instance, to allow
(C)   clients, like to allow
(D)   clients, such as to be allowing
(E)   clients; which might, as an instance, be the allowing of

Grammatical construction; Rhetorical construction

This sentence correctly joins two independent clauses with a semicolon. The first clause makes a generalization; the second clause gives a particular example that supports the generalization.

A   **Correct.** This sentence correctly has two independent clauses with linked ideas joined with a semicolon.

B   In trying to condense two main clauses into one, this construction produces an ungrammatical sequence of words with no clear meaning.

C   The preposition *like* should not be used to introduce the infinitive phrase *to allow . . .*; the comparative preposition *like* is properly used to draw a comparison between two nouns.

D   *Such as to be allowing* is not a correct idiomatic expression.

E   The semicolon is followed by a wordy, incorrect construction rather than an independent clause.

The correct answer is A.

14.   The themes that Rita Dove explores in her poetry <u>is universal, encompassing much of the human condition while occasionally she deals</u> with racial issues.

(A)   is universal, encompassing much of the human condition while occasionally she deals

(B)   is universal, encompassing much of the human condition, also occasionally it deals

(C)   are universal, they encompass much of the human condition and occasionally deals

(D)   are universal, encompassing much of the human condition while occasionally dealing

(E)   are universal, they encompass much of the human condition, also occasionally are dealing

Agreement; Grammatical construction

The plural subject of the sentence, *themes*, requires the plural verb *are* in place of *is*. Because the *themes* of Dove's poetry *encompass* the human condition and *deal* with racial issues, there is no need to make this a compound sentence by introduce a new grammatical subject, *she*, in a final clause. A single subject with two parallel verbs is the clearest and most efficient form for this sentence.

A   The plural subject disagrees with the singular verb. The sentence should retain the focus on the single subject *themes* rather than introduce a new subject and clause at the end.

B   The plural subject disagrees with the singular verb. Because *also occasionally it deals with . . .* introduces a new main clause, the comma between *condition* and *also* is an insufficient connector (creating a comma splice).

C   The comma between *universal* and *they* is an insufficient connector, creating a comma splice; the singular verb *deals* does not agree with the plural subject *they*.

D   **Correct.** The plural verb *are* agrees with the plural subject. The sentence is effectively worded and grammatically correct.

E   The comma between *universal* and *they* creates a comma splice. There is no subject for the verb *are dealing*.

The correct answer is D.

15.   It is well known in the supermarket industry that how items are placed on shelves and <u>the frequency of inventory turnovers can be</u> crucial to profits.

(A)   the frequency of inventory turnovers can be

(B)   the frequency of inventory turnovers is often

(C)   the frequency with which the inventory turns over is often

(D)   how frequently is the inventory turned over are often

(E)   how frequently the inventory turns over can be

Parallelism; Agreement

Two activities are considered *crucial*, and those two activities should appear as grammatically parallel elements in the sentence. The first is *how items are placed on shelves*, so the second should be *how frequently the inventory turns over*.

A   *The frequency . . .* is not parallel to *how items. . . .*

B   *The frequency . . .* is not parallel to *how items . . .* , and *is* does not agree with the compound subject.

C   *The frequency . . . over* is lengthy, wordy, and not parallel, and *is* does not agree with the compound subject.

D   *Is the inventory* is not parallel to *items are placed*.

E   **Correct.** In this sentence, the two clauses, *how items are placed on shelves* and *how frequently the inventory turns over*, are parallel.

The correct answer is E.

16. Iguanas have been an important food source in Latin America since prehistoric times, and it is still prized as a game animal by the campesinos, who typically cook the meat in a heavily spiced stew.

    (A) it is still prized as a game animal
    (B) it is still prized as game animals
    (C) they are still prized as game animals
    (D) they are still prized as being a game animal
    (E) being still prized as a game animal

Agreement; Grammatical construction

The pronouns and nouns that refer to the plural noun *iguanas* must be plural, as should the verb following the (corrected) pronoun in the second clause. Thus, the sentence should read: *Iguanas . . . they are still prized as game animals.*

A   *It is* and *a game animal* do not agree with *iguanas.*

B   *It is* does not agree with *iguanas* or *game animals.*

C   **Correct.** In this sentence, *they are* and *game animals* properly agree with *iguanas.*

D   *A game animal* does not agree with *iguanas*; *being* is unnecessary and awkward.

E   *A game animal* does not agree with *iguanas.* The second independent clause requires a subject and a verb, not the participle *being.*

The correct answer is C.

17. Travelers to Mars would have to endure low levels of gravity for long periods of time, avoid large doses of radiation, contend with the chemically reactive Martian soil, and perhaps even having to ward off contamination by Martian life-forms.

    (A) contend with the chemically reactive Martian soil, and perhaps even having to ward
    (B) contend with the chemically reactive Martian soil, and perhaps even warding
    (C) contend with the chemically reactive Martian soil, and perhaps even ward
    (D) contending with the chemically reactive Martian soil, and perhaps even to ward
    (E) contending with the chemically reactive Martian soil, and perhaps even warding

Parallelism; Grammatical construction

This sentence provides a list of three conditions Mars travelers would certainly have to contend with, along with one additional thing they might have to do—*ward off contamination by Martian life-forms.* The items in the list are most clearly and effectively structured in parallel—as phrases beginning with infinitive verb forms—*to endure,* (*to*) *avoid,* (*to*) *contend,* (*to*) *ward off.* Because the sentence introduces all these actions as something travelers *would have to* do, repeating the *hav[ing] to* construction in the final item of the list is redundant.

A   The phrase *having to* is not parallel with the other items in the list, and it unnecessarily repeats the sense of the introductory phrase, which identifies all items in the list as things travelers *would have to* do.

B   The verb form *warding* is not parallel with the other items in the list.

C   **Correct.** The sentence uses proper grammar and parallel construction.

D   The participial form *contending* violates the parallel structure of the list of infinitive phrases. The reader is misled into thinking that *contending with chemically reactive Martian soil* describes what travelers would have to do to avoid radiation doses.

E   The participial phrases *contending with* and *warding off* violate the parallel structure established by the list of infinitive phrases.

The correct answer is C.

18. Except for a concert performance that the composer himself staged in 1911, Scott Joplin's ragtime opera *Treemonisha* was not produced until 1972, sixty-one years after its completion.

    (A) Except for a concert performance that the composer himself staged
    (B) Except for a concert performance with the composer himself staging it
    (C) Besides a concert performance being staged by the composer himself
    (D) Excepting a concert performance that the composer himself staged

(E)   With the exception of a concert performance with the staging done by the composer himself

Idiom; Rhetorical construction

This sentence requires attention to idiom and to conciseness. *Except for* is correctly followed by a noun, *concert performance*; *that the composer himself staged* is a clause that clearly and concisely describes the performance.

A   **Correct.** In this sentence, the correct idiom is used in a clear and concise expression.

B   *With . . . it* is an awkward and wordy construction, and *staging* suggests ongoing action rather than action completed in 1911.

C   *Being staged* suggests ongoing rather than completed action.

D   *Excepting* usually appears in negative constructions; it is not the correct idiom in this sentence.

E   This sentence is awkward and wordy.

The correct answer is A.

19.   Chinese, the most ancient of living writing systems, consists of tens of thousands of ideographic characters, <u>each character a miniature calligraphic composition inside its</u> own square frame.

(A)   each character a miniature calligraphic composition inside its

(B)   all the characters a miniature calligraphic composition inside their

(C)   all the characters a miniature calligraphic composition inside its

(D)   every character a miniature calligraphic composition inside their

(E)   each character a miniature calligraphic composition inside their

Agreement

The underlined part of the original sentence acts as a modifier, or a phrase in apposition, describing Chinese ideographic characters. The modifier correctly uses the singular for all three terms: *character*, *composition*, and *its* all agree.

A   **Correct.** In this sentence, the nouns *character* and *composition* and the pronoun *its* agree.

B   *Characters* and *their* are plural, but *composition* is singular.

C   While *characters* is plural, *composition* and *its* are singular.

D   *Character* and *composition* are singular, but *their* is plural.

E   *Character* and *composition* are singular, but *their* is plural.

The correct answer is A.

20.   Declining values for farm equipment and land, <u>the collateral against which farmers borrow to get through the harvest season, is</u> going to force many lenders to tighten or deny credit this spring.

(A)   the collateral against which farmers borrow to get through the harvest season, is

(B)   which farmers use as collateral to borrow against to get through the harvest season, is

(C)   the collateral which is borrowed against by farmers to get through the harvest season, is

(D)   which farmers use as collateral to borrow against to get through the harvest season, are

(E)   the collateral against which farmers borrow to get through the harvest season, are

Agreement; Rhetorical construction

Because a lengthy construction appears between the subject and the verb, it may be hard to see at first that the plural subject *values* does not agree with the singular verb *is*. *Values* requires *are*.

A   The singular verb *is* does not agree with the plural subject *values*.

B   *Is* does not agree with *values*; the clause is awkward and redundant.

C   *Is* does not agree with *values*; the clause is awkward and wordy.

D   *Use as collateral to borrow against* is redundant; the wording is awkward.

E   **Correct.** In this sentence, the plural subject *values* agrees with the plural verb *are*.

The correct answer is E.

21. While depressed property values can hurt some large investors, they are potentially devastating for homeowners, whose equity—in many cases representing a life's savings—can plunge or even disappear.

(A) they are potentially devastating for homeowners, whose

(B) they can potentially devastate homeowners in that their

(C) for homeowners they are potentially devastating, because their

(D) for homeowners, it is potentially devastating in that their

(E) it can potentially devastate homeowners, whose

Rhetorical construction; Agreement

This sentence is correct and concise. *They* clearly refers to *property values*, and *whose* refers to *homeowners*.

A **Correct.** The relationship between nouns and pronouns is correct in this sentence; the expression is concise and clear.

B *Can potentially* is redundant; *in that their* is wordy, awkward, and ambiguous.

C *Their* appears to refer to *they* (*property values*) rather than to *homeowners*.

D *It* does not agree with *property values*; *in that their* is wordy and awkward.

E *It* does not agree with *property values*; *can potentially* is redundant.

The correct answer is A.

22. Japanese researchers are producing a series of robots that can identify human facial expressions, to which they will then respond; their goal is primarily creating a robot that will empathize with us.

(A) expressions, to which they will then respond; their goal is primarily creating

(B) expressions, then responding to them; primarily to create

(C) expressions and then respond to them; the researchers' primary goal is to create

(D) expressions as well as giving a response to them; their primary goal is creation of

(E) expressions and responding to them; primarily, the researchers' goal is creating

Logical predication; Rhetorical construction

This sentence uses two complete clauses to present two main topics—the capabilities of robots designed by Japanese researchers and the goal that motivates this design. The first clause most effectively uses a succession of parallel verbs to describe what the robots can do: *identify* expressions and *respond* to them. Beginning the second clause with the possessive pronoun *their* creates ambiguity, because it is not clear whether the pronoun refers to the robots or the researchers.

A The pronouns *they* and *their* in this version of the sentence are ambiguous, possibly referring to both researchers and robots.

B The phrase *then responding to them* should be converted to a main verb to parallel *identify* and to make clear that the robots can do these two things. The semicolon should be followed by a complete clause, but in this version of the sentence it is followed by an adverbial phrase.

C **Correct.** The wording is concise and unambiguous.

D The phrase *as well as giving a response to them* is wordy; the pronoun *their* is ambiguous.

E *Responding* is the wrong verb form—it should be an infinitive to parallel *identify*.

The correct answer is C.

23. Consumers may not think of household cleaning products to be hazardous substances, but many of them can be harmful to health, especially if they are used improperly.

(A) Consumers may not think of household cleaning products to be

(B) Consumers may not think of household cleaning products being

(C) A consumer may not think of their household cleaning products being

(D) A consumer may not think of household cleaning products as

(E) Household cleaning products may not be thought of, by consumers, as

Idiom; Agreement

The sentence uses an idiom that is correctly expressed as *think of x as y*. The use of *to be* is incorrect.

A *To be* is incorrect in the idiom *to think of x as y.*

B *Being* is incorrect in the idiom *to think of x as y.*

C *Being* is incorrect in the idiom *to think of x as y. Their* does not agree with *a consumer.*

D **Correct.** This sentence uses the idiom correctly: *think of household products as.*

E The passive-voice construction is awkward and wordy.

The correct answer is D.

24. In recent years cattle breeders have increasingly used crossbreeding, <u>in part that their steers should acquire certain characteristics</u> and partly because crossbreeding is said to provide hybrid vigor.

   (A) in part that their steers should acquire certain characteristics

   (B) in part for the acquisition of certain characteristics in their steers

   (C) partly because of their steers acquiring certain characteristics

   (D) partly because certain characteristics should be acquired by their steers

   (E) partly to acquire certain characteristics in their steers

Parallelism; Rhetorical construction

The sentence gives two reasons that cattle breeders use crossbreeding; these reasons should be introduced in parallel ways with the word *partly*. The infinitive *to acquire* clearly and concisely conveys the purpose of the crossbreeding.

A *In part* should be *partly.* Use of the relative clause *that their steers should acquire . . .* is ungrammatical.

B *In part* should be *partly.* Use of prepositional phrases is wordy and awkward.

C *Because of* suggests that crossbreeding has occurred because the steers have already acquired certain characteristics.

D Passive voice *should be acquired by* is awkward and illogical.

E **Correct.** In this sentence, the word *partly* is used to introduce both reasons; the phrase *to acquire certain characteristics* is clear and concise.

The correct answer is E.

25. <u>Like Auden, the language of James Merrill</u> is chatty, arch, and conversational—given to complex syntactic flights as well as to prosaic free-verse strolls.

   (A) Like Auden, the language of James Merrill

   (B) Like Auden, James Merrill's language

   (C) Like Auden's, James Merrill's language

   (D) As with Auden, James Merrill's language

   (E) As is Auden's the language of James Merrill

Logical predication; Rhetorical construction

The intent of the sentence is to compare the *language* used by the two authors; both write in a *chatty, arch, and conversational* way. Using the phrase *like Auden's* to begin the comparison creates a concise statement, and the parallel construction of *Merrill's* also reduces wordiness and enhances clarity. Since the possessive *Auden's* matches the possessive *Merrill's*, the word *language* is not needed following the word *Auden's.*

A *Auden* is illogically compared to *language.*

B *Auden* is illogically compared to *language.*

C **Correct.** This sentence states the comparison correctly and concisely, making it clear that Auden's language is being compared with Merrill's language.

D It is unclear what the adverb phrase *as with Auden* modifies.

E While the sentence attempts to compare Auden's language with Merrill's, its phrasing is wordy and confusing.

The correct answer is C.

26. The Baldrick Manufacturing Company has for several years followed a policy <u>aimed at decreasing operating costs and improving</u> the efficiency of its distribution system.

    (A) aimed at decreasing operating costs and improving

    (B) aimed at the decreasing of operating costs and to improve

    (C) aiming at the decreasing of operating costs and improving

    (D) the aim of which is the decreasing of operating costs and improving

    (E) with the aim to decrease operating costs and to improve

Parallelism; Rhetorical construction

This correct sentence uses the grammatically parallel elements *decreasing* and *improving* to describe the two aims of the company's policy.

A   **Correct.** *Decreasing* and *improving* are grammatically parallel; *aimed at* is a correct and concise expression.

B   *The decreasing* and *to improve* are not parallel.

C   Using *the* before *decreasing* creates a gerund, which is not parallel to the participle *improving*.

D   *The aim of which* is awkward and wordy; *the decreasing* is not parallel to *improving*.

E   *With the aim to* is not the correct idiom; the correct idiom is *with the aim of* followed by an *ing* verb form such as *decreasing*.

The correct answer is A.

27. <u>Obtaining an investment-grade rating will keep the county's future borrowing costs low, protect</u> its already-tattered image, and increase its ability to buy bond insurance.

    (A) Obtaining an investment-grade rating will keep the county's future borrowing costs low, protect

    (B) To obtain an investment-grade rating will keep the county's future borrowing costs low, and protect

    (C) Having obtained an investment-grade rating will, in keeping the county's future borrowing costs low, protect

    (D) To obtain an investment-grade rating would keep the county's future borrowing costs low, protecting

    (E) Obtaining an investment-grade rating, keeping the county's borrowing costs low, would be protecting

Verb form; Parallelism

This sentence lists three benefits the county will experience when it obtains an investment-grade rating. The auxiliary verb *will* applies to all of these future benefits, so all of the verbs listing those benefits must take infinitive verb forms to parallel (*will*) *keep*. Moreover, the possessive *county's* in the first verb phrase must be paralleled in the successive phrases with the possessive pronoun *its*.

A   **Correct.** The sentence uses correct verb forms and correct parallel structure.

B   The infinitive subject *To obtain* suggests that obtaining an investment grade rating is an objective in and of itself, not a means to achieve the desired benefits; the repetition of *and* between the phrases in the list is unnecessarily wordy.

C   The correct verb form to anticipate future consequences is the present-tense gerund *obtaining* rather than the present-perfect form *having obtained*. This version of the sentence is not only confusing, it is also wordy.

D   The faulty parallelism is confusing; *protecting* introduces an adjective phrase describing the subject of the sentence, but this makes *increase* into a verb with no subject.

E   This sentence implies that obtaining an investment-grade rating and keeping costs low are the same thing; this version of the sentence makes the referent of the possessive pronoun *its* uncertain because the possessive pronoun no longer identifies with the possessive noun in a grammatically parallel series.

The correct answer is A.

28. Eating saltwater fish may <u>significantly reduce the risk of heart attacks and also aid for</u> sufferers of rheumatoid arthritis and asthma, according to three research studies published in the *New England Journal of Medicine*.

    (A) significantly reduce the risk of heart attacks and also aid for
    (B) be significant in reducing the risk of heart attacks and aid for
    (C) significantly reduce the risk of heart attacks and aid
    (D) cause a significant reduction in the risk of heart attacks and aid to
    (E) significantly reduce the risk of heart attacks as well as aiding

Diction; Parallelism

The word *aid* can be a noun or a verb; here it should be a verb that is parallel to the verb *reduce*. If *aid* were a noun, it would parallel *risk* and so would mean illogically that eating fish reduces *aid for sufferers* as well as *the risk of heart attacks*.

A   *Aid for* seems to be a noun, parallel to the noun *risk*, indicating that *eating saltwater fish* reduces *aid for sufferers*.

B   *Aid for* seems to be a noun, parallel to the noun *risk*, indicating that *eating saltwater fish* reduces *aid for sufferers*.

C   **Correct.** In this sentence, *aid* is used as a verb, parallel to the verb *reduce*. *Sufferers* is the direct object of *aid*; no preposition is needed.

D   *Aid to* is incorrectly used as a noun, suggesting that *eating saltwater fish* reduces *aid to sufferers*.

E   While this sentence conveys the correct meaning, it lacks the parallel structure found in the correct answer.

The correct answer is C.

29. According to some economists, the July decrease in unemployment <u>so that it was the lowest in two years</u> suggests that the gradual improvement in the job market is continuing.

    (A) so that it was the lowest in two years
    (B) so that it was the lowest two-year rate

    (C) to what would be the lowest in two years
    (D) to a two-year low level
    (E) to the lowest level in two years

Idiom; Rhetorical construction

In this sentence, *decrease* is used as a noun and cannot grammatically be modified by the adverbial *so that*. The simple prepositional phrase *to the lowest level in two years* is a precise, concise alternative.

A   The use of *so that it was* to modify a noun is ungrammatical, and *it* could refer to either *decrease* or *unemployment*.

B   The use of *so that it was* to modify a noun is ungrammatical. *It* could refer to either *decrease* or *unemployment*, and the word *rate* is unclear.

C   Use of the conditional *would* to state a fact is nonstandard; *lowest* should refer to a noun such as *level*.

D   The meaning of *to a two-year low level* is unclear, and the phrase is unidiomatic.

E   **Correct.** This sentence uses a clear, simple phrase that conveys an unambiguous meaning.

The correct answer is E.

30. Thomas Eakins' powerful style and his choices of subject—the advances in modern surgery, the discipline of sport, the strains of individuals in tension with society or even with themselves—<u>was as disturbing to his own time as it is</u> compelling for ours.

    (A) was as disturbing to his own time as it is
    (B) were as disturbing to his own time as they are
    (C) has been as disturbing in his own time as they are
    (D) had been as disturbing in his own time as it was
    (E) have been as disturbing in his own time as

Agreement; Verb form

The compound subject of this sentence, *style* and *choices*, is followed by singular verbs, *was* and *is*, and a singular pronoun, *it*. The compound subject requires the plural verbs *were* and *are* and the plural pronoun *they*.

A   The verbs and pronoun are singular, but the subject is plural.

B   Correct. Verbs (*were, are*) and pronoun (*they*) agree with the plural subject in this sentence.

C   *Has been* is singular and illogically indicates that Eakins' time continues today.

D   *Had been* indicates a time anterior to some other past time; *it was* is singular and the wrong tense.

E   *Have been* illogically indicates that Eakins' time continues into the present day.

The correct answer is B.

31.   Nearly two tons of nuclear-reactor fuel have already been put into orbit around the Earth, and the chances of a collision involving such material increase greatly <u>as the amount of both space debris and satellites continue to rise</u>.

(A)   as the amount of both space debris and satellites continue to rise

(B)   as the rise continues in both the amount of satellites and space debris

(C)   as the amount of space debris and the number of satellites continue to rise

(D)   with the continually increasing amount of space debris and the number of satellites

(E)   with the amount of space debris continuing to increase along with the number of satellites

Diction; Rhetorical construction

This sentence opens with a main clause stating a condition (two tons of nuclear-reactor fuel orbiting the Earth) and follows this with a second main clause stating possible consequences of combining this condition (amount of space debris) with a second condition (rising number of satellites). Because debris is not a countable noun, it must be described as an *amount*; satellites are countable, so they must be referred to as a number, not an amount.

A   *Amount* is an inappropriate descriptor for satellites.

B   *Amount* is an inappropriate descriptor for satellites. *Both* should be followed by two nouns, but here it is followed by only one, so the comparison is grammatically incorrect.

C   Correct. The sentence is unambiguous and grammatically correct and uses *amount* and *number* correctly.

D   By attaching the adjective *increasing* only to *amount of space debris*, the sentence fails to indicate that the number of satellites is also growing. This leaves the function of *and the number of satellites* uncertain and confusing.

E   This version of the sentence is indirect, wordy, and confusing.

The correct answer is C.

32.   <u>Like Rousseau, Tolstoi rebelled</u> against the unnatural complexity of human relations in modern society.

(A)   Like Rousseau, Tolstoi rebelled

(B)   Like Rousseau, Tolstoi's rebellion was

(C)   As Rousseau, Tolstoi rebelled

(D)   As did Rousseau, Tolstoi's rebellion was

(E)   Tolstoi's rebellion, as Rousseau's, was

Logical predication; Rhetorical construction

The preposition *like* correctly compares two equal nouns, in this case, two writers. The comparison must be between two equal elements; it cannot be between a person and an event. The original sentence is direct, clear, and concise.

A   Correct. The two writers are compared clearly and succinctly in this sentence.

B   *Tolstoi's rebellion* rather than *Tolstoi* is compared to *Rousseau*.

C   When used as a conjunction, *as* should introduce clauses, not phrases or nouns.

D   *Tolstoi's rebellion* is compared to *Rousseau*. To be correct, this construction would have to be *as did Rousseau, Tolstoi rebelled*, but this is a wordy alternative.

E   *Tolstoi's rebellion . . . was against* is awkward and wordy; *Tolstoi rebelled against* is more direct.

The correct answer is A.

33. The Wallerstein study indicates that even after a decade young men and women still experience some of the effects of a divorce occurring when a child.

    (A)   occurring when a child
    (B)   occurring when children
    (C)   that occurred when a child
    (D)   that occurred when they were children
    (E)   that has occurred as each was a child

Logical predication; Agreement

The original sentence has two problems. (1) The phrasing implies that the young men and women had divorced in childhood. (2) The word *child* does not agree with the plural antecedent *men and women*.

A   *Child* does not agree with *men and women*, and the phrase *occurring when a child* is illogical.

B   The phrase *occurring when children* is illogical.

C   *Child* does not agree with *men and women*.

D   **Correct.** This sentence corrects both problems by making it clear that the divorce took place when the men and women were children and by using *they* and *children* to agree with *men and women*.

E   *Each* does not agree with *men and women*; *has occurred* is not the correct verb tense.

The correct answer is D.

34. Lacking information about energy use, people tend to overestimate the amount of energy used by equipment, such as lights, that are visible and must be turned on and off and underestimate that used by unobtrusive equipment, such as water heaters.

    (A)   equipment, such as lights, that are visible and must be turned on and off and underestimate that

    (B)   equipment, such as lights, that are visible and must be turned on and off and underestimate it when

    (C)   equipment, such as lights, that is visible and must be turned on and off and underestimate it when

    (D)   visible equipment, such as lights, that must be turned on and off and underestimate that

    (E)   visible equipment, such as lights, that must be turned on and off and underestimate it when

Parallelism; Agreement

This sentence has errors in parallelism and in subject-verb agreement. The clause *that are visible* is not parallel to the adjective *unobtrusive*. Two kinds of equipment are being contrasted, *visible* and *unobtrusive*, so to be parallel (and concise) each adjective should appear directly before the noun it modifies, *equipment*. The noun *equipment* is singular and requires a singular verb.

A   *That are visible* is not parallel to *unobtrusive*, and *are* does not agree with *equipment*.

B   *That are visible* is not parallel to *unobtrusive*, and *it when used by* is not parallel to *the amount . . . used by*. The singular noun *equipment* requires a singular verb.

C   *That is visible* is not parallel to *unobtrusive*; *it when used by* is not parallel to *the amount . . . used by*.

D   **Correct.** In this sentence, the two adjectives *visible* and *unobtrusive* are parallel, and placing *visible* before *equipment* eliminates the verb and solves the agreement problem. The construction *overestimate the amount of energy used by . . . and . . . underestimate that used by* provides parallel structure.

E   *It when used by* is not parallel to *the amount . . . used by*.

The correct answer is D.

35. The rise in the Commerce Department's index of leading economic indicators suggest that the economy should continue its expansion into the coming months, but that the mixed performance of the index's individual components indicates that economic growth will proceed at a more moderate pace than in the first quarter of this year.

    (A)   suggest that the economy should continue its expansion into the coming months, but that

    (B)   suggest that the economy is to continue expansion in the coming months, but

    (C)   suggests that the economy will continue its expanding in the coming months, but that

    (D)   suggests that the economy is continuing to expand into the coming months, but that

    (E)   suggests that the economy will continue to expand in the coming months, but

Agreement; Grammatical construction; Verb form

The singular subject *the rise* requires the singular verb *suggests*, not the plural *suggest*. This sentence is best composed of a main clause followed by a subordinate clause, the coordinating conjunction *but*, and then another main clause followed by a subordinate clause. When *that* is repeated after *but*, this structure is lost and a grammatically incorrect one put in its place. The second half of the sentence uses the future tense *will proceed*, so the first half should use *will continue*, the future tense reinforced by the phrase *in the coming months*. The infinitive phrase *to expand* is the clearest of the alternatives.

A   *Suggest* does not agree with *the rise*. *That* should be omitted to create a main clause, and the verb should be the future tense *will continue*.

B   *Suggest* does not agree with *the rise*. The phrase *is to continue expansion* is not as clear as the more direct *will continue to expand*.

C   *Suggest* does not agree with *the rise*, and use of *that* results in a subordinate clause when a main clause is required. *Its expanding* is awkward.

D   *That* used after *but* results in an incomplete grammatical construction, and the verb should be the future tense *will continue*.

E   **Correct.** This sentence is complete and correct, with the subject and verb in agreement and the verbs in the future tense.

The correct answer is E.

36.   Polio, although it is eradicated in the United States, it continues elsewhere and is able to be brought into the country by visitors.

(A)   Polio, although it is eradicated in the United States, it continues elsewhere and is able to be

(B)   Polio, although eradicated in the United States, it still continues elsewhere and can be

(C)   Although still continuing elsewhere, polio has been eradicated in the United States and could be

(D)   Although having been eradicated in the United States, polio still continues elsewhere and is capable of being

(E)   Although eradicated in the United States, polio continues elsewhere and could be

Grammatical construction; Rhetorical construction

This sentence makes two main claims about a single subject, *polio* (that it continues elsewhere, and that it can be brought back into the United States). The claim that polio has been eradicated in the United States is a condition of the other two claims and is best expressed in a subordinate clause.

A   The second appearance of *it* as the subject of *continues* and *is* leaves *polio* as a subject with no verb.

B   The pronoun *it* is ungrammatical because *polio* already occupies the subject position for the verbs *continues* and *can be brought*.

C   The sequence of events in this version of the sentence is confusing. The possibility of polio being reintroduced in the United States is a consequence of its continuing elsewhere, but this version of the sentence obscures that connection.

D   Although not grammatically incorrect, this version of the sentence is wordy and indirect.

E   **Correct.** The sentence is clear, concise, and grammatically correct.

The correct answer is E.

37.   Some buildings that were destroyed and heavily damaged in the earthquake last year were constructed in violation of the city's building code.

(A)   Some buildings that were destroyed and heavily damaged in the earthquake last year were

(B)   Some buildings that were destroyed or heavily damaged in the earthquake last year had been

(C)   Some buildings that the earthquake destroyed and heavily damaged last year have been

(D)   Last year the earthquake destroyed or heavily damaged some buildings that have been

(E)   Last year some of the buildings that were destroyed or heavily damaged in the earthquake had been

Diction; Verb form

The buildings cannot be both *destroyed* and *heavily damaged* at the same time; they must be one *or* the other. The ideas of this sentence are most clearly expressed using two verb tenses: the simple past, *were*, for the earthquake occurring last year; and the past perfect, *had been*, for the time prior to that when the buildings were constructed.

A The buildings are illogically said to be both *destroyed* and *damaged*.

B Correct. This sentence properly states that the buildings were either destroyed *or* damaged and clarifies that they *had been constructed* before the earthquake struck.

C Buildings cannot be both destroyed *and* damaged. The verb tense makes it seem that they were constructed after the earthquake.

D The verb tense illogically indicates that the buildings *have been constructed* since the earthquake.

E This structure indicates that construction of the buildings, rather than the earthquake, occurred *last year*.

The correct answer is B.

38. A study commissioned by the Department of Agriculture showed that if calves exercise and <u>associated with other calves, they will require less medication and gain weight quicker than do</u> those raised in confinement.

(A) associated with other calves, they will require less medication and gain weight quicker than do

(B) associated with other calves, they require less medication and gain weight quicker than

(C) associate with other calves, they required less medication and will gain weight quicker than do

(D) associate with other calves, they have required less medication and will gain weight more quickly than do

(E) associate with other calves, they require less medication and gain weight more quickly than

Verb form; Diction

The first and last verbs in the series of verbs that describe the calves are in the present tense, so the two in the middle should be as well: the calves *exercise . . . associate . . . require . . . gain weight*. Adverbs, not adjectives, describe how an action is carried out. These calves gain weight *more quickly*, not *quicker*, than other calves. The comparison is between *calves* and *those* (referring to another set of calves); the verb *do* ungrammatically interrupts the comparison and should be eliminated.

A *Associated* and *will require* do not match *exercise* and *gain*. The adjective *quicker* should be the adverb *more quickly*, and *do* must be omitted from the comparison.

B *Associated* is in the past rather than the present tense; *quicker* is used in place of the correct *more quickly*.

C *Required* and *will gain* are not in the present tense; *quicker* is used in place of the correct *more quickly*. *Do* must be omitted.

D *Have required* and *will gain* should be in the present tense; *do* must be omitted.

E Correct. In this sentence, the verbs are all in the present tense; an adverb correctly modifies the verb phrase; and the comparison is logical and grammatically correct.

The correct answer is E.

39. A recent study has found that within the past few years, many doctors <u>had elected early retirement rather than face</u> the threats of lawsuits and the rising costs of malpractice insurance.

(A) had elected early retirement rather than face

(B) had elected early retirement instead of facing

(C) have elected retiring early instead of facing

(D) have elected to retire early rather than facing

(E) have elected to retire early rather than face

Verb form; Parallelism

For action that started in the past and continues into the present, it is correct to use the present perfect tense: *have elected*. When a choice is presented using the *rather than* construction—*the doctors have chosen x rather than y*—the *x* and the *y* must be parallel. In this case, the doctors have chosen *to retire* rather than (*to* understood) *face*. *To* does not need to be repeated in order to maintain parallelism because it is understood.

A   *Had elected* shows an action completed in the past; *early retirement* is not parallel to *face*.

B   *Had elected* shows an action completed in the past; *retirement* and *facing* are not parallel.

C   *Have elected* must be followed by an infinitive (*to retire*).

D   *Facing* and *to retire early* are not parallel.

E   **Correct.** In this sentence, *have elected* shows action continuing into the present; *to retire* and (*to* understood) *face* are parallel.

The correct answer is E.

40.   The Gorton-Dodd bill requires <u>that a bank disclose to their customers how long they will delay access to funds from deposited checks</u>.

(A)   that a bank disclose to their customers how long they will delay access to funds from deposited checks

(B)   a bank to disclose to their customers how long they will delay access to funds from a deposited check

(C)   that a bank disclose to its customers how long it will delay access to funds from deposited checks

(D)   a bank that it should disclose to its customers how long it will delay access to funds from a deposited check

(E)   that banks disclose to customers how long access to funds from their deposited check is to be delayed

Agreement; Rhetorical construction

A bank is singular and must be followed by the singular pronouns *its* and *it* rather than the plural pronouns *their* and *they*.

A   *Their* and *they* do not agree with *a bank*.

B   *Their* and *they* do not agree with *a bank*, and the singular *check* is illogical since customers do not share one check.

C   **Correct.** In this sentence, the pronouns *its* and *it* agree with *a bank*, and *deposited checks* is a logical fit with *customers*.

D   *Requires a bank that it should* is not a grammatical construction. The singular *check* is illogical since the customers do not share one check.

E   The passive voice *is to be delayed* conceals the bank's role in delaying access. The singular *check* with the plural *their* is illogical.

The correct answer is C.

41.   Unlike a funded pension system, in which contributions are invested to pay future beneficiaries, <u>a pay-as-you-go approach is the foundation of Social Security</u>.

(A)   a pay-as-you-go approach is the foundation of Social Security

(B)   the foundation of Social Security is a pay-as-you-go approach

(C)   the approach of Social Security is pay-as-you-go

(D)   Social Security's approach is pay-as-you-go

(E)   Social Security is founded on a pay-as-you-go approach

Logical predication

This sentence contrasts two systems, *a funded pension system* and *Social Security*. The sentence must be structured so that the contrast is logical and grammatical. After the first (*funded pension*) system is introduced and described, the second (*Social Security*) system must be introduced. The original sentence makes the mistake of contrasting *a funded pension system* with *a pay-as-you-go approach*.

A   *A funded pension system* is contrasted with an *approach* rather than with *Social Security*.

B   *A funded pension system* is contrasted with *the foundation* rather than with *Social Security*.

C   *A funded pension system* is contrasted with *the approach* rather than with *Social Security*.

D   *A funded pension system* is contrasted with *Social Security's approach* rather than with *Social Security*.

E   **Correct.** The two systems are contrasted in a logical, grammatical way in this sentence.

The correct answer is E.

42. Twenty-two feet long and 10 feet in diameter, the AM-1 is one of the many new <u>satellites that is a part of 15 years effort of subjecting the interactions of Earth's atmosphere, oceans, and land surfaces</u> to detailed scrutiny from space.

(A)   satellites that is a part of 15 years effort of subjecting the interactions of Earth's atmosphere, oceans, and land surfaces

(B)   satellites, which is a part of a 15-year effort to subject how Earth's atmosphere, oceans, and land surfaces interact

(C)   satellites, part of 15 years effort of subjecting how Earth's atmosphere, oceans, and land surfaces are interacting

(D)   satellites that are part of an effort for 15 years that has subjected the interactions of Earth's atmosphere, oceans, and land surfaces

(E)   satellites that are part of a 15-year effort to subject the interactions of Earth's atmosphere, oceans, and land surfaces

Rhetorical construction; Logical predication

This sentence describes one satellite and identifies it as part of a larger space project designed to scrutinize Earth's ocean, land, and atmospheric interactions. The relative pronoun *that* refers to satellites, so it should be followed by a plural verb. The idiomatic expression is *effort to* rather than *effort of.* The correct adjectival term is *15-year* rather than *15 years*.

A   The relative pronoun *that* refers to satellites, so it should be followed by the plural verb *are*; *effort to* is the correct idiomatic expression; as an adjective, *15 years* becomes *15-year.*

B   In this version of the sentence, it is unclear what the relative pronoun *which* refers to—if it refers to *satellites*, it should be followed by a plural verb. Presenting the object of the verb *subject* as a phrase beginning with *how* and ending with the verb *interact* produces a sentence that seems to be about how various conditions react to detailed scrutiny from space.

C   This sentence too seems to be making a nonsensical statement about how conditions are interacting to detailed scrutiny. It is not clear whether *part* refers to *satellites* or the *AM-1.*

D   This version is wordy and confusing because of the sequence of relative clauses beginning with *that.*

E   **Correct.** The sentence is clearly worded and logically coherent.

The correct answer is E.

43. Though the term "graphic design" may <u>suggest laying out corporate brochures and annual reports, they have come to signify widely ranging</u> work, from package designs and company logotypes to signs, book jackets, computer graphics, and film titles.

(A)   suggest laying out corporate brochures and annual reports, they have come to signify widely ranging

(B)   suggest laying out corporate brochures and annual reports, it has come to signify a wide range of

(C)   suggest corporate brochure and annual report layout, it has signified widely ranging

(D)   have suggested corporate brochure and annual report layout, it has signified a wide range of

(E)   have suggested laying out corporate brochures and annual reports, they have come to signify widely ranging

Agreement; Diction; Verb form

The subject of the sentence is the singular noun *term*, which must be followed by the singular *it has* rather than the plural *they have*. *Widely ranging* could describe a conversation that moves from one topic to another; in this context, it is incorrect because the work does not move from one place to another. *A wide range of work* shows that the work consists of many different kinds of projects.

A   *They have* does not agree with *term*; *widely ranging work* is imprecise.

B   Correct. In this sentence, *it has* agrees with *term*, and the phrase *a wide range of work* suggests a variety of projects.

C   *Has signified* suggests a completed action and thus distorts the meaning; *widely ranging work* is imprecise.

D   *Have suggested* does not agree with *term*. The verb tenses suggest a completed action rather than an ongoing one.

E   *Have suggested* and *they have* do not agree with *term*; *widely ranging work* is imprecise.

The correct answer is B.

44.   In contrast to large steel plants that take iron ore through all the steps needed to produce several different kinds of steel, <u>processing steel scrap into a specialized group of products has enabled small mills to put capital into new technology and remain</u> economically viable.

(A)   processing steel scrap into a specialized group of products has enabled small mills to put capital into new technology and remain

(B)   processing steel scrap into a specialized group of products has enabled small mills to put capital into new technology, remaining

(C)   the processing of steel scrap into a specialized group of products has enabled small mills to put capital into new technology, remaining

(D)   small mills, by processing steel scrap into a specialized group of products, have been able to put capital into new technology and remain

(E)   small mills, by processing steel scrap into a specialized group of products, have been able to put capital into new technology and remained

Logical predication

This sentence contrasts *large steel plants* with *small mills*. Since the first half of the sentence begins with *in contrast to large steel plants*, the second half should begin with *small mills* to make the contrast immediately obvious and thus easy to understand.

A   *Large steel plants* should be contrasted with *small mills*, not with *processing steel scrap*.

B   *Large steel plants* appear to be contrasted with *processing steel scrap* rather than with *small mills*; *remaining* and *to put* are not parallel.

C   *Large steel plants* appear to be contrasted with the *processing of steel scrap*; *remaining* and *to put* are not parallel.

D   Correct. In this sentence, *large steel plants* are clearly contrasted with *small mills*, and *to put* is parallel with (*to* understood) *remain*.

E   *Remained* violates the parallelism with *to put*, and its past tense is not compatible with the present perfect verb *have been able*.

The correct answer is D.

45.   Under high pressure and intense heat, graphite, the most stable form of pure carbon, changes into the substance commonly referred to as diamond and <u>remaining this way whether or not</u> the heat and pressure are removed.

(A)   remaining this way whether or not

(B)   remaining like that even as

(C)   remaining as such whether or not

(D)   remains in this way although

(E)   remains thus even when

Parallelism; Rhetorical construction

This sentence tells of two things that happen to graphite under intense heat and pressure, and these are best presented as parallel predicates— *changes* and *remains*. *Thus* is the most economical way to say *this way*, *like that*, *as such*, or *in this way*.

A   *Remaining* should be a main verb, parallel with *changes*.

B   *Remaining* should be parallel with the other main verb, *changes*; *even as* suggests the meaning of *while*, which is not the intent of the sentence.

C   *Remaining* should be parallel with *changes*; *whether or not* is unnecessarily wordy.

D   *In this way* is unnecessarily wordy; *although* indicates that the heat and pressure are always or definitely removed, but this makes little sense in relation to the rest of the sentence.

E   **Correct.** The sentence coherently refers to the possibility of heat and pressure being removed. The sentence is clear and concise and properly uses parallel verb forms.

The correct answer is E.

46. The psychologist William James believed that facial expressions not only provide a visible sign of an emotion, actually contributing to the feeling itself.

(A) emotion, actually contributing to the feeling itself

(B) emotion but also actually contributing to the feeling itself

(C) emotion but also actually contribute to the feeling itself

(D) emotion; they also actually contribute to the feeling of it

(E) emotion; the feeling itself is also actually contributed to by them

Idiom; Grammatical construction

This sentence should depend on the correlative construction *not only x . . . but also y*, where *x* and *y* are parallel. However, the faulty construction in the original sentence does not properly include the second element, *but also*, and so produces a sentence fragment. James says that facial expressions have two effects: they provide a sign of emotion and they contribute to emotion. Thus, in this sentence, *not only* should be followed by (*x*) *provide a visible sign of an emotion*, and *but also* should be followed by (*y*) *actually contribute to the feeling itself*.

A   The *not only . . . but also* construction is violated, creating a sentence fragment.

B   *But also actually contributing* is not parallel to *not only provide*; because *contributing* is a participle and not a verb, the result is a sentence fragment.

C   **Correct.** The *not only . . . but also* construction is parallel, resulting in a complete sentence.

D   The *not only* construction needs to be completed with *but also* and should not be interrupted by a semicolon. *The feeling of it* is awkward and wordy.

E   Use of the semicolon in the *not only . . . but also* construction is not correct; the passive voice *is also actually contributed to* is awkward and not parallel to *provide*.

The correct answer is C.

47. Wisconsin, Illinois, Florida, and Minnesota have begun to enforce statewide bans prohibiting landfills to accept leaves, brush, and grass clippings.

(A) prohibiting landfills to accept leaves, brush, and grass clippings

(B) prohibiting that landfills accept leaves, brush, and grass clippings

(C) prohibiting landfills from accepting leaves, brush, and grass clippings

(D) that leaves, brush, and grass clippings cannot be accepted in landfills

(E) that landfills cannot accept leaves, brush, and grass clippings

Idiom; Verb form

This sentence misuses the idiomatic construction *prohibits x from doing y*; an alternative construction with the same meaning is *forbids x to do y*. The verb from the first construction, *prohibiting*, is incorrectly joined with the infinitive form required in the second construction, *to accept*. The correct statement is *prohibiting landfills from accepting. . . .*

A   *Prohibiting . . . to accept* is not the correct idiom.

B   *Prohibiting that . . . accept* is not the correct idiom.

C   **Correct.** *Prohibiting . . . from accepting* is the correct idiom to use in this sentence.

D   *Bans that . . . cannot be accepted* is not a correct idiom and does not make sense.

E   *Bans that . . . cannot accept* is an incorrect idiom, and *cannot* following *bans* is illogical.

The correct answer is C.

48. Reporting that one of <u>its many problems had been the recent</u> extended sales slump in women's apparel, the seven-store retailer said it would start a three-month liquidation sale in all of its stores.

    (A) its many problems had been the recent
    (B) its many problems has been the recently
    (C) its many problems is the recently
    (D) their many problems is the recent
    (E) their many problems had been the recent

Agreement; Verb form; Diction

The correct use of pronoun reference, verb tense, and modifier make the sentence clear and easy to understand. The singular possessive pronoun *its* refers to the singular noun *retailer*. The past perfect verb *had been* indicates action completed before the action in the simple past tense *said*. The adjective *recent* modifies *extended sales slump*.

A **Correct.** *Its* agrees with *retailers*; the past perfect *had been* indicates action prior to the simple past *said*; and *recent* modifies *extended sales slump*.

B The adverb *recently* modifies only the adjective *extended*, suggesting illogically that the sales slump has been *recently extended*.

C *Is* shows present, rather than completed, action, and the adverb *recently* modifies only the adjective *extended*, distorting meaning.

D *Their* does not agree with *retailer*, and *is* shows present, rather than completed, action.

E The plural *their* does not agree with the singular *retailer*.

The correct answer is A.

49. In developing new facilities for the incineration of solid wastes, we must avoid the danger of shifting environmental problems from <u>landfills polluting the water to polluting the air with incinerators</u>.

    (A) landfills polluting the water to polluting the air with incinerators
    (B) landfills polluting the water to the air being polluted with incinerators
    (C) the pollution of water by landfills to the pollution of air by incinerators

    (D) pollution of the water by landfills to incinerators that pollute the air
    (E) water that is polluted by landfills to incinerators that pollute the air

Parallelism; Rhetorical construction

When the construction is *from x to y*, *x* and *y* must be grammatically parallel. In this case, *x* and *y* are the two environmental problems: *x* is *the pollution of water by landfills* and *y* is *the pollution of air by incinerators*. Starting the parallel phrases with *the pollution* emphasizes the similarity of the problem; each of the other elements, *of water/of air* and *by landfills/by incinerators*, emphasizes difference.

A Lack of parallelism makes these two phrases difficult to understand.

B *Landfills polluting . . .* is not parallel to *the air being. . . .*

C **Correct.** The correct use of parallel structure clarifies the meaning of the sentence.

D *Pollution of . . .* is not parallel to *incinerators that. . . .*

E *Water that is polluted . . .* is not parallel to *incinerators that pollute. . . .*

The correct answer is C.

50. The bank holds $3 billion in loans that are seriously delinquent or in such trouble that <u>they do not expect payments when</u> due.

    (A) they do not expect payments when
    (B) it does not expect payments when it is
    (C) it does not expect payments to be made when they are
    (D) payments are not to be expected to be paid when
    (E) payments are not expected to be paid when they will be

Agreement; Logical predication; Verb form

The plural pronoun *they* cannot be used to refer to the singular noun *bank*. The structure of *they do not expect payments when due* is awkward and unclear.

A   *Bank* requires the singular pronoun *it*, not the plural pronoun *they*. The structure of *when due* creates ambiguity in meaning.

B   *Payments* is a plural noun, so the singular *it is* is incorrect.

C   **Correct.** In this correct sentence, pronouns and their referents agree, as do subjects and their verbs. The addition of the modifying phrase *to be made* clarifies the meaning of the sentence.

D   The active voice is preferable here, since the passive voice leaves it unclear who does not expect the payments to be made. *Payments . . . to be paid* is redundant. *Are not to be* incorrectly suggests that the writer is prescribing that the payments not be expected.

E   The active voice is preferable here, since the passive voice leaves it unclear who does not expect the payments to be made. *Payments . . . to be paid* is redundant. *Will be* is not the correct verb form.

The correct answer is C.

51.   In a 5-to-4 decision, the Supreme Court ruled <u>that two upstate New York counties owed restitution to three tribes of Oneida Indians for the unlawful seizure of</u> their ancestral lands in the eighteenth century.

(A)   that two upstate New York counties owed restitution to three tribes of Oneida Indians for the unlawful seizure of

(B)   that two upstate New York counties owed restitution to three tribes of Oneida Indians because of their unlawful seizure of

(C)   two upstate New York counties to owe restitution to three tribes of Oneida Indians for their unlawful seizure of

(D)   on two upstate New York counties that owed restitution to three tribes of Oneida Indians because they unlawfully seized

(E)   on the restitution that two upstate New York counties owed to three tribes of Oneida Indians for the unlawful seizure of

Idiom; Rhetorical construction

The underlined part of the sentence correctly introduces a subordinate clause with *that* to identify the Supreme Court's ruling. The idiomatic expression *owed restitution to x for y* is also correctly used.

A   **Correct.** This sentence properly uses a subordinate clause introduced by *that* and contains the correct idiom.

B   *Owed restitution to x because of y* is not the correct idiom, and the pronoun reference *their* is ambiguous.

C   *That* is omitted, resulting in an awkward construction; the pronoun reference *their* is ambiguous.

D   *Ruled on . . . that* begins an awkward construction, and the pronoun reference *they* is ambiguous.

E   *Ruled on . . . that* begins an awkward and imprecise construction.

The correct answer is A.

52.   Recently discovered fossil remains strongly suggest that the Australian egg-laying mammals of today are a branch of the main stem of mammalian evolution <u>rather than developing independently from</u> a common ancestor of mammals more than 220 million years ago.

(A)   rather than developing independently from

(B)   rather than a type that developed independently from

(C)   rather than a type whose development was independent of

(D)   instead of developing independently from

(E)   instead of a development that was independent of

Idiom; Parallelism

The original point is that the mammals mentioned are thought to be an offshoot of *the main stem of mammalian evolution* and not a descendent of *a common ancestor of* [all] *mammals*. This sentence makes a contrast using the construction *x rather than y* or *x instead of y; x* and *y* must be parallel in either case. The mammals are (*x*) *a branch* rather than (*y*); here *y* should consist of an article and a noun to match *a branch*. The second half of the contrast may be rewritten *a type that developed independently from* to complete the parallel construction. The idiom *independently from* is different in meaning from the idiom *independent of*; the logic of this sentence requires the use of *independently from*.

A   *Developing independently from* is not parallel to *a branch*.

B   Correct. This idiomatically correct sentence properly uses *a type* in parallel to *a branch*.

C   The verb *developed* is preferable to the awkward and wordy relative clause using the noun *development*; *independent of* distorts the original meaning.

D   *Developing independently from* is not parallel to *a branch*.

E   While *a development* may appear to parallel *a branch, a development that was independent of . . .* expresses a meaning contrary to that expressed in the original sentence. The verb *developed* is preferable to the noun *development*.

The correct answer is B.

53.   The normative model of strategic decision-making suggests that executives examine a firm's external environment and internal <u>conditions, and in using the set of objective criteria they derive from these analyses, can decide</u> on a strategy.

(A)   conditions, and in using the set of objective criteria they derive from these analyses, can decide

(B)   conditions, and they use the set of objective criteria derived from these analyses in deciding

(C)   conditions and, in using the set of objective criteria derived from these analyses, deciding

(D)   conditions and, using the set of objective criteria derived from these analyses, decide

(E)   conditions and, in their use of the set of objective criteria they derive from these analyses, they decide

Grammatical construction; Verb form

The noun clause introduced by *that* has one subject (*executives*) and two main verbs (*examine* and *decide*). These verbs need to be in parallel form. The information about using *objective criteria* describes the *executives* and is therefore most efficiently presented as a participial phrase (*using . . .*) rather than a prepositional phrase (*in using . . .*).

A   This version is unnecessarily wordy and indirect. There is no need to repeat the subject, *executives*, with the pronoun *they*.

B   This version is unnecessarily wordy because it creates a compound sentence by repeating the subject, using the pronoun *they* to refer to *executives*.

C   By using the coordinating conjunction *and*, this version of the sentence creates the need for a second subject and main verb; this second subject is absent. The participle *deciding* cannot function as a main verb.

D   Correct. The sentence is grammatically correct and uses proper verb forms to express a clear and logically coherent message.

E   This version of the sentence is wordy and indirect, largely because of the repetition of the pronoun *they*.

The correct answer is D.

54.   A patient accusing a doctor of malpractice will find it difficult to prove damage <u>if there is a lack of some other doctor to testify</u> about proper medical procedures.

(A)   if there is a lack of some other doctor to testify

(B)   unless there will be another doctor to testify

(C)   without another doctor's testimony

(D)   should there be no testimony from some other doctor

(E)   lacking another doctor to testify

Rhetorical construction; Idiom

The underlined clause is wordy and awkward; *lack of some other doctor* is not a correct idiomatic expression. This clause must be replaced by a more concise construction. *If there is a lack of* can be replaced by the preposition *without*; *some other doctor* is better expressed as *another doctor*; and *testimony* can be substituted for *to testify*. The result, *without another doctor's testimony*, clearly expresses in four words what the original statement poorly conveyed in eleven.

A   The clause is wordy and awkward; *lack of some other doctor* is not idiomatic.

B   The construction *y will happen unless x happens first* requires the present tense following the *unless* clause, rather than the future tense used here.

C   **Correct.** This sentence uses a phrase that is clear and concise.

D   This alternative is awkward and wordy.

E   *Lacking* illogically and incorrectly modifies *damage*.

The correct answer is C.

55.   The energy source on *Voyager 2* is not a nuclear reactor, in which atoms are actively broken <u>apart; rather</u> a kind of nuclear battery that uses natural radioactive decay to produce power.

(A)   apart; rather
(B)   apart, but rather
(C)   apart, but rather that of
(D)   apart, but that of
(E)   apart; it is that of

Grammatical construction; Logical predication

The correct version of this sentence focuses on a contrast by using the construction *not x, but rather y*. A comma, not a semicolon, should separate the two parallel parts of the contrast; using a semicolon results in a sentence fragment unless a subject and verb are provided in the construction that follows the semicolon.

A   Using a semicolon results in a sentence fragment.

B   **Correct.** This sentence is grammatical and logically coherent. The contrast is clearly drawn in the construction *not a nuclear reactor . . . , but rather a kind of nuclear battery*.

C   *That of* has no referent and results in an illogical construction.

D   *That of* has no referent.

E   No word is used to indicate contrast; *that of* has no referent.

The correct answer is B.

56.   Archaeologists in Ireland believe that a recently discovered chalice, which dates from the eighth century, was probably buried <u>to keep from</u> being stolen by invaders.

(A)   to keep from
(B)   to keep it from
(C)   to avoid
(D)   in order that it would avoid
(E)   in order to keep from

Grammatical construction; Logical predication

The phrase *to keep from being stolen* is incomplete and does not indicate what might be stolen. Inserting a pronoun makes it clear that it is the chalice that might be stolen.

A   The pronoun *it* is needed for clarity.

B   **Correct.** The sentence is clarified by inserting the word *it*, which refers back to *chalice*.

C   This suggests that the chalice acts to prevent its own theft. The pronoun *it* is needed for clarity.

D   This suggests that the chalice acts to prevent its own theft. The pronoun *it* is needed for clarity. *In order that it would* is wordy.

E   The pronoun *it* is needed for clarity.

The correct answer is B.

57. <u>According to its proponents, a proposed new style of aircraft could, by skimming along the top of the atmosphere, fly between most points on Earth in under two hours.</u>

   (A) According to its proponents, a proposed new style of aircraft could, by skimming along the top of the atmosphere, fly between most points on Earth in under two hours.

   (B) By skimming along the top of the atmosphere, proponents of a proposed new style of aircraft say it could fly between most points on Earth in under two hours.

   (C) A proposed new style of aircraft could fly between most points on Earth in under two hours, according to its proponents, with it skimming along the top of the atmosphere.

   (D) A proposed new style of aircraft, say its proponents, could fly between most points on Earth in under two hours because of its skimming along the top of the atmosphere.

   (E) According to its proponents, skimming along the top of the atmosphere makes it possible that a proposed new style of aircraft could fly between most points on Earth in under two hours.

Rhetorical construction; Logical predication

The main point of this sentence is that a proposed aircraft could fly between any two points on Earth in under two hours; that information should be presented in the main clause. Qualifications of this point (who says it, how it can be accomplished) are a secondary focus and should therefore be presented in adverbial phrases.

A   **Correct.** The sentence is clear, direct, and logically coherent.

B   This sentence makes *proponents* the main subject of the sentence; the opening prepositional phrase, *By skimming . . .*, nonsensically describes *proponents*.

C   The prepositional phrase (*with it . . .*) is indirect and wordy and too far from the noun phrase it modifies (*style of aircraft*).

D   The explanation of how the aircraft could accomplish its feat is awkwardly expressed in the final phrase (*because of its . . .*).

E   This version is wordy and repetitive (*possible* and *could* repeat the same meaning); because the antecedent for *its* is so far from the opening phrase, the reference is unclear.

The correct answer is A.

58. Lawmakers are examining measures that would require banks to disclose all fees and account requirements in writing, <u>provide free cashing of government checks, and to create basic savings accounts to carry</u> minimal fees and require minimal initial deposits.

   (A) provide free cashing of government checks, and to create basic savings accounts to carry

   (B) provide free cashing of government checks, and creating basic savings accounts carrying

   (C) to provide free cashing of government checks, and creating basic savings accounts that carry

   (D) to provide free cashing of government checks, creating basic savings accounts to carry

   (E) to provide free cashing of government checks, and to create basic savings accounts that carry

Parallelism; Verb form

The correct version of the sentence uses parallel structure to describe what new legislation would require banks to do. The first requirement is written as *to disclose*; the other two requirements must be parallel in form. In this case, the other two requirements can be given as either *to provide . . . to create* or *provide . . . create*, with the *to* understood. In addition, using the same infinitive form for a different purpose in *to carry* is potentially confusing; using *that carry* is a clearer construction.

A   *Provide* and *to create* are not parallel. *To carry* is unclear and can be seen as making the illogical claim that the purpose of creating the accounts is to carry minimal fees and require minimal deposits.

B   *Provide* and *creating* are not parallel.

C   *Creating* is not parallel with *to provide*.

D   *To provide* and *creating* are not parallel in form. *To carry* is unclear and can be seen as making the illogical claim that the purpose of creating the accounts is to carry minimal fees and require minimal deposits.

E   Correct. Parallelism is maintained in this sentence by following *to disclose* with *to provide* and *to create*. In this setting, the form *that carry* is more readily understood than *to carry*.

The correct answer is E.

59. Certain pesticides can become ineffective if used repeatedly in the same place; one reason is suggested by the finding that there are much larger populations of pesticide-degrading microbes in soils with a relatively long history of pesticide use than in soils that are free of such chemicals.

   (A) Certain pesticides can become ineffective if used repeatedly in the same place; one reason is suggested by the finding that there are much larger populations of pesticide-degrading microbes in soils with a relatively long history of pesticide use than in soils that are free of such chemicals.

   (B) If used repeatedly in the same place, one reason that certain pesticides can become ineffective is suggested by the finding that there are much larger populations of pesticide-degrading microbes in soils with a relatively long history of pesticide use than in soils that are free of such chemicals.

   (C) If used repeatedly in the same place, one reason certain pesticides can become ineffective is suggested by the finding that much larger populations of pesticide-degrading microbes are found in soils with a relatively long history of pesticide use than those that are free of such chemicals.

   (D) The finding that there are much larger populations of pesticide-degrading microbes in soils with a relatively long history of pesticide use than in soils that are free of such chemicals is suggestive of one reason, if used repeatedly in the same place, certain pesticides can become ineffective.

   (E) The finding of much larger populations of pesticide-degrading microbes in soils with a relatively long history of pesticide use than in those that are free of such chemicals suggests one reason certain pesticides can become ineffective if used repeatedly in the same place.

Logical predication; Rhetorical construction

The sentence is correctly constructed; it has two independent clauses connected by a semicolon. *If used repeatedly in the same place* clearly and correctly modifies *certain pesticides*.

A   Correct. The sentence is correctly constructed; the modifier *if used repeatedly in the same place* is correctly placed.

B   *If used repeatedly in the same place* modifies *one reason* when it should modify *certain pesticides*.

C   *If used repeatedly in the same place* modifies *one reason* when it should modify *certain pesticides*. The absence of *in* in the phrase *than those . . .* makes the comparison unclear.

D   *If used repeatedly in the same place* ambiguously modifies *one reason* when it should clearly modify *certain pesticides*.

E   The comparison *the finding of much larger populations . . . than in those that . . .* is improperly constructed in a way that makes *the finding* appear to refer awkwardly to a discovery of larger populations rather than to a research conclusion about the presence of such populations.

The correct answer is A.

60. In the textbook publishing business, the second quarter is historically weak, because revenues are low and marketing expenses are high as companies prepare for the coming school year.

   (A) low and marketing expenses are high as companies prepare

   (B) low and their marketing expenses are high as they prepare

   (C) low with higher marketing expenses in preparation

   (D) low, while marketing expenses are higher to prepare

   (E) low, while their marketing expenses are higher in preparation

Parallelism; Logical predication

This sentence is correctly written. It uses parallel structure to give two reasons why textbook publishers have weak second quarters: *revenues are low* and *expenses are high*. The construction *as companies prepare for the coming school year* is clear, as opposed to the awkward constructions using the ambiguous plural pronouns *they* and *their*.

A **Correct.** This sentence uses the parallel forms *are low . . . are high* and employs the unambiguous *companies* as the subject of *prepare*.

B *Their* seems illogically to refer to *revenues*. The subject of *prepare* is the ambiguous *they*.

C *Higher* is not parallel to *low*, and it gives no indication of what the comparison is supposed to be (Higher than what?). This construction makes it appear, illogically, that the low revenues have higher marketing expenses.

D *Higher* is not parallel to *low* and is illogical. The infinitive construction *to prepare . . .* is awkward.

E *Higher* is not parallel to *low* and is illogical since no comparison is being made; *their* has no clear referent.

The correct answer is A.

61. Almost a decade after New York State passed laws to protect patients by reducing the grueling hours worked by medical residents, <u>twelve hospitals have been investigated by state medical officials, finding that all twelve consistently break the laws, many residents work longer than 24 hours straight, and that more than half the surgical residents work</u> more than 95 hours a week.

   (A) twelve hospitals have been investigated by state medical officials, finding that all twelve consistently break the laws, many residents work longer than 24 hours straight, and that more than half the surgical residents work

   (B) an investigation by state medical officials of twelve hospitals have found all twelve consistently breaking the laws, that many residents work longer than 24 hours straight, with more than half the surgical residents working

   (C) an investigation of twelve hospitals by state medical officials has found that all twelve consistently break the laws, that many residents work longer than 24 hours straight, and that more than half the surgical residents work

   (D) twelve hospitals were investigated by state medical officials who found all twelve breaking the laws, with many residents working longer than 24 hours straight, and more than half the surgical residents work

   (E) an investigation by state medical officials has found that, of twelve hospitals, all twelve consistently break the laws, that many residents work longer than 24 hours straight, with more than half the surgical residents working

Parallelism; Logical predication

This sentence is primarily concerned with presenting the findings of an investigation, so the main subject should be *investigation*, and the main verb should be *has found*. The findings are most efficiently presented in a parallel series of relative clauses beginning with *that*.

A The phrase *finding that all . . .* has nothing to attach to in this sentence, because *hospitals* has been made the subject of the sentence; the items in the list of findings are not presented in parallel form.

B The singular subject requires a singular verb; the items in the list of findings are not presented in parallel form.

C **Correct.** The sentence's structure makes it clear and logical.

D The preposition *with* governs both examples of how the hospitals break the law, so parallelism requires that both verbs assume the *ing* ending.

E The sentence is repetitive and indirect; the list of findings is not presented in parallel form.

The correct answer is C.

62. Parliament did not accord full refugee benefits to twelve of the recent immigrants because it believed that <u>to do it rewards</u> them for entering the country illegally.

(A)   to do it rewards

(B)   doing it rewards

(C)   to do this would reward

(D)   doing so would reward

(E)   to do it would reward

Diction; Verb form

The problem in the underlined section is how to refer back to the verb *accord*. The clearest and most standard way is to use the adverb *so*, rather than a pronoun such as *it* or *this*. The verb *rewards* is incorrectly in the indicative mood, the mood used to state a fact; in the context of a hypothetical action, the conditional *would reward* is more appropriate.

A   The pronoun *it* does not have a clear antecedent; the adverb *so* is preferable. *Rewards* should be *would reward*.

B   The pronoun *it* does not have a clear antecedent; the adverb *so* is preferable. *Rewards* should be *would reward*.

C   The pronoun *this* does not have a clear antecedent; the adverb *so* is preferable.

D   **Correct.** The adverb *so* is correctly used to refer back to the verb *accord*; the conditional *would reward* is appropriate in referring to something contrary to fact.

E   The pronoun *it* does not have a clear antecedent; the adverb *so* is preferable.

The correct answer is D.

63.   Many policy experts say that shifting a portion of health-benefit costs back to the workers helps to control the employer's costs, but also helps to limit medical spending by making patients more careful consumers.

(A)   helps to control the employer's costs, but also helps

(B)   helps the control of the employer's costs, and also

(C)   not only helps to control the employer's costs, but also helps

(D)   helps to control not only the employer's costs, but

(E)   not only helps to control the employer's costs, and also helps

Idiom; Parallelism

The correlative pair *not only . . . but also* can be used to describe the two effects: *not only helps to control . . . but also helps to limit*. These effects should be grammatically and logically parallel. It is incorrect to use *but also* by itself. Alternatively, the two effects, stated in parallel ways, could simply be linked by *and also*.

A   *But also* must be used as part of the correlative pair *not only . . . but also*.

B   *Helps the control of* is awkward and is not parallel to *to limit*.

C   **Correct.** This sentence uses the *not only . . . but also* construction correctly and expresses the two effects in parallel ways.

D   *Not only* should precede *helps*.

E   The *not only . . . but also* construction requires the phrase *but also*, rather than *and also*.

The correct answer is C.

64.   Ms. Chambers is among the forecasters who predict that the rate of addition to arable lands will drop while those of loss rise.

(A)   those of loss rise

(B)   it rises for loss

(C)   those of losses rise

(D)   the rate of loss rises

(E)   there are rises for the rate of loss

Logical predication; Parallelism

The forecaster is making predictions about two different rates. The forecast changes in the rates can be compared using the construction *the rate of x will drop while the rate of y rises*; *x* and *y* should be parallel.

A   There is no referent for *those*.

B   *It* refers *to the rate of addition*, creating a nonsensical statement.

C   There is no referent for *those*. *Of losses* should be singular to parallel *of addition*.

D   **Correct.** This sentence uses a construction that clearly states the predicted changes in the rates; the rates are expressed in parallel ways.

E   *There are rises for* is wordy and unidiomatic.

The correct answer is D.

65. The market for recycled <u>commodities like aluminum and other metals remain</u> strong despite economic changes in the recycling industry.

 (A) commodities like aluminum and other metals remain

 (B) commodities like those of aluminum and other metals are remaining

 (C) commodities such as aluminum and other metals remains

 (D) commodities, such as aluminum and other metals, remain

 (E) commodities, like the commodities of aluminum and other metals, remains

Agreement; Rhetorical construction

The singular subject *market* requires the singular verb *remains*. While there has been some dispute over the use of *like* to mean "for example," this is an acceptable use.

A The plural verb does not agree with the singular subject.

B *Like those of* indicates that aluminum and other metals possess commodities rather than exemplify them; the plural verb *are remaining* does not agree with the singular subject *market*.

C **Correct.** The verb agrees with the subject, and *such as* properly expresses the relationship between *recycled commodities* and *aluminum and other metals*.

D The plural verb *remain* does not agree with the singular subject *market*.

E The repetition of *commodities* is wordy and with the use of *like* this phrasing could suggest that the *market for recycled commodities* is like or equivalent to *the commodities of aluminum and other metals*.

The correct answer is C.

66. <u>Unlike auto insurance, the frequency of claims does not affect the premiums for personal property coverage,</u> but if the insurance company is able to prove excessive loss due to owner negligence, it may decline to renew the policy.

 (A) Unlike auto insurance, the frequency of claims does not affect the premiums for personal property coverage,

 (B) Unlike with auto insurance, the frequency of claims do not affect the premiums for personal property coverage,

 (C) Unlike the frequency of claims for auto insurance, the premiums for personal property coverage are not affected by the frequency of claims,

 (D) Unlike the premiums for auto insurance, the premiums for personal property coverage are not affected by the frequency of claims,

 (E) Unlike with the premiums for auto insurance, the premiums for personal property coverage is not affected by the frequency of claims,

Logical predication; Agreement

The sentence has been written so that *auto insurance* is contrasted with *the frequency of claims*. The correct contrast is between *the premiums for auto insurance* and *the premiums for personal property coverage*.

A *Auto insurance* is illogically contrasted with *the frequency of claims*.

B *Unlike with* is an incorrect idiom; *auto insurance* is contrasted with *the frequency of claims*; the singular subject *frequency* does not agree with the plural verb *do*.

C *The frequency of claims* is contrasted with *the premiums for personal property coverage*.

D **Correct.** The contrast between *the premiums for auto insurance* and *the premiums for personal property coverage* is clearly and correctly stated in this sentence.

E *Unlike with* is an incorrect idiom; the plural subject *premiums* does not agree with the singular verb *is not affected*.

The correct answer is D.

67. Faced with an estimated $2 billion budget gap, the city's mayor <u>proposed a nearly 17 percent reduction in the amount allocated the previous year to maintain the city's major cultural institutions and to subsidize</u> hundreds of local arts groups.

(A)   proposed a nearly 17 percent reduction in the
        amount allocated the previous year to maintain
        the city's major cultural institutions and to
        subsidize

(B)   proposed a reduction from the previous year of
        nearly 17 percent in the amount it was allocating
        to maintain the city's major cultural institutions
        and for subsidizing

(C)   proposed to reduce, by nearly 17 percent, the
        amount from the previous year that was
        allocated for the maintenance of the city's major
        cultural institutions and to subsidize

(D)   has proposed a reduction from the previous year
        of nearly 17 percent of the amount it was
        allocating for maintaining the city's major
        cultural institutions, and to subsidize

(E)   was proposing that the amount they were
        allocating be reduced by nearly 17 percent from
        the previous year for maintaining the city's major
        cultural institutions and for the subsidization

Rhetorical construction; Parallelism

The original sentence contains no errors. It uses
the parallel construction *to maintain* and *to
subsidize* to show clearly the two areas where the
17 percent reduction in funds will be applied. In
addition, the *17 percent reduction* is closely followed
by *the amount allocated the previous year,* making it
clear what is being reduced by 17 percent.

A   Correct. The sentence uses parallel
       construction and a well-placed modifier.

B   *To maintain* and *for subsidizing* are not
       parallel. The sentence is imprecise, and *it*
       does not have a clear antecedent.

C   *For the maintenance* and *to subsidize* are not
       parallel, and the sentence is wordy.

D   *For maintaining* and *to subsidize* are not
       parallel, *it* not have a clear antecedent,
       and the sentence structure makes it unclear
       just what the writer is claiming.

E   *Maintaining* and *the subsidization* are not
       parallel, *they* does not have a clear
       antecedent, and the sentence structure
       makes it unclear just what the writer is
       claiming.

The correct answer is A.

68.   By offering lower prices and a menu of personal
        communications options, such as caller identification
        and voice mail, the new telecommunications company
        has not only captured customers from other phone
        companies but also forced them to offer competitive
        prices.

(A)   has not only captured customers from other
        phone companies but also forced them

(B)   has not only captured customers from other
        phone companies, but it also forced them

(C)   has not only captured customers from other
        phone companies but also forced these
        companies

(D)   not only has captured customers from other
        phone companies but also these companies
        have been forced

(E)   not only captured customers from other phone
        companies, but it also has forced them

Parallelism, Verb form

The sentence intends to show the effect of the new
telecommunications company on the other phone
companies. In the original sentence, however, the
antecedent of the pronoun *them* is unclear; it may
refer to *companies* or to *customers*. If it refers to
customers, the sentence structure illogically has the
new company forcing customers to offer
competitive prices.

A   The referent of *them* is unclear.

B   The referent of *them* is unclear, and the use
       of *it* is redundant.

C   **Correct.** The verbs are parallel in this
       sentence, and *these companies* is clearly the
       object of the verb *forced*.

D   The sentence does not maintain parallelism,
       unnecessarily changing from active voice
       (*has captured*) to passive voice (*have been
       forced*).

E   The referent of *them* is unclear. *Captured* and
       has forced are not parallel in verb tense, and
       the use of *it* is redundant.

The correct answer is C.

69. The Anasazi settlements at Chaco Canyon were built on a spectacular scale, with more than 75 carefully engineered structures, of up to 600 rooms each, were connected by a complex regional system of roads.

(A) scale, with more than 75 carefully engineered structures, of up to 600 rooms each, were

(B) scale, with more than 75 carefully engineered structures, of up to 600 rooms each,

(C) scale of more than 75 carefully engineered structures of up to 600 rooms, each that had been

(D) scale of more than 75 carefully engineered structures of up to 600 rooms and with each

(E) scale of more than 75 carefully engineered structures of up to 600 rooms, each had been

Logical predication; Grammatical construction

This sentence makes a claim about the scale (size, extent) of the Anasazi settlements and then illustrates that claim with a description of the settlements' structures. The second part of the sentence, introduced by the preposition *with*, describes the structures first in terms of their rooms, and then in terms of the roads that connect them together. To describe the noun *structures*, the participial form *connected* should be used, turning the verb into an adjective.

A The verb *were connected* has no subject, since *structures* is the object of the preposition *with*.

B Correct. The sentence is logically coherent and grammatically correct.

C The comma preceding *each* makes *each* a subject, but it has no verb, since *that* is the subject of *had been connected*.

D This sentence suggests that the scale or size of the settlements is made up of structures, rather than uses the structures as an example of the settlements' grand scale; it also nonsensically indicates that each room is connected by a complex system of roads.

E This run-on sentence suffers from a comma splice, as the phrase following the comma is a main clause; the reference of the pronoun *each* is ambiguous.

The correct answer is B.

70. The gyrfalcon, an Arctic bird of prey, has survived a close brush with extinction; its numbers are now five times greater than when the use of DDT was sharply restricted in the early 1970s.

(A) extinction; its numbers are now five times greater than

(B) extinction; its numbers are now five times more than

(C) extinction, their numbers now fivefold what they were

(D) extinction, now with fivefold the numbers they had

(E) extinction, now with numbers five times greater than

Agreement; Diction; Logical predication

The original sentence contains no errors. The semicolon correctly connects the closely related ideas in the two independent clauses. *The gyrfalcon* is the antecedent for *its* in the second phrase.

A Correct. The original sentence correctly uses a singular pronoun, *its*, to refer to the singular antecedent *gyrfalcon*, and it properly uses the construction *its numbers are . . . greater than*.

B The use of *more* instead of *greater* inappropriately implies that there are now more numbers, rather than more gyrfalcons.

C The pronoun *their* is plural, and thus incorrect, since the antecedent *gyrfalcon* is singular. *Fivefold what they were* is awkward and nonstandard and implies that there are now more numbers, rather than more gyrfalcons.

D The pronoun *they* is plural, and thus incorrect, since the antecedent *gyrfalcon* is singular. The comma introduces a confusing phrase seeming to modify *extinction*. *Fivefold the numbers they had* is awkward and nonstandard and implies that there are now more numbers, rather than more gyrfalcons.

E The comma introduces a confusing phrase seeming to modify *extinction*.

The correct answer is A.

71. Analysts blamed May's sluggish retail sales on unexciting merchandise as well as the weather, <u>colder and wetter than was usual in some regions, which slowed</u> sales of barbecue grills and lawn furniture.

    (A) colder and wetter than was usual in some regions, which slowed

    (B) which was colder and wetter than usual in some regions, slowing

    (C) since it was colder and wetter than usually in some regions, which slowed

    (D) being colder and wetter than usually in some regions, slowing

    (E) having been colder and wetter than was usual in some regions and slowed

Logical predication; Diction

The sentence must clearly indicate that the inclement weather had slowed retail sales. Relative pronouns, such as *which*, should follow as closely as possible the nouns to which they refer. The adjective *usual*, rather than the adverb *usually*, is required when modifying a noun. The phrase *wetter than usual* is correct and concise.

A   The insertion of *was* is unnecessary and misleading. The referent of *which* is unclear, because *regions*, not *weather*, is the nearest noun.

B   Correct. This sentence is concise, correct, and idiomatic, and *which* has a clear referent, *the weather*.

C   With the linking verb *was*, the adjective *usual* is needed in place of the adverb *usually*. The referent of *which* is unclear because *regions*, not *weather*, is the nearest noun.

D   This construction is unclear and can be seen as unintentionally indicating that the analysts were colder and wetter. The adjective *usual* should be used instead of the adverb *usually* to modify the noun *weather*.

E   This construction is unclear and can be seen as unintentionally indicating that the analysts were colder and wetter. The insertion of *was* is unnecessary and misleading.

The correct answer is B.

72. State officials report that soaring <u>rates of liability insurance have risen to force</u> cutbacks in the operations of everything from local governments and school districts to day-care centers and recreational facilities.

    (A) rates of liability insurance have risen to force

    (B) rates of liability insurance are a force for

    (C) rates for liability insurance are forcing

    (D) rises in liability insurance rates are forcing

    (E) liability insurance rates have risen to force

Rhetorical construction; Verb form; Idiom

This sentence does not clearly present its main point. It should be revised to eliminate redundancy, clarify cause-and-effect relationships, and use the word *rates* correctly. The idea expressed in the verb *have risen* is already fully contained in the adjective *soaring*, so that verb should be omitted. Replacing it with *are forcing* shows clearly what the *soaring rates* are doing. When *rate* means a *price charged*, it is followed by the preposition *for*.

A   *For* should be used following *rates*; *of* is misleading. *Have risen* is redundant.

B   *For* should be used following *rates*; *of* is misleading. The wordy construction *are a force for* is not nearly as clear as the more concise *are forcing*.

C   **Correct.** The sentence is concise and uses the appropriate preposition following *rates*, and the present progressive verb tense makes it clear that this is an ongoing situation.

D   *Rises* is used unidiomatically and adds nothing to the idea already expressed in the adjective *soaring*.

E   *Have risen* adds nothing to the idea expressed in the adjective *soaring*.

The correct answer is C.

73. After suffering $2 billion in losses and 25,000 layoffs, the nation's semiconductor industry, which makes chips that run everything from <u>computers and spy satellites to dishwashers, appears to have</u> made a long-awaited recovery.

    (A) computers and spy satellites to dishwashers, appears to have

    (B) computers, spy satellites, and dishwashers, appears having

    (C) computers, spy satellites, and dishwashers, appears that it has

    (D) computers and spy satellites to dishwashers, appears that it has

    (E) computers and spy satellites as well as dishwashers, appears to have

Idiom; Grammatical construction; Verb form

This sentence correctly makes use of the idiomatic expression *from . . . to . . .* to describe the range of products made by the semiconductor industry. The main verb *appears* is intransitive and is most efficiently followed by the infinitive form *to have made*, which introduces a description of the subject, *the semiconductor industry*.

A **Correct.** The sentence is grammatically correct and uses the idiomatic expression correctly.

B The phrase *everything from* anticipates idiomatic completion with the second preposition *to*; without the *to* it could refer to components coming from the listed items, but this reading is unlikely; *appears having* is an incorrect verb form and makes the clause ungrammatical.

C This version is unidiomatic because *from* is not completed by *to*; *appears that it has* is an awkward and incorrect verb form.

D *Appears that it has* is an incorrect verb form.

E *As well as* is awkward and imprecise here; it is the wrong completion for the idiomatic expression *from . . . to . . . .*

The correct answer is A.

74. While some academicians believe that business ethics should be integrated into every business course, others say that students will take ethics seriously <u>only if it would be taught as a separately required course.</u>

    (A) only if it would be taught as a separately required course

    (B) only if it is taught as a separate, required course

    (C) if it is taught only as a course required separately

    (D) if it was taught only as a separate and required course

    (E) if it would only be taught as a required course, separately

Rhetorical construction; Verb form; Diction

Conditional constructions require specific verb tenses. For a present condition, like this debate between academicians, the subordinate clause introduced by *if* uses the present indicative, and the main clause uses the future tense: *y will happen* (main clause) *only if x happens* (subordinate clause). Logically, the *course* is to be both *separate* and *required*, so the two adjectives should equally modify the noun and thus be separated by a comma: *separate, required course*.

A The verb tense in the *if* clause is incorrect. The adverb *separately* should be the adjective *separate*.

B **Correct.** This sentence has the correct verb tense, and the two adjectives equally modify the noun.

C The placement of *only* distorts the meaning; it should precede *if*. *A course required separately* is unclear.

D The verb tense in the *if* clause is incorrect. The placement of *only* distorts the meaning.

E The verb tense in the *if* clause is incorrect. The placement of *only* distorts the meaning. The adjective *separate* should be used instead of the adverb *separately* and should precede the noun.

The correct answer is B.

75. Scientists have observed large concentrations of heavy-metal deposits in the upper twenty centimeters of Baltic Sea sediments, which are consistent with the growth of industrial activity there.

    (A) Baltic Sea sediments, which are consistent with the growth of industrial activity there

    (B) Baltic Sea sediments, where the growth of industrial activity is consistent with these findings

    (C) Baltic Sea sediments, findings consistent with its growth of industrial activity

    (D) sediments from the Baltic Sea, findings consistent with the growth of industrial activity in the area

    (E) sediments from the Baltic Sea, consistent with the growth of industrial activity there

Rhetorical construction; Logical predication

As the sentence is written, *which* seems to refer somewhat illogically to the *sediments*. Inserting the noun *findings* makes the reference clear. Where has the growth of industrial activity taken place? *There* is too vague and makes it seem that the industry is taking place in the sediments. Replacing *there* with the more specific *in the area* solves this problem.

A *Which* has no logical referent. *There* is too vague.

B *Where* has no logical referent.

C *Its* does not have a referent.

D **Correct.** This sentence is logical and clear. *Findings* refers back to the scientists' observations, and *in the area* provides a clear reference to the place in question.

E The phrase beginning with *consistent* illogically describes the Baltic Sea.

The correct answer is D.

76. Under a provision of the Constitution that was never applied, Congress has been required to call a convention for considering possible amendments to the document when formally asked to do it by the legislatures of two-thirds of the states.

    (A) was never applied, Congress has been required to call a convention for considering possible amendments to the document when formally asked to do it

    (B) was never applied, there has been a requirement that Congress call a convention for consideration of possible amendments to the document when asked to do it formally

    (C) was never applied, whereby Congress is required to call a convention for considering possible amendments to the document when asked to do it formally

    (D) has never been applied, whereby Congress is required to call a convention to consider possible amendments to the document when formally asked to do so

    (E) has never been applied, Congress is required to call a convention to consider possible amendments to the document when formally asked to do so

Verb form; Idiom; Grammatical construction

The meaning of this sentence is distorted by the use of incorrect verb tenses. The use of the present perfect *has been required* following *was never applied* makes the time sequence unclear at best. The correct idiom is *call . . . to consider*, not *call . . . for considering*. The pronoun *it* has no clear referent. The more standard expression *to do so* more clearly and correctly refers to what Congress must do.

A The verb tenses are incorrect. *Call for considering* should be *call to consider*. *It* has no clear referent.

B The verb tenses are incorrect. The idiom *call to consider* is violated. *It* has no clear referent. The sentence is unnecessarily wordy.

C The first verb tense is incorrect. *Whereby* introduces a sentence fragment. The idiom *call to consider* is violated. *It* has no clear referent.

D *Whereby* introduces a sentence fragment.

E **Correct.** In this sentence, the verb tenses are appropriate and coherent with one another. The correct idiom is used. *To do so* correctly refers to what Congress is required to do.

The correct answer is E.

303

77. Geologists believe that the warning signs for a major earthquake may include sudden fluctuations in local seismic activity, tilting and other deformations of the Earth's crust, <u>changing the measured strain across a fault zone and varying</u> the electrical properties of underground rocks.

    (A) changing the measured strain across a fault zone and varying

    (B) changing measurements of the strain across a fault zone, and varying

    (C) changing the strain as measured across a fault zone, and variations of

    (D) changes in the measured strain across a fault zone, and variations in

    (E) changes in measurements of the strain across a fault zone, and variations among

Parallelism; Logical predication

This sentence uses four phrases to describe the *warning signs* for an earthquake. These phrases should be parallel. The first sign is *sudden fluctuations in local seismic activity*; the second is *tilting and other deformations of the Earth's crust*. *Tilting* in this case is used as a noun, just as *deformations* and *fluctuations* are nouns. The first two signs are parallel. The third and fourth warning signs resemble *tilting* in the *ing* form, but they are not parallel because they are used as verbs rather than as nouns: *changing . . . the strain*; *varying . . . the properties*. To make the latter two signs parallel, nouns must replace verbs: *changes in . . . variations in*.

A *Changing* and *varying* are used as verbs and so are not parallel to the nouns *fluctuations* and *tilting*.

B The four signs are not parallel; the substitution of *measurements of the strain* distorts the meaning.

C *Changing* is used as a verb and so does not parallel the nouns *fluctuations*, *tilting*, and *variations*.

D **Correct.** In this sentence, the four nouns— *fluctuations, tilting, changes, variations*—are parallel, and the meaning of *the measured strain* is not distorted.

E This sentence says illogically that *changes in measurement* are a warning sign; it should say that changes in the strain are a warning sign.

The correct answer is D.

78. The root systems of most flowering perennials either become too crowded, <u>which results in loss in vigor, and spread</u> too far outward, producing a bare center.

    (A) which results in loss in vigor, and spread

    (B) resulting in loss in vigor, or spreading

    (C) with the result of loss of vigor, or spreading

    (D) resulting in loss of vigor, or spread

    (E) with a resulting loss of vigor, and spread

Idiom; Parallelism

This sentence uses the construction *either x or y*; *x* and *y* must be grammatically parallel. In this case, *and spread* must be *or spread*. The antecedent of *which* is unclear; replacing *which results* with *resulting* clarifies the meaning.

A *Either* is incorrectly followed by *and*; *which* has no clear referent.

B *Or spreading* is not parallel to *either become*.

C *With the result of* is wordy and awkward. *Or spreading* is not parallel to *either become*.

D **Correct.** The phrase *resulting in loss of vigor* concisely modifies the first clause; the either/or construction is correct and parallel in this sentence.

E *Either* is incorrectly followed by *and*; *with a resulting loss* is wordy.

The correct answer is D.

79. The computer company has announced that it will purchase the color-printing division of a rival company for $950 <u>million, which is part of a deal that will make</u> it the largest manufacturer in the office color-printing market.

    (A) million, which is part of a deal that will make

    (B) million, a part of a deal that makes

    (C) million, a part of a deal making

    (D) million as a part of a deal to make

    (E) million as part of a deal that will make

Rhetorical construction; Verb form

The relative pronoun *which* requires a clear antecedent, but none appears in the original version of the sentence. The company's announcement is entirely geared to the future—it *will* purchase the division as part of a deal that *will* make it the largest manufacturer.

A   There is no antecedent for the relative pronoun *which*.

B   Like a relative pronoun, the appositive phrase (*a part . . .*) must have a noun or noun phrase as a clear antecedent; the verb *makes* should be future tense.

C   The appositive phrase requires a clear antecedent; *making* does not indicate future tense.

D   This sentence is a little awkward (the article *a* in *a part* is unnecessary) and says something rather different; *as a part of a deal to make* suggests that the deal itself includes making the company the *largest manufacturer* rather than its being the outcome of the deal.

E   **Correct.** The future tense is used throughout and the sentence structure is clear.

The correct answer is E.

80. Any medical test will sometimes fail to detect a condition when it is present and indicate that there is one when it is not.

(A)   a condition when it is present and indicate that there is one

(B)   when a condition is present and indicate that there is one

(C)   a condition when it is present and indicate that it is present

(D)   when a condition is present and indicate its presence

(E)   the presence of a condition when it is there and indicate its presence

Grammatical construction; Logical predication

In this sentence the pronoun *it* does not always refer to *condition*, but, for the sake of clarity and correctness, it should. *Detect a condition when it is present* is correct and should be followed by a corresponding construction: *indicate that it is present when it is not*. The construction of *there is one* leaves *it* without a referent.

A   *There is one* leaves *it* in the final clause without a referent.

B   *Detect a condition* is more precise because it emphasizes the condition itself; *there is one* leaves *it* without a referent.

C   **Correct.** The three uses of the pronoun *it* refer clearly to *condition*, and the two parts of the sentence correspond.

D   *When a condition is present* emphasizes the time of the detection rather than the condition itself. The final *it* has no referent.

E   *Presence* illogically repeats the same idea as *when it is there*. The final *it* has no referent.

The correct answer is C.

81. Since 1986, when the Department of Labor began to allow investment officers' fees to be based on how the funds they manage perform, several corporations began paying their investment advisers a small basic fee, with a contract promising higher fees if the managers perform well.

(A)   investment officers' fees to be based on how the funds they manage perform, several corporations began

(B)   investment officers' fees to be based on the performance of the funds they manage, several corporations began

(C)   that fees of investment officers be based on how the funds they manage perform, several corporations have begun

(D)   fees of investment officers to be based on the performance of the funds they manage, several corporations have begun

(E)   that investment officers' fees be based on the performance of the funds they manage, several corporations began

Verb form; Logical predication

Since 1986 indicates action begun in the past and continuing into the present, and the form of the verb must show that continuity, as the present perfect tense does: since 1986, corporations *have begun.* In the original sentence, the pronoun *they* lacks a clear referent. While *they* should refer unambiguously to *investment officers,* grammatically its referent is somewhat unclear because *investment officers'* is a possessive modifying *fees,* and the plural noun *fees* intervenes between *officers'* and the pronoun.

A   *Have begun* should replace *began; they* has no clear referent.

B   *Have begun* should replace *began; they* has no clear referent.

C   *Allow that . . . be based on* is not a correct idiom; it should be *allow . . . to be based on.*

D   Correct. Substituting *fees of investment officers* in this sentence allows the pronoun *they* to refer to the *officers; have begun* properly indicates a continuing situation.

E   *Allow that . . . be based on* is an incorrect idiom. *They* has no clear referent. *Began* does not indicate the continuity necessary after *since 1986.*

The correct answer is D.

82.   Downzoning, zoning that typically results in the reduction of housing density, allows for more open space in areas where <u>little water or services exist</u>.

(A)   little water or services exist

(B)   little water or services exists

(C)   few services and little water exists

(D)   there is little water or services available

(E)   there are few services and little available water

Diction; Agreement

In this sentence, the adjective *little* correctly modifies the noun *water* because *water* is not a countable quantity. However, the noun *services* is a countable quantity and must be modified by *few,* not by *little.* Logically, the areas described would suffer from both *little water* and *few services* at the same time, so the correct conjunction is *and,* not *or.* This compound subject requires a plural verb.

A   *Services* should be modified by *few,* not *little.*

B   The singular verb *exists* does not agree with the plural subject *services.* When a compound subject is joined by *or,* the verb agrees with the closer subject.

C   When a compound subject consists of two distinct units joined by the conjunction *and,* the verb must be plural.

D   *Little* cannot modify *services.*

E   Correct. In this sentence, *few* correctly modifies *services; and* correctly joins *services* and *water.*

The correct answer is E.

83.   In theory, international civil servants at the United Nations are prohibited from continuing to draw salaries from their own governments; in practice, however, some governments merely substitute living allowances <u>for their employees' paychecks, assigned by them</u> to the United Nations.

(A)   for their employees' paychecks, assigned by them

(B)   for the paychecks of their employees who have been assigned

(C)   for the paychecks of their employees, having been assigned

(D)   in place of their employees' paychecks, for those of them assigned

(E)   in place of the paychecks of their employees to have been assigned by them

Logical predication; Rhetorical construction

It is difficult to tell which parts of this sentence go together because of errors and confusion in the underlined portion. *Living allowances* is the counterpart of *paychecks,* so it is better to say *governments . . . substitute living allowances for the paychecks of their employees* because it makes the substitution clearer. This change also makes it easier to correct the modification error that appears in the phrase *assigned by them,* which incorrectly modifies *paychecks* rather than *employees.* The modifying clause *who have been assigned* clearly describes *employees* and fits into the remaining part of the sentence, *to the United Nations.*

A   *Assigned by them* incorrectly and illogically modifies *paychecks*.

B   **Correct.** In this sentence, the meaning is clearer, because *paychecks* is separated from *employees*. The relative clause clearly modifies *employees*.

C   *Having been assigned* illogically modifies *governments*.

D   The correct construction is *substitutes x for y*, not *substitutes x in place of y*. The construction following *paychecks* is wordy and awkward.

E   The correct construction is *substitutes x for y*, not *substitutes x in place of y*. The construction following *employees* is wordy and awkward.

The correct answer is B.

84. The computer company's present troubles are a result of technological stagnation, marketing missteps, and managerial blunders <u>so that several attempts to revise corporate strategies have failed to correct it</u>.

(A) so that several attempts to revise corporate strategies have failed to correct it

(B) so that several attempts at revising corporate strategies have failed to correct

(C) in that several attempts at revising corporate strategies have failed to correct them

(D) that several attempts to revise corporate strategies have failed to correct

(E) that several attempts at revising corporate strategies have failed to correct them

Agreement; Rhetorical construction

This sentence lists three causes of the company's troubles and asserts that strategies to correct the causes of the problems have failed. The clearest, most efficient way to explain this is to refer to the causes with the relative pronoun *that*, positioning it as an object of the verb *failed to correct*.

A   The singular pronoun *it* has no clear antecedent; the conjunction *so* typically indicates that a consequence will follow, but this is not the case.

B   The conjunction *so* is inappropriate because no consequences are given; the verb *correct* has no object.

C   *In that* is an inappropriate connector because it is not followed by an indication of how the company's troubles result from the three problems listed in the first part of the sentence.

D   **Correct.** The sentence is clearly and efficiently worded, and the referent of the pronoun *that* is clear.

E   Because *attempts* is the subject of the final clause, and *that* is the object of its verb (*have failed to correct*), the pronoun *them* has no function.

The correct answer is D.

85. According to a study by the Carnegie Foundation for the Advancement of Teaching, companies in the United States are providing job training and general education for nearly eight million people, about <u>equivalent to the enrollment of</u> the nation's four-year colleges and universities.

(A) equivalent to the enrollment of

(B) the equivalent of those enrolled in

(C) equal to those who are enrolled in

(D) as many as the enrollment of

(E) as many as are enrolled in

Diction; Logical predication

This sentence compares two groups of people. The best phrase to use for a comparison of two countable quantities (such as people) is *as many as*. The number of *people* in job training should be compared to the number of *people* in colleges, but the original sentence mistakenly compares *people* to *enrollment*.

A   The sentence compares *people* to *enrollment*. *Equivalent to* does not make it clear that the two groups are being compared with respect to numbers.

B   *The equivalent* is the wrong term for the intended comparison; it should be made clear that the comparison concerns the numbers of people in both groups and not some broader concept.

C   *Equal* is generally used for uncountable quantities, such as *equal justice*, not countable quantities, such as people.

D   *People* are incorrectly compared with *enrollment* rather than with other people.

E   **Correct.** In this sentence, *as many as* compares countable quantities. *People* are compared with people, the understood subject of *are enrolled*.

The correct answer is E.

86. Intar, the oldest Hispanic theater company in New York, has moved away from the Spanish classics and <u>now it draws on the works both of contemporary Hispanic authors who live abroad and of those</u> in the United States.

(A) now it draws on the works both of contemporary Hispanic authors who live abroad and of those

(B) now draws on the works of contemporary Hispanic authors, both those who live abroad and those who live

(C) it draws on the works of contemporary Hispanic authors now, both those living abroad and who live

(D) draws now on the works both of contemporary Hispanic authors living abroad and who are living

(E) draws on the works now of both contemporary Hispanic authors living abroad and those

Grammatical construction; Idiom; Parallelism

The pronoun *it* before the second verb results in an ungrammatical construction; removing the pronoun removes the error. The scope of *those* is unclear (authors, or contemporary Hispanic authors). The correct version of the sentence makes it clear that the company *draws on the works of contemporary Hispanic authors* who live in two different places. *Those who live abroad* is parallel to *those who live in the United States.*

A   Because there is no comma after *classics*, the use of *it* creates an ungrammatical construction. The construction following *both* is unclear.

B   **Correct.** In this sentence, Intar is the subject of *draws on*; parallel constructions follow *both . . . and.*

C   *It* creates an ungrammatical construction; *those living abroad* is not parallel to *who live.*

D   The construction following *both* is not parallel to the construction following *and.*

E   *Now* modifies the verb and should precede it. The parallelism of the *both . . . and* construction is violated.

The correct answer is B.

87. Last year, land values in most parts of the pinelands rose almost <u>so fast, and in some parts even faster than what they did</u> outside the pinelands.

(A) so fast, and in some parts even faster than what they did

(B) so fast, and in some parts even faster than, those

(C) as fast, and in some parts even faster than, those

(D) as fast as, and in some parts even faster than, those

(E) as fast as, and in some parts even faster than what they did

Idiom; Parallelism

This sentence says *x* rose *almost so fast y*, which is not a correct idiomatic construction; *x* rose *almost as fast as y* is the correct idiom for this comparison. The two elements being compared, *x* and *y*, must be parallel, but the noun *land values* (*x*) is not parallel to *what they did* (*y*). *Land values* in the pinelands (*x*) must be compared with *those* (the pronoun correctly replacing *land values*) outside the pinelands (*y*).

A   *So fast* is used instead of *as fast*. *What they did* is not parallel to *land values.*

B   *So fast* is not the correct idiom for comparison.

C   *As fast* must be followed by *as* in this comparison.

D   **Correct.** *As fast as* is the correct comparative conjunction used in this sentence; *those* is parallel to *land values.*

E   *What they did* is not parallel to *land values.*

The correct answer is D.

88. <u>Clouds are formed from the evaporation of the oceans' water that is warmed by the sun and rises high into the atmosphere, condensing in tiny droplets on minute particles of dust.</u>

   (A) Clouds are formed from the evaporation of the oceans' water that is warmed by the sun and rises high into the atmosphere, condensing in tiny droplets on minute particles of dust.

   (B) Clouds form by the sun's warmth evaporating the water in the oceans, which rises high into the atmosphere, condensing in tiny droplets on minute particles of dust.

   (C) Warmed by the sun, ocean water evaporates, rises high into the atmosphere, and condenses in tiny droplets on minute particles of dust to form clouds.

   (D) The water in the oceans evaporates, warmed by the sun, rises high into the atmosphere, and condenses in tiny droplets on minute particles of dust, which forms clouds.

   (E) Ocean water, warmed by the sun, evaporates and rises high into the atmosphere, which then condenses in tiny droplets on minute particles of dust to form as clouds.

Rhetorical construction; Logical predication

This sentence describes a multistep process by which ocean water is transformed into clouds. These steps are most clearly presented in chronological order, with *ocean water* as the main subject of the sentence.

A   This sentence provides no sense of steps and illogically suggests that the oceans' water evaporates after it rises high into the atmosphere.

B   The antecedent for the relative pronoun *which* is ambiguous, again suggesting that oceans rise high.

C   **Correct.** The sequence of steps in a cloud's formation is clear.

D   The nonchronological order of the steps by which clouds are produced is confusing, suggesting that dust forms clouds.

E   The relative pronoun *which* grammatically refers to *atmosphere*, creating a nonsensical claim that the atmosphere, rather than the water, condenses.

The correct answer is C.

89. <u>If Dr. Wade was right, any apparent connection of the eating of</u> highly processed foods and excelling at sports is purely coincidental.

   (A) If Dr. Wade was right, any apparent connection of the eating of

   (B) Should Dr. Wade be right, any apparent connection of eating

   (C) If Dr. Wade is right, any connection that is apparent between eating of

   (D) If Dr. Wade is right, any apparent connection between eating

   (E) Should Dr. Wade have been right, any connection apparent between eating

Verb form; Idiom

This sentence also uses the idiomatic construction *connection between x and y*; *x* and *y* must be parallel. Thus, *connection* must be followed by *between* rather than *of*, and *the eating of* (*x*) must be made parallel to *excelling at* (*y*). *The eating* is a gerund, or noun form, but *eating* is a participle and thus parallel to the participle *excelling*.

A   *Connection* must be followed by *between*; *the eating of* is not parallel to *excelling*.

B   *Should Dr. Wade be right* should not be followed by the present indicative verb *is*. *Connection of* is not the correct idiom.

C   *Apparent connection* is preferable to the wordy *connection that is apparent*.

D   **Correct.** In this sentence, the verb is present tense, and the correct idiom is used; *eating* is also parallel to *excelling*.

E   *Should Dr. Wade have been right* should not be followed by the present indicative verb *is*. *Apparent* should precede *connection* rather than follow it.

The correct answer is D.

90. The commission proposed <u>that funding for the park's development, which could be open to the public early next year, is</u> obtained through a local bond issue.

   (A) that funding for the park's development, which could be open to the public early next year, is

   (B) that funding for development of the park, which could be open to the public early next year, be

(C)   funding for the development of the park, perhaps open to the public early next year, to be

(D)   funds for the park's development, perhaps open to the public early next year, be

(E)   development funding for the park, which could be open to the public early next year, is to be

Logical predication; Verb form

Which modifies the noun that precedes it; in this sentence, the clause beginning with *which* illogically refers to *development* rather than *the park*. This error can be corrected by substituting *development of the park* (*which* follows *park*) for *park's development* (*which* follows *development*). When a verb such as recommend, request, or *propose* is used in the main clause, the verb following *that* in the subordinate clause is subjunctive (*be*) rather than indicative (*is*).

A   *Which* modifies *development* instead of *park*. *Be* is required, not *is*.

B   **Correct.** In this sentence, *which* clearly modifies *park*; the subjunctive *be* correctly follows *proposed that*.

C   *Be* is required, not the infinitive *to be*.

D   *That* is omitted, making the construction awkward and unclear. The phrase modifies *development*, not *park*.

E   *Development funding* distorts the meaning. *Be* is required, not *is to be*.

The correct answer is B.

91.   Seismologists studying the earthquake that struck northern California in October 1989 are still investigating some of its mysteries: the unexpected power of the seismic waves, the upward thrust that threw one man straight into the air, and the strange electromagnetic signals detected hours before the temblor.

(A)   the upward thrust that threw one man straight into the air, and the strange electromagnetic signals detected hours before the temblor

(B)   the upward thrust that threw one man straight into the air, and strange electromagnetic signals were detected hours before the temblor

(C)   the upward thrust threw one man straight into the air, and hours before the temblor strange electromagnetic signals were detected

(D)   one man was thrown straight into the air by the upward thrust, and hours before the temblor strange electromagnetic signals were detected

(E)   one man who was thrown straight into the air by the upward thrust, and strange electromagnetic signals that were detected hours before the temblor

Parallelism; Grammatical construction

Some of the earthquake's *mysteries* are described in a series of three correctly parallel elements: (1) *the unexpected power . . .* , (2) *the upward thrust . . .* , and (3) *the strange electromagnetic signals. . . .* Each of the three elements begins with an article (*the*), a modifier, and a noun. This parallelism is crucial, but each mystery is allowed the further modification most appropriate to it, whether a prepositional phrase (1), a clause (2), or a participial phrase (3).

A   **Correct.** This sentence correctly provides a parallel series of three mysteries.

B   *The* is omitted before *strange*. The verb *were detected* makes the last element not parallel to the previous two.

C   Because they use complete independent clauses, the last two elements are not parallel to the first, and the sentence is ungrammatical.

D   The constructions beginning *one man* and *hours before* are not parallel to the construction beginning *the unexpected power*.

E   The grammatical constructions describing the mysteries are not parallel.

The correct answer is A.

92.   Schistosomiasis, a disease caused by a parasitic worm, is prevalent in hot, humid climates, and it has become more widespread as irrigation projects have enlarged the habitat of the freshwater snails that are the parasite's hosts for part of its life cycle.

(A)   the freshwater snails that are the parasite's hosts for part of its life cycle

(B)   the freshwater snails that are the parasite's hosts in part of their life cycle

(C)   freshwater snails which become the parasite's hosts for part of its life cycles

(D)   freshwater snails which become the hosts of the parasite during the parasite's life cycles

(E)   parasite's hosts, freshwater snails which become their hosts during their life cycles

Rhetorical construction; Agreement

This sentence explains the increased incidence of schistosomiasis as a consequence of the enlarged habitat of the kind of freshwater snails that host the parasitic worm responsible for the disease. The definite article is necessary before *freshwater snails* because the sentence identifies a particular type of snail, namely, those that host the parasite. The correct preposition to express duration in combination with *host* is *for*, not *in*. As the parasite is referred to as singular, the possessive pronoun in the final phrase must also be singular.

A   Correct. The sentence is clear with all pronouns and verbs in agreement.

B   The preposition *in* is inappropriate for expressing duration; the plural possessive pronoun *their* does not agree with the singular antecedent *parasite*.

C   A definite article should precede *freshwater snails* to identify a particular type of snails; the plural *cycles* is inappropriate because *its* refers to a singular parasite, which only has one life cycle.

D   A definite article is needed before *freshwater snails*; repetition of the word *parasite* makes the final phrase unnecessarily wordy; *cycles* should be singular.

E   The repetition of *hosts* makes the final phrase unnecessarily wordy; *cycles* should be singular; *their hosts* should be *its hosts*; the referent for the second appearance of *their* is unclear—does it refer to *snails* or the *parasite*?

The correct answer is A.

93.   Two new studies indicate that many people become obese more <u>due to the fact that their bodies burn calories too slowly than overeating</u>.

(A)   due to the fact that their bodies burn calories too slowly than overeating

(B)   due to their bodies burning calories too slowly than to eating too much

(C)   because their bodies burn calories too slowly than that they are overeaters

(D)   because their bodies burn calories too slowly than because they eat too much

(E)   because of their bodies burning calories too slowly than because of their eating too much

Parallelism; Rhetorical construction

To compare two explanations for weight gain, this sentence uses the construction *more x than y*; *x* and *y* must be parallel. Here, *x* is *due to the fact that their bodies burn calories too slowly* and *y* is *overeating*. *Due to the fact that* uses five words to say what *because* does in one; *because* is a better choice to introduce both elements. The single-word *y* can be made parallel to the clause *x* by introducing a subject, verb, and adverb: *because they eat too much*.

A   *Due to the fact that* is wordy and awkward. The two parts of the comparison are not parallel.

B   *Due to* is not the correct idiom. The two parts of the comparison are not parallel.

C   *That* has no referent. The two parts of the comparison are not parallel.

D   Correct. In this sentence, the two parts of the comparison are parallel and concise.

E   This alternative, though parallel, is awkward and wordy. *Bodies* should be *bodies'* because in this construction *burning* can most reasonably be construed as a gerund rather than a participle; the possessive case is required before a gerund.

The correct answer is D.

94.   Judge Bonham denied a motion <u>to allow members of the jury to go home at the end of each day instead of to confine them to</u> a hotel.

(A)   to allow members of the jury to go home at the end of each day instead of to confine them to

(B)   that would have allowed members of the jury to go home at the end of each day instead of confined to

(C)   under which members of the jury are allowed to go home at the end of each day instead of confining them in

(D) that would allow members of the jury to go home at the end of each day rather than confinement in

(E) to allow members of the jury to go home at the end of each day rather than be confined to

Parallelism; Logical predication

The logic of this sentence has two possible options for the *members of the jury*: they can go home or be confined to a hotel. The first option is expressed using the infinitive *to go home*; the second option should use the parallel form (*to* understood) *be confined*. Since the *members of the jury* are not doing the confining themselves, the passive form must be used. The construction *x instead of y*, when *x* and *y* are infinitives, is clumsy; the idiomatic construction *x rather than y* is better here. Both constructions require *x* and *y* to be parallel.

A The passive form *to be confined* is required. *To allow members of the jury . . . to confine them* illogically indicates that the jurors are doing the confining.

B The infinitive form *to be confined* is required, rather than the past participle. The sentence is awkward and wordy.

C *Members of the jury* is the illogical object in *confining them. Confining* is not parallel to *to go home.*

D The noun *confinement* is not parallel to *to go home.*

E **Correct.** *Be confined to* uses the infinitive form just as *to go home* does; the *to* before *be confined* is understood and does not need to be repeated. The *x rather than y* construction is appropriately used in this sentence.

The correct answer is E.

95. Proponents of artificial intelligence say they will be able to make computers that can understand English and other human languages, recognize objects, and reason <u>as an expert does—computers that will be used to diagnose equipment breakdowns, deciding whether to authorize a loan, or other purposes such as these</u>.

(A) as an expert does—computers that will be used to diagnose equipment breakdowns, deciding whether to authorize a loan, or other purposes such as these

(B) as an expert does, which may be used for purposes such as diagnosing equipment breakdowns or deciding whether to authorize a loan

(C) like an expert—computers that will be used for such purposes as diagnosing equipment breakdowns or deciding whether to authorize a loan

(D) like an expert, the use of which would be for purposes like the diagnosis of equipment breakdowns or the decision whether or not a loan should be authorized

(E) like an expert, to be used to diagnose equipment breakdowns, deciding whether to authorize a loan or not, or the like

Parallelism; Rhetorical construction

The sentence presents three functions of intelligent computers, but these functions (*to diagnose . . . , deciding . . . , or other purposes*) are not written in parallel ways. Moreover, the final function is vague. Turning this final function into an introductory statement and using parallel forms for the two elements *diagnosing* and *deciding* creates a stronger sentence. Either the clause, *as an expert does*, or the prepositional phrase, *like an expert*, is correct and idiomatic in this sentence.

A The series *to diagnose . . . , deciding . . . , or other purposes* should be expressed in parallel ways.

B *Which* has no clear referent.

C **Correct.** Moving *for such purposes as* to an introductory position strengthens the sentence; *diagnosing* and *deciding* are parallel.

D *The use of which would be for purposes like* is wordy and awkward. *Which* has no clear referent.

E *To be used, deciding,* and *or the like* are not parallel.

The correct answer is C.

96. Floating in the waters of the equatorial Pacific, an array of buoys collects and transmits data on long-term interactions between the ocean and the <u>atmosphere, interactions that affect</u> global climate.

    (A) atmosphere, interactions that affect
    (B) atmosphere, with interactions affecting
    (C) atmosphere that affects
    (D) atmosphere that is affecting
    (E) atmosphere as affects

Grammatical construction; Agreement

The underlined portion of the sentence is an appositive, a terminal noun phrase restating the kind of data being collected and providing additional information about it. This is a clear and economical way to provide the extra information.

A **Correct.** The sentence is grammatically correct and logically coherent.

B The prepositional phrase, *with . . .* has no clear noun or noun phrase to attach to and is therefore ungrammatical.

C Using the restrictive *that* after *atmosphere* illogically suggests that there are many atmospheres to differentiate from and the one in question in this sentence is the one affecting global climate.

D The restrictive *that* also follows *atmosphere* as in answer C.

E The phrase *as affects global climate* functions as an adverb, but there is no verb for it to modify.

The correct answer is A.

97. <u>Unlike the United States, where farmers can usually depend on rain or snow all year long, the rains in most parts of Sri Lanka</u> are concentrated in the monsoon months, June to September, and the skies are generally clear for the rest of the year.

    (A) Unlike the United States, where farmers can usually depend on rain or snow all year long, the rains in most parts of Sri Lanka

    (B) Unlike the United States farmers who can usually depend on rain or snow all year long, the rains in most parts of Sri Lanka

    (C) Unlike those of the United States, where farmers can usually depend on rain or snow all year long, most parts of Sri Lanka's rains

    (D) In comparison with the United States, whose farmers can usually depend on rain or snow all year long, the rains in most parts of Sri Lanka

    (E) In the United States, farmers can usually depend on rain or snow all year long, but in most parts of Sri Lanka the rains

Logical predication; Rhetorical construction

The intent of the sentence is to compare seasonal rainfall patterns in the United States and Sri Lanka. There are many ways to set up such comparisons: *unlike x, y; in comparison with x, y; compared to x, y;* and so on. The *x* and *y* being compared must be grammatically and logically parallel. An alternative way of stating the comparison is the use of two independent clauses connected by *but*. The original sentence compares *the United States* to *rains in most parts of Sri Lanka*; this illogical comparison cannot convey the writer's intention.

A This sentence illogically compares *the United States* to *rains in most parts of Sri Lanka*.

B Comparing *United States farmers* to *the rains in most parts of Sri Lanka* is not logical.

C The sentence awkwardly and illogically seems to be comparing most parts of the United States with *most parts of Sri Lanka's rains*.

D This sentence compares *the United States* and *the rains in most parts of Sri Lanka*.

E **Correct.** This sentence uses two independent clauses to make the comparison. The first clause describes conditions in the United States, and the second clause describes conditions in Sri Lanka. The comparison is clear and logical.

The correct answer is E.

98. Although Napoleon's army entered Russia with far more supplies than <u>they had in their previous campaigns,</u> it had provisions for only twenty-four days.

    (A) they had in their previous campaigns,
    (B) their previous campaigns had had,
    (C) they had for any previous campaign,
    (D) in their previous campaigns,
    (E) for any previous campaign,

Agreement; Verb form

The sentence incorrectly switches between the plural pronouns *they* and *their* and the singular *it* to refer to the army. The past perfect verb tense *had had* is preferable to the simple past *had*, because this action occurred before the action in the main clause. In the context of *supplies for a campaign*, the preposition *for* is preferable to the preposition *in*. In cases such as this, where the sentence has multiple errors, it is often helpful to look among the answer choices for an alternate construction.

A Pronouns referring to the noun *army* should be *it* and *its*, not *they* and *their*; the verb should be *had had*.

B *Their* does not agree with the singular pronoun *it*, which treats *army* as a singular noun.

C *They* does not agree with the singular noun and the other pronoun. The verb should be *had had*.

D The preposition used should be *for*, not *in*. *Their* should be *its*.

E **Correct.** This simple construction avoids the problems of pronoun agreement and verb tense; it is clear, correct, and concise.

The correct answer is E.

99. After the Civil War, contemporaries of Harriet <u>Tubman's maintained that she has</u> all of the qualities of a great leader: coolness in the face of danger, an excellent sense of strategy, and an ability to plan in minute detail.

    (A) Tubman's maintained that she has
    (B) Tubman's maintain that she had
    (C) Tubman's have maintained that she had

    (D) Tubman maintained that she had
    (E) Tubman had maintained that she has

Idiom; Verb form

The apostrophe in a possessive noun such as *Tubman's* indicates that the word *of* has been omitted. It is correct to write *Tubman's* or *of Tubman*; it is incorrect to write *of Tubman's*. The verbs *maintained* and *had* describe actions that were completed in the past and occurred at about the same time. Since Tubman died long ago, she *had*, not *has*, the qualities of a great leader. Her contemporaries were people who lived at the same time as Tubman; the simple past should be used to describe their actions.

A *Of Harriet Tubman's* is an incorrect possessive. *Has* should be the simple past tense *had*.

B *Of Harriet Tubman's* is an incorrect possessive. *Maintain* should be simple past tense *maintained*.

C *Of Harriet Tubman's* is an incorrect possessive. *Have maintained* should be simple past tense *maintained*.

D **Correct.** In this sentence, the possessive is properly expressed with the phrase *of Tubman*; *maintained* and *had* both use the simple past tense.

E Simple past tense should be used in place of both verbs.

The correct answer is D.

100. Sixty-five million years ago, according to some scientists, an asteroid bigger than Mount Everest slammed into North America, <u>which, causing plant and animal extinctions, marks</u> the end of the geologic era known as the Cretaceous Period.

    (A) which, causing plant and animal extinctions, marks
    (B) which caused the plant and animal extinctions and marks
    (C) and causing plant and animal extinctions that mark
    (D) an event that caused plant and animal extinctions, which marks
    (E) an event that caused the plant and animal extinctions that mark

Logical predication; Agreement

This sentence describes a two-part sequence of events, the second of which has led to a particular categorization of geological time. In order to clarify that it is not the first event (asteroid strike) that produced the time division (end of the Cretaceous Period), but the first event's consequences (biological extinctions), the sentence needs an appositive form to restate the content of the main clause (*an event*), followed by a two-part chain of relative clauses (*that caused . . . that mark . . .*).

A   The antecedent for the relative pronoun *which* is ambiguous; it is therefore unclear what *marks* the end of the Cretaceous Period.

B   The antecedent of *which* is unclear; the compound verbs *caused* and *marks* fail to indicate that the extinctions, not the asteroid strike, are significant markers of geological time.

C   Following the conjunction *and* with a participial rather than a main verb is grammatically incorrect because it violates parallelism and produces a fragment at the end of the sentence.

D   *Which*, referring to *extinctions*, should be followed by a plural verb.

E   **Correct.** The sentence is unambiguous, and the verbs agree with their subjects.

The correct answer is E.

101. The Federalist papers, a strong defense of the United States Constitution <u>and important as a body of work in political science as well, represents</u> the handiwork of three different authors.

(A) and important as a body of work in political science as well, represents

(B) as well as an important body of work in political science, represent

(C) and also a body of work of importance in political science is representing

(D) an important body of work in political science and has been representative of

(E) and as political science an important body of work too, represent

Rhetorical construction; Grammatical construction

The subject of this sentence is *the Federalist papers*. Although the work is sometimes referred to by the title *The Federalist Papers*, the fact that *papers* is not capitalized indicates that in this case it is intended as a descriptive reference to the collection of papers, not as a title. Thus, it should have a plural verb. The subject is followed by a long modifying phrase set off by commas; both elements of the phrase should be parallel. Thus, *important as a body of work* should be revised so that it is parallel to *a strong defense*.

A   *Important as a body of work* is not parallel to *a strong defense*; it is also wordy and awkward. *Represents* should be the plural verb *represent* to agree with *the Federalist papers*.

B   **Correct.** The plural verb *represent* agrees with the plural subject. *An important body of work* is parallel to *a strong defense*. The sentence is clear and concise.

C   The present progressive *is representing* wrongly suggests a developing situation. *A body of work of importance in political science* is wordy and awkward. The closing comma of the pair is omitted.

D   Omission of *and* is incorrect; *has been representative of* uses an incorrect tense and introduces an awkward construction.

E   The inverted word order is awkward and is not parallel to *a strong defense*.

The correct answer is B.

102. As business grows more complex, students <u>majoring in specialized areas like those of finance and marketing have been becoming increasingly</u> successful in the job market.

(A) majoring in specialized areas like those of finance and marketing have been becoming increasingly

(B) who major in such specialized areas as finance and marketing are becoming more and more

(C) who majored in specialized areas such as those of finance and marketing are being increasingly

(D) who major in specialized areas like those of finance and marketing have been becoming more and more

(E) having majored in such specialized areas as finance and marketing are being increasingly

Verb form; Diction

The subordinate clause *as business grows more complex* uses the present tense verb *grows* to describe an ongoing situation. The main clause describes an effect of this growing complexity; the verbs in the main clause should also use present-tense verbs. The present perfect progressive *have been becoming* is incorrect. The preferred way to introduce examples is with the phrase *such as*, rather than with the word *like*, which suggests a comparison.

A *Like* should be replaced by *such as. Have been becoming* is an incorrect verb tense.

B **Correct.** In this sentence, *major* and *are becoming* are present-tense verbs; *such . . . as* is the preferred form for introducing examples.

C *Majored* is a past-tense verb; *those of* is unnecessary and awkward. *Becoming* is preferable to *being* for describing an unfolding pattern of events.

D *Like* should be replaced by *such as. Those of* is unnecessary and awkward. *Have been becoming* is an incorrect verb tense.

E *Having majored* is an awkward past participle. *Becoming* is preferable to *being* for describing an unfolding pattern of events.

The correct answer is B.

103. Inuits of the Bering Sea were in isolation from contact with Europeans longer than Aleuts or Inuits of the North Pacific and northern Alaska.

(A) in isolation from contact with Europeans longer than

(B) isolated from contact with Europeans longer than

(C) in isolation from contact with Europeans longer than were

(D) isolated from contact with Europeans longer than were

(E) in isolation and without contacts with Europeans longer than

Idiom; Logical predication

The construction *in isolation from* is awkward; the idiomatic way to express this idea is *isolated from.* The comparison is ambiguous; it could mean the Bering Sea Inuits were isolated from Europeans longer than they were isolated from Aleuts and other Inuits or that they were isolated from Europeans longer than Aleuts and other Inuits were isolated from Europeans. Adding *were* after *than* will solve this problem.

A *In isolation from* is not the correct idiom. The comparison is ambiguous.

B The comparison is ambiguous.

C *In isolation from* is not the correct idiom.

D **Correct.** The idiom *isolated from* is correctly used in this sentence. The comparison is clear and unambiguous.

E *In isolation . . . without* is incorrect and confusing. The comparison is ambiguous.

The correct answer is D.

104. Although the first pulsar, or rapidly spinning collapsed star, to be sighted was in the summer of 1967 by graduate student Jocelyn Bell, it had not been announced until February 1968.

(A) Although the first pulsar, or rapidly spinning collapsed star, to be sighted was in the summer of 1967 by graduate student Jocelyn Bell, it had not been announced until February 1968.

(B) Although not announced until February 1968, in the summer of 1967 graduate student Jocelyn Bell observed the first pulsar, or rapidly spinning collapsed star, to be sighted.

(C) Although observed by graduate student Jocelyn Bell in the summer of 1967, the discovery of the first sighted pulsar, or rapidly spinning collapsed star, had not been announced before February 1968.

(D) The first pulsar, or rapidly spinning collapsed star, to be sighted was observed in the summer of 1967 by graduate student Jocelyn Bell, but the discovery was not announced until February 1968.

(E) The first sighted pulsar, or rapidly spinning collapsed star, was not announced until February 1968, while it was observed in the summer of 1967 by graduate student Jocelyn Bell.

Verb form; Logical predication; Rhetorical construction

This sentence presents conditions that are followed by an unexpected outcome: a delayed announcement of the discovery of a pulsar. A compound sentence using a coordinating conjunction *but* is an effective way to present the conditions of the first pulsar sighting and then information about the subsequent announcement of the discovery. The sentence must clarify that it is not about *the first pulsar*, but *the first pulsar . . . to be sighted*. The verbs in the sentence must all be in past tense; using a past-perfect verb to present information about the announcement of the discovery indicates that this announcement illogically took place before the pulsar was first sighted.

A   The subject of the opening dependent clause is *pulsar*, and the verb is *was*. The clause needs to indicate not just that the pulsar existed but that it was observed by Bell; the past perfect verb tense is inappropriate in the concluding clause.

B   The opening participial phrase functions as an adjective, but it has no logical noun or noun phrase to attach to; Bell herself was not announced in 1968.

C   Grammatically, the opening participial phrase describes the first noun that follows, but it makes no sense to say that *the discovery* of the pulsar was *observed*; *discovery of the first sighted pulsar* is also imprecise; one does not discover a first sighting.

D   **Correct.** The sentence presents the sequence of events clearly and in the past tense.

E   This sentence presents events in a way that is confusing; as a conjunction, *while* indicates simultaneous events, but this sentence is about events that occurred in a sequence.

The correct answer is D.

105.   The physical structure of the human eye enables it to sense light of wavelengths up to 0.0005 millimeters; <u>infrared radiation, however, is invisible because its wavelength—0.1 millimeters—is too long to be registered by the eye.</u>

(A)   infrared radiation, however, is invisible because its wavelength—0.1 millimeters—is too long to be registered by the eye

(B)   however, the wavelength of infrared radiation—0.1 millimeters—is too long to be registered by the eye making it invisible

(C)   infrared radiation, however, is invisible because its wavelength—0.1 millimeters—is too long for the eye to register it

(D)   however, because the wavelength of infrared radiation is 0.1 millimeters, it is too long for the eye to register and thus invisible

(E)   however, infrared radiation has a wavelength of 0.1 millimeters that is too long for the eye to register, thus making it invisible

Logical predication; Rhetorical construction

This sentence requires attention to clear references and appropriate modification. Here *its* clearly refers to *infrared radiation*; it is the *radiation* that is *invisible*, and the *wavelength* that is *too long*.

A   **Correct.** This sentence clearly and grammatically explains why infrared radiation is invisible.

B   *Making it invisible* modifies *eye*, rather than *wavelength*.

C   *It* lacks a clear referent.

D   *It* is imprecise. *Thus invisible* modifies *wavelength*, rather than *infrared radiation*.

E   Using a restrictive clause suggests that not all wavelengths of *0.1 millimeters* are *too long for the eye to register*. *It* lacks a clear referent.

The correct answer is A.

106. <u>As well as heat and light, the sun is the source of a continuous stream</u> of atomic particles known as the solar wind.

  (A) As well as heat and light, the sun is the source of a continuous stream

  (B) Besides heat and light, also the sun is the source of a continuous stream

  (C) Besides heat and light, the sun is also the source of a continuous streaming

  (D) The sun is the source not only of heat and light, but also of a continuous stream

  (E) The sun is the source of not only heat and light but, as well, of a continuous streaming

Idiom; Logical predication; Rhetorical construction

The underlined section must be revised to eliminate modification errors and to clarify meaning by using parallel construction. *As well as heat and light* cannot logically modify the sun, as grammar requires; the sentence seems to suggest that heat, light, and the sun are the source of the solar wind. The sentence can be improved by employing the construction *not only x . . . but also y*; *x* and *y* should be parallel.

A *As well as heat and light* is misplaced and potentially confusing.

B *Besides heat and light* is confusing. The word order of *also the sun* is awkward.

C *Besides heat and light* is unclear. *Streaming* should be the more straightforward *stream*.

D **Correct.** This sentence uses the *not only . . . but also* construction to solve the modification error; *of heat and light* is parallel to *of a continuous stream*.

E *As well* is incorrect in the *not only . . . but also* construction. *Heat and light* is not parallel to *of a continuous streaming*. *Streaming* should be the more straightforward *stream*.

The correct answer is D.

107. Bluegrass musician Bill Monroe, whose repertory, views on musical collaboration, and vocal style <u>were influential on generations of bluegrass artists, was also an inspiration to many musicians, that included Elvis Presley and Jerry Garcia, whose music differed significantly from</u> his own.

  (A) were influential on generations of bluegrass artists, was also an inspiration to many musicians, that included Elvis Presley and Jerry Garcia, whose music differed significantly from

  (B) influenced generations of bluegrass artists, also inspired many musicians, including Elvis Presley and Jerry Garcia, whose music differed significantly from

  (C) was influential to generations of bluegrass artists, was also inspirational to many musicians, that included Elvis Presley and Jerry Garcia, whose music was different significantly in comparison to

  (D) was influential to generations of bluegrass artists, also inspired many musicians, who included Elvis Presley and Jerry Garcia, the music of whom differed significantly when compared to

  (E) were an influence on generations of bluegrass artists, was also an inspiration to many musicians, including Elvis Presley and Jerry Garcia, whose music was significantly different from that of

Agreement; Rhetorical construction; Grammatical construction

The original sentence logically intends to explain that Monroe's work influenced generations of artists in his own musical field and that he inspired many musicians in other musical fields. Who or what influenced or inspired whom must be more clearly stated. Additionally, the original sentence lacks precision, being overly wordy and using phrases that are not idiomatic. Concise and consistent verb forms, as well as the use of subordinate phrases rather than clauses, improve the precision of the sentence.

A The phrase *were influential on* is wordy and is not idiomatic; the use of verb forms *were* (the predicate of *repertory*, *views*, and *style*) and *was* (the predicate of *Monroe*) is confusing.

B   **Correct.** The use of the concise verb forms of *influenced* and *inspired* simplifies and clarifies the sentence. The concise use of *including* avoids the pronoun error and unnecessary wordiness.

C   The subject and verb do not agree in *repertory, views,* and *style . . . was* (compound subject with singular verb). *Was influential to* and *different . . . in comparison to* are unnecessarily wordy.

D   There is incorrect subject-verb agreement in *repertory, views,* and *style . . . was* (compound subject with singular verb). *Was influential to* and in *when compared to* are unnecessarily wordy. *The music of whom* is cumbersome and stilted.

E   The phrase *were an influence on* is wordy and not idiomatic. The phrases *was also an inspiration to* and *was significantly different* are unnecessarily wordy. The phrase *from that of* is unclear and confusing.

The correct answer is B.

108.   Sound can travel through water for enormous distances, prevented from dissipating its acoustic energy as a result of boundaries in the ocean created by water layers of different temperatures and densities.

(A)   prevented from dissipating its acoustic energy as a result of

(B)   prevented from having its acoustic energy dissipated by

(C)   its acoustic energy prevented from dissipating by

(D)   its acoustic energy prevented from being dissipated as a result of

(E)   preventing its acoustic energy from dissipating by

Logical predication; Rhetorical construction

This sentence opens with a statement that sound can travel long distances through water and then explains why that is so: water layers in the ocean prevent acoustic energy from dissipating. Because *dissipating* is an intransitive verb, *acoustic energy* cannot be its object.

A   *Dissipating* is not a transitive verb, so *acoustic energy* cannot function as its object.

B   This version of the sentence is wordy, awkward, and indirect; *from having . . . by* erroneously suggests that the boundaries in the ocean are attempting to dissipate sound energy.

C   **Correct.** Here, *acoustic energy* is effectively modified by the participial *prevented from dissipating. . . .*

D   This version of the sentence is wordy, awkward, and indirect; *being dissipated as a result of* makes it unclear whether the boundaries contribute to energy loss or prevent it.

E   This version of the sentence nonsensically explains that sound prevents the dissipation of its own energy.

The correct answer is C.

109.   The nephew of Pliny the Elder wrote the only eyewitness account of the great eruption of Vesuvius in two letters to the historian Tacitus.

(A)   The nephew of Pliny the Elder wrote the only eyewitness account of the great eruption of Vesuvius in two letters to the historian Tacitus.

(B)   To the historian Tacitus, the nephew of Pliny the Elder wrote two letters, being the only eyewitness accounts of the great eruption of Vesuvius.

(C)   The only eyewitness account is in two letters by the nephew of Pliny the Elder writing to the historian Tacitus an account of the great eruption of Vesuvius.

(D)   Writing the only eyewitness account, Pliny the Elder's nephew accounted for the great eruption of Vesuvius in two letters to the historian Tacitus.

(E)   In two letters to the historian Tacitus, the nephew of Pliny the Elder wrote the only eyewitness account of the great eruption of Vesuvius.

Logical predication; Rhetorical construction

The challenge in this sentence lies in the correct placement of a prepositional phrase. In the original version, the placement of *in two letters to the historian Tacitus* appears to suggest that Vesuvius erupted in the letters themselves. Placing the phrase at the beginning of the sentence solves the problem.

A   The sentence suggests that the eruption of Vesuvius took place in the letters themselves.

B   Beginning the sentence with *to the historian Tacitus* is clumsy and unclear. The verb phrase *being* . . . seems illogically to modify *the nephew*, creating the awkward suggestion that *the nephew* was *the eyewitness accounts*.

C   The sentence's meaning is unclear due to an extended sequence of prepositional phrases.

D   *An account* is a narrative record; *to account for* means to be the cause of. Using both in the same sentence is confusing and here suggests that the nephew caused the eruption. The sentence also suggests that the eruption of Vesuvius took place in the letters themselves.

E   **Correct.** The placement of the prepositional phrase at the beginning of the sentence clarifies the meaning of the sentence; the construction of the rest of the sentence is straightforward.

The correct answer is E.

110. Being a United States citizen since 1988 and born in Calcutta in 1940, author Bharati Mukherjee has lived in England and Canada, and first came to the United States in 1961 to study at the Iowa Writers' Workshop.

(A)   Being a United States citizen since 1988 and born in Calcutta in 1940, author Bharati Mukherjee has

(B)   Having been a United States citizen since 1988, she was born in Calcutta in 1940; author Bharati Mukherjee

(C)   Born in Calcutta in 1940, author Bharati Mukherjee became a United States citizen in 1988; she has

(D)   Being born in Calcutta in 1940 and having been a United States citizen since 1988, author Bharati Mukherjee

(E)   Having been born in Calcutta in 1940 and being a United States citizen since 1988, author Bharati Mukherjee

Verb form; Rhetorical construction

Being . . . since 1988 and born in Calcutta in 1940 is an awkward, wordy construction, which presents an unclear and potentially confusing chronological order. Since in the correct version of the sentence the original phrase (*being* . . .) has been made into a main clause, a semicolon should separate it from the second main clause beginning *she has lived*.

A   The phrases are expressed in an illogical and potentially confusing sequence.

B   *Having been* suggests that the citizenship came chronologically before the birth. The pronoun *she* is the subject of the first clause; since the author's name is mentioned only after the semicolon, *she* has no clear referent.

C   **Correct.** In this sentence, the sequence of events is expressed logically, grammatically, and concisely in each independent clause.

D   The progressive verb forms *being born* and *having been* illogically suggest continuous action and fail to establish a logical time sequence. The sentence is wordy and awkward.

E   The progressive verb forms *having been born* and *being* illogically suggest continuous action and fail to establish a logical time sequence. The sentence is wordy and awkward.

The correct answer is C.

111. Initiated five centuries after Europeans arrived in the New World on Columbus Day 1992, Project SETI pledged a $100 million investment in the search for extraterrestrial intelligence.

(A)   Initiated five centuries after Europeans arrived in the New World on Columbus Day 1992, Project SETI pledged a $100 million investment in the search for extraterrestrial intelligence.

(B) Initiated on Columbus Day 1992, five centuries after Europeans arrived in the New World, a $100 million investment in the search for extraterrestrial intelligence was pledged by Project SETI.

(C) Initiated on Columbus Day 1992, five centuries after Europeans arrived in the New World, Project SETI pledged a $100 million investment in the search for extraterrestrial intelligence.

(D) Pledging a $100 million investment in the search for extraterrestrial intelligence, the initiation of Project SETI five centuries after Europeans arrived in the New World on Columbus Day 1992.

(E) Pledging a $100 million investment in the search for extraterrestrial intelligence five centuries after Europeans arrived in the New World, on Columbus Day 1992, the initiation of Project SETI took place.

Logical predication; Grammatical construction

The original sentence becomes illogical when phrases do not modify what they are intended to modify. This sentence mistakenly says that *Europeans arrived in the New World on Columbus Day 1992*. It also says that Project SETI was *initiated five centuries after . . . Columbus Day 1992*. To make the modifiers grammatically and logically correct, the sentence may be revised: *Initiated on Columbus Day 1992, five centuries after Europeans arrived in the New World, Project SETI. . . .*

A   Project SETI cannot have been *initiated five centuries after . . . 1992*, nor did Europeans first arrive in 1992.

B   *Initiated . . .* modifies *$100 million investment* instead of *Project SETI*.

C   **Correct.** The modifiers are grammatically and logically correct in this sentence.

D   *Pledging . . .* incorrectly modifies *the initiation*. This is a sentence fragment.

E   *Pledging . . .* incorrectly modifies *the initiation*. Europeans appear to have arrived on Columbus Day 1992. The construction is awkward, unbalanced, and imprecise.

The correct answer is C.

112. In the 1980s the federal government was the largest single provider of day care for children, offering child care, health, and educational services to hundreds of thousands of children from poor households through the Head Start program and which supported private day-care facilities through child-care tax credits, state block grants, and tax breaks for employers who subsidized day-care services.

(A) In the 1980s the federal government was the largest single provider of day care for children, offering

(B) The federal government was the largest single provider of day care for children in the 1980s, which offered

(C) In the 1980s the federal government was the largest single provider of day care for children and offered

(D) The largest single provider of day care for children in the 1980s was the federal government, offering

(E) In the 1980s the largest single provider of day care for children was the federal government, which offered

Grammatical construction; Parallelism

The main point of this sentence is to identify the federal government as the largest single provider of children's day care. It goes on to illustrate this with two examples that need to be presented in grammatically parallel form. Because the second example is given as a relative clause beginning with *which supported private*, the first example must be similarly presented. The opening statement must therefore present *government* as the predicate noun so that *which* clearly refers to *government* in both of the examples.

A   The two examples are not in parallel form; the first begins with a present participial, *offering*, while the second is presented as a relative clause, *which supported. . . .*

B   The antecedent for the relative pronoun *which* is ambiguous.

C   The first example, introduced as a compound verb of the subject *federal government*, is not parallel with the second example, presented in a relative clause.

D   The first example, presented as a present participial (*offering*) is not parallel with the second example, presented in a relative clause.

E   **Correct.** The sentence is grammatically correct and the examples are parallel.

The correct answer is E.

113. In A.D. 391, <u>resulting from the destruction of the largest library of the ancient world at Alexandria,</u> later generations lost all but the *Iliad* and *Odyssey* among Greek epics, most of the poetry of Pindar and Sappho, and dozens of plays by Aeschylus and Euripides.

(A)   resulting from the destruction of the largest library of the ancient world at Alexandria,

(B)   the destroying of the largest library of the ancient world at Alexandria resulted and

(C)   because of the result of the destruction of the library at Alexandria, the largest of the ancient world,

(D)   as a result of the destruction of the library at Alexandria, the largest of the ancient world,

(E)   Alexandria's largest library of the ancient world was destroyed, and the result was

Logical predication; Rhetorical construction; Grammatical construction

Because it is introduced by a participle, the phrase that begins *resulting from* illogically modifies *later generations*. Substituting the idiom *as a result of* for *resulting from* corrects this error. *The largest library of the ancient world at Alexandria* is both cumbersome and ambiguous because it suggests that the *ancient world* was located *at* (and only at) *Alexandria*. This problem is best corrected by breaking the series of phrases into two distinct parts: *the library at Alexandria, the largest of the ancient world*. Here, the second phrase clearly modifies the first.

A   *Resulting from* illogically modifies *later generations*. The series of prepositional phrases is confusing and ambiguous.

B   *The destroying of* is wordy and awkward. *And* creates a second main clause, which would need to be appropriately punctuated with a comma before *and*.

C   *Because of the result of* is redundant.

D   **Correct.** *As a result of* begins the phrase clearly and correctly in this sentence; the *library* rather than the *ancient world* is properly located *at Alexandria*; *the largest of the ancient world* correctly modifies *library*.

E   *Alexandria's largest library of the ancient world* is an illogical reference. *The result was* must be followed by *that*.

The correct answer is D.

Appendix A Percentile Ranking Tables

Table 1
Percentages of Examinees Tested from January 2005 through December 2007 (including Repeaters) Who Scored Below Specified Verbal Scores

Verbal Scaled Score	Percentage Below	Verbal Scaled Score	Percentage Below
46–60	99	26	40
45	98	25	36
43	96	24	33
42	95	23	29
41	92	22	27
40	89	21	23
39	87	20	19
38	83	19	16
37	81	18	15
36	78	17	12
35	74	16	10
34	69	15	8
33	66	14	7
32	64	13	5
31	58	12	4
30	56	11	3
29	53	10	2
28	48	7–9	1
27	43	0–6	0

Number of Candidates = 650,395
Mean = 27.8
Standard deviation = 9.1

Table 2
Percentages of Examinees Tested from January 2005 through December 2007 (including Repeaters) Who Scored Below Specified Quantitative Scores

Quantitative Scaled Score	Percentage Below	Quantitative Scaled Score	Percentage Below
51–60	99	30	29
50	94	29	25
49	88	28	24
48	84	27	20
47	79	26	19
46	77	25	16
45	75	24	15
44	70	23	13
43	68	22	11
42	63	21	10
41	61	20	9
40	59	19	8
39	55	18	7
38	53	17	5
37	51	16	4
36	46	15	4
35	42	14	4
34	40	13	3
33	38	11–12	2
32	34	7–10	1
31	30	0–6	0

Number of Candidates = 650,395
Mean = 35.6
Standard deviation = 10.7

Table 3
Percentages of Examinees Tested from January 2005 through December 2007 (including Repeaters) Who Scored Below Specified Total Scores

Total Scaled Score	Percentage Below	Total Scaled Score	Percentage Below
760–800	99	500	36
750	98	490	34
740	97	480	31
730	96	470	29
720	95	460	25
710	92	450	23
700	90	440	21
690	88	430	19
680	86	420	17
670	85	410	15
660	83	400	13
650	80	390	12
640	76	380	10
630	75	370	9
620	72	360	8
610	69	350	7
600	66	340	6
590	63	330	5
580	60	320	4
570	58	310	3
560	54	300	3
550	51	290	3
540	48	280	2
530	44	270	2
520	42	230–250	1
510	39	200–220	0

Number of Candidates = 650,395
Mean = 535.2
Standard deviation = 120.1

Table 4
Percentages of Examinees Tested from January 2005 through December 2007 (including Repeaters) Who Scored Below Specified AWA Scores

AWA Scaled Score	Percentage Below
6.0	87
5.5	80
5.0	55
4.5	42
4.0	21
3.5	13
3.0	6
2.5	4
2.0	3
1.5	3
1.0	3
0.5	3
0.0	0

Number of Candidates = 650,395
Mean = 4.4
Standard deviation = 1.2

To register for the GMAT test go to www.mba.com

Appendix B   Answer Sheets

Reading Comprehension Answer Sheet

1.	27.	53.	79.
2.	28.	54.	80.
3.	29.	55.	81.
4.	30.	56.	82.
5.	31.	57.	83.
6.	32.	58.	84.
7.	33.	59.	85.
8.	34.	60.	86.
9.	35.	61.	87.
10.	36.	62.	88.
11.	37.	63.	89.
12.	38.	64.	90.
13.	39.	65.	91.
14.	40.	66.	92.
15.	41.	67.	93.
16.	42.	68.	94.
17.	43.	69.	95.
18.	44.	70.	96.
19.	45.	71.	97.
20.	46.	72.	98.
21.	47.	73.	99.
22.	48.	74.	100.
23.	49.	75.	101.
24.	50.	76.	102.
25.	51.	77.	103.
26.	52.	78.	104.

Critical Reasoning Answer Sheet

1.	22.	43.	64.
2.	23.	44.	65.
3.	24.	45.	66.
4.	25.	46.	67.
5.	26.	47.	68.
6.	27.	48.	69.
7.	28.	49.	70.
8.	29.	50.	71.
9.	30.	51.	72.
10.	31.	52.	73.
11.	32.	53.	74.
12.	33.	54.	75.
13.	34.	55.	76.
14.	35.	56.	77.
15.	36.	57.	78.
16.	37.	58.	79.
17.	38.	59.	80.
18.	39.	60.	81.
19.	40.	61.	82.
20.	41.	62.	83.
21.	42.	63.	

Sentence Correction Answer Sheet

1.	30.	59.	88.
2.	31.	60.	89.
3.	32.	61.	90.
4.	33.	62.	91.
5.	34.	63.	92.
6.	35.	64.	93.
7.	36.	65.	94.
8.	37.	66.	95.
9.	38.	67.	96.
10.	39.	68.	97.
11.	40.	69.	98.
12.	41.	70.	99.
13.	42.	71.	100.
14.	43.	72.	101.
15.	44.	73.	102.
16.	45.	74.	103.
17.	46.	75.	104.
18.	47.	76.	105.
19.	48.	77.	106.
20.	49.	78.	107.
21.	50.	79.	108.
22.	51.	80.	109.
23.	52.	81.	110.
24.	53.	82.	111.
25.	54.	83.	112.
26.	55.	84.	113.
27.	56.	85.	
28.	57.	86.	
29.	58.	87.	

Get MORE—
More practice, more questions, and more answers!

FROM THE CREATORS OF THE TEST!

QUANTITATIVE REVIEW
2ND EDITION

The only study guide with 300 past GMAT® questions —and their answers— by the creators of the test.

~The~ OFFICIAL Guide

THE OFFICIAL GUIDE FOR GMAT® QUANTITATIVE REVIEW 2ND EDITION

• Actual questions from past GMAT tests, including 75 questions new to this edition

• 300 past Problem Solving and Data Sufficiency questions and answer explanations spanning Arithmetic, Algebra, Geometry, and Word Problems.

• Questions organized in order of difficulty to save study time

From the Graduate Management Admission Council®

978-0-470-44976-9 • 216 pages • $17.95

Anyone preparing for the Graduate Management Admission Test® (GMAT®) knows it's important to study with the experts. With *The Official Guide for GMAT® Quantitative Review*, 2nd Edition, you'll get **more** questions, answers, and explanations straight from the source.

The only official quantitative review for the GMAT exam, this book targets your study and helps you improve your quantitative skills by focusing on your ability to solve equations, interpret data, and determine probability with assurance and ease.

Also Available!

MORE THAN 1 MILLION COPIES SOLD WO...

13TH EDITION
REVIEW

The **only** study guide by the creators of the test

• More than 900 questions from past GMAT® exams

• **NEW!** Companion website includes 50 Integrated Reasoning questions

• Diagnostic section helps you assess where to focus your test-prep efforts

~The~ OFFICIAL Guide

From the Graduate Management Admission Council®

978-1-118-10979-3
840 pages • $42.95

e Available in print and e-book formats.

WILEY
Now you know